DEVOTIONS FOR Busy People

Written by
Lowell Lundstrom

Edited by
Sally Petersen

Lowell Lundstrom Ministries, Inc.
Sisseton, South Dakota 57262

DEVOTIONS FOR BUSY PEOPLE

Copyright ©1986 by Lowell Lundstrom

Published by Lowell Lundstrom Ministries, Inc.
Sisseton, South Dakota 57262

All rights reserved. No portion of this book may be reproduced in any form without the written permission of the publisher.

Printed in the United States of America.

All biblical quotations are taken from the King James Version unless otherwise noted.

Dear Friend:

This devotional book may change your life; I know because writing it changed mine.

A Christian writer is a channel of the Holy Spirit. When God begins to pour forth His truth it is a spiritual experience for the writer as well as the reader.

I have enjoyed writing this devotional book very much. I recall these lines from somewhere:

> "To know—read
> to be clear—speak
> to be exact—write"

This has been an "exacting" experience for me that I hope will be an uplifting experience for you. I am certain the truths you learn each day will inspire your faith and strengthen your life.

Sincerely,

Lowell Lundstrom

Lowell Lundstrom

1/THE TREASURE OF TIME!

"But this I say, brethren, the time is short ... " (1 Corinthians 7:29).

Also read: Hos. 10:12; Mark 1:15

This New Year is your gift from God. You should cherish it. You should never feel sad over growing older; think of your many friends who have been denied the privilege. A walk through your local cemetery will take the self-pity out of your heart.

Clare Booth Luce, the wife of Henry Luce, former publisher of *Time* and *Life* magazine, says that when you grow older your future is in your past. Thank God, because of Jesus Christ, we truly have a future; the best is yet to come!

Because time has a way of slipping away, you'll have to make a special effort to make the most of it.

First, establish your priorities. Just what do you want to accomplish this New Year?

1. Spiritually _____
2. Socially (with your family) _____
3. Intellectually _____
4. Financially _____

If you don't have a game plan for the New Year, beginning this very day, you'll waste this treasure God has given you. When Jesus died on the cross He cried, *"It is finished"* (John 19:30). He had completed His task.

What is yours? Decide now.

Take a moment—go back and fill in the lines under the special headings. Otherwise, you will fail to complete the task God has called you to do.

Be tough on yourself. When Queen Elizabeth of England lay dying she cried, "I'd give all of my empire for twenty more minutes of time."

Can you imagine what she would give for the year that God has probably given to you? And because this may be your last year of life—make it the best ever by setting specific goals and then accomplish them.

•

Remember: TIME IS A TREASURE THAT SHOULDN'T BE WASTED.

2/HOW TO GET YOUR PRAYERS ANSWERED!

"The effectual fervent prayer of a righteous man availeth much" (James 5:16).

Also read: Ps. 145:18 & 19; Mt. 7:7 & 8; Jn. 15:7

If you're facing a tough situation and need to get your prayers answered, here's a life-changing verse for today.
1. TO BE EFFECTUAL you need to be specific. Don't pray "around the world" when you need a specific answer. Zero in. Target your prayers! Jesus said, *"Whatever you bind on earth will be bound in heaven, and whatever you loose on earth will be loosed in heaven"* (Matthew 16:19, NKJ). So you'd better decide what you want done and get to work binding and loosing. *Remember, God isn't going to do it without you, and you can't do it without God. So you are partners in prayer!*
2. YOU NEED TO BE FERVENT. You need to pray with fire and emotion. Dead prayers don't go anywhere. When Hannah wanted a son, she prayed so fervently that her lips moved and trembled, but her voice was not heard. Eli the high priest thought she was drunk, but she was possessed with a magnificent obsession.

   Do you really want an answer to your prayers? Then you must pray with a fervency that may be greater than what you've been accustomed to. You may have to raise your hands. *"I will therefore that men pray every where, lifting up holy hands, without wrath and doubting."* (1 Timothy 2:8). You may even want to lift up your voice and yell out your petition! *"And being let go, they went to their own company, and...they lifted up their voices to God"* (Acts 4:23,24).
3. BE RIGHTEOUS! I know it is popular in Christian circles to say, "There is none righteous. No, not one." But it is also true that there are some righteous. God said Noah was righteous in Genesis 7:1; in Psalm 1:6, He speaks of the way of the righteous, and, *"the righteous cry, and the Lord...delivereth them"* (Psalm 34:17).

It is a fact that when you walk with God and obey Him, you have a residual righteousness that comes from God—but is truly your own. If you want your prayers answered, make certain that your heart is right with God.

•

Remember: "THE EFFECTUAL FERVENT PRAYER OF A RIGHTEOUS MAN AVAILETH MUCH."

3/ARE YOU GOD'S FRIEND?

"Abraham...was called the Friend of God" (James 2:23).

Also read: 2 Chron. 20:7; Is. 41:8

Do you realize there are times when God can be lonely? In heaven God is surrounded by the heavenly host, but what about friends here on earth?

When Sodom and Gommorah became such wicked cities the cry of their suffering inhabitants reached heaven. God said, *"I will go down...and see whether they have done altogether according to the cry of it."* (Gen. 18:21). In other words, God said, "I'm going to go down and check it out."

The Bible says, *"and the Lord appeared unto Abraham—and he lift up his eyes and, lo, three men stood by him."* (Theologians say that each of the angelic men stood for one of the triune Godhead: God the Father, God the Son and God the Holy Spirit.)

Then God said, *"Shall I hide from Abraham the thing I'm going to do?"* (Gen. 18:17). Abraham was such a close friend that God wanted to talk to him about Sodom and Gommorah.

That's when Abraham began to interceed in prayer to God for the lives of the righteous, and their families. The most striking thing about this event is that God wasn't going to act without talking it over with Abraham first.

I ask myself, "Would God come down and talk with me about the situation in the United States before He did something drastic?"

Abraham was God's personal friend. In a land full of sinners and rebels, God was comfortable with Abraham, for he was His friend. Because of Abraham's petitions, God promised that the cities would not be destroyed for as few as ten righteous souls.

Let's try to be God's friend, so that when He comes near us, He'll feel welcome. To become a friend of God, we need to walk and talk with Him each day.

•

Remember: BE GOD'S FRIEND!

4/YOU CAN DO EVERYTHING!

"I can do all things through Christ which strengtheneth me" (Philippians 4:13).

Also read: Ps. 119:103-105; Rom. 10:17; Heb. 4:12

Do you realize the greatest power in the universe dwells within you this very moment? The maker of heaven and earth, the power who holds the universe together, the mighty one who hung the worlds on nothing is abiding in you by the Holy Spirit.

This is why you can do everything. What habit, what sin, what inferiority complex, what situation has more power than God, and God is in you?

Now you may be wondering as I often do, "What is it that keeps this magnificent power from manifesting itself more clearly in my life?"

Unbelief. Our theology, doctrines and creeds are all locked up in our minds instead of burning in our hearts. We are theologians and philosophers rather than demonstrators of God's power.

This is why Paul the apostle said, *"My speech and my preaching was not with enticing words of man's wisdom, but in demonstration of the Spirit and of power: That your faith should not stand in the wisdom of men, but in the power of God"* (1 Cor. 2:4 & 5).

What is the task that you are facing? What is the impossible habit or situation that you need to release God's power toward?

Say this aloud, "The greatest power of the universe dwells in me this very moment and I can do everything. Now, in Jesus' name, I release God's almightly power toward this situation. I take authority over it in Jesus' name. I bind it to God's will. I loose it from Satan and declare I will have victory over this situation today or in the very near future."

When you start praying and speaking like this, you will discover that God will be inspired to begin moving on your behalf.

•

Remember: YOU CAN DO EVERYTHING!

5/THE FIRE OF DESIRE!

"What things soever ye desire, when ye pray, believe that ye receive them and ye shall have them" (Mark 11:24).

Also read: Jn. 14:16 & 17; 16:7,13; Acts 4:31

Desire is the fire that gives power to your prayers. If you don't have a burning desire to receive the things you are praying for, you'll never hold on long enough to get an answer from God.

It is the fire of desire that keeps you asking, seeking, knocking. If your fires are burning low, here are a few ways you can fan the flames.

1. Be Honest. Admit you're feeling dead in your soul and ask God to breathe a fresh breath of the Holy Spirit upon your soul.
2. Read some of the great prayers in the Bible. For instance: Daniel fighting demon powers in chapter 9; Moses helping God to change His mind in Exodus 22, or Jesus praying for us in John 17.
3. Ask Christians to share the greatest answers to their prayers. This will encourage you to pray more fervently.
4. Consider the tragic results of failing to pray. It might be hard to pray, but the results of not praying will be much worse.

A wise man has said, "The reason so few people get what they want is because they don't want it hard enough!"

Actually, when you and I pray, we are throwing our hearts and souls into a spirit world dominated by the devil, demons and darkness. This is what makes it so difficult. When Jesus finished praying in the Garden of Gethsemane, the pressure was so great that blood oozed from the pores of His temples.

Oh, God, give us the holy desire, the holy fire to pray until we get an answer! Holy Spirit, lead us into the presence of God and help us in our weaknesses.

"The Holy Spirit helps us with our daily problems and in our praying. For we don't even know what we should pray for, nor how to pray as we should; but the Holy Spirit prays for us with such feeling that it cannot be expressed in words." (Rom. 8:26, TLB).

•

Remember: THE SPIRIT WILL PROMPT YOUR FIRE OF DESIRE!

6/THE NAME ABOVE ALL NAMES!

". . . Blessed be thy glorious name, which is exalted above all blessing and praise" (Nehemiah 9:5).

Also read: Phil. 2:9-11

Bernard Johnson has been called the Billy Graham of Brazil. His crowds have numbered up to 150,000. He spoke at the Chapel of Trinity Bible College (where I was recently elected president) and shared some inspiring thoughts about the name of Jesus:

"Philosophers and atheists have declared they would put an end to His name. One famous atheist was Voltaire, the famous French infidel and philosopher. Voltaire said, 'I am going to destroy the Bible, the name of Jesus and the Christian Church. And one hundred years after I die, the name of Jesus will never be spoken again and the Bible might be found in some old museum.'

"But here's what happened: As Voltaire lay dying, surrounded by friends and relatives, he became so demon possessed that he had to be held down. It took dozens of men taking shifts to hold him in place. In the last moment before he died he cried out, 'People, I can feel the flames of hell licking on my ankles and my legs.'

"What a tragic death. And one hundred years after his death, when he declared the name of Jesus would never be mentioned again, and that the Bible would not be found except in an old museum, Voltaire's house was purchased by the World Bible Society and became the headquarters of the World Bible Society in Paris, France.

"Since then, millions of Bibles have been distributed from the headquarters now in Voltaire's house. The name of Jesus is not destroyed; it is increasing day by day."

•

Remember: THE NAME OF JESUS IS ABOVE ALL NAMES!

7/YOUR TRIALS ARE YOUR TREASURE!

"The trial of your faith, being much more precious than of gold...though it be tried with fire" (1 Peter 1:7).

Also read: Ps. 18:28-32; 56:11-13; Is. 43: 2-4

If you're in the midst of a fiery trial you can be encouraged by this fact: your trials will be your treasure.

When Constantine became the Emperor of Rome, his soldiers found an old man who had been imprisoned for his Christian faith. He had suffered greatly at the hands of his tormentors, who had attached a large ball and chain to his leg.

Wanting to right the wrong, Constantine ordered that the ball and chain be weighed, and whatever the weight, the man be given in gold. His trial became his treasure.

Jesus said, *"I council thee to buy of me gold tried in the fire, that thou mayest be rich"* (Rev. 3:18).

The gold He is speaking of here are the characteristics of Godliness that come from the fiery trials. Jesus said this gold makes you rich.

Booker T. Washington said, "Character is the sum total of all we struggle against." Just like a weightlifter's muscles develop under the pressure and strain of the barbells, your character develops from the trials you struggle through. And just as it is impossible to develop muscles without strain, it is impossible to develop character without struggle.

I know it's hard to understand why it has to be this way. This is why Peter the Apostle tells us, *"Beloved, think it not strange concerning the fiery trial which is to try you...But rejoice...that, when his (Christ's) glory shall be revealed, you may be glad also with exceeding joy"* (I Peter 4:12-13).

•

Remember: YOUR TRIALS ARE YOUR TREASURES!

8/HOW TO BE BEAUTIFUL!

"How beautiful are the feet of them that preach the gospel of peace, and bring glad tidings of good things!" (Romans 10:15).

Also read: Prov. 16:24; 18:4; Mt. 12:34

This year, billions of bucks will be spent by people seeking beauty. If you'd like to be more beautiful, there are ways you can help yourself without spending a fortune on a facelift. The Bible says, *"How beautiful are the feet of them that preach the gospel of peace, and bring glad tidings of good things."*

Did you ever think the Bible could tell you how to have beautiful feet? By nature your feet are somewhat ugly. But even your "uglies" become beautiful when they're committed to bringing glad news.

Being energetic is a great way to beautify your face. Have you noticed how so many people are tired and worn out? Their lack of energy causes their faces to fall, their smiles to vanish and their eyes to glaze over.

Today you have the "Divine Energizer" moving in your heart and soul. He will light up your face and your life until you glow with the radiance of heaven. The Bible says of Stephen, *"And all that sat in the council, looking stedfastly on him, saw his face as it had been the face of an angel"* (Acts 6:15).

You won't get this glow from Max Factor; you need the Divine Factor. Revlon can't do it; a Revelation is necessary. It's not Oil of Olay; it's knowing that everything is OK. Clinique is unique, but the Holy Spirit has the true technique to make you beautiful.

What good news will you bear today? Will you share Christ or a word of encouragement with anyone? Beautiful words will beautify your feet.

•

Remember: THE GOOD NEWS YOU BRING AND THE ENERGY OF THE HOLY SPIRIT WILL MAKE YOU AS BEAUTIFUL AS AN ANGEL.

9/BONES

"The hand of the Lord was upon me, and carried me out in the spirit of the Lord, and set me down in the midst of the valley which was full of bones" (Ezekiel 37:1).

Also read: Is. 66:12-14; Eph. 5:30

Ezekiel was told to prophesy to a valley full of bones. It must have been discouraging to preach to bones, but I think ministers today know the feeling—every organization has four different kinds of bones:

First, the *wishbones:* people who wish somebody else, doing the work, would do it their way.

Second, the *jawbones:* those who do all the talking but little else.

Third, the *knucklebones:* people who knock everything done by those who are working.

Fourth, the *backbones:* the faithful people who get under the load and do the work.

What kind of "bone" are you? If you haven't been the kind of person you want to be, there's a way you can be changed. As the prophet Ezekiel preached God's Word, the bones came together. As you read God's Word and pray, you will also be changed. *"So I prophesied...and they lived...an exceeding great army"* (Ezekiel 37:10).

Sometime ago God gave a vision to a minister friend of mine while I was preaching at a convention. He saw thousands of sheep coming toward him. Their wool was all white and fluffy. But as they neared, their wool turned into helmets of steel and their faces changed from that of sheep into determined soldiers.

I believe this dream may mean that God is going to transform His sheep into determined soldiers of the cross and that we are going to see a great last-day revival before Jesus returns.

•

Remember: READ GOD'S WORD AND ALLOW HIS SPIRIT TO MOVE IN YOUR LIFE—THIS WILL BRING YOUR BONES TOGETHER WITH OTHERS' UNTIL WE BECOME A GREAT ARMY.

10/AGING AIN'T ALL BAD!

"White hair is a crown of glory and is seen most among the godly" (Proverbs 16:31, TLB).

Also read: Ps. 73:24-26; 90:14; Ti. 2:2-4; 2 Cor. 5:1

Growing old is not all bad. There are a few good things about aging. Someone has said, "Birthdays are good for you. He who has the most lives the longest!"

But as a friend told me, "Good comes out of everything." Today's devotional is my effort to squeeze good out of a sometimes tragic situation.

1. **Aging dampens the fires of desire so you can concentrate more fully on the eternal dimensions of life.**
2. **Aging should make you easier to live with.** Young people react to everything and try to win every argument and triumph in every battle. But the good thing about growing older is that you mellow with age. You begin to lose some of your sharp edges and things go easier if you walk with the Lord.

    The tragic thing about growing older without God is that you become bitter and resentful. Like one man said, "The devil doesn't have any happy old people." The reason why is because sinful old people have nothing to be happy about.
3. **Age gives you a pulpit of influence.** One famous author said that no one listened to her or read her books until she turned gray.
4. **Age helps you prepare to meet God.** Think of how many would rush straight to hell if God did not slow them down to prepare for judgment day.

> A traveler in the East came upon this poignant epitaph:
> "Oh traveler, as you pass by
>   As you are now so once was I
> As I am now, so you will be
>   Prepare yourself to follow me."
> But he saw that someone had added these lines:
> "To follow you, I'm not content
>   Until I know which way you went."

•

Remember: GROWING OLD AIN'T ALL BAD—WHEN YOU GROW OLD WITH GOD.

11/WHEN YOU'RE SICK OF SPIRITUAL THINGS!

"God; who has made us able ministers of the new testament; not of the letter, but of the spirit; for the letter killeth, but the spirit giveth life" (2 Corinthians 3:6).

Also read: Ps. 44:20 & 21; Mal. 3:7; Heb. 10:23

Do you ever get sick of reading spiritual books? Maybe after reading all these pages, you'd like to toss this devotional book of mine into the lake.

I must confess there have been many times when I've become so weary of spiritual books I've felt like throwing out the whole bunch.

But I'm wise to "Old Lowell" and his fickle ways of the flesh. I know how to get the best of him when he acts spiritually nauseated.

1. **I don't condemn myself for feeling unspiritual.** Never once has God said we are to feel spiritual. He simply says, *"Keep my commandments"* (see Jn. 14:15). Feelings come and go like the wind that shifts from hour to hour. Actions are more important than feelings, so as long as I act right, I really don't care how I feel.
2. **I'll turn to "pure theology": The Bible.** I have found when other authors have failed to reach me, God's Word penetrates my hardness quicker than anything else. The Holy Spirit is aware of my carnal condition; when I make a decision to read God's Word and pray, the Spirit helps make the Word come alive.
3. **I'll speed-read a good book.** If your spiritual palate is not up to eating God's Word, you can speed-read a book, turning the pages as fast as you can. Within a few minutes, you'll run across something that you like and will create a spiritual hunger for more. Don't be afraid of priming your pump.
4. **An honest prayer helps.** There's nothing wrong in praying, "Oh God, I'm as dead as a piece of wood. Give me a holy hunger for spiritual things." I've prayed this prayer often.

How many times have you not been hungry and then were invited to eat? Out of courtesy you pulled your chair up to the table and taken a small helping of some food and "Bang!" your appetite hit. Be honest enough to recognize that your spiritual man is much like the natural one. Force-feed yourself a few steaks from God's Word. Decide to seek God as a matter of principle, and the Lord will honor your decision and move in your heart.

•

Remember: ALLOW THE LIFE OF GOD'S SPIRIT TO ENTER YOUR DEVOTIONS.

12/DON'T BE AN EAGLE IN A SPARROW'S NEST!

"As God's Messenger I give each of you God's warning: Be honest in your estimate of yourselves" (Romans 12:3, TLB).

Also read: Matt. 19:30; 23:11 & 12; Mark 9:35

Little Paul was swinging on his swing, ignoring his mother as she called. Finally, in a moment of frustration his mother said, "Paul, if I could buy you for what you're worth, and sell you for what you think you're worth, I could make a fortune."

The child had an inflated opinion of himself. How do you view yourself? Do you think more or less of yourself than you should? To think more results in pride—to think less results in feelings of inferiority. The balance is hard to find.

The problem with many people is they think they are too big to do little things. The problem with others is they think they're too little to do big things.

How do you get a true picture of yourself? By studying the life of Jesus Christ. Did Jesus set himself up on a throne to be served?

Never.

The book of John records that Jesus *". . . riseth from supper, and laid aside his garments: and took a towel, and girded himself ... and began to wash the disciples feet"* (John 13:3-5).

Wow! What a man.

Only a man who is truly sure of himself can serve others. Inferior-feeling people feel threatened when asked to serve, but Jesus taught that service is a sign of self-confidence.

Are you serving others? Today, as you go about your duties, take the towel and serve others. It is proof that you truly feel good about yourself.

•

Remember: DON'T BE AN EAGLE IN A SPARROW'S NEST.

13/YOU ARE GOD'S AGENT!

"Ye have not chosen me, but I have chosen you, and ordained you, that ye should go and bring forth fruit, and that your fruit should remain: that whatsoever ye shall ask the Father in my name, he may give it (to) you" (John 15:16)

Also read: Deut. 13:4; Ps. 100; Rom. 12:10-13

Get ready, for today's text is one of the most powerful in the entire Bible. Jesus says:

1. **You have not chosen me, but I have chosen you.** Why should a God as holy as the Lord choose sinners like you and me? We were outcasts of the Kingdom, rebels, doomed to be damned. But Jesus Christ has chosen you and me to be His agents here on planet earth. What a great honor!
2. **Jesus has ordained you to the work of the ministry.** Maybe you've never realized this truth before now. You probably thought your pastor was the ordained one, but the Bible says that Jesus has ordained you. He has selected you to be His personal agent to represent Him in your home, your job, or wherever you go. You are God's agent.
3. **Jesus has ordained you to go!** The danger of your life is that you get into a habit, a routine that limits your scope and sphere of influence. Jesus says, "Get out and go!" Each day of your life—including today—try to meet new people.

    Drive home a different way and make a few extra stops. At work or school, take a different hour for lunch, or, if that's impossible, sit in a different place when you eat. Go out of your way to talk to someone.

    Go. Go. Go. Get out of your rut. Make certain that you meet different people each day.
4. **You are to make converts.** Jesus said, "Go and bring forth fruit, and your fruit should remain." It is your responsibility to bring others to Christ. It is the pastor's and evangelist's job to teach you how to do it.

    Are you bringing forth fruit? Are you winning lost souls to Christ? The realization that you are God's agent, chosen and ordained for the task of soulwinning, will transform you from an unmotivated failure into a powerfully successful Christian.

And how are you to accomplish all this? Jesus said, *"Whatsoever ye shall ask the Father in my name, He will give it (to) you"* (Jn. 16:23). Prayer is the secret to unlocking the power of God in your life. Start praying this very moment. Say, "Lord Jesus, You have chosen me to be Your agent to win many others to Christ. I dedicate my heart, soul, mind and body to this task, that You will be pleased and God will be glorified."

•

Remember: YOU ARE GOD'S AGENT!

14/PAIN—THE PRICE OF PROGRESS!

"For we know that the whole creation groaneth and travaileth in pain together until now" (Romans 8:22).

Also read: 2 Cor. 4:8-10; 17-18; Heb. 12:6-8; 11-13

Read the following paragraphs carefully. They are so important, I have a copy pasted in the front of my Bible.

"We live in a culture that worships comfort. During this century, we have seen the greatest assault on discomfort in the history of the human race. We have learned to control our environment with central heating and air conditioning; we have reduced drudgery with machines and computers; we have learned to control pain, depression, and stress; we even provide electronic antidotes to boredom with television sets and video games.

"Most of this is to the good, but unfortunately it has created an impression that the purpose of life is to attain a blissful state of nirvana, a total absence of struggle and strain. The emphasis is on consuming, not producing; on short term hedonism rather than long term satisfaction. We seek immediate gratification of our desires with no penalties.

"Life doesn't work that way—at least not for many, and not for long. One of Benjamin Franklin's favorite sayings was 'There's no gain without pain.' And it's as true today as it was when it appeared in *Poor Richard's Almanac*. The great goal of becoming what one is capable of becoming can be achieved only by those willing to pay the price; and the price always involves sacrifice, discomfort, unpleasantness, and yes, even pain."

(Excerpt from *Doing It Now Scribners* by Edwin C. Bless.)

No one likes pain, but it's the price of progress, and you will move ahead in life depending on how much pain you are willing to bear. Athletes push the pain barrier every time they train or appear in competition.

As I write these devotionals, my shirt is often wet with sweat. I hurt as I reach into my inner resources to find ways to express eternal truth. But pain is the price of progress.

•

Remember: TO SUCCEED IN LIFE YOU MUST MAKE PAIN YOUR FRIEND.

15/PROTECT YOUR PEARLS!

"Give not that which is holy unto the dogs, neither cast ye your pearls before swine, lest they trample them under their feet, and turn against to tear you" (Matthew 7:6).

Also read: Prov. 21:20; Matt. 6:21

Once, years ago in Kansas, some young men and women were driving around, drinking and "having fun" when they saw me and stopped their car. They wanted to talk.

In my zeal to win them to the Lord I spent two hours sharing truths and experiences that were my treasures. After all my sharing they simply laughed and drove off into the darkness.

Looking back, I can see that I was foolish to waste my time sharing my spiritual secrets. They were using me to make their boring night interesting.

I learned that there are some things you don't tell an unbeliever. There are secrets of your soul that are pearls—not to be cast out to be walked on by those without faith.

The Bible tells us God loved Hezekiah, but the king made a great mistake. He forgot to protect his "pearls." The King of Babylon heard of King Hezekiah's greatness and sent several of his ambassadors to check out the story. This impressed Hezekiah and his ego was so swelled by the visit the Bible in 2 Kings says, *"And Hezekiah shewed them all his treasures—his silver, gold, spices, aromatic oils, armory—everything ..."*

The prophet Isaiah went to King Hezekiah and said, *"The time will come when everything in this palace shall be carried to Babylon...nothing shall be left. Some of your own sons will be taken away and made into eunuchs who will serve in the palace of the King of Babylon"* (2 Kings 20:13-18, TLB).

King Hezekiah forgot to protect his "pearls"—the treasures of God's temple. The lesson is this: be careful with whom you share your innermost treasures. The Spirit of God will help you to know which listeners are truly sincere.

•

Remember: PROTECT YOUR PEARLS!

16/HELP SOMEONE LAUGH!

"A merry heart doeth good like a medicine: but a broken spirit drieth the bones" (Proverbs 17:22).

Also read: Prov. 15:13 & 15; Jas. 5:13

For fifty years George Burns has been one of the greatest humorists in show business. On a recent TV interview he said, "You can be sad alone, but it takes someone else to help you laugh."

How many will you help laugh today? I meet many people who say, "I can never remember a joke." Why? Because they've never felt jokes were important.

There's so much sadness and depression in the world. You can lift the load by helping someone laugh. Did you know laughter can actually make a person feel better physically? Arnold Glasgow calls laughter "...a tranquilizer with no side effects."

Here are a few jokes I hope you will enjoy:

"Marriage is the only war where you sleep with the enemy."

"My wife know who's boss in our house. The other day she came to me on her knees and said, 'Come out from under that bed you coward."

"I'm so poor, I can't even pay attention."

"A wife is a person who stands by her husband through all of the troubles she wouldn't have had if she hadn't married him."

Now if these lines are not funny to you, find some other good, witty sentences and practice them until they work for you.

The Bible says a cheerful spirit is like medicine but a broken spirit dries up the bones. Have you allowed the troubles of your life to infect your spirit or can you laugh at life and at yourself? Today, try your best to help someone laugh.

•

Remember: HELP SOMEONE LAUGH TODAY.

17/SPEAK UP!

"For Herod...laid hold on John (the Baptist), and bound him, and put him in prison for Herodias' sake, his brother Phillip's wife. For John said unto him, It is not lawful for thee to have her" (Matthew 14:3 & 4).

Also read: Deut. 6:6-9; 11:18 & 19; Mt. 5:13-16

The Bible emphatically declares that in the last days, sin will abound and the love of many will wax cold (see Matt. 24:12), that some shall depart from the faith, *"giving heed to seducing spirits, and doctrines of devils"* (Tim 4:1).

What is the devil's doctrine? The same that he spoke to Eve in the garden when he said, *"If you partake of the forbidden, ye shall not surely die"* (Gen. 3:4).

The Bible tells us what sin is; the commandments have never been watered down to suggestions. John the Baptist was the greatest prophet ever born. He was jailed and later beheaded for preaching out against the sin of immorality. (see Matt. 11:1-15).

John's courageous stand against evil won the admiration of Jesus Christ. Jesus said, *"Truly, of all men ever born, none shines more brightly than John the Baptist"* (Matt. 11:11, TLB).

John the Baptist took an uncompromising stand against sin and was proclaimed to be greater than any prophet ever born.

These are slippery days when many compromises are being made about premarital sex, adultery, alcoholism, pornography, abortion, homosexuality, gambling, etc. Are you speaking up for Christ on the burning issues of the day, or do you let the conversation slide toward more comfortable topics like the weather and sports?

Martin Luther said, "If I profess with the loudest voice and clearest exposition every portion of the truth of God except precisely that little point which the world and the devil are at that moment attacking, I am not confessing Christ, however boldly I may be professing Christ."

If you have been hiding your light under a bushel, the devil has gagged you. Shake yourself free from your cowardice and speak up.

•

Remember: SPEAK UP TODAY!

18/PRESS OR REGRESS

"I press toward the mark for the prize of the high calling of God in Christ Jesus" (Philippians 3:14).

Also read: Luke 13:24; Col. 1:29

What is your goal for today? Tomorrow? Five years from now? The reason I ask is that you need a goal to press toward. If you don't press you'll regress.

Webster's dictionary defines regress as "to go back." It also describes pressing as "to act upon through steady pushing or thrusting force." In our easy-going affluent age, pressing is not popular; especially among lazy Christians.

My associate, Carl Malz, has come to the conclusion that all our problems can be traced to arrogance or apathy. Either we're so arrogant we don't see the problem or we are so apathetic that when we see the problem, we don't care.

We're already many days into the New Year. Have you defined your goal? Are you pressing toward it? Don't be depressed by the fact that your goal may be distant. Inch by inch—anything's a cinch.

Press—or you'll regress.

To encourage you, let me make an acrostic out of "press".

> P—*Pinpoint your daily goal.* The saying is "to start is to have the job half-done."
>
> R—*Reject discouragement.* When Edison was asked if he was discouraged over his 10,000 experiments to invent the electric light bulb, he said, "No. I've just learned 10,000 ways it's not done."
>
> E—*Express confidence.* Once you express your faith openly and decide that you will be victorious, you will find people moving towards you.
>
> S—*Share with others!* If you give your love, joy and advice to others, they'll soon become your allies.
>
> S—*Seek advice.* So few people take advantage of the success of others. If there has been a key to my success in life it has been my determination to seek the advice of other successful people.

Don't forget these ideas if you want to be a success!

•

Remember: PRESS OR YOU'LL REGRESS

19/HOW TO OVERCOME YOUR FEARS!

"There is no fear in love; but perfect love casteth out fear: because fear hath torment. He that feareth is not made perfect in love" (1 John 4:18).

Also read: Ps. 91:4-7; 2 Tim. 1:7; Rom. 8:29-39

The Bible says, "Fear has torment." If you have been tormented by fear there's a way you can escape. But it will require confrontation. Why? Because flight will only increase your fright.

Someone has said, "Fear is false evidence appearing real." Repeat this sentence aloud: "Fear is false evidence appearing real."

The root of fear is falsehood. Psychologists will tell you there are only two basic forces in this world: fear and love. You will be dominated by one or the other.

If you're afraid of something, aggressively examine the facts about it. Knowledge dispels falsehoods. The fewer lies you believe about a situation, the more you will relax.

But you cannot deal with fear politely, it is a tormentor that you must aggressively attack without mercy!

If you allow fear to keep you from traveling when road conditions are poor, it won't be long before a rainstorm will keep you off the highway, and then heavy traffic. Soon your fear will spread until you dislike getting out at all, and finally, you'll be a hermit hiding out at home.

Some people give in to their fears so often that one dentist has this sign outside his door: "We Cater To Cowards."

David the Psalmist faced his fears and said, *"Yea, though I walk through the valley of the shadow of death, I will fear no evil: for thou art with me; thy rod and thy staff they comfort me"* (Ps. 23:4).

Pray about the decisions you make. If God wants you to take a trip or make a deal, remember that He is in charge: if He leads you to do something, it will turn out well.

•

Remember: OVERCOME YOUR FEARS BY LEARNING THE FACTS, LIVING AGGRESSIVELY, AND PRAYING.

20/CAN YOU LEGISLATE MORALITY?

"Flee fornication" (1 Corinthians 6:18).

Also read: 1 Kng. 8:60 & 61; Lk. 6:47-49; Heb. 12:9 & 10

Promotors of evil have a quick one-liner they like to throw at anyone who stands in favor of righteousness. They'll glibly say, "You know, you can't legislate morality."

They have a half-truth here but they are trying to present it as a whole one and it doesn't fly. Here's why.

Deadly diseases of the body are quarantined. When smallpox, the black plague, and other diseases swept continents, the infected were quarantined. In Florida diseased orange trees are burned.

Sin is a spiritual disease that needs to be quaratined—just like other physical diseases. For instance, 25,000 people are killed and 800,000 are maimed each year by drivers who drink. Now, finally, after many years, the states are getting tough on drunken drivers, passing strict laws. In states where tough laws have been written, traffic deaths have dropped dramatically.

The least we can do for people who lack self-control is to make it more difficult for them to practice their vice.

Let's not forget that the divine lawgiver did legislate morality when He gave the 10 commandments. Was God at fault when He wrote the commandments in stone saying "Thou shalt not"? Never. He knew there were certain things you and I should not do. He made it plain that there are certain physical and spiritual diseases that should not be allowed to exist—in order to prevent the deadly infection of sin from spreading.

•

Remember: WHILE SOME MORAL BEHAVIOR CANNOT BE LEGISLATED, IT CAN BE RESTRICTED.

21/CREATED TO SUCCEED!

"... faith, if it hath not works is dead" (James 1:20).

Also read: Jos. 1:9; Jas. 2:14-26

It seems that Christians are divided between two philosophies today. One emphasizes the inner life of holiness and prayer—the other encourages hard work and success. Each have their weaknesses. The "holiness" people (and I count myself as one of them, *"for without holiness no one will see the Lord"* (Heb. 12:14, NIV)) are slow to face their responsibilities. When faced with failure or a problem they'll say, "Maybe this is God's will—we ought to pray about it ..."

The "success" people fail to see the importance of holiness and prayer. They are often carnal, allowing unclean habits and sins into their lives and seldom spend much time in prayer.

To be a Super Saint you need both philosophies. You need a pure life and prayer, but you also need persistence and the ability to perceive the laws of success.

During the first years of my Christian life I committed myself to the "holiness" group. But then I began to study "success" theories. I could see that they actually had more practical things going for them than the fundamentalists did; but I disliked their basic philosophy that "man by his willpower can create a new world" (humanism) because I knew this was a lie. I admired their zeal but could not embrace their error.

I was about to give up on the "success" activist philosophy altogether until I read Genesis 1:26 and 28 where God said, *"Let us make man IN OUR IMAGE, after our likeness ... and let them have dominion ... and replenish the earth ... and SUBDUE IT"* (emphasis mine).

Then I thought, if I have been created in God's image and God is a success—then I should succeed too!

You and I were created to succeed; but to truly succeed we must live holy lives of prayer and be persistent and wise in all that we do. The answer to life is not one philosophy or the other—but both.

●

Remember: YOU WERE CREATED TO SUCCEED IN ALL THAT YOU DO!

22/PADDLE WHILE YOU PRAY!

"Then the Lord said to Moses, 'Quit praying and get the people moving! Forward, march!' " (Exodus 14:15, TLB).

Also read: Joshua 2:18

I want to expand on the two philosophies I mentioned in yesterday's devotional. A deep understanding of these two philosophies is fundamental to your ultimate success.

One camp says, "*God* must do it." The other camp says, "*I* must do it." The truth is—"*Both* must do it" because God works His will through man.

> The story is told of two men in a canoe who were not aware they had drifted dangerously close to a great falls. The water had picked up speed and was swirling wildly, carrying their canoe along. If they plunged over the falls they'd surely die. Sensing the danger one man cried, "Let's pray!" The other man, equally afraid, yelled, "Paddle while you pray!"

His understanding was the best. When Ronald Reagan was running for President several of his staff members were extremely frustrated at the "born-again" Christian community. They told reporters, "We can't get these Christians to do anything. All they want to do is sit in church and sing 'Amazing Grace' and pray—but we can't get them out to pound on doors enlisting voters."

I really believe if America is lost it will be because Christians abandoned their responsibilities. It's good to pray—but we'd better "pound" the street with our shoeleather if we hope to save this country.

> Another story illustrates this point. A Christian man was inspired to build a rock garden on an unusable piece of his property. He worked for over two years, creating beautiful arrangements out of rocks and planting flowers and vines. When he finished he invited his Christian friend over to see it. When the friend walked in he exclaimed, "Isn't it wonderful what God can do!" To which the man replied, "Yeah, you should have seen it when just God had it!"

Your life is much like the rock garden before the man went to work, and your success is like the two men in the canoe drifting toward the falls. You'd better "paddle while you pray" or you're sure to fall.

•

Remember: GOD WORKS HIS WILL THROUGH MEN—SO "PADDLE WHILE YOU PRAY."

23/DO YOU HAVE A DARING DREAM?

"I will pour out my spirit upon all flesh; and your sons and your daughters shall prophesy, your old men shall dream dreams, your young men shall see visions." (Joel 2:28).

Also read: Prov. 3:5 & 6; 16:3; Is. 48:17; Jn. 16:3

Dreams are dynamite! They can propel you into orbit quicker than any other force. Do you have a daring dream?

There is an old adage that says,
"Some men die in battle
   Fighting evil kings
Most men die of boredom
   Doing little things!"

I have taken surveys across the United States and Canada and have found that less than one in ten Christians has a daring dream. Most believers just plod through the routines of life mechanically and without feeling.

God created you and me from the dust of the earth, and He knows how important a daring dream is to our lives. This is why He said, "In the last days I will pour out my Spirit upon all flesh and three things will happen:

1. Your youth shall speak forth My word (prophesy).
2. Your old men shall dream dreams. (Only God knows how much an aging person needs a dream. The older you get the more life shrinks.)
3. Your young men shall see visions." (To have clear cut vision of the future, knowing God's perfect plan for your life is the most essential element of personal motivation.)

If you do not have a daring dream, the key to receiving one is to seek God until you are filled with the Spirit. Dreams and visions are the result of living a Spirit-filled life. The more God's Spirit takes ahold of you, the more of what God is planning is made real to you, and the more you can see how you fit in with His future.

•

Remember: SEEK GOD FERVENTLY AND YOU'LL RECEIVE A DARING DREAM.

24/WHO IS JESUS

"Neither is there salvation in any other: for there is none other name under heaven given among men, whereby we must be saved" (Acts 4:12).

Also read: Ps. 11:9; Jn. 1:12; Acts 3:16

Although Jesus Christ is described throughout the Bible in many ways, He is still the Lord.

He's the seed of the woman (Gen); the passover Lamb (Ex.); High Priest (Lev.); the cloud by day and Pillar of Fire by night (Num.); a prophet like unto Moses (Deut.); the Captain of our Salvation (Josh.). He is the Lawgiver (Jud.); the Kinsman Redeemer (Ruth); a prophet like unto Samuel (1 & 2 Sam.); the Great King (1 & 2 Kings); the Incomparable Monarch (1 & 2 Chron.); Our Faithful Scribe (Ezra); our builder (Neh.); our escape from death (Est.); the Holy One (Job); and our Eternal Wisdom (Prov.). He is also our Total Life (Ecc.); Lover of our souls (Song of Sol.); Prince of Peace (Is.); the Eternal Branch (Jer.); the One who weeps on our behalf (Lam.); the God of four faces (Ez.); the fourth man in the fiery furnace (Dan.); the faithful Husband (Hos.); the Baptizer in the Holy Spirit (Amos); the Mighty to save (Obad.); the great Missionary (Jon.). He is Messenger of beautiful feet (Mic.); the Avenger of God's people (Nah.); the stirring Evangelist (Hab.); the burning Bush (Zeph.); the Restorer of God's inheritance (Hag.); the eternal Fountain (Zech.); and the Son of Righteousness (Mal.).

Anne Sullivan was a dedicated teacher who worked with Helen Keller, the blind and deaf mute. You probably have heard the story of the breakthrough when Anne pumped cold water on Helen's hand and spelled out the first word that Helen understood.

One day Anne was "talking" to Helen about God via the spelling system. When Anne asked her if she believed in Jesus, Helen replied, "I've always known Him—but now I know His Name."

Praise God, you and I know Jesus Christ as our Personal Savior.

•

Remember: JESUS IS HIS NAME; ALL THE DESCRIPTIONS ONLY HELP US TO LOVE AND KNOW HIM BETTER.

25/THE WAY TO LIVE!

"He that believeth on me, the works that I do shall he do also: and greater works than these shall he do; because I go unto my Father" (John 14:12).

Also read: Mt. 25:35-40; Heb. 6:10; 1 Jn. 3:16-18

Jesus lived the one perfect life and He is our example today. We know from the words of Jesus that He came:
1. **To do God's will**
   "I seek not my own will, but the will of the Father which hath sent me" (John 5:30).
2. **To speak God's Word**
   "For I have given unto them the words which thou gavest me; and they have received them" (John 17:8).
3. **To work in God's name**
   "I have manifested thy name...and I have declared unto them thy name, and will declare it; that the love wherewith thou hast loved me may be in them, and I in them" (John 17:6, 26).

Christ is our perfect pattern. Today you should:
1. **Do God's will.** Think of yourself as "God at work," "God at school," "God at play." If you decide to do God's will today in the things you do and the things you say, this will be one of the best days of your life.
2. **Speak God's Word.** Truth is what you need to share with others. You don't have to be spouting off Scriptures all of the time. Much of what Jesus said was simple truth about life. Speak the truth in quietness and meekness, and if the person you are sharing with is open, share God's Word.
3. **Work in Jesus' name.** Jesus said, *"And whatsoever ye shall ask in my name, that will I do, that the Father may be glorified in the Son. If ye shall ask anything in my name, I will do it"* (John 14: 13 & 14).

You really are an agent of Jesus Christ, working in His name. This will affect everything you do and say. In fact, today's text declares that the very works that Jesus did, you are to do also.

Jesus fed the hungry, healed the sick, helped the fallen, spoke the truth, cast out evil spirits, etc. Just as Jesus was God wrapped in skin, your attitude, words and actions are to be like His.

So how should you live? Just as Jesus lived when He was here on earth. Imagine Jesus working on your job, living in your house, going to your school. If you pattern your life after His, you will find the same joy He discovered.

•

Remember: DO THE WORKS THAT JESUS DID.

26/WHY YOU'RE BEING BURNED AND BATTERED AROUND!

"For we are his workmanship" (Ephesians 2:10).

Also read: Is. 43:2-4; Na.1:7; 2 Cor. 4:8 & 9

Are you in the fire? Are you being beaten down by circumstances beyond your control? Before you give up and bail out, it's important that you understand what God is doing in your life.

Today's text says that we are His workmanship. God is working on you and me to make us like Jesus Christ. A moment's reflection on this will tell you that great changes must be made.

Wilkinson steel swords are famous for their resiliency and strength. These swords are made by heating the steel and hammering it until the molecules are arranged in order. This process is repeated over and over again until the swords seldom, if ever, break.

How will God change us from cheap pot metal, the kind you find in toys, into tough spring steel? The only way is by putting us in the fire and allowing events to pound on us until all the impurities have been driven out.

Your strength comes from your struggles. Your power comes from the pounding. Your faithfulness is developed in the fiery trials you've been going through.

Jesus said, *"They shall lay their hands on you, and persecute you, delivering you up to the synagogues, and into prisons...and ye shall be betrayed both by parents, and brethren, and kinsfolks, and friends; and some of you shall they cause to be put to death. And ye shall be hated of all men for my name's sake. But there shall not an hair of your head perish. In...patience possess ye your souls"* (Luke 21:12,16-19).

If you're going through a fiery trial, don't fear. The Lord is watching over every detail so you will develop into strong steel for His glory.

•

Remember: YOU ARE HIS WORKMANSHIP.

27/DON'T COME EMPTYHANDED!

"And none shall appear before me empty" (Exodus 34:20).

Also read: Ex. 34:20; Deut. 16:16

When I was a child I used to attend church with my Catholic grandparents. Grandpa would always hand me a nickel to put in the offering plate when it came by. He didn't want any of his granchildren to appear unthankful for God's blessings.

I've never forgotten those times. And when I found these words in Exodus, *"And none shall appear before me empty"*—I realized Grandpa was right: no one should freeload on the Lord.

Do you make a special effort to prepare the offerings you give to God? The last minute shuffling at offering time, looking for your checkbook or a little change shows that you're probably not keyed to giving.

I used to be this way but then I instructed our bookkeeper to assign the first ten percent of my paycheck to the projects God had laid on my heart. So now the Lord gets the first tenth of my earnings.

The truth is God knows the gifts you bring to Him (or send to soulwinning ministries), are actually the seeds for your own prosperity. The Bible says, *"Remember this—if you give little, you will get little. A farmer who plants just a few seeds will get only a small crop, but if he plants much, he will reap much"* (2 Cor. 9:6, TLB).

So don't come before the Lord emptyhanded. If you have been praying today, wondering if He has heard your prayers, check and see if your giving is "up to date". Money won't buy God's favor, but your obedience to His command to give tithes will bless Him (see Mal. 10).

•

Remember: DON'T COME BEFORE THE LORD EMPTYHANDED.

28/HOW TO KEEP FROM STRIKING OUT!

"For our light affliction, which is but for a moment, worketh for us a far more exceeding and eternal weight of glory" (2 Corinthians 4:17).

Also read: Prov. 16:32; Rom. 12:19-24; Eph. 4:31 & 32

Baseball is big business. The clubs are run by powerful multimillionaires with king size egos. Whoever aspires to be the commissioner of baseball has to be a "man's man" in the most nitty-gritty sense of the word.

When baseball commissioner Bowie Kuhn was preparing to leave office, after ruling the diamond empire for 18 years, he offered these bits of advice to his successor, Peter Ubberroth: "Stick to your guns; be courageous. Don't let anyone push you around. Be thick-skinned. And, above all, have a good sense of humor, because you're going to need it."

These words have tremendous significance to anyone who wants to win at the game of life.

The Apostle Paul had to defend himself against the accusations of false brethren who were trying to undermine his position as the leader of the Corinthian church. He wrote:

They say they serve Christ? But I have served him far more! (Have I gone mad to boast like this?) I have worked harder, been put in jail oftener, been whipped times without number, and faced death again and again and again.

Five different times the Jews gave me their terrible thirty-nine lashes. Three times I was beaten with rods. Once I was stoned. Three times I was shipwrecked. Once I was in the open sea all night and the whole next day...

Then, besides all this, I have the constant worry of how the churches are getting along (2 Cor. 11:23-25, 28).

Speaking of all these trials, Paul was able to say, *"For our light affliction, which is but for a moment, worketh for us for a more exceeding and eternal weight of glory"* (2 Cor. 4:17). Why was Paul able to succeed and not strike out? Because he stuck to his guns, was courageous, didn't let anyone push him around, was thick-skinned and had enough sense of humor to call his troubles a "light affliction."

•

Remember: KUHN'S ADVICE AND YOU WON'T STRIKE OUT!

29/WHAT ARE YOU MAKING OF YOURSELF?

"Steady plodding brings prosperity" (Proverbs 21:5 TLB).

Also read: Ec. 7:8 & 9; Is. 40:31; Heb. 6:12; 12:1

Are you happy with the progress you are making in life? Remember, the advances you make are a result of your decisions and you are the only one responsible for them.

Failures blame their circumstances, their upbringing, or whatever for their inability to rise. But most successful people will tell you they reached the top by lots of hard work and tears.

Our text today says, *"Steady plodding brings prosperity."* This has really been true in my own life.

I grew up on a farm in South Dakota, plowing and tilling the soil. I wanted to do something to "break out of the furrow"—so I learned how to play the guitar. I didn't have a music teacher so every step was a slow one—just plodding along learning a new chord here and a new song there.

Before long I organized my first little country-rock dance band and kept plodding on until we had a good following.

But then God was good enough to win me to Christ and Connie and I began in the ministry. At first we only had a rambler station wagon and a couple of guitars. But we kept plodding on, year after year. Five, ten, fifteen, twenty years, until now it's been twenty nine years in the ministry.

Yes, we do have a nationwide ministry on TV, conduct many crusades and seminars and I am president of an exciting Bible college (Trinity Bible College in Ellendale, North Dakota), but all of this success has been simply God's blessings upon a plodder.

Are you willing to make quality decisions, think quality thoughts, choose quality friends and keep plodding on? If so, you will surely succeed!

•

Remember: IF YOU DON'T LIKE YOUR LIFE, KEEP ON PLODDING UNTIL YOU MAKE THE NECESSARY CHANGES.

30/YOU HAVE INSIDE INFORMATION

"The fool hath said in his heart, There is no God. They are corrupt, they have done abominable works, there is none that doeth good" (Psalm 14:1).

Also read: Prov. 15:1-12; Rom. 1:19-21

The atheist who denies the existence of God usually considers himself to be intellectually superior to a believer. But the Bible calls him a fool. Here's why:

Let's say I met a man on the street one day and said, "I'm really glad to see you. Let me tell you what John Olsen said to me." Wouldn't he be foolish to hold up his hand and say, "Don't tell me that. I know John Olsen doesn't exist!"

I'd reply, "But I just spoke with him a few minutes ago!"

And he'd say, "Well, I've never met him, I haven't seen him; I deny he exists!"

This would be downright stupid! Yet this is what an atheist says when he denies the existence of God. You and I know God exists because we have "inside information." We can feel the Spirit of God moving within us. This is something unbelievers will never understand until they experience Christ for themselves. The Bible says, *"But the man who isn't a Christian can't understand and can't accept these thoughts from God, which the Holy Spirit teaches us. They sound foolish to him, because only those who have the Holy Spirit within them can understand what the Holy Spirit means"* (1 Cor. 2:14, TLB).

The American Atheist magazine recently devoted almost every article of one issue denying the existence of God. Each poisoned pen wrote about someone he declared did not exist. Amusing, but sad.

The real reason many deny the existence of God is they don't want to be held accountable for their actions. Once you admit the existence of God, you will have to alter your lifestyle—a living God implies a pending Judgment Day.

Do you believe in God? I'm sure you do, but the way you live proves your faith is real more than all the words you say!

•

Remember: YOU KNOW GOD EXISTS BECAUSE YOU HAVE INSIDE INFORMATION.

31/THE SWORD BEARS YOUR NAME!

"And they cried, The sword of the Lord and of Gideon" (Judges 7:20).

Also read: Mk. 16:15; Gal 6:1-6

Why is it that so few Christians are motivated? About all that nine out of ten Christians do is sit in their pew.

One of the main reasons for this lethargy is the failure of Christians to see their responsibilitiy in winning the world to Christ. Another reason is that Christians are reluctant to give credit to others who try hard and win big.

When someone does a great job, they'll seldom say, "Tom did it." They'll usually say something like, "The Lord is really moving in our community." This leaves Tom feeling like his extra efforts have been annihilated. Not that Tom thought he did it alone, but if he hadn't put forth the extra effort and sacrificed himself, the victory would not have been won.

Note the Lord has said, *"I AM the Lord: That is my name: and my glory will I not give to another."* (Is. 42:8, emphasis mine).

But it is also true that God does not work alone. The combination effort is best expressed in these two lines:

"Without God, we cannot.

Without us, God will not."

We are partners in bringing the gospel to the world. God works through man and man calls on God to answer his requests. After the resurrection, the disciples *"went forth and preached everywhere, the Lord working with them, confirming the Word with signs following* (Mark 16:20).

Do you consider the gospel "Your gospel"? Have you committed your life so deeply to God that you fully identify with the success or failure of the church? There are a lot of Lone Ranger believers who like to ride alone without really identifying themselves with the Kingdom of God.

Don't be so modest as to think God is going to win your neighbors and friends without you. God needs you and you need God. You are a Kingdom team.

●

Remember: THE SWORD BEARS YOUR NAME!

32/DON'T BURY YOUR BONES!

"He that covereth his sins shall not prosper: but whoso confesseth and forsaketh them shall have mercy" (Proverbs 28:13).

Also read: Lk. 9:23-25; 2 Cor. 4:2; 1 Jn. 2:15-17

Recently a converted alcoholic said, "Most people bury their bad habits like a dog buries his favorite bone, and whenever things get tough, they'll dig up their bone of an evil habit and go to chewing it again."

Have you buried any of your favorite bones? If you have covered up lust, bitterness, greed, pride, envy etc., you'd better abandon them rather than just burying them. The Bible says if you cover your sins, you will not prosper, but if you confess and *forsake* them, you will find mercy. When the children of Israel came out of Egypt on their way to Canaan, they came to Jericho. Joshua, the commander, told the people that any of the silver or treasures found in Jericho were to belong to God.

But Achan took a beautiful Babylonian robe and approximately $200 of silver and $500 worth of gold (Josh. 7:21). Then he dug a hole (like a dog) and buried the treasures. But he could not dig a hole deep enough to hide his disobedience. Achan's covetousness caused the wrath of God to fall upon the Israelites and they lost a battle to the tiny city of Ai.

When Joshua asked why they had lost the Lord said:

"Israel hath sinned, and they have also transgressed my covenant which I commanded them: for they have even taken of the accursed thing, and have also stolen, and (lied) also, and they have put it even among their own stuff...O Israel: thou canst not stand before thine enemies, until ye take away the accursed thing from among you" (Josh. 7:11-13)..

You need to abandon your bones instead of burying them or you'll never be able to stand before your enemies (Satan, demons, evil-minded people and others).

Are you winning spiritually, physically, financially today? If not, it might be that you've buried some of your favorite bones.

•

Remember: DON'T BURY YOUR BONES—ABANDON THEM TODAY!

33/SMOKESCREENS

"Therefore you have no excuse, O man, whoever you are, when you judge another; for in passing judgment upon him you condemn yourself, because you, the judge, are doing the very same things" (Romans 2:1, RSV).

Also read: Matt. 7:3-5

An unusual story is told of Diogenes and Plato, two popular philosophers of ancient Greece. Plato had a beautiful couch which was plated with gold and embellished with precious jewels. He would have this ornate couch carried from place to place to where he would speak and would rest upon it while he lectured. Plato was more popular with the people than Diogenes, and it always irked the younger philosopher.

One night at a party of elite community leaders, Diogenes looked in and saw Plato strolling among the crowd, his guilded couch resting in the corner. Suddenly Diogenes burst in, ran over to the couch and jumped up and down upon it, crying out, "Diogenes stomps on Plato's pride!" Plato responded by saying, "Yes, and with greater pride."

The righteous indignation of the younger philosopher was only a smokescreen for his jealousy.

When religious leaders brought a woman to Jesus who had been caught in the very act of adultery, they weren't interested in justice, they were actually plotting murder. Their accusations against her were only a smokescreen used to trap Jesus by appearing to be against the law of Moses. This is why He said, *"He that is without sin among you, let him first cast a stone at her"* (John 8:7).

If you are using a smokescreen of righteous indignation to cover up your true feelings about someone else—don't. It's not worth it. Be honest enough to admit how you feel and then receive the strength of God to handle your feelings.

•

Remember: SCENES ARE OFTEN SMOKESCREENS.

34/HOW TO GET RID OF YOUR SIN!

"Come now, and let us reason together, saith the Lord; though your sins be as scarlet, they shall be as white as snow; though they be red like crimson, they shall be as wool" (Isaiah 1:18)

Also read: Ps. 103:12; Is. 43:25; Jer. 33:8

God says, "Be reasonable; listen to Me and start looking at your sins the way I do."

A student at Trinity Bible College in Ellendale, North Dakota came up with the best simplified outline of how to handle your sin: (1) admit it, (2) commit it, (3) forget it.

I'm sure you are reasonable enough to admit you have sinned. The Bible says, *"All have sinned and come short of the glory of God"* (Rom. 3:23). Notice your sin is twofold: not only have you sinned against God by your actions, but you have failed by falling short of the glory of God by not becoming all you were intended to be.

So if you'll admit before God that you are a sinner and that you have failed to achieve the glory of God, then you have made a great stride toward getting rid of your sins. You cannot eradicate what you refuse to admit.

Second, are you willing to commit your transgression to the cleansing power of the blood of Christ?

Because your sin is primarily spiritual, it requires a spiritual solution. You cannot cleanse yourself. It takes God; this is why Jesus Christ died upon the cross for you and me. *"God was in Christ, reconciling the world unto himself"* (II Cor. 5:19).

If you will commit your awful sins to Christ, the innocent blood He shed will cleanse away the stains on your soul.

Third, forget your sins! You won't accomplish a thing grieving endlessly about your transgression. Penitence doesn't help a bit. Be sure in your heart that you are forgiven. Don't let Satan convince you otherwise!

Now is the time for you to allow God to cleanse your soul. Use this basic outline to experience the cleansing power of Jesus Christ.

•

Remember: TO GET RID OF YOUR SIN: ADMIT IT, COMMIT IT, AND FORGET IT!

35/WHY TITHE?

"Bring ye all the tithes into the storehouse" (Malachi 3:10).

Also read: Prov. 11:24 & 25; 29:7; Mt. 6:19-21

If you were God and were building a Kingdom on earth you'd need finances to get the work done. This is the reason tithing is so important.

1. **It is critically important to others.** Your financial support is needed to send to missionaries, evangelists, Christian workers and pastors into communities throughout the world. The Bible says, "*And how shall they preach, except they be sent?"* (Rom. 10:15).

    When you give you are enabling others to hear the gospel—just like someone was sent to reach you, or the one who led you to Christ, you and I have the privilege and responsibility to send others forth. If you and I withhold our finances, the multitudes of lost souls will point their finger at us in judgment and cry, "Why didn't you care?"

2. **Think of what your tithing does for God.** Our Father in heaven has given us health, strength, a clear mind and an opportunity to make a living from His earth. When we give God the first tenth (the word "tithe" means "tenth") we are expressing our gratitude for what He has done.

    The Bible says, *"God loveth a cheerful giver."* Because giving is part of God's nature, He is thrilled when we act as He would.

3. **Think of what tithing does for you!** God says, *"Bring ye all the tithes into the storehouse, that there may be meat in mine house* (that the needs of my kingdom be met) *and prove me now,* (or literally put me to the test)...*if I will not open to you the windows of heaven, and pour you out a blessing that there shall not be room enough to receive it. And I will rebuke the devourer for your sake"* (Malachi 3:10 & 11).

Have you ever considered all the forces that devour your paycheck? Taxes, breakdowns, unexpected crises, sickness, disease, accidents, etc. God says, "If you will begin to give 10% of your income to my work, I will rebuke the devourer. And I will open the windows of heaven and pour you out a blessing greater than you can receive."

Wow! This is the kind of blessing I want on my life and family. Don't you?

Begin giving regularly to God from each and every paycheck. Honor God with the first fruits, the first 10% and He will honor you with the first blessing.

•

Remember: TITHING REVEALS YOUR LOVE FOR GOD, YOURSELF AND OTHERS.

YOU CAN OVERCOME!

"I write unto you...because you have overcome the wicked one" (1 John 2:13).

Also read: 1 Jn. 4:4, 5:4

A friend of mine recently said, "God's grace works for those who are overcome—but the promises of God are for the overcomers."

If you want to be an overcomer, study the Bible until you know the promises of God. Then when the enemy comes, you'll be able to defend yourself against his attacks.

Here's some great overcoming promises:

"No weapon that is formed against thee shall prosper" (Is. 54:17).

"(I have) not seen the righteous forsaken, nor his seed begging bread" (Ps. 37:25).

"Delight thyself also in the Lord; and he shall give thee the desires of thine heart" (Ps. 37:4).

"Greater is he that is in you than he that is in the world" (1 Jn. 4:4).

If these promises feel dead to your soul, there is a way you can make them "come alive:" by entering into the spirit of worship and praise.

This has been the secret of my spiritual strength throughout the 28 years of this ministry. Whenever I have been so burdened with cares that I felt I couldn't carry my load another day, I have found one of these verses of Scripture and then praised God in prayer, hands raised heavenward until it came alive in my soul.

Suddenly, like a mighty volt of electricity, the Spirit makes the invisible, visible; the impossible, possible and I'm alive in God again.

How about you? These promises were given to help you be an overcomer. Regardless of how you feel, claim one and pray it alive—you will overcome victoriously.

•

Remember: GOD'S GRACE IS FOR THOSE OVERCOME: HIS PROMISES ARE FOR THE OVERCOMERS.

37/RELIGION IS SIMPLE

"But I fear, lest by any means, as the serpent beguiled Eve through his subtilty, so your minds should be corrupted from the simplicity that is in Christ" (2 Corinthians 11:3).

Also read: Rom. 3:24 & 25; 10:9; Eph. 2:8 & 9

You'll often hear people say, "Religion is too complicated. With so many different religions, churches and sects contradicting each other, it's impossible to know the way to God."

I know religion may appear confusing at first, but if you break it down, it comes to this: either you think you can save yourself through religious deeds or you believe that God must save you through Christ.

Another way to say it is, "works or deeds." It is important that you understand the difference. It's simply this: if you can save yourself through prayers, penance and personal deeds, then Jesus Christ's life, death, and resurrection were in vain!

The fact is: Jesus died for your sins and mine because we could *not* save ourselves. *"Therefore by the deeds of the law there shall be no flesh be justified in his (God's) sight"* (Romans 3:20).

Another Scripture says, *"Not by works of righteousness which we have done, but according to his mercy he saved us"* (Tit. 3:5).

If you're trying to save yourself, how many brownie points, how many good deeds, does it take before God forgives one sinful thought or deed? It's impossible to know because God's plan is that salvation be a gift—not something you receive as a prize for good conduct.

It takes Jesus Christ abiding within you by the Holy Spirit to create the character within you that is pleasing to God. *"This is the secret: that Christ in your hearts is your only hope of glory"* (Colossians 1:27 TLB).

If you make it any more complicated than this, you are moving away from the simplicity that is in Christ.

•

Remember: RELIGION IS SIMPLE, BUT LIVING UP TO THIS SIMPLICITY TAKES A LIFETIME.

38/DON'T WASTE YOUR WISHES!

"I press toward the mark for the prize of the high calling of God in Christ Jesus" (Philippians 3:14).

Also read: Eph. 3:14-19; 2 Pet. 1:2-5; 3:18

Do you really know what you want in life? Unless you really think it through and zero in on your goals, you'll waste your wishes.

There is an amusing story of three men who were lost at sea, adrift in a lifeboat, hundreds of miles from shore. Death was only hours away for they had run out of food and water.

Suddenly they heard the clanging of a bottle alongside their rowboat and saw a little genie inside waiting to be released. They were overjoyed, knowing he could grant their wishes.

When they popped the bottle open, the genie jumped out and said, "Thank you for helping me. Now ask what you will, and I will give each of you one request."

The first man said, "I'm almost dead from exposure. I wish I was home."

Plinko! He was gone.

The second said, "His request can not be improved on. I wish I was home too."

Plinko! He was gone.

The third looked around and realizing he was alone, said, "It's really lonely out here, I sure wish the other two guys were back with me."

The foolish man wasted his wish.

How about you? Are you wasting the one great lifetime God has given you by failing to concentrate on the main goal of living? The apostle Paul said he "pressed toward the mark." What is your mark or goal?

You might be tempted to waste your time wanting things, but you should concentrate your energy on becoming rather than accumulating. Use what time you have been given to develop your character, determination and skills. Most important of all, be sure to spend time growing closer to God. Don't waste the life He has given you!

•

Remember: CONCENTRATE ON YOUR GOALS OR YOU WILL WASTE YOUR WISHES.

39/DRY TIMES WORK FOR YOUR GOOD!

"And even though Jesus was God's Son, he had to learn from experience what it was like to obey, when obeying meant suffering. It was after he had proved himself perfect in this experience that Jesus became the Giver of eternal salvation" (Hebrews 5:8-9 TLB).

Also read: Jas. 1:1-4, TLB

When you're going through a dry time in your relationship with God it's good to remember what the Lord is trying to accomplish. It might be best illustrated by this story:

Have you ever seen one of the old-time butcher blocks used in some meat markets? A butcher-block is that big square chunky table, in natural wood color, where the meat is cut up.

There is a special process that is used to bind the different pieces of the butcher-block together. First the wood is selected, then cut to proper lengths. Next it is placed in a kiln where it is heated so that the boards shrink.

After the shrunken block is dry, it is soaked in a brine water so that it swells again. Then it is placed back into the kiln to shrink dry.

This process is repeated many times until the craftsman is able to stamp these words on the block, "Will not swell or shrink."

God often puts you and me through this same process of soaking and shrinking. One day he soaks us with His blessings and the next day He puts us into a fiery situation so we'll shrink. He repeats this process over and over again until He can say, "This saint will not swell or shrink!"

If you don't feel very strong at times, if the going gets hard and the times are dry, don't question why. God is trying to produce a solid saint that will not swell or shrink.

•

Remember: THE DRY TIMES WORK FOR YOUR GOOD.

40/HOW TO RELAX

"Casting all your care upon him; for he careth for you" (1 Peter 5:7).

Also read: Psa. 23:2-4; Matt. 11:28-30; John 14:27;

Have you been under a lot of stress lately? Has it been hard for you to sleep at night? If you haven't been getting your rest, here are some helpful tips on how to relax.

I believe the art of relaxing is a three-fold experience: physical, mental and spiritual. What I am about to say may sound amusing but in an effort to help you, let me share what works for me:

1. *Physical Relaxation*

It helps me if I exercise until my body sweats. Jogging is a good way to get your body warmed up. If this is too strenuous for you, try walking briskly until you perspire. (Check with your doctor before you begin any exercise program.)

Then I eat a meal with a lot of potatoes and starchy foods. Remember, sleeping pills are made from the ingredients found in starchy foods, so when you eat things like potatoes and bread you're taking nature's sleeping pill.

Then I take a hot bath.

2. *Mental Relaxation*

If I'm under stress, I need to get my mind off my problems and give my brain a rest. I crawl into bed, put on extra blankets and listen to something on the TV or radio that I'm not the least bit interested in (a sporting event or a lesson on basket weaving). This helps to block out thoughts of worry.

3. *Spiritual Relaxation*

Finally, I read my Bible. I read about the promises of God and then thank Him for them in prayer.

Soon sleep rolls over me in gentle waves and I take a short nap.

When I awake I'm relaxed and ready to fight the good fight of faith again.

Try these suggestions the next time stress overcomes you.

●

Remember: YOU CAN LEARN HOW TO RELAX.

41/AFFLICTIONS CAN WORK FOR YOUR GOOD

"But the more they afflicted them, the more they multiplied and grew" (Exodus 1:12).

Also read: Rom. 8:28

Can you imagine the desperate situation the Hebrews were in as slaves of Pharoah? Day after day they cringed under the taskmaster's lash. Week after week they groaned under their heavy burdens. Everything was going wrong—but in one way it worked for their good. The Bible says the more Pharoah afflicted them the more they multiplied and grew.

How do you suppose this happened? *I believe their afflictions brought them nearer to God.* People pray more during times of trouble. I'm sure that every lash of the whip prompted a prayer. And even though they were in terrible trouble, these Jews were never closer to God!

Their afflictions kept them in better physical shape. I doubt that there was one overweight, out of shape, Jew among them. The Bible says the Egyptians made the children of Israel serve with rigor (or hardship).

The Living Bible tells the story this way, *"So the Egyptians made slaves of them and put brutal taskmasters over them to wear them down under heavy burdens while building the store - cities Pithom and Raamses. But the more the Egyptians mistreated and oppressed them, the more the Israelis seemed to multiply!"* (Ex. 1:11 & 12).

If men and women are close to God, praying all day, every day, and in great physical condition from hard work, they are also more sexually active.

So the Hebrews' afflictions worked for their own good; not that they would want slavery again—but there were spiritual, physical and sexual benefits brought on by their afflictions. Be sure to know that God is with you in your afflictions and can use them for your good.

•

Remember: YOUR AFFLICTIONS CAN WORK FOR YOUR GOOD.

42/THE AMERICAN DILEMMA

"Righteousness exalteth a nation: but sin is a reproach to any people" (Proverbs 14:34).

Also read: Ps 72:11, 17; Rom. 16:26

I recently read a handbook called *Christianity In America*. This interesting volume concludes with these perspective paragraphs:

"People want world peace but prepare for world war. They want intimacy but find isolation. People have shrunken the world by electronic wizardry, but their omniscience is so unbearable that they expand their minds by drugs to escape it. They are conversant with the whole world but unknown to their next door neighbors.

"Americans constitute the wealthiest nation on earth but forget their own poor. They claim to be one nation under God, but are many nations under many gods. They say that they believe in the rule of law, but why then are they the most unruly, the most violent, nation in the Western World?

"They want freedom, but find themselves paralyzed by the endless possibilities that confront them. Freedom is defined as not choosing, as dropping out of the rat race. The rich die from too much weight and the poor from too little nourishment.

"How will mankind shape its future in this world, a world marked by brilliance without wisdom, power without conscience? The key to the secrets of life and death is at hand, but can humans be trusted with such knowledge? Is mankind not, at one and the same time, adrift on the seas of high technology and shipwrecked on the reefs of low morality?" (Eerdman's Handbook to Christianity in America, published 1983.)

America needs a personal relationship with Jesus Christ to help her sort out the confusion of these changing times. Jesus said, *"I am the way, the truth, and the life"* (Jn. 14:6).

Let's pray America finds the way.

•

Remember: RIGHTEOUSNESS EXALTS A NATION!

43/DISCIPLINE YOURSELF

"Like an athlete I punish my body, treating it roughly, training it to do what it should—not what it wants to. Otherwise I fear that after enlisting others for the race, I myself might be declared unfit and ordered to stand aside" (1 Corinthians 9:27 TLB).

Also read: Heb. 12:7-13, TLB

Today is Ash Wednesday, the first day of Lent. Roman Catholic, Russian and Greek Orthodox, and many Protestant Christians observe Lent as a time for fasting and making penitence. Whether or not you observe Lent you should learn the value of discipline.

Paul the apostle said, *"In a race, everyone runs, but only one person gets first prize. So run your race to win. To win the contest you must deny yourselves many things that would keep you from doing your best. An athlete goes to all this trouble just to win a blue ribbon or a silver cup, but we do it for a heavenly reward that never disappears. So I run straight to the goal with purpose in every step. I fight to win. I'm not just shadow-boxing or playing around"* (1 Cor. 9:24-26 TLB).

Paul sounds like a professional athlete. Rocky Marciano, former heavyweight champion of the world, said, "I have always adhered to two principles. The first one is to train hard and get into the best possible physical condition. The second is to forget all about the other fellow until you face him in the ring and the bell sounds for the fight."

William Penn, a Quaker and the first governor of Pennsylvania said, "No pain, no palm; no thorns, no throne; no gall, no glory; no cross, no crown."

George Allen, the great football coach said, "Every time you win, you're reborn; when you lose you die a little."

If you've been losing in your Christian life, it may be that you haven't disciplined your life. Don't go on dying a little each day. This is the first day of Lent—can you think of a better time to get yourself under control?

•

Remember: "IF IT DOESN'T HURT, YOU'RE NOT DOING IT RIGHT."

44/HOLD STEADY

"And having done all... stand" (Ephesians 6:13).

Also read: Psa. 18:2; Prov. 18:10; 2 Thess. 3:3; Jude 24, 25.

I have talked with professional gamblers and they say there is a mysterious force that often displays itself in gambling. A player can "get hot" and the dice, cards, or roulette wheel will actually work in his favor to bring him great riches. Could it be that Satan manipulates things or are there psychological or natural forces that transform a "cold" man into a "hot" one?

The reason I ask is that there also appear to be mysterious forces that work against you if things start going wrong. For instance: if I'm late for an appointment, that will be the day I'll hit every red light, my car will run out of gas and I'll have a flat tire before I arrive.

Maybe it's all in my head—but I don't think so. I think there are many unseen forces, both natural and supernatural, that you must deal with in your life. If you find yourself on the bottom end of things, the Bible says "Stand!" If Satan or the forces of life are throwing themselves against you, it is a great victory to stand your ground even if you don't gain an inch.

Mohammed Ali, the great heavyweight boxer, used to leave himself open for his opponents to punch away at his midsection. He would stand and hold his ground. When they could not put him away, Ali would laugh and say, "You can't hurt me—ha, ha, you can't hurt me."

It would demoralize them.

If Satan is punching away at your midsection—hold your ground. Stand! Because *"Greater is he* (the Lord Jesus Christ) *that is in you, than he that is in the world"* (1 John 4:4).

•

Remember: HOLD STEADY!

45/EXPRESS YOUR LOVE!

"For this is the message that you have heard from the beginning, that we should love one another" (1 John 3:11).

Also read: Jn. 15:12; Rom. 13:8; 1 Pet. 1:22; 1 Jn. 4:21

Valentine's Day is dedicated to the expression of our love to one another. The cards and flowers and candies are a lift during a month that is somewhat dreary (at least in the northern half of this continent).

While stationed in Taiwan, an American serviceman noticed a Chinese man taking a hot bowl of rice to the graveside of departed relatives each weekend. After several weeks the American asked "Why are you wasting your rice? Your loved ones cannot come out of their graves to eat." Hearing this the Chinaman said, "They eat my rice when they smell your flowers."

Jesus taught us to love one another and to express our love by giving, forgiving, and even washing one another's feet. The Bible says, *"When Jesus knew that he should depart out of this world unto the Father, having loved his own which were in the world, HE LOVED THEM UNTO THE END.*

"Jesus knowing that the Father had given all things into his hands, and that he was come from God, and went to God: He arose from supper, and laid aside his garments: and took a towel. . . and began to wash the disciples feet" (John 13:1-5, emphasis mine).

Some Christians have practiced foot washing as a ceremony and I am not opposed to this. HOWEVER the PRINCIPAL should be practiced today. In our family and team we will rub someone's neck or back—or even feet. We'll often do one another's dirty job of washing the car, cleaning the bathtub, etc.

> If you have a friend worth loving,
> Love him, yes, and let him know
> That you love him, ere life's evening
> Tinge his brow with sunset glow.
> Why should good words ne'er be said
> Of a friend till he's dead?
>
> —Daniel W. Hoyt

•

Remember: EXPRESS YOUR LOVE. IT WAS THE LORD'S WAY FROM THE BEGINNING.

46/BLESS YOUR FRIENDS

"Ye shall bless the children of Israel" (Numbers 6:23).

Also read: John 17:11, 21-23; Rom. 15:5-7; Heb. 10:24-25

People hear so much bad news today that you should make a genuine effort to bless everyone you come in contact with.

Bless them with your smile! Remind yourself to look bright. It's so easy for cares to cause your mouth to sag. Flash a smile to the people you meet today.

Bless them with their name! There is no sweeter sound to the people you meet than their name. Say, "Hi, Tom!" or "Hi, Sue!", etc. It will lift their spirits.

Bless them with an encouraging word. People usually feel the way they think, so if you want to help them feel better, help them to think better. Compliment them on something they're wearing or on a good deed they've done.

Bless them with an uplifting story or illustration. Maybe you've heard a good joke or a heart-touching story. (Remember, be brief!) Give them something to learn or laugh about.

Bless them with a hug! The New Testament says, *"Greet one another with a kiss of love"* (1 Pet. 5:14). Many people need to feel your touch. They're hurting, and your tender and brief embrace will tell them you really care. (You should be careful about touching a member of the opposite sex who holds a natural attraction to you. If you meet someone who really "rings your emotional bell" you'd better just shake hands.)

Bless them with a word of blessing! *"And the Lord spake unto Moses, saying, Speak unto Aaron and unto his sons, saying, In this wise ye shall bless the children of Israel, saying unto them, The Lord bless thee, and keep thee: The Lord make his face shine upon thee, and be gracious unto thee: The Lord lift up his countenance upon thee, and give thee peace"* (Num. 6:22-26).

•

Remember: BLESS YOUR FRIENDS TODAY!

47/GIVE HIM YOUR STAINS

"And we know that all things work together for good to them that love God" (Romans 8:28).

Also read: Rom. 8:31-39

There is a special home in Scotland that people come from all over the world to see. Years ago, because of an accident, a wall was badly stained.

Sire Edwin Landseer, a great artist of the day, was visiting the home at the time of the accident. He didn't say anything to his hostess, but when he was alone, began to paint on the stained wall.

With an old piece of charcoal and a few touches and strokes, he transformed the disfigure and wall into a beautiful piece of art. The stain was used as a background for a waterfall; surrounding it were fir trees and crags and a handsome stag.

Today this sketch is regarded as one of Landseer's most successful interpretations of highland life; people come from all over the world to admire the stain that was glorified.

This wall is a reminder that there is hope in any situation. If a mere man an change a ruined wall into something better, think of what God, our Creator, can do with our stains!

God is the greatest artist of all time. It doesn't matter how far you have fallen, or how miserably you have failed; God is able to make a masterpiece out of your stains—if you'll surrender to Him!

My friend Bill Gaither wrote a song titled "Something Beautiful":

"Something beautiful, something good
All my confusion, he understood.
All I had to offer him, was brokenness and strife
But he made something beautiful, of my life."

•

Remember: YOUR STAINS ARE NOT TOO GREAT FOR THE MASTER DESIGNER TO CONVERT INTO A MASTERPIECE.

48/SEEK WISDOM

"Wisdom is the principal thing; therefore get wisdom: and with all thy getting get understanding" (Proverbs 4:7).

Also read: Prov. 2:6; 3:13; 15:2; 18:15

Today I've dedicated this devotional to Abraham Lincoln—the man who had the courage to go to war, to divide our country for a time that he might stamp out the evil of slavery and unite us.

Lincoln knew that as long as the evil of slavery existed in this country we would never be a strong nation. He was right. The issue of freedom from slavery is also important in your life and mine: as long as a man or woman is a slave to some habit or desire they are not free.

Lincoln was a very wise man. His godly mother helped to establish the foundation of righteousness within him, and this enabled Lincoln to "sense the truth" in most situations.

Here are some of his observations:

"As I would not be a slave, so I would not be a master. This expresses my idea of Democracy."

"I'm a slow walker, but I never walk back."

"What kills a skunk is the publicity it gives itself."

"He has the right to criticize, who has the heart to help."

"Every man is said to have his peculiar ambition."

When asked during the Civil War if God was on his side, he said, "We trust sir, that God is on our side. It is more important to know that we are on God's side."

"The possibility that we may fail in the struggle ought not to deter us from the support of a cause we believe to be just."

"I have been driven many times to my knees by the overwhelming conviction that I had NOWHERE to go. My own wisdom and that of all about me seemed insufficient for the day."

•

Remember: WISDOM IS THE MOST IMPORTANT THING.

49/THE IMPORTANCE OF YOUR STAND

"And he stood between the dead and the living; and the plague was stayed" (Numbers 16:48).

Also read: Matt. 5:14-16; Luke 12:8-9; Acts 1:8

The setting for today's text took place after Korah and other men rebelled against Moses. The earth opened up and swallowed the rebels and all of their loved ones alive.

The next day the people blamed Moses for killing Korah. This angered God so greatly that He sent a plague upon the people, killing them. When Moses realized what was happening, he told Aaron to take incense from off the altar and make an atonement (reconciliation) for the people. The Bible says, *"And (Aaron) stood between the dead and the living; and the plague was stayed"* (Num. 16:48).

As a believer, you stand between the living and the dead. You have a divine mission to bring a wayward world back to God. He *"hath given to us the ministry of reconciliation...Now then we are ambassadors for Christ...we pray you in Christ's stead, be ye reconciled to God"* (2 Cor. 5:18 & 20).

How are you doing in witnessing to your friends about Jesus Christ? There are many ways you can help them without alienating yourself from them socially.

First, *share Christian books.* You probably have several good books that are gathering dust at your house. Give these "paper preachers" to your friends.

Second, *clue them in on good TV programs.* Many friends use the Lundstrom TV programs as vehicles of witnessing.

Third, *invite them to special meetings.* My wife, Connie, and I came to Jesus Christ through Connie's sister's invitation to special meetings in their church. Andrew's bringing his brother Peter to Jesus was the beginning of a great apostle (see John 1:40-42).

Fourth, *share your personal testimony.* You don't have to be a great speaker to share how Jesus came into your heart and life. Just speak from your heart.

•

Remember: HELP RECONCILE PEOPLE TO GOD—STAND BETWEEN THE LIVING AND THE DEAD.

50/PREACH THE WORD!

"Preach the word; be instant in season, out of season; reprove, rebuke, exhort with all longsuffering and doctrine. For the time will come when they will not endure sound doctrine; but after their own lusts shall they heap to themselves teachers, having itching ears; And they shall turn away their ears from the truth, and shall be turned unto fables" (2 Tim. 4:2-4).

Also read: Mt. 24:4-14; 1 Tim. 4:1-3; 2 Tim. 3:1-5

Today's text is a long one because we are living in the very days this Scripture is describing. People are turning away from the truth because they have itchy ears, and they want to hear something new. Most of the new things appeal to their lusts, exactly as the Scriptures say.

For instance: one of the popular lies today is that "gain is of God." Paul, the apostle, described the last day perversion by warning us of the false teachers who would come with *"corrupt minds, and destitute of the truth, SUPPOSING THAT GAIN IS GODLINESS: from such withdraw thyself"* (1 Tim. 6:5, emphasis mine).

Follow Paul's advice to Timothy: *"Do you want to be truly rich? You already are if you are happy and good. After all, we didn't bring any money with us when we came into the world, and we can't carry away a simple penny when we die. So we should be well satisfied without money if we have enough food and clothing. But people who long to be rich soon begin to do all kinds of wrong things to get money, things that hurt them and make them evil-minded and finally send them to hell itself. For the love of money is the first step towards all kinds of sin. Some people have even turned away from God because of their love for it and as a result have pierced themselves with many sorrows. "Oh, Timothy, you are God's man. Run from all these evil things and work instead at what is right and good, learning to trust him and love others and to be patient and gentle"* (1 Tim. 6:6-11, TLB).

•

Remember: LISTEN TO PREACHERS WHO PREACH GOD'S TRUE WORD.

51/WHEN OTHERS CURSE YOU

"And perhaps the Lord will see that I am being wronged and will bless me because of these curses" (2 Samuel 16:12, TLB).

Also read: 1 Pet. 2:18-20, TLB; 5:10; Heb. 5:8

This was the lowest point in David's life. His own beloved son, Absalom, had become a traitor. Absalom was leading a massive rebellion against his own father and David was fleeing for his life.

Trouble has a way of bringing out the true feelings of your antagonists and this happened to David. As his small band of men moved through the hills, Shimei, the grandson of King Saul, walked along, cursing and throwing rocks and dirt at David and shouting lies.

Then one of David's soldiers said, *"Why should this dead dog curse my lord the king?" Abishai demanded, "Let me go over and strike off his head!"*

"No!" the king said, "If the Lord has told him to curse me, who am I to say no? My own son is trying to kill me, and this Benjaminite is merely cursing me. Let him alone, for no doubt the Lord has told him to do it. And perhaps the Lord will see that I am being wronged and will bless me because of these curses."

"So David and his men continued on, and Shimei kept pace with them on a nearby hillside, cursing as he went and throwing stones at David and tossing dust into the air. The king and all those who were with him were weary by the time they reached Bahurim" (2 Sam. 16:7-14, TLB).

Just like David, you will have dark days in your life, when others will curse you and accuse you of wrongdoing when you are innocent. Notice what David said:

First, he said the Lord may have prompted the attack to humble him.

Second, the Lord would be prompted to have mercy because of the wrongdoing of others against him.

•

Remember: THE CURSES OF OTHERS WILL PROMPT THE MERCIES OF GOD ON YOUR BEHALF.

52/ARE YOU ONE OF THE NINE?

"Were there not ten cleansed? but where are the nine?" (Luke 17:17).

Also read: 1 Chron. 23:30; Psa. 26:2-7; 69:30; 100:4

I'm sure you know this story: Jesus healed 10 lepers but only one returned to thank Him, prompting Jesus to say, "Where are the nine?"

Have you taken time to thank people who have blessed your life?

Thank your mother and father. If they are still living, write, call or visit them today. Come right out and say how much you appreciate their sacrifices on your behalf. However badly they may have treated you, they did some good things for you.

One of the happiest moments I ever had with Mom and Dad was the night I stopped by their home and said, "I'm really glad you fell in love, got married and had me. I wouldn't be here today if you hadn't given yourself for me." They smiled in a way I had never seen them smile before.

Thank your teachers. Have you ever written to those dedicated teachers who labored over your test papers?

Thank your pastor. Write him a letter, or better yet, buy him a turkey or a roast and pin a note on it saying, "Thanks for feeding my soul. I want to feed your body."

Thank your children. You have a million happy memories of their childhood; why not tell them one or two and thank them for making you happy!

Thank your community officials. When is the last time you wrote a note to your mayor, councilman, police chief or fire chief? Leaders like these need your love.

Thank me! That's right. You'll be surprised how few people thank me for the efforts I make in God's work. Here I am on my bed in the bus, writing this devotional. My hand is cramped from writing, my soul is weary from reaching out for new truths, my mind is fatigued from thinking, my stomach is hurting for food. (I've delayed eating for 4 hours so I could complete several of these devotionals. I'm really not feeling sorry for myself—just stating facts.)

MOST OF ALL—THANK THE LORD!

God likes to hear your words of appreciation as well as Jesus Christ and the Holy Spirit. When is the last time you thanked the Holy Spirit for bringing you to Jesus? Do you ever express your gratitude to Him? Remember, He is a person too. *"When HE is come, he will reprove the world of sin, and of righteousness, and of judgment"* (John 16:8, emphasis mine).

•

Remember: JESUS ASKED, "WHERE ARE THE NINE?"

53/THE WISDOM OF WASHINGTON

"Wisdom is the principal thing: THEREFORE GET WISDOM...Exalt her and she shall promote thee: she shall promote thee to honour, when thou dost embrace her" (Proverbs 4:7-8, emphasis mine).

Also read: Prov. 1:1-7

Today I've dedicated this devotional to some of George Washington's words of wisdom: "Associate yourself with men of good quality if you esteem your own reputation—for it is better to be alone than in bad company."

"To persevere in one's duty and be silent, is the best answer to calumny." (Calumny: Webster's Dictionary defines this word as, "The act of uttering false charges or misrepresentations maliciously calculated to damage another's reputation.")

"Labor to keep alive in your breast that little spark of celestial fire called conscience."

"We ought not to look back unless it is to derive useful lessons from past errors, and for the purpose of profiting by dear bought experience."

"Be courteous to all, but intimate with few, and let those few be well tried before you give them your confidence. True friendship is a plant of slow growth, and must undergo and withstand the shocks of adversity before it is entitled to the appellation (The act of calling by a name)." (In other words, you cannot call someone your real friend until your friendship has had time to grow and endured many trials.)

"We must never despair: our situation has been compromising before, and it has changed for the better; so I trust it will again. If new difficulties arise, we must put forth a new exertion and proportion our efforts to the exigencies (demands) of the times."

"I shall never ask, never refuse, nor ever resign an office."
"Few men have virtue to withstand the highest bidder."

•

Remember: WASHINGTON'S WORDS OF WISDOM.

54/GOD HAS PROMISED TO SAVE YOUR LOVED ONES

"Believe on the Lord Jesus and you will be saved, and your entire household" (Acts 16:31, TLB).

Also read: Matt. 10:22; 24:13; Acts 2:21; 11:14

If you have a loved one who doesn't know Christ, today's devotional will be priceless to you. God has promised to save your family if you'll pray. Here are some of God's greatest promises:

Proverbs 11:21 says, *"You can also be very sure that God will rescue the children of the godly"* (TLB).

When one father was burdened for his lost children God gave him this unusual verse from Exodus 10:25. It was Moses responding to Pharaoh, who didn't want to let the Hebrew people go. Moses said, *"We must take our flocks and herds for sacrifices and burn offerings to Jehovah our God. NOT A HOOF SHALL BE LEFT BEHIND"* (TLB, emphasis mine). When the father claimed this verse for his children, they began to get saved.

Isaiah 62:6-7 is another encouraging verse, *"Ye that make mention of the Lord, keep not silence, And GIVE HIM NO REST, till he establish....Jerusalem a praise in the earth"* (emphasis mine). This means that God says not to give Him any rest until He makes your lost loved one a praise in the earth. Wow! What a glorious word of encouragement.

Once when I was going through a difficult time with one of our children, I was tempted to get bitter over the apparent failure of God to "get moving" on my behalf. I kept saying to God, "If Your child was in trouble, I'd help You out. Why aren't You helping me?" Then God led me to this beautiful verse in Psalm 18:25, *"With the merciful thou wilt shew thyself merciful; with an upright man thou wilt shew thyself upright."*

This really encouraged me because then I realized that God would treat me the same as I treated His children. Because I try to deal with his lost children fairly—witnessing to them and encouraging them—I knew God would deal with my child in a fair and upright way.

•

Remember: HAVE FAITH IN GOD FOR YOUR LOVED ONE'S SALVATION.

55/THE POOR ARE GOD'S SIGNPOSTS

"And every one that was in distress, and every one that was in debt, and every one that was discontented, gathered themselves unto (David); and he became a captain over them" (1 Samuel 22:2).

Also read: Psa. 34:6-10; 107:4-8; Matt. 5:3; 6:31-34; Jas. 2:5

Have you ever wondered why so many poor people join "on-fire" evangelical churches? Here's why: I believe when the Gospel is preached in power, the poor will be attracted by its message of hope.

This is what happened in David's day. Everyone that was distressed, discontented and in debt joined his army. They knew that David was their only hope of deliverance. He was their only chance of becoming free.

Centuries later, Jesus Christ came from heaven to show men the way back to God. He was called "The Son of David" and the same desperate crowd followed Him. While John the Baptist was in prison, he began to wonder if Jesus was really the Messiah, if he had announced the right one. So he sent his disciples to enquire about it. Jesus responded by saying, *"Go and shew John again those things which ye do hear and see: The blind receive their sight, and the lame walk, the lepers are cleansed, and the deaf hear, the dead are raised up, and the poor have the gospel preached to them. And blessed is he, whosoever shall not be offended in me"* (Matt. 11:4-6).

The Bible says of Jesus, *"The common people heard him gladly"* (Mark 12:37). The mission of Jesus Christ was summed up in His very first sermon at the synagogue in Nazareth:

"The Spirit of the Lord is upon me, because he hath anointed me to
  *preach the gospel to the poor;
  *he hath sent me to heal the brokenhearted,
  *to preach deliverance to the captives,
  *and recovering of sight to the blind,
  *to set at liberty them that are bruised,
  *To preach the acceptable year of the Lord" (Luke 4:18).

The next time you see a poor, shabbily dressed person in church, show love towards him, for his presence is a sign the Gospel is being declared in power—offering hope and encouragement to all.

●

Remember: THE POOR ARE GOD'S SIGNPOSTS THAT THE GOSPEL IS BEING PREACHED!

56/LIVE ENTHUSIASTICALLY!

"Work hard and cheerfully at all you do, just as though you were working for the Lord and not merely for your masters, remembering that it is the Lord Christ who is going to pay you, giving you your full portion of all he owns. He is the one you are really working for" (Colossians 3:23,24 TLB).

Also read: Ne. 8:10; Pr. 15:13; 17:22; Mt. 25:21

Did you hear about the woman who walked into a butcher shop and ordered two pounds of hamburger? The butcher turned around to a helper and said, "Wrap up two pounds of enthusiasms!"

"Why do you call it enthusiasms?" the woman asked.

"Because we put everything into it!" the butcher said with a smile.

How do you plan to live today? Just putting in your time or giving it all you've got? Most of the people you will rub shoulders with today are dead on their feet; this is why you need to live enthusiastically. You can help spark them with your energy.

You can help them even if you're hurting. About a year ago I broke my ankle and had to hobble around on crutches. So I put signs beneath the handles that said, "I wanted to be in the theatre; now I'm part of the cast!"; "Don't laugh, this could have happened to you!" Everywhere I hobbled, people broke out laughing.

One thing that keeps employees from giving their very best to their work is the feeling that they're underpaid. Today's text says that you should work as though you were working for the Lord and not for men, and that Jesus Christ will pay you well on Judgment Day.

Make an effort to live enthusiastically today. Smile at the people you meet (especially the grouch who makes everyone miserable) and give your job a 110% effort. Remember, even if your boss doesn't pay you well, God will.

•

Remember: "PUT EVERYTHING INTO IT!"

57/BLESS THE LORD!

"I will bless the Lord at all times: his praise shall continually be in my mouth" (Psalm 34:1).

Also read: Deut. 8:10; Neh. 9:5; Psa. 96:2; 115:18

"**B**eing God ain't no picnic" is an adage I've never forgotten. In fact, the more I think about it the more I realize how important it is to bless the Lord.

The Psalmist David discovered this secret. He said, *"Bless the Lord, O my soul: and all that is within me, bless his holy name. Bless the Lord, O my soul, and forget not all his benefits"* (Psa. 103:1-3).

I recently shared this truth of encouraging God with some of my partners and discovered they had never thought of it. Many envision God as all-powerful, all-complete, without problems or feelings of grief as you and I experience.

> Here's what the Bible says, *"When the Lord God saw the extent of human wickedness, and that the trend and direction of men's lives were only towards evil, He was sorry He had made them. IT BROKE HIS HEART."* (Gen. 6:5, TLB emphasis mine).
>
> *"But they rebelled against him and grieved his Holy Spirit. That is why he became their enemy and personally fought against them"* (Isa. 63:10, TLB).
>
> *"Don't cause the Holy Spirit sorrow by the way you live"* (Eph. 4:30, TLB).
>
> *"And when he (Jesus) was come near, he beheld the city, and wept over it."* (Luke 19:41).

These Scriptures and many more will show you how grieved God is with our world today. There is so much sorrow for God; you should determine to bring Him great joy.

You can do this by blessing His name. Praise God for all He is doing. Thank Him for enduring so many insults. Appreciate God for His mercy and patience.

If you will bless the Lord with all that is within you, I know God will bless you with all that is within Him.

•

Remember: BLESS THE LORD—SO MANY ARE CURSING AND BREAKING HIS COMMANDMENTS; YOUR WORDS OF APPRECIATION WILL CARRY A LOT OF WEIGHT IN HEAVEN.

58/REMEMBER THE WORD!

"Thy word have I hid in mine heart, that I might not sin against thee" (Psalm 119:11).

Also read: Josh. 1:8; Psa. 32:8; 119:105; Prov. 6:22, 23

Shakespeare said, "I am part of everything I have seen and heard." This is why you must guard your eyes and ears against evil; this is also why you must program your eyes and ears to assimilate good.

In John 15:20 Jesus said, *"Remember the word that I said unto you."* Are you making any efforts to memorize the Word of God?

If you will memorize just one good Scripture a week, you'll know 52 powerful verses in one year. Imagine how they will revolutionize your life!

The best way to memorize God's Word is:

> Print out the Scripture on a card. (The act of writing it impresses it on you mind better.)
> Place the card where you can see it: on your bathroom mirror, by your kitchen sink, or on the dash of your car.
> Quote it aloud as often as you can. You can also quote it during your conversation with friends.
> Review your cards regularly.

Scripture memorization is something we often talk about and seldom do. I don't spend much time memorizing Scripture, but I do implant God's Word deeply into my soul during all my sermon preparations.

I also do a lot of underlining in my Bible. This helps to implant God's Word in my mind. (It will also help your relatives after you die, because the first book they'll reach for after your death is your Bible. You should mark it well—it will show where you've been with God and inspire your family to seek Him too.)

I have also found that the Holy Spirit will anoint certain passages of the Word to my life at certain times. For several weeks God will anoint the book of Numbers and I'll study it. Then the Spirit will move me to the book of Ephesians or Colossians. God knows the difficulties I am going through at any given time and gives me the specific Scriptures that speak to my needs.

Whatever else you do, spend time with God's Word. It's a clear-cut command to you from Jesus Christ.

●

Remember: JESUS SAID, "REMEMBER THE WORD!"

59/DO YOU LOVE YOUR HATES?

"Ye have heard that it hath been said,....love thy neighbor, and hate thine enemy. But I say unto you, Love your enemies, bless them that curse you, do good to them that hate you, and pray for them which despitefully use you, and persecute you" (Matthew 5:43-44).

Also read: Prov. 25:21; Luke 6:27, 35-37

Recently I had lunch with a Roman Catholic Bishop who headed the diocese where we were conducting a crusade. We had a great time visiting together. The Bishop shared how Vatican II, led by the late Pope Paul, was a breath of fresh air to his church.

Then he told me an unforgettable story about what happened on his return from that historic conference in Rome.

A very devout German nun who had given her life helping the elderly and the poor came up to him and said, "Bishop, what is this news I hear from Pope Paul telling us that we Catholics should love Protestants? Is this true?" The Bishop confirmed that she had heard correctly. The Pope *was* urging Catholics to love Protestants.

Then, this deeply dedicated nun, who had given her life helping others, turned to the Bishop. With a perplexing look and hurt in her voice said, "But Bishop—they are taking away all of our hates."

What a life-changing story! It shows that good people sometimes feel at ease hating certain people, and they are disturbed if they are urged to give up their grudges.

How about you? Do you love your hates? Are there certain groups—Catholics, Protestants, Jews, Masons, drug addicts, prostitutes, gamblers, drunkards, homosexuals and others—that you have subconsciously written on your hate list?

If so, then do what Jesus said. Begin to love your enemies, bless them, pray for them—even if they persecute you. In doing so you will become like Jesus Christ.

•

Remember: GOD ALLOWS YOUR ENEMIES TO EXIST SO YOU CAN LEARN TO LOVE THEM.

HOW TO HAVE FAITH

"Have faith in God" (Mark 11:22).

Also read: Rom. 10:17; Heb. 11:1

We hear the words above every day, but the question is, "Just *how* do I go about having faith in God? How can I say I believe, when I honestly doubt?"

Jesus helps us answer this question.

First, *He tells you to speak to the mountain in your life.*

"For verily I say unto you, That WHOSOEVER SHALL SAY UNTO THIS MOUNTAIN, Be thou removed, and be thou cast into the sea; and shall not doubt in his heart, but shall believe that those things which he SAITH shall come to pass: he shall have whatsoever he SAITH" (Mark 11:23, emphasis mine).

Whatever your need is—speak to it! When your words of faith are spoken, you've moved faith out of the unseen invisible area of your life into the arena of reality.

Second, *Release your desires!*

Desire has power to fuel your faith. Jesus said, *"Whatsoever things YOU DESIRE when you pray, believe that you receive them, and ye shall have them"* (Mark 11:24 emphasis mine). Do you really want God to work a miracle for you? Then keep desiring it, keep praying. Don't give up. Desire is to faith what fuel is to a fire. Pour it on and watch it burn.

Third, *Forgive.*

If you have hard feelings against anyone or know of anyone who has bitterness against you, forgive him or ask his forgiveness.

If you want a miracle, you need God to work on your behalf—and the only way He'll do this is if you forgive others and keep the channel of forgiveness open.

So, it's not so hard to have faith in God. If you'll follow this three-step plan, you will strengthen your faith.

•

Remember: HAVING FAITH IN GOD OUR FATHER IS NOT DIFFICULT FOR HIS OBEDIENT CHILDREN.

61/RIGHTEOUS BEYOND QUESTION

"There was a man... whose name was Job; and that man was perfect and upright, and one that feared God, and (shunned) evil" (Job 1:1).

Also read: Rom. 10:10; 1 Cor. 1:30; Gal. 3:6, 7; Phil. 3:9

There are some people who are confused about the trials of Job. They say that fear caused his troubles, because he said, *"For the thing which I greatly feared is come upon me, and that which I was afraid of is come unto me"* (Job 3:25).

However, to say that Job's fears caused his trials is as foolish as saying that a man's fears that he might one day be involved in an accident caused a truck to crash into him.

Besides, the Bible clearly declares in God's own words that Job was righteous. *After* Satan destroyed Job's family and possessions, God said, *"Have you considered my servant Job, that there is none like him in the earth, a perfect and an upright man, one that feareth God, and (shuns) evil? ...and still he holdeth fast his integrity, ALTHOUGH YOU MOVED ME AGAINST HIM, TO DESTROY HIM **WITHOUT CAUSE**"* (Job 2:3, emphasis mine).

Notice that God said there was no cause within Job for the things that he suffered.

Finally, in the end, God became angry at Eliphaz and his friends for accusing Job of wrongdoing and wouldn't accept their prayers. God said, *"My anger is kindled against thee, and against thy two friends: for ye have not spoken of me the thing that is right, as my servant Job hath...go to my servant Job...and my servant Job shall pray for you: for him will I accept"* (Job 42:7 & 8).

Job was righteous beyond question. Why then did he have so many trials? Because God was proving to Satan that Job was truly righteous and that Job would serve God no matter what happened!

If you're going through severe trials, don't let anyone question your integrity. God may be proving a point with you just as He did with Job.

•

Remember: JOB WAS RIGHTEOUS BEYOND QUESTION.

62/HERE'S WHAT HAPPENED TO YOUR SINS!

"Much more then, being now justified by his blood, we shall be saved from wrath through him" (Romans 5:9).

Also read: 2 Cor. 5:17; 2 Tim. 1:9; Tit. 3:5 & 6

Have you ever stopped to consider what the Bible says has happened to your sins since you received Christ?

1. YOUR SINS HAVE BEEN REMOVED AS FAR AS THE EAST IS FROM THE WEST.

    This means your sins have been placed beyond reach. You cannot measure the distance from east to west—you'll go in an endless circle.

    The Psalmist David said, *"as far as the east is from the west, so far hath he removed our transgressions from us"* (Ps. 103:12).

2. YOUR SINS HAVE BEEN CAST INTO THE DEPTHS OF THE SEA!

    The prophet Micah says, *"He will have compassion upon us; he will subdue our iniquities; and thou wilt cast all their sins into the depths of the sea"* (Mi. 7:19).

    Mount Everest is approximately 29,000 feet high—but the Meriana Trench in the Pacific is 36,000 feet deep—about 7 miles in depth.

    Just imagine all of your sins cast into this deep, dark hole. Hallelujah! They're buried in the deepest place of the earth.

3. GOD HAS PUT YOUR SINS OUT OF HIS MIND.

    The Lord says, *"I will forgive their iniquity, and I will remember their sin no more"* (Jer. 31:34).

    Isn't it wonderful to realize that God has forgotten every evil thing that you and I have done against Him. And I should add this point: If God forgives and forgets your sins—don't you think you should do the same? If you refuse to forgive and forget your sins you're setting yourself up as more judgmental than God.

4. YOUR SINS HAVE BEEN BLOTTED OUT OF EXISTENCE!

    Have you ever written something you didn't want read by someone else, and you blotted out the words by scribbling over them with ink? This is what God has done with your sins when you received Christ.

5. YOUR SINS HAVE BEEN MADE JUST AS IF THEY'D NEVER BEEN.

    Today's text says we are "justified by his blood." This word justified means "just-as-if-I'd-never-sinned!" WOW!

Your sins are out of reach, out of sight, out of mind, out of existence—and you are just-as-if-you'd never sinned. If you've been carrying a heavy load of guilt—give up your burden and rejoice. Christ has set you free!

•

Remember: YOUR SINS ARE MADE JUST AS IF THEY'D NEVER BEEN.

63/LEARN TO LOVE TO WORK

"And the Lord God took the man, and put him in the garden of Eden to dress it and to keep it" (Genesis 2:15).

Also read: Jas. 1:22-25

As I am writing this, my son, Lowell Jr, 16, is busy trying to shovel the snow off the driveway.

I want him to learn how to work. The other day when the snow had packed the driveway, I went out and helped him. For two hours I worked beside him until it was cleared. Then I said, "Be sure to shovel the snow when it is fresh fallen; that way you don't have to chip it." But he failed to do this, so today I'm letting him do it alone. I'm hoping this will remind him of his responsibility and that it will teach him to love work.

Do you love to work? I hope so. Here are some ideas about work that may help:

First, *Work is a blessing!* When God placed Adam in the garden of Eden, He gave him the job of maintaining it. God knew Paradise would not be enjoyable without work to do.

Second, *Work provides your living!* Think of the millions of people who are praying for a job, any job—the job you have right now. Your work provides your food, clothing, and shelter.

Third, *Work builds character!* I've never seen a lazy man with character. If you can't get "high" on sweat and sore muscles, you'll also be easy on yourself in other areas.

Right now I can hear the scraping of Lowell Jr's shovel. I know in a few moments he will come in out of the cold, with a red face and maybe complaining a bit, but later he'll be proud that he completed his task. Work does more for the man than man does for the job.

•

Remember: WORK IS A BLESSING.

64/PROBLEMS ARE PART OF GOD'S PLAN

"Now no chastening for the present seemeth to be joyous, but grievous: nevertheless afterward it yieldeth the peaceable fruit of righteousness" (Hebrews 12:11).

Also read: Job 2:10; Psa. 34:19; Rom. 5:3-4; 1 Pet. 2:20-21

Your problems are your friends. If you think you're out of God's will because you have problems, remember the Israelites. God planned their problems just to see how they would respond. *"And thou shalt remember all the way which the Lord thy God led thee these forty years in the wilderness, to humble thee, and to prove thee, to know what was in thine heart, whether thou wouldst keep his commandments, or no"* (Deut. 8:2).

You can see that God planned their problems in advance. This phrase came to me clearly one day, "Problems are part of God's plan to make a man." If you're having problems, rejoice—it shows God is working in your life.

If I asked you, "Do you want to be like Jesus?" I'm sure you'd say, "Yes, I want to be like my Savior!"

Okay. Now read this verse, *"And even though Jesus was God's Son, he had to learn from experience what it was like to obey, when obeying meant suffering. It was after he had proved himself perfect in this experience that Jesus became the Giver of eternal salvation to all those who obey him"* (Heb. 5:8, TLB).

If Jesus had to learn from the experiences of suffering, how can you and I claim to be exempt? This does not mean that you should lie down and accept every problem that comes your way, but if you cannot escape, then use your problems to your advantage. As one author wrote, "The bumps are what you climb on."

•

Remember: PROBLEMS ARE PART OF GOD'S PLAN TO MAKE A MAN.

65/HOW TO FIND GREATER JOY!

"Whatsoever ye shall ask the Father in my name, he will give to you... Ask and ye shall receive, that your joy may be full" (John 16:23 & 24).

Also read: Ps. 5:11 & 12; Pro. 15:3; Jn. 15:11 & 12

Are you happy with the joy you are experiencing in your Christian life? If you feel flat and lack excitement and joy, it could be that your prayers are too small.

That's right, your prayers are too small because you probably have become contented with things as they are and have failed to tackle the big problems that trigger big miracles that produce great excitement and joy.

Realize that if you're happy with yourself and what you have, God cannot do anything more for you. God moves on your requests. If you are not storming heaven for miracles in your life and others, you will remain the same until you die.

You might say, "But I'm content with what I have; why should I ask for more?"

Stop! Your prayer requests should not be for just the blessings of God upon yourself. Why not pray for the salvation, healing and prosperity of relatives and friends—and the billions of lost souls? If you already have what you need, pray that they receive the same.

Jesus said to pray for the conversion of the whole world. He said, *"The harvest truly is great but the labourers are few: pray ye therefore the Lord of the harvest, that he would send forth labourers into his harvest"* (Lk. 10:2).

Soon you will see things begin to happen, and instead of living a ho-hum boring life, you'll begin to witness miracles as a result of your prayers. God will work with you and soon you'll be partners making exciting things happen on a daily basis.

•

Remember: TO FIND GREATER JOY, START PRAYING FOR MIRACLES.

66/YOUR BODY BELONGS TO CHRIST

"I beseech you therefore, brethren, by the mercies of God, that ye present your bodies a living sacrifice, holy, acceptable unto God, which is your reasonable service" (Romans 12:1-2).

Also read: Eph. 4:20-32; Col. 3:5-13

There are two kinds of hypocrites: one who deliberately intends to deceive others, and one who is deceived and doesn't know it. I knew a man who claimed to be a devoted Christian but had a terrible reputation around town for charging high rent on the shacks he rented to the poor. No matter what he said about God, his renters wouldn't listen.

During the Lenton season, many Christians give up certain pleasures to honor Christ. But the greatest sacrifice we can make to God is ourselves. God honors every gift you offer, but there is more to self-denial than giving up candy bars, movies, dances or chocolate cake. The call of God is to give your body, soul, mind and spirit to Christ as a daily sacrifice.

You shouldn't think x-rated thoughts because you have given your *mind* to Christ. You shouldn't read dirty literature or watch unclean TV shows because you have given your *eyes* to Christ. You shouldn't curse or tell coarse stories because you have given your *tongue* to Christ. You shouldn't steal because your *hands* belong to the Lord. And when your *feet* have been given to God, they will never take you to worldly places of amusement.

Have you considered your committment to Christ in these terms? If you belong to Jesus Christ, it requires more than attending a one-hour church service or even serving God in your own way. It's all or nothing. Lest we think this is too extreme, Paul the Apostle says this is our "reasonable service."

•

Remember: WHAT YOU DO WITH YOUR BODY REVEALS HOW COMMITTED YOU ARE TO JESUS CHRIST.

67/BE FAITHFUL UNTIL DEATH

"Be thou faithful unto death, and I will give you a crown of life" (Revelation 2:10).

Also read: Josh. 1:9; Jer. 32:27; 2 Cor. 5:7

Paul the apostle said, *"Fight the good fight of faith, lay hold on eternal life"* (1 Tim. 6:12). Sometimes in this great struggle against sin and Satan, you're tempted to give up-- but you must remember the words of our Savior, *"Be faithful until death and I will give you a crown of life."*

When the going's really tough it helps to consider the crown you will receive for suffering. Think of Jesus who suffered the death of crucifixion so you could be saved. Think of the martyrs who were boiled in oil, sawn in two, skinned alive, pulled apart or burned at the stake.

The Russian people suffered terribly at the hands of the German Soldiers when Adolph Hitler ordered them to attack Russia. As many as 30 million Russian men, women and children died. But they died valiantly—fighting insurmountable forces.

Recently some children were playing around an old battlefield and found an empty cartridge with this message scrawled on a piece of paper and stuffed inside: "First there were three of us, then only two. Now I'm the only one left and I'll soon be gone. The tanks keep coming. Friends, avenge us. We never took a step back."

Dying is not easy—it was even hard for Jesus to die. Jesus prayed three tines that God would take the cup of death from Him. The Bible says, *"And he went a little further, and fell on his face, and prayed, saying. O my Father, if it be possible, let this cup pass from me: nevertheless not as I will, but as thou wilt"* (Matt. 26:39).

Remember what Coronation Day will be like when the heroes of the faith step forward before God's throne to receive their crowns and all of heaven thunders its ovation of appreciation.

•

Remember: BE FAITHFUL UNTIL DEATH.

68/PERSONALIZE THE PROMISES!

"O how I love thy law! it is my meditation all the day"
(Psalm 119:97).

Also read: Rom. 4:16; Heb. 6:12; 2 Pet. 1:4-8

If you love God's Word, you need to personalize the promises. One way I do this is by marking my Bible and underlining the Scriptures that are especially meaningful to me.

There are special days when a Bible promise simply jumps out at you and explodes with faith in your heart. When this happens, mark the day and year in your margin and claim this verse as your very own. Later, after God has fulfilled His promises, you will see where the light shone brightly even in your darkest hour. Personalizing and marking the promises of God will help build your faith.

There's another reason why you should mark your Bible; as soon as you die, the first thing your relatives will try to get their hands on is your Bible, so leave good markings. It will help them to find God.

I also use up the blank pages in the front and back of my Bible for favorite quotes. Many of the famous quotations in this devotional book were first logged in my Bible.

Another way you can personalize passages of Scripture is to write down the date and the minister who spoke when the passage came alive in your soul. Include a brief outline of his message.

Colored pens and highlighters also make the Scriptures come alive. Then at a glance you're able to see what becomes meaningful to your life.

Some people do not like to mark their Bibles because they consider the Word of God to be holy. Yes, it really is, but the paper is only paper and a promise personalized has much more power than cold print on white paper.

The purpose of God's promises is to help us become God-like. So personalize every promise you can—it will help God become more personal to you.

•

Remember: PERSONALIZE THE PROMISES!

69/STAND UP FOR YOUR BELIEFS!

"But Peter and the apostles replied, 'We must obey God rather than men" (Acts 5:29, TLB).

Also read: Isa. 1:19; 1 Thess. 2:2; Heb. 5:9

It takes courage to stand up against popular opinion. Recently this splendid ad copy by United Technologies was run in the *Wall Street Journal.* You'll want to share it with your friends:

> Submit to pressure from peers and you move down to their level.
> Speak up for your own beliefs and you invite them up to your level.
> If you move with the crowd, you'll get no further than the crowd.
> When 40 million people believe in a dumb idea, it's still a dumb idea.
> Simply swimming with the tide leaves you nowhere.
> So if you believe in something that's good, honest and bright, stand up for it.
> Maybe your peers will get smart and drift your way.

This was the determined commitment of the early Christians. When Peter and John were commanded not to speak about Jesus again, they replied, *"You decide whether God wants us to obey you instead of Him! We cannot stop telling about the wonderful things we saw Jesus do and heard Him say"* (Acts 4:19, TLB).

Have you been "giving ground" to the opinions of those who surround you at work or school? Have you been appeasing the God-haters by refusing to speak up?

> Once after I was first converted the only job I could get was working for a godless farmer. He cursed continually and tried to make things hard for me. Sometimes he would say, "Wasn't it easier to run your dance band than to do this hard work?"
>
> One day as we were working he began cursing with an air that told me he was taunting God. Rather than deny the Lord, I started praising God. The farmer would say, "Blankety-blank-blank" and I would say, "Praise you, Lord. I love You, Jesus!" This went on for several minutes until finally he threw his wrench to the ground and yelled, "Lundstrom, you're fired!"
>
> I replied by saying, "The reason you're firing me is that you see Jesus in my life and you won't repent!"

I stood up for my belief in God and got fired. But that very day I was offered a job for twice as much money for half as many hours. God rewarded my obedience to Him.

•

Remember: STAND UP FOR WHAT YOU BELIEVE NO MATTER WHAT IT COSTS!

70/THERE'S POWER IN THE NAME OF JESUS

"Wherefore God also hath highly exalted him, and given him a name which is above every name: That at the name of Jesus every knee should bow, of things in heaven, and things in earth, and things under the earth" (Philippians 2:9 & 10).

Also read: Ex. 20:7; Luke 24:47; John 1:12; 2:23; 20:31

I had preached this text for 27 years and thought I knew it until a member of the Lundstrom band pointed out a wonderful discovery he had made.

(Maybe you should read this text again before going furthur. It's so dynamic I want you to get the full impact of it.)

I knew that when Jesus returns everyone will bow, including atheists like Madalyn Murray O'Hair, communists like Khrushchev and Brezhnev, politicians and world leaders like de Gaulle, Churchhill, Roosevelt and others. But I thought that these powers would not bow until Jesus returned "in person."

But I didn't see this truth: the Bible says, *"AT THE NAME OF JESUS every knee shall bow"* (emphasis mine). I interpreted that Scripture to mean that at the presence of Jesus every knee would bow. But the Bible says *the name.*

The name of Jesus, used in faith, is powerful enough to cause every knee to bow. Today you and I have been given His name as our authority. Jesus said, *"And whatsoever ye shall ask in my name, that will I do, that the Father may be glorified in the Son"* (John 14:13).

What are you doing with the name of Jesus? Are you using it to wage war against Satan, sin and all his hellish host? Are you using the name of Jesus to bind and loose according to Matthew 16:19, that *"Whatsoever thou shalt bind on earth shall be bound in heaven: and whatsoever thou shalt loose on earth shall be loosed in heaven?"*

You can use the name of Jesus to do mighty things. Demons must flee, kingdoms must concede and heaven must honor the holy matchless name of Jesus. Use it to God's glory.

•

Remember: THERE'S POWER IN THE NAME OF JESUS!

71/THE ABCs OF SUCCESS!

"Learn to be wise...and develop good judgment and common sense! I cannot overemphasize this point" (Proverbs 4:5 TLB).

Also read: Ps. 27:14; 31:24; Is. 41:10

Bobby Knight, basketball coach for the University of Indiana, has coached a lot of championship teams. He says, "The most important thing in life is not the will to win but the will to prepare to win!"

Are you aware of the ABCs of success? They are:

A—Ability
B—Breaks
C—Courage

If you hope to win over the competition (and there's plenty of it), you must develop your abilities to peak performance. If you want to succeed you must have enough willpower to discipline your life spiritually, mentally and physically.

Getting a break is another key: to be in the right place at the right time. Solomon said, *"I looked throughout the earth and saw that the swiftest person does not always win the race, nor the strongest man the battle, and that wise men are often poor, and skillful men are not necessarily famous; but it is all by chance, by happening to be at the right place at the right time."* (Ecc. 9:11 TLB).

But don't get discouraged. Courage plays a big part. The best way to develop courage is to tackle problems a little bigger than your abilities, and hang on until you win. After you have had a series of successes, you won't be afraid of difficulties. In fact, you will welcome them as challenges.

Decide today to prepare yourself to win; when you have developed your abilities, and you get your breaks (opportunities) and are courageous, you will join the circle of champions.

•

Remember: ABILITY, BREAKS AND COURAGE ARE THE ABCs OF SUCCESS.

72/TRY A LONG-DISTANCE SHORTCUT

"Don't worry about anything; instead, PRAY ABOUT EVERYTHING; tell God your needs and don't forget to thank him for his answers" (Philippians 4:6, emphasis mine).

Also read: Matt. 6:6; Matt. 21:22; Luke 18:1

So often we wait until we've tried everything else before we pray. The truth is that prayer should be our first response to a crisis.

A lighthouse keeper in Northern England went out one stormy winter night to check some of his weather instruments. The wind was blowing so hard it slammed the door behind him. When he returned to the door, half frozen, he found it locked. His wife was busy working upstairs and could not hear his cries or pounding.

Realizing he would freeze to death if he didn't act quickly, he spied the pay telephone used by visitors. The only way he could reach his wife was by phoning long distance to London who would then connect him to his wife upstairs. He tried a long-distance shortcut and it worked.

Do you pray about everything? Do you ever feel that you don't want to bother God? The truth is that He enjoys being bothered.

> One day one of my most dedicated employees was having a terrible time. He was at the point of total frustration. He was trying to find the writer and publisher of a Gospel song we had recorded.
>
> I said, "Jim, did you get the information yet?" He replied, "It's nowhere to be found. I've called everyone! No one has even heard of the song! I have exhausted all of my resources."
>
> I said, "No, you haven't! You haven't asked *me*." I proceeded to tell him who had recorded the song and where he could find the information.
>
> Within 30 minutes he had the facts.

Learn to pray about everything. It won't tire God to hear your prayers. In fact, it will give Him an opportunity to show His power on your behalf.

•

Remember: TRY A LONG-DISTANCE SHORTCUT. PRAY TO GOD IN HEAVEN IF YOU WANT TO REACH SOMEONE CLOSE TO YOU!

73/THE FURNACE OF AFFLICTION

"Beloved, think it not strange concerning the fiery trial which is to try you, as though some strange thing happened unto you: But rejoice, inasmuch as ye are partakers of Christ's sufferings; that, when his glory shall be revealed, ye may be glad also with exceeding joy" (1 Peter 4:12 & 13).

Also read: Psa. 138:7; Isa. 43:2, 4; Psa. 138:7; 2 Cor. 4:8-9

Do you know how the hardened steel blades of Wilkinson's swords are made? The steel is heated until it is white hot and then it is pounded until it cools. The process is repeated over and over again until the steel is so tough it seldom breaks.

The same is true of your life; you are toughened by the heat and pounding that you get. The Lord told Israel, *"Behold, I have refined thee...I have chosen thee in the furnace of affliction"* (Isa. 48:10).

If you have been in a furnace of affliction, don't despair or be afraid of what is happening. God is overseeing the process of purification in your life.

It is said that chemists have to be careful while purifying precious metals. They must regulate the heat being applied to the gold and silver. If the heat is too intense it will burn the impurities into the metal and ruin its value. If they don't apply enough heat the metal will not be purified and it will be worthless.

In ancient days the man in charge of purifying silver would heat it until it reached its purest possible state. How did he know when to quit? When the silver was pure enough, he could see his own reflection. Hallelujah!

God may be allowing some heat to come into your life. If so, don't despair! He is the master chemist and will not ruin you. He will only purify you until He can see the reflection of Jesus in your life.

•

Remember: GOD'S IN CHARGE OF THE FURNACE OF AFFLICTION.

ZANE GREY'S GOSPEL

"Ye have not yet resisted unto blood" (Hebrews 12:4).

Also read: 1 Pet. 4:1-17; 5:10 & 11; Heb. 2:9 & 10

As a boy I remember the thrills I received from reading the western novels of Zane Grey. I don't know much about this man, but I sense he must have gone through his share of suffering because this is what he has written. I call it "Zane Grey's Gospel."

> "To bear up under loss, to fight the bitterness of defeat and the weakness of grief, to be victor over anger, to smile when tears are close, to resist evil men and base instincts, to hate hate and to love love, to go on when it would seem good to die, to seek ever after the glory and the dream, to look up with unquenchable faith in something evermore about to be that is what any man can do, and so be great."
>
> Zane Grey

Zane Grey says you and I need to "look up with unquenchable faith." This fits in with this passage in Hebrews, that says we are surrounded by a grandstand filled with heavenly spectators who are, I'm sure praying for us and cheering us on: *"Since we have such a huge crowd of men of faith watching us from the grandstands, let us strip off anything that slows us down or holds us back, and especially those sins that wrap themselves so tightly around our feet and trip us up; and let us run with patience the particular race that God has set before us.*

"Keep your eyes on Jesus, our leader and instructor. He was willing to die a shameful death on the cross because of the joy he knew would be his afterwards; and now he sits in the place of honor by the throne of God. If you want to keep from becoming fainthearted and weary, think about his patience as sinful men did such terrible things to him. After all, you have never yet struggled against sin and temptation until you sweat great drops of blood" (Heb. 12:1-4, TLB).

These are profound words. Use them to be reassured that real faith doesn't give up or quit. Don't forget that the same Christ who brought others to victory is at work in your heart today.

•

Remember: LOOK UP AND GET A GREATER VIEW OF REALITY.

75/YOU DON'T DARE HATE!

"But if ye forgive not men their trespasses, neither will your Father forgive your trespasses" (Matthew 6:15).

Also read: Matt. 6:14; 18:21-22; Mark 11:25-26; Eph. 4:32; Col. 3:13

Living with hate in your heart is like living in hell. If you're going to live a happy life you must learn how to forgive.

I found this quote recently, "Hate is like acid: It can damage the vessel in which it is stored as well as destroy the object on which it is poured."

Where does hate come from? I believe it comes from failing to forgive. Once you store up a hurt in your heart it begins to ferment and spoil into the poison of hate. Once hatred seizes your spirit *you* are the victim more than the one you are hating. Hate will twist your heart, soul and mind until you become a monster of revenge.

> Jesus said, *"Ye have heard that it hath been said, Thou shall love thy neighbour, and hate thine enemy.*
> *"But I say unto you, love your enemies, bless them that curse you, do good to them that hate you, and pray for them which despitefully use you, and persecute you.*
> *"That ye may be the children of your Father which is in heaven: for he maketh His sun to rise on the evil and on the good, and sendeth rain on the just and on the unjust.*
> *"For if ye love them which love you, what reward have ye? do not even the publicans (or tax gatherers) the same?*
> *"...Be ye therefore perfect, even as your Father which is in heaven is perfect"* (Matthew 5:43-48).

You can see why you dare not hate others, no matter what they have done against you.

First, hatred poisons your own soul. The acid destroys your vessel as well as the one on which it is poured.

Second, if you want to be like God, remember He is generous to His enemies. Man plots revenge but God seeks ways to forgive.

Third, your forgiveness will be your greatest witness. When your enemy sees your God-like act of mercy he'll say, "Why would you forgive me?" Then you'll have the opportunity to share your testimony.

•

Remember: DON'T HATE—THE PRICE IS TOO HIGH.

JOB'S COMFORTERS

"Now when Job's three friends heard of all this evil that was come upon him, they came...to mourn with him and to comfort him" (Job 2:11).

Also read: Deut. 31:6; Psa. 27:10; Matt. 7:1; 28:20

When trouble comes your way, watch out for the comforters that follow. Job's three friends, Eliphaz, Bildad and Zophar came as soon as they heard the bad news. At first they grieved with him but before long their unbelief began to express itself.

They accused Job of committing sin—saying that he was not righteous and that his calamity was caused by his unrighteousness.

Eliphaz said, *"Who ever perished, being innocent? or where were the righteous cut off?"* (Job 4:7).

Bildad said, *"If you were pure and upright; surely now he would awake for thee, and make...thy righteousness prosperous"* (Job 8:6).

Zophar said, *"Should (your) lies make men hold their peace? ...For thou has said, My doctrine is pure, and I am clean"* (Job 11:3 & 4).

Each of Job's friends insisted that his calamities had come upon him because of his sin. But the Bible clearly declares Job was righteous. The very first verse of the book of Job tells us that he was *"perfect and upright, and one that feared God and eschewed* (shunned) *evil."* God also told Satan, after the devil had destroyed Job's family and taken all of his possessions, *"(Consider) my servant Job, that there is none like him in the earth, a perfect and an upright man, one that feareth God, and (avoids) evil? and still he holdeth fast his integrity, although thou movedst me against him, to destroy him, WITHOUT CAUSE"* (Job 2:3, emphasis mine).

NOTE: God said Job was perfect and that Satan's attack had no justification.

Were Job's friends right in accusing Job of secret sin? NO! If your "comforters" turn into your "accusors," don't listen to them.

•

Remember: JOB'S COMFORTERS WERE WRONG; CHANCES ARE, YOUR COMFORTERS ARE WRONG TOO!

77/THE GRACE OF FORGETTING

"This one thing I do, forgetting those things which are behind, (I reach) forth unto those things which are before"
(Philippians 3:13).

Also read: Psa. 32:1, 2; Isa. 1:18; 43:25; Heb. 8:12

If you want to live a healthy Christian life you must learn how to forget. Chances are, if you're like me, you've done things you're ashamed of. If you're a sensitive soul, your blunders and sins will torment you greatly.

Paul discovered the grace of forgetting. He said, "I forget the things which are behind." Someone has said, "He who dwells in the past—comes last." If you have failed God you must ask His forgiveness, accept it and then move on.

Imagine that your past is a cassette tape that's running through your mind. Now do this: Reach up between your eyes and pull that imaginary tape out of your mind and destroy it—forever!

The human psyche is such that it fastens itself on certain memories and replays them over and over again until they drive you mad. You must take hold of those ugly hurtful memories and cast them away. Satan also loves to have us dwelling in past failures. He blinds our eyes to the beautiful life of our future in the Lord.

If God has forgiven you and cast your sins in the sea of forgetfulness, if He has separated your sins as far as the east is from the west (an unlimited distance—see Psa. 103:12), what gives you the right to remember the sins God has forgotten and separated Himself from?

Your flesh-mind is foolish and fickle. Not only does it want to sin, but after it sins it will replay the event over and over again. The more it replays the event the more unworthy you feel of God's love (which is Satan's objective).

So—stop it!

Don't allow the cassette tape to play anymore. God has forgiven you and forgotten your sinful past. You must do the same.

•

Remember: PAUL LEARNED TO FORGET HIS PAST SO IT WOULD NOT HINDER HIM FROM PRESSING FORWARD IN GOD.

78/DO YOU NEED A SNAKE?

"The effectual fervent prayer of a righteous man or woman availeth much" (James 5:16, TLB).

Also read: Ps. 109:4; Prov. 15:8

I think the reason our prayers fail to penetrate heaven is that we fail to focus the power of our faith.

So often when I pray my mind begins to wander and conjures up a thousand other things I should be doing, or else it will drift around to several things. When I concentrate on the real need I get action.

The story is told of a missionary who was traveling through a strange country when nightfall came upon him. He found an abandoned cottage and settled there for the night.

That night as he lay sleeping, a large cobra unraveled from the rafters above and came slinking down onto the missionary's chest. When he awakened he was staring into the deadly eyes of the cobra.

He began to pray silently and earnestly, for he knew that one tiny move would prompt the cobra to strike. But as he prayed he did not have difficulty with his mind wandering as it so often had in times past!

Suddenly he saw the dark figure of a man in the door. It was a thief intent on robbing him. In the darkness the thief could not see the cobra when he reached for the missionary's wallet. The cobra struck and drove his poisonous fangs deep into the thief's wrist. The man screamed and ran out into the night. The cobra slithered away, satisfied, and the missionary began to praise God for the snake.

Are your prayers reaching heaven or are they being diluted by your wandering, restless mind? If so, maybe you need a "snake": a situation so serious your mind won't wander.

•

Remember: SNAKES MIGHT HELP YOU PRAY.

79/WHAT YOU SOW—GROWS!

"Whatsoever a man soweth, that shall he also reap. For he that soweth to his flesh shall of the flesh reap corruption; but he that soweth to the Spirit shall of the Spirit reap life everlasting" (Galatians 6:7 & 8).

Also read: Psa. 92:12; Phil. 1:6, 9, 10; Col. 1:9-11; 2 Pet. 3:18

Your life is like a garden. Whatever you sow—grows! If you don't like the crop that is springing up in your life, then you need to change the seed.

I remember, as a boy, planning a garden every spring. I would order seeds from a catalog and when the small packages came, they would always show the completely grown vegetable on the cover—in beautiful living color. I would place the packages on sticks by the rows so I would know what was growing.

What do you really want to grow in your life? Righteousness, peace, and Holy-Ghost joy? Then you must plant the right seeds.

If you're wasting time watching stupid and sensual TV programs, you will grow weeds of evil. If you read trashy novels and gossip magazines, you will grow sin. If you listen to worldly music, you will grow iniquity.

Whatever you put into your heart comes out of your life. So watch what you sow!

Give God Your Eyes—That you will behold things that are pure and edifying.

Give God Your Ears—that you will only listen to those songs and words that uplift the Lord.

Give God Your Money—that you will not waste it on empty materialistic things.

Give God Your Heart—that you will put your faith and trust in Him and not in this world's temporal pleasures.

Plant yourself firmly in the solid ground of the Scriptures. Water your soul generously with the tears of repentance. Weed out the distractions of hectic daily living. Then watch yourself grow in the warm sunlight of God's love.

•

Remember: WHAT YOU SOW—GROWS!

THE BIBLE'S DESCRIPTION OF CHRISTIANS

"And the disciples were called Christians first in Antioch" (Acts 11:26).

Also read: Ac. 20:7; Gal. 2:16; 1 Jn. 4:7

You and I have a lot of names—more than you might have imagined. For instance:
1. *We are called saints for our holiness.*
    Paul the apostle writes: *"But fornication, and all uncleanness, or covetousness, let it not be once named among you, as becometh saints"* (Eph. 5:3).
2. *We are called believers for our faith!*
    The Bible says of Abraham: *"And he believed in the Lord; and he counted it to him for righteousness"* (Gen. 15:6).
    Jesus said, *"For the Father himself loveth you, because ye have loved me, and have believed that I came out from God"* (Jn. 16:27).
3. *We are called brethren for the love.*
    Jesus said, *"A new commandment I give unto you. That ye love one another; as I have loved you, that ye also love one another. By this shall all men know that you are my disciples, if ye have love one to another"* (Jn. 13:34 & 35).
4. *We are called disciples for our knowledge.*
    "And it came to pass, that, as he was praying in a certain place, when he had ceased, one of his disciples said unto him, Lord, teach us to pray, as John also taught his disciples" (Lk. 11:1).
5. *We are called children for our relationship.*
    "For you are all the children of God by faith in Jesus Christ" (Gal. 3:26).
6. *We are called heirs for our possessions.*
    "The Spirit itself beareth witness with our spirit, that we are the children of God: And if children, then heirs; heirs of God, and joint-heirs with Christ; if so be that we suffer with him, that we may be also glorified together" (Rom. 8:16 & 17).
    We have many names, and each one is full of glorious meaning.

•

Remember: GOD HAS MANY WONDERFUL NAMES FOR CHRISTIANS.

81/THE MYSTERIOUS SECRET

"This mystery... which is "Christ in you, the hope of glory" (Colossians 1:27).

Also read: Gal. 2:20; Phil. 1:21

Yousuf Karsh is a Canadian photographer of world renown. He has photographed famous people from Winston Churchill to Ronald Reagan. In fact, he has made it his lifetime quest to search out greatness.

Karsh says, "I believe the past has no claim on greatness, for such arresting personalities are always among us. Nor can we yet judge what lessons remain to be learned from the young. I know only that my quest continues.

"The endless fascination of these people for me lies in what I call their inward power. It is part of the elusive secret that hides in everyone, and it has been my life's work to try to capture it on film. The mask we present to others and too often to ourselves may lift for only a second—to reveal that power in an unconcious gesture, a raised brow, a surprised response, a moment of repose. THIS is the moment to record."

The secret of the Christian faith—the mystery is— Christ in you, the hope of glory. The only lasting thing in this universe is the Christ who dwells in your heart by the Holy Spirit.

Don't take your faith for granted. Buddah cannot live in Buddists and Mohammed cannot dwell in Moslems, for Buddah and Mohammed are dead. But Jesus Christ can live in you because He is alive!

Just think: through Jesus you become like God. *"Beloved, now are we the sons of God, and it doth not yet appear what we shall be: but we know that, when he shall appear, we shall be like him"* (1 Jn. 3:2).

Today, draw closer to Him through prayer and reading His word—find out what it's like to have Christ, the hope of glory, living in you.

●

Remember: CHRIST IN YOU IS YOUR INWARD POWER AND BEAUTY. HE WILL GIVE YOU THE INNER GLOW THAT PHOTOGRAPHERS SEEK!

82/VISUALIZE YOUR VICTORY!

"For I can do everything God asks me to do with the help of Christ" (Philippians 4:13, TLB).

Also read: Ps. 91:2-4; Pro. 30:5; Jer. 17:7 & 8

Do you believe today's text? Do you feel that you can do everything God asks you to do with the help of Christ? Where do you stand on the Ladder of Achievement?

100% I did!	40% What should I do?
90% I will!	30% I wish I could.
80% I can!	20% I don't know how.
70% I think I can.	10% I can't!
60% I might.	0% I won't!
50% I think I might.	

If you are going to succeed in life you must visualize your victory. An experiment was tried with two basketball teams. One team practiced hard, running up and down the floor, and won. The second team was told to just sit quietly and visualize each move they'd make during a winning game. The second team won by an even greater margin than the team that worked out.

Try this:
1. Visualize yourself on the throne with Jesus Christ, ruling and reigning with Him throughout eternity.
   "To him that overcometh will I grant to sit with me in my throne, even as I also overcame" (Rev. 3:21).
2. Visualize Jesus Christ living in your body, thinking, speaking, working, and helping others.
   "I live; yet not I, but Christ liveth in me: and the life which I now live in the flesh I live by the faith of the Son of God" (Gal. 2:20).
3. Visualize Jesus Christ facing your greatest problem.
   "For God is at work within you, helping you want to obey him, and then helping you do what he wants" (Phil. 2:13, TLB).

Visualizing your victory will help you overcome the difficulties that life has set in your path.

Look again at the Ladder of Achievement. Visualize yourself with Jesus Christ moving up every step until at last you are ruling together in heaven.

•

Remember: VISUALIZE YOUR VICTORY!

83/PLEASE PRAY FOR ME

"Now I beseech you, brethren, for the Lord Jesus Christ's sake, and for the love of the Spirit, that ye strive together with me in your prayers to God for me; That I may be delivered..." (Romans 15:30).

Also read: 1 Sam. 12:23; 1 Kings 13:6, Col. 1:9; 1 Thess. 5:25

Paul begged the Christians in Rome to pray for him that he be delivered from unbelievers and accepted by the saints in Jerusalem, *"That I may come unto you with joy by the will of God, and may with you be refreshed"* (verse 32).

Paul said their prayers would help deliver and refresh him. This is how I feel about *your* prayers for this ministry. I am certain your pastor and missionary friends appreciate your prayers too.

The Bible tells of the time when Moses and the children of Israel came out of Egypt on their way to the Promised Land. On their journey they came across the Amalekites, who gathered their armies to make war.

> The Bible says, *"Then came Amalek, and fought with Israel...*
>
> *"And Moses said unto Joshua, Choose...men, and go out and fight with Amalek: tomorrow I will stand on the top of the hill with the rod of God in mine hand.*
>
> *"So Joshua* (and his men)*...fought with Amalek: and Moses, Aaron, and Hur went up to the top of the hill.*
>
> *"And it came to pass, when Moses held up his hand, that Israel prevailed: and when he let down his hand, Amalek prevailed.*
>
> *"But Moses' hands were heavy; and they took a stone, and put it under him, and he sat thereon: and Aaron and Hur stayed* (held) *up his hands...and Joshua discomfited* (crushed) *Amalek and his people"* (Ex. 17:8-13).

When Aaron and Hur held up the hands of Moses, their leader, Israel prevailed. I need you to lift up my ministry with your prayers. Together we can defeat Satan and bring glory to God. We can prevail over the wicked one and win many souls to Christ. But I need your prayers—just as Paul needed the prayers of his Christian friends. Please pray for me and other ministers of God today.

•

Remember: TOGETHER, OUR PRAYERS CAN HELP DEFEAT SATAN.

84/RIGHT IS ALWAYS RIGHT!

"Therefore to him that knoweth to do good, and doeth it not, to him it is sin" (James 4:17).

Also read: Ex. 15:26; Deut. 6:18; Eph. 6:1

For more than 23 years, Connie and I struggled to decide which way was right to pass the food around the table. We'd study books about manners and then forget what the books said. Just when we thought we had it down we'd visit someone's house and they'd change the direction and we'd be confused again.

One day while visiting a very proper family we asked the hostess, "Tell us, which direction should the food be passed around the table?" She smiled and said, "Right is always right!" That did it. It stuck in our minds. Now, after the mealtime prayer, we don't have to sit there boogle-eyed, wondering which way to pass the food. When anyone hesitates someone says, "Right is always right."

This phrase also works well for daily living. If you always tell the truth, you don't need such a good memory. Tell what's right and it won't trip you up. "It's never right to do wrong to do right."

Ananias and Sapphira tried to deceive the early church when they said that they had given all when they had kept back part of the price. They tried to make themselves appear committed when they were not. You know what happened—they were struck dead (see Acts 5:1-11).

Right is always right in the long run. You can compromise truth or actions, but sooner or later everyone is going to know the truth. Make it your life's creed that "right is always right". You'll have a conscience at peace with God and your fellow man.

"It's never right to do wrong to do right."

•

Remember: RIGHT IS ALWAYS RIGHT!

85/WATCH YOUR SPIRIT!

"But my servant Caleb, because he had another spirit with him, and hath followed me fully, him will I bring into the land...and his seed shall possess it" (Numbers 14:24).

Also read: Matt. 6:14-15; Eph. 4:31-32; 1 Pet. 1:7-9

I have met so many men and women down through my years of ministry who are talented and personable and even committed to Christ, but who have a "twist" in their inner spirit. Sometimes it's hard to pinpoint what it is, but I can feel it when I talk with them.

Beware of Bitterness. Paul said, *"Look diligently lest any man foil the grace of God; lest any root of bitterness springing up trouble you, and thereby many be defiled"* (Heb. 12:15).

If someone has hurt you deeply and you haven't fully forgiven them—the bitterness you hold in your soul will ferment until it defiles your spirit. Quickly forgive them—now—before it ruins your radiant spirit.

Beware of Disobedience. I have found that a person who is really walking in obedience to God has an open spirit; you can peer deeply into his soul. But as soon as a man does wrong he pulls the blinds. Soon you find yourself talking to a person in hiding—even though you are face to face.

If you study the context for today's text you'll see that God was totally exasperated with Israel. He said they would all die in the desert and never see the promised land. But He commended Caleb for his excellent spirit because,

> Caleb had *another spirit*—a spirit of faith. Caleb and Joshua believed God while the other 10 spies doubted. If you want God to admire you, believe that He will do what He has promised.
>
> God said, *"Caleb...hath followed me fully."* Caleb kept God's commandments; this earned him a first-rank position with the Lord.

●

Remember: WATCH YOUR SPIRIT! IT IS LIKE A TRANSMITTER, EMITTING SIGNALS OF BITTERNESS OR BLESSINGS.

86/THE CRAZINESS OF COMPETITIVENESS

"Be kindly affectioned one to another with brotherly love; in honour preferring one another" (Romans 12:10).

Also read: Ps. 55:14; Jn. 17:21-23; 1 Cor. 1:10

Christian competition is crazy. In the 29 years I have traveled as an evangelist, I have been grieved by the way churches, ministries and fellow Christians compete with one another.

The big problems among Christians seldom involve who will preach and sing at the jail but who will sing "the special" on Sunday morning, or who will play the organ or piano—in short, who will receive the attention of the local congregation.

The Bible says we are to be kindly affectioned one to another. The Living Bible says, *"Love each other with brotherly affection and take delight in honoring each other."*

It's hard for some people to honor others because they feel it depletes themselves; they feel threatened by another's success.

But if you want to be above others, then you're just like Lucifer. He said, *"I will ascend into heaven, I will exalt my throne above the stars of God...I will ascend...I will be like the most High"* (Is. 14:13 & 14).

The devil was an angel who wanted to be above others—and he became horribly corrupt. The balanced truth is you should want to succeed but not at the expense of others. You should want to reach the top—not to look down on others and say, "Look at me, I've made it!" but to say, "God, I hope you're proud of me, and I hope I can use my success to help many more reach the top."

It's sad to see petty infighting among Christians because there's a whole world to win.

Since there are nearly 5 billion people in the world and only 1 billion are Christians, why should anyone be competitive? There is plenty of opportunity for everyone to minister in some way.

•

Remember: REJOICE WHEN OTHERS ARE EXALTED.

87/WHY JESUS DIED

"Christ...who through the eternal Spirit offered himself without spot to God, will cleanse your mind and conscience to serve the living God" (Hebrews 9:14 Literal).

Also read: Rom. 14:6-9, 1 Cor. 1:23

Today as we celebrate Good Friday, let's review some of the things Jesus accomplished when He died for us on the cross.

1. *Jesus opened the way into the Holy of Holies.* Before Jesus died, only one man could enter into God's presence once each year. The high priest would kill a perfect lamb and cautiously enter into the Holy of Holies.

This sacred area (where God dwelt) was separated by a heavy curtain. When Jesus died, the Bible says, *"Behold, the veil of the temple was torn in two from the top to the bottom: and the earth quaked, the rocks were torn apart"* (Matt. 27:51, Literal).

The tearing open of the veil was a literal illustration to the Jewish people, and to the world, that Jesus had opened the way for all of us to enter into God's presence. You no longer need a representative here on earth to go before God on your behalf; Jesus made you a priest of the most High God (See Rev. 1:6).

2. *Jesus appeased the righteous wrath of a holy God.* Whenever you and I sin it angers God. The Bible says, *"God is angry with the wicked every day"* (Ps. 7:11).

However, how could God be just and punish sin and yet be merciful to save sinners? The Bible says, *"He* (Jesus) *is the one who took God's wrath against our sins upon himself, and brought us into fellowship with God"* (1 Jn. 2:2).

Have you taken advantage of all that Jesus has done for you? Are you fellowshipping with God as a personal friend? The best way to thank Jesus for His sufferings is to fully enter into your privileges as a believer today.

•

Remember: JESUS DIED TO OPEN UP THE HOLY OF HOLIES SO YOU COULD BE A PERSONAL FRIEND OF GOD.

88/THE CARE OF ALL THE CHURCHES

"Beside those things that are without, that which cometh upon me daily, the care of all the churches"
(2 Corinthians 11:28).

Also read: 2 Cor. 4:8-9; Gal. 6:9; 1 Pet. 1:6-9

If you're going through difficulties you should review what Paul went through. He gives a list of his trials saying,
* Of the Jews five times I received 39 stripes
* Three times I was beaten with rods
* Once I was stoned
* Three times I suffered shipwreck
* A night and day I have been in the deep
* In journeyings often
* In perils of waters
* In perils of robbers
* In perils by my own countrymen
* In perils by the heathen
* In perils in the wilderness
* In perils in the sea
* In perils among false religious leaders
* In weariness and painfulness
* In prayer
* In hunger and thirst
* In fastings often
* In cold and nakedness (see 2 Cor. 11:24-27).

Paul concluded the list of his trials by saying that in addition to all those things he had the care of all the churches. In some ways the daily care of daily problems weighed as heavily upon Paul as the great shipwrecks he had experienced. At least in the shipwrecks there was tension and excitement, and it kept his adrenalin flowing.

But "daily care" is more dull and drab. It has a tendency to wear down your spirit with its monotonous routine.

Is this what you're facing at this time? Do you have a non-evangelical situation that goes on and on, without end; where there doesn't seem to be any change in sight? Jesus said, *"Who then is that faithful and wise steward, whom his lord shall make ruler over his household?"* (Luke 12:42).

Rulers are those who faithfully carry the day-by-day cares and responsibilities of life—whatever they may be.

So don't be wearied by the ordinary—your faithfulness in daily routines is preparing you to rule upon a throne.

•

Remember: MIXING YOUR PRAYERS WITH YOUR CARES WILL HELP LIFT THE LOAD.

89/HE IS RISEN!

"He is not here: for he is risen" (Matthew 28:6).

Also read: Acts 2:31; Romans 1:4; 1 Peter 1:13

I believe Easter morning will be remembered in eternity as the greatest moment in history. On this day Jesus broke the death barrier: He made it possible for you and me to live again.

Paul the Apostle said, *"The fact is that Christ did actually rise from the dead, and has become the first of millions who will come back to life someday"* (1 Cor. 15:20 TLB).

The resurrection of Jesus Christ promises that you will be united with your loved ones in heaven someday. If your family is saved, you'll be united around the throne of God as a happy unit again. Just think:

Your parents will be young and strong, your husband or wife will be smiling by your side, your children will be happy and healthy, and all the saints of God will be rejoicing with you—embracing you and shouting praises to Christ our King.

There is NO greater hope given man than life after death, and the resurrection of Jesus makes it all real!

IT'S REALLY GOING TO HAPPEN!

We have the promise in God's Word that it is going to happen: *"But if the Spirit of him that raised up Jesus from the dead dwell in you, he that raised up Christ from the dead shall also quicken your mortal bodies by his Spirit that dwelleth in you"* (Rom. 8:11).

Jesus Christ has conquered our greatest enemy—death. Because He lives, you and I are guaranteed a new world, a new life, a new heaven, a new earth, a new covenant, and a new hope of life everlasting.

HALLELUJAH! HALLELUJAH! HALLELUJAH!

●

Remember: HE IS RISEN!

WHEN YOUR FAITH FALLS

"But when he saw the wind boisterous, he was afraid; and beginning to sink, he cried, saying, Lord, save me" (Matthew 14:30).

Also read: Matt. 17:20; Rom. 4:5; 10:17

If your faith has been sinking don't be too alarmed. Peter's faith failed him several times but he still became a great apostle.

The story of our text is a familiar one. A storm overtook the disciples as they tried crossing Lake Galilee in their small fishing boat. As they fought for their lives they were shocked to see Jesus coming towards them—walking on the water.

At first they thought Jesus was a ghost, but Peter had enough faith to say, *"Lord, if it be you, bid me come unto you on the water."*

When Jesus said *"Come,"* Peter started walking towards Him on the water. Then Peter's faith began to falter and he cried, *"Lord, save me."* Immediately Jesus caught him and said, *"O thou of little faith, wherefore didst thou doubt?"* (see Matt. 14:28-32).

Notice how the gentle rebuke of Jesus stands out, *"Why did you doubt?"* This very question reveals that having faith is closely tied to your will. If faith was outside of Peter's control our Lord wouldn't have asked the question.

Don't ever let your faith-breakdown hurt your pride. Don't say, "I'll never try believing for something like that again." If Peter had done that, he would have never preached the sermon that won 3,000 to Jesus Christ (Acts 2), nor would he have raised Dorcas from the dead (Acts 9).

So, if your faith fails, it is because you did not will to believe as you should. You can strengthen your faith by reinforcing your will. Because your will acts upon knowledge, or your faith acts upon facts, the best way to recover from a faith-failure is to review the truths of God's Word. Hearing testimonies of what God has done for others will help your faith to grow.

•

Remember: GOD WILL WORK A MIRACLE WHEN YOU BELIEVE.

91/ARE YOU WAVERING?

"Let him ask in faith, nothing wavering" (James 1:6).

Also read: Matt. 9:25, 29; Mark 9:23; Heb. 11:6; Jas. 1:1-8

I was going through a very difficult time recently and needed a miracle from God. For over a year I'd struggled with two problems that wouldn't go away:

First, a loved one that needed to be saved.

Second, I needed a miracle of financial help.

I prayed and prayed and prayed and prayed without receiving an answer. Then the Lord guided me to this portion of Scripture in James: *"If any of you lack...let him ask of God, that giveth to all men liberally...and it shall be given him.*

"BUT LET HIM ASK IN FAITH, nothing wavering. For he that wavereth is like a wave of the sea driven with the wind and tossed.

"For let not that man think that he shall receive anything of the Lord" (Jas. 1:5-7, emphasis mine).

When I read these Scriptures I could see that conditions were tossing me about like a piece of driftwood on the ocean. One day I'd be "up," believing God would answer prayer. The next day I'd be "down," wondering if God would keep His promises.

The Holy Spirit impressed me that I should "lock-on" to God's promises and not let go—no matter what the conditions dictated. This helped me a lot.

I hope this helps you too! If you believe that God answers prayer—and He does!—then lock-on to His promises and keep on believing while you pray. Persistance is needed if your prayers are to be answered. Put your faith in God alone. He will honor your faith.

•

Remember: DON'T WAVER IN YOUR FAITH!

92/THE FANTASTIC FAITH OF ABRAHAM

"By faith Abraham, when he was tried, offered up Isaac" (Hebrews 11:17).

Also read: Matt. 9:28-29; Mark 9:23; 11:22-24; 1 Pet. 1:7-9

In Bible days, a man without a son was considered as good as dead—he knew that when he died there would be no one to carry on his name or his influence on this earth.

You'll recall that God called Abraham to leave his home in Ur of the Chaldees to journey to Canaan—the Land of Promise (see Gen. 15:17). God also assured Abraham that he would have a son (see Gen. 16:17).

But the years went by and Abraham grew older. Finally God appeared to him when he was 99 years old and repeated His promise. It sounded so impossible that Abraham and Sarah could have a child in their old age that, *"Abraham fell upon his face, and laughed, and said in his heart, Shall a child be born unto him that is an hundred years old and shall Sarah, that is ninety years old, bear?"* (Gen. 17:17). Even Sarah laughed.

But God said, *"Is any thing too hard for the Lord?"* (Gen. 18:14).

When Sarah conceived and Isaac was finally born, his parents' joy was overflowing. As Isaac grew older, he became the very hope of Abraham's life.

Then God commanded Abraham to offer his son as a sacrifice.

Can you imagine how Abraham must have felt? But he obeyed God without question.

H. Clay Turnbull writes, "For Abraham to surrender his son, and so to become again a childless, hopeless old man was a difficult thing. ONLY A FAITH THAT WOULD NEITHER QUESTION NOR REASON, ONLY A LOVE THAT WOULD NEITHER FAIL NOR WAVER COULD MEET AN ISSUE LIKE THAT."

Are you facing a similar situation in your life? Are you being called upon to give up someone or something that you cherish? Just believe in Him and obey God as Abraham did. You will be blessed for your faith.

•

Remember: ABRAHAM TRUSTED GOD AND WAS REWARDED FOR HIS FAITHFULNESS.

93/GLORY IN THE LORD!

"Let him that glorieth glory in this, that he understandeth and knoweth me" (Jeremiah 9:24).

Also read: Ps. 145:11; 149:5; Prov. 3:35; Jer. 9:23

Nonchristian people glory in three things: wisdom, strength and power. But the Bible says, *"But let him that glorieth glory in this, that he understandeth and knoweth me, that I am the Lord which exercise lovingkindness, judgment, and righteousness, in the earth: for in these things I delight, saith the Lord"* (Jer. 9:24).

The three things God delights in are: love, fairness, and holiness.

The great question of life is, "What are you seeking most?" Are you seeking the world's system (money, strength, power) or God's Kingdom (love, fairness, holiness)?

This should not confuse you, but in some ways it is possible to seek both—if your motives are right. The Bible says, *"The fear of the Lord is the beginning of wisdom"* (Ps. 111:10). You should seek to be as wise as possible, acknowledging God as the source.

It is also true that your body is the temple of God (so you should keep it in shape), and wealth is a means of spreading the Gospel throughout the world.

However, these things are not an end in themselves but a means of serving God. The true perspective is to seek love, fairness and holiness, and then when you're fully committed, use your wisdom, strength and wealth to serve God. As Jesus said, *"You cannot serve God and mammon"* (Matt. 6:24) but you should seek to serve God WITH mammon.

Best of all, you should delight in knowing the Lord—that you're His child, and part of His Kingdom. There's an old statement that says, "If God has called you into His work—don't backslide to become a king."

Today you have a chance to accomplish eternal good. As you minister to the needs of others, rejoice! You're wealthier than a billionaire because you know the Lord and He knows you!

•

Remember: GLORY IN THE LORD!

STOP, LOOK, AND LIVE!

"Look unto Me, and be...saved...for I am God, and there is none else" (Isaiah 45:22).

Also read: Jn. 3:16; Rom. 10:9; Tit. 3:5 & 6

If this were the last article you read before death, it would be important for me to ask, "Are you saved?" And if you say you are, on what basis are you trusting the salvation of your soul?

The Bible warns, *"Be not deceived"* (Gal. 6:7). What if you are and don't know it? What if you've been led by a religious system that has blinded you to the true way of salvation? I urge you to stop, look, and live!

When the Jews were delivered out of Egypt by the power of God, they had to make a long journey across a wilderness to the promised land of Caanan.

> The Bible says, *"The people were very discouraged; they began to murmur against God and to complain against Moses... So the Lord sent poisonous snakes among them to punish them, and many of them were bitten and died."*
>
> *"Then the people repented and asked Moses to pray for them. The Lord told Moses, 'Make a bronze replica of one of these snakes and attach it to the top of a pole; anyone who is bitten shall live if he simply looks at it.*
>
> *"So Moses made the replica, and whenever anyone who had been bitten looked at the bronze snake, he recovered!"* (see Num. 21:2-9).

Notice the saving of their lives depended on stopping to look at God's provision. Jesus said this is the way you are saved from sin. It's not by efforts of your own, but by the miracle power of God's grace in your life.

Are you looking and trusting only in Jesus Christ to save you? Remember He bled and died in your place. If you want to be saved from the pain and poison of sin and damnation, lift your eyes towards Him.

•

Remember: STOP, LOOK, AND LIVE!

95/DESIRE SPIRITUAL GIFTS

"Follow after charity, and desire spiritual gifts..."
(1 Corinthians 14:1).

Also read: Rom. 1:11-12; 1 Cor. 12

Spiritual gifts have always created a lot of controversy in the church. Paul lists the nine gifts of the Spirit in 1 Corinthians 12, verses 8 and 9:
1. Word of Wisdom
2. Word of Knowledge
3. Faith
4. Healing
5. Working of Miracles
6. Prophecy
7. Discerning of Spirits
8. Speaking in Different Tongues
9. Interpretation of Tongues

All nine of these gifts are supernatural. Wisdom, knowledge and faith are not the results of that natural wisdom that one is born with—or that which he gathers in college. The gifts of God's Spirit are supernatural in every way.

Paul says you should desire spiritual gifts. If you're like me, you need all the help from God you can get! However, the danger is that you select or reject gifts on the basis of your *personal preference*.

For instance, many Christians would like to have the gift of faith. But what if the Holy Spirit would like to manifest Himself through you by giving you the gifts of healing, speaking in tongues, or the power to do miracles? These latter gifts are controversial issues and are, to a great measure, laid aside.

My feeling about spiritual gifts is that I need and want all of God I can get. I'm seeking Him for all that He will provide. I'm not going to pick and choose the ones I prefer. I'm going to let God, my Father who loves me and knows me, choose the gifts He wants to give me, no matter how much criticism I get.

•

Remember: DESIRE SPIRITUAL GIFTS AND TRUST GOD TO GIVE YOU THE GIFTS HE WANTS YOU TO HAVE.

96/THE 11TH COMMANDMENT

"A new commandment I give unto you, That ye love one another; as I have loved you, that ye also love one another" (John 13:34).

Also read: Lev. 19:18; Deut. 6:5; Matt. 5:43-44

Have you ever wondered why Jesus gave us this 11th commandment? Why didn't God include it with the original 10 that He gave to Moses?

The reason He did not include it then is that God is very practical. He knew it would take an extra measure of the Holy Spirit to enact such a commandment—so He waited until Jesus (the greatest most perfect expression of Himself) came before He shared these words.

How does Jesus make it easier for us to love one another? Here's how:

* *Jesus reveals how much God loves us.* Would you be willing to purposely send your only son to a place where you knew he would be tortured and killed?

Through Jesus we can see God's overwhelming love for us.

* *Jesus lifts the condemnation of guilt and judgment.* The Bible says, *"He that believeth on Him is not condemned"* (John 3:17). Isn't it fantastic to know that God doesn't condemn you for even ONE of the evil things you've done? When you realize how undeserving you were and how free God has made you, you can't condemn others—you can only love them.

* *Jesus fills us with the Holy Spirit!* Jesus was God but He was also filled with God. The Holy Spirit manifested the loving nature of God through Jesus. Jesus said, *"I will pray the Father, and he shall give you another Comforter"* (John 14:16). When the Holy Spirit abides in your heart you will love others as God loves them.

So love people today as God loves them. Pick out a critical, miserable person and lavish your love upon him. In doing this you will glorify God and prove that the love of God dwells in you.

•

Remember: JESUS ENABLES YOU TO FULFILL THE 11TH COMMANDMENT.

97/FROM A DOT TO DUST—WHEN THEN?

"Then he...came trembling, and fell down before Paul and Silas, and brought them out, and said, 'Sirs, what must I do to be saved?" (Acts 16:29 & 30).

Also read: Jn. 3:36; 1 Cor. 15:1-4; 1 Jn. 5:11-13

Stop and study the period at the end of this sentence. Yes, the dot you just passed. Here is another one just in case you missed it.

When you and I were conceived we were smaller than this tiny dot, and when we finish this world we'll become a pile of ashes.

The greatest question is—what then? Will you disappear as dust in the wind? Or is there life beyond the grave?

I believe there is. I instinctly believe it, and others who have had life after death experiences (who have died and gone to heaven), as the Apostle Paul did, confirm it. *"Fourteen years ago I was taken up to heaven for a visit. Don't ask me whether my body was there or just my spirit, for I don't know; only God can answer that. But anyway, there I was in paradise, and heard things so astounding that they are beyond a man's power to describe or put in words"* (2 Cor. 12:2).

Jesus Christ—who was crucified and buried, whose grave was guarded by soldiers, who arose from the tomb on the third day as He foretold—said, *"I am the resurrection, and the life: he that believeth in me, though he were dead, yet shall he live: And whosoever liveth and believeth in me shall never die"* (Jn. 11:25 & 26).

How do we find salvation? How do we prepare to meet God? Jesus Christ declares, *"I am the Way, the Truth, and the Life: No man cometh unto the Father, but by Me"* (Jn. 14:6).

Right now you and I are somewhere between the dot and dust. The moment we die we'll face the Creator of the universe who will ask if we received Christ, His son, as our personal Savior. I'll answer "yes"—will you? If you haven't received Christ yet, do so today!

●

Remember: WITHOUT CHRIST, DOTS AND DUST DON'T STAND A CHANCE.

98/WINNER'S LOSE

"For what is a man profited, if he shall gain the whole world, and lose his own soul? or what shall a man give in exchange for his soul?" (Matthew 16:26).

Also read: Matt. 10:37-39; Phil. 1:21; 1 Pet. 4:1-2

I walked into a restaurant today and saw a man wearing a T-shirt with this inscription, "He who has the most toys when he dies—wins!"

I laughed because the statement expressed so bluntly the world's philosophy of life. Eric Toffler, the working man's philosopher, said, "Life is one short bus ride. The tragedy is that most people spend most of their time fighting for the best seats."

What is your goal in living? Are you gathering toys (houses, cars, clothes, boats, guns, etc.)? Are you seeking position (recognition for your accomplishments)? Are you seeking comfort and security (the "good life," and protection from the unpredictable)?

Jesus said the only way to live is to give your life up to God and others. This was His way. He said, *"If any man will come after me, let him deny himself, and take up his cross, and follow me.*

"For whosoever will save his life shall lose it: and whosoever will lose his life for my sake shall find it" (Matt. 16:24-25).

How do you lose your life for Christ? Here are a few ideas to help you:

>**Be An Intercessor.* When you enter your prayer closet to intercede on behalf of others you are giving yourself in a most sacrificial way. Remember—Jesus is our full-time intercessor in heaven.
>**Make Disciples of Others.* It takes a lot of time to teach others God's Word. You may have to give up many of your cherished evenings to establish someone else in Christ.
>**Give Up Your Most Cherished Dreams.* Maybe there is something YOU want to accomplish in your life that is different from what God wants. If so, giving up your dream will be very difficult. But keep this in mind—the person you will become through obedience to Jesus Christ will be far more than what you'll be on your own.

•

Remember: IN GOD'S ESTIMATION, WINNERS LOSE AND LOSERS WIN.

99/TRY A LITTLE HUMBLENESS

"Humble men are very fortunate!" He told them, "for the Kingdom of Heaven is given to them" (Matthew 5:3, TLB).

Also read: Jas. 4:10; 1 Peter. 5:6; Col. 3:12

The meek are not weak; they are the ones who will rule the world. I like the Living Bible paraphrase that uses the word humble instead of *meek*. Webster's dictionary defines the word *humble* as, "not proud or haughty: not arrogant or assertive."

You know the meek shall inherit the earth in the world to come (for they are the only ones fit to rule and reign); but did you realize the meek shall inherit the earth in the world here and now?

In my 26 years of travel in the U.S., Canada and around the world, I have found the most successful people are usually the most humble. Their modest opinion of themselves causes them to reach out for answers beyond them.

> Yousuf Karsh, the world famous photographer, was ready to do Albert Einstein's portrait. He says, "At Princeton's Institute for Advanced Study, I have found Einstein a simple, kindly, almost childlike man, too great for any of the postures of eminence. One did not have to understand his science to feel the power of his mind or the force of his personality.
>
> "He spoke sadly yet serenely, as one who had looked into the universe for past mankind's small affairs"(emphasis mine).

How humble are you? Take this opportunity to examine yourself. Jesus said, *"But those who think themselves great shall be disappointed and humbled; and those who humble themselves shall be exalted"* (Matt. 23:12, TLB).

Isn't it better to humble yourself and let others praise you than to praise yourself and have others humble you?

There was no man on earth more humble than our Lord when He laid aside His power as the Son of God to become our Savior on that tortuous cross.

Humble yourself today and give praise and thanks to our Lord Jesus Christ!

•

Remember: A HUMBLE SPIRIT WILL LEAD YOU TO THE PERFECT PLEASURES YOU WILL FIND IN GOD.

100/THE DANGER OF IDEALISM

"I am made all things to all men, that I might by all means save some" (1 Corinthians 9:22).

Also read: Acts 2:42-47; Jn. 17:21-23; 1 Jn. 1:3, 7

There is a danger in being too right, too correct, too technical in your faith. Paul the apostle was a pragmatist. He literally said, "I've become everything to everybody—that I might win some."

By this Paul didn't mean that he compromised his stand of salvation through faith in Christ, but in all secondary matters he was willing to bend so that he might reach more of the unreached.

For instance, if you'll study the book of Acts and the epistles, you'll see that circumcision was the big controversy of the early church. In the beginning, the Christians were primarily Jewish, and each of the Jewish men had already been circumcised. But Paul preached that this should not be required of the Gentiles. This caused a firestorm of controversy everywhere Paul preached.

> The Bible says, *"They* (elders) *praised God but then said, 'You know, dear brother how many thousands of Jews have also believed, and they are all very insistent that Jewish believers must continue to follow the Jewish traditions and customs. Our Jewish Christians here at Jerusalem have been told that you are against the laws of Moses, against our Jewish customs, and that you forbid the circumcision of their children. Now what can be done? For they will certainly hear that you have come.*
>
> *"We suggest this: We have four men here who are preparing to shave their heads and take some vows. Go with them to the temple and have your head shaved too, and pay for theirs to be shaved.*
>
> *"Then everyone will know that you approve of this custom for the Hebrew Christians and that you yourself obey the Jewish laws and are in line with our thinking in these matters...*
>
> *"So Paul agreed to their request"* (Acts 21:20-26 TLB).

Amazing! Paul had his head shaved to communicate Christ to the Jews and yet preached Christ to the Gentiles without mentioning circumcision. Was he right? I believe so. He was truly becoming all things to reach all men.

Meditate on this truth prayerfully: "Idealism is greatly increased the further one is removed from the problem" (Thatcher Constretch).

•

Remember: IDEALISM FORGETS THAT PEOPLE ARE MORE IMPORTANT THAN RULES.

101/CAST OUT—OR BE CAST OUT!

"But the children of the kingdom shall be cast out into outer darkness: there shall be weeping and gnashing of teeth" (Matthew 8:12).

Also read: Lk. 4:18 & 19; Jn. 3:3; Rom. 1:18-20

The question arises, "How can you and I win against the enemy within our hearts, the church, the world and even heaven?"

The answer is simple: the enemy must be cast out. You and I must cast out every force contrary to God or eventually be cast out of the Kingdom ourselves. The decree is simple: cast out or be cast out!

It is possible to call yourself a Christian and be in the church actively participating in the work of evangelism and still not be right with God. Jesus spoke of Judgment Day very seriously with these words, *"Many will say to me in that day, Lord, Lord, have we not prophesied in thy name? and in thy name have cast out devils? And in thy name done many wonderful works?*

"And then will I profess unto them, I never knew you: depart from me, ye that work iniquity" (Matt. 7:22 & 23).

From these passages you can clearly see that people involved with the church, preaching, working miracles, doing good deeds, and fundamentally sound, even calling Jesus "Lord," could be cast out of the Kingdom of God into everlasting punishment.

How terrifying! Why will they be cast out? Because they didn't cast the flesh and the devil out of their hearts and lives. They'll be cast out because they embraced a system instead of the Savior. This is why Jesus said, "Depart from me, I never knew you." They knew the Christian religion, it's power and miracles and teachings, but they didn't know Christ.

The lesson is simply this: you must win the war within your heart by serving the Savior—and not just the Christian system—and you must cast out the enemy now or you will be cast out later.

•

Remember: CAST OUT THE FLESH AND THE DEVIL OR YOU WILL BE CAST OUT!

SPARE YOUR WORDS

"He that hath knowledge spareth his words" (Proverbs 17:27).

Also read: Prov. 21:23; I Pet. 3:10

The Spartans of ancient Greece had a virtue that many 20th century Christians should adopt today. They were strict disciplinarians who did not fear pain or danger.

The city of Sparta was also known as Lacedaemon, from which we get the word "laconic." This means someone who is concise, or spares his words. Proverbs 13:3 confirms this virtue by saying, *"He that keepeth his mouth, keepeth his life: but he that openeth wide his lips shall have destruction."*

Do you waste a lot of words? One pastor said he could eliminate 90% of the gossip that plagued the congregation if everyone limited his phone calls to 3 minutes.

Somewhere I read that the shortest description of a naval battle in World War II was a message that said, "Sighted sub—sank same." Jesus would approve of such brevity. He said, *"But let your communication be Yea, yea; Nay, nay: for whatsoever is more than these cometh of evil"* (Matt 5:37).

The best way to keep yourself from sinning is to talk less. *"In the multitude of words there (lacks) no sin: but he that refrains his lips is wise."* (Prov. 10:19)

Have you fallen into the trap of repeating garbage? Another wise pastor I heard of had a sign on the door of his office that said, "I will listen to anything you say about anybody as long as you sign your name and address." Few gossiping church members felt free about unloading on him!

Today, try something new: control the conversation you have with others. Whenever they begin to talk about others or repeat negative news, simply switch the conversation by saying, "What is the best thing you like about your job? or "What's the three best things you and I can do for others?"

You'll be surprised how these questions will spare you a lot of words as well as a lot of grief.

•

Remember: THE FEWER NEGATIVE WORDS THE BETTER.

103/HOW YOU CAN SPEAK WITH AUTHORITY

"For he taught them as one having authority, and not as the scribes" (Matthew 7:29).

Also read: Rom. 1:1, 6, 18-22; 1 Cor. 9:19; Phil. 2:7

Have you ever noticed that some Christians speak with more authority than others? How do some take command and radiate more power and assurance with their words?

There is a reason for this dynamic power. It is this: Coming *under* the authority of God's Word gives you authority *with* God's Word. If you are obeying God's commandments you will speak with confidence. If not, your words will be hollow.

Jesus loved God and obeyed His Word fully. This gave Him such authority and power that when the soldiers were sent to arrest Him, they returned empty-handed saying, *"No man ever spoke like this man!"* (John 7:46, RSV).

There are many personality courses you can take and books you can study, such as those by Dale Carnege and Zig Ziglar. You could try to "win friends and influence people" and become a more confident person by studying self-help and how-to books. But the greatest lesson in improving your impact upon others comes from studying God's Word.

You can learn how to speak and act with authority. In Matthew 20:25-28 we read these words of Jesus,

"Ye know that the princes of the Gentiles exercise dominion over them, and they that are great exercise authority upon them.

"But it shall not be so among you: but whosoever will be great among you, let him be your minister;

"And whosoever will be chief among you, let him be your servant:

"Even as the Son of man came not to be ministered unto, but to minister, and to give his life as a ransom for many."

The power of an influential Christian lies not in his ability to study and absorb suggestions from others, but in his willingness to become a servant. This doesn't make sense in the eyes of the world, but it's true.

If you want to become a person of authority, become a person of God's Word and service to others.

•

Remember: TO SPEAK WITH AUTHORITY, USE THE QUIET VOICE OF THE SERVANT.

104/SPEAK THE WORD

"Speak the word only, and my servant shall be healed" (Matthew 8:8).

Also read: Matt. 6:8; 7:7-11; 21:22

___

Of all the multitudes that followed Jesus during His earthly ministry, only one man had such great faith that it caused Jesus to marvel.

When Jesus entered the city of Capernaum He met a Roman soldier, a centurian (in charge of 100 men), who asked Jesus if He would heal his servant.

Jesus quickly answered, *"I will come and heal him."*

The centurian answered, *"Lord, I am not worthy that you should come under my roof: but speak the word only, and my servant shall be healed.*

"For I am a man under authority having soldiers under me: and I say to this man, Go, and he goeth; and to another, Come, and he cometh; and to my servant, Do this, and he doeth it.

"When Jesus heard it he marvelled, and said to them that followed, Verily I say unto you, I have not found so great faith, no, not in Israel.

"...And Jesus said unto the centurian, Go thy way; as you have believed, so be it done unto you. And his servant was healed in that very hour" (see Matt. 8:5-13).

Let me ask you something. If the President of the United States came to you and promised that if you would go to your nearest bank he would cover any check you cashed up to 1 million dollars, would you believe him and write your check?

What if the President wrote you a letter telling you the same thing? Would you believe him and write your check?

God in heaven has given you His written Word, *"I am the Lord that healeth thee"* (Ex. 15:26).

Do you believe His written Word? Will you act upon His message just as you would the President's? If you will believe God's Word, you will receive the miracle of healing.

•

Remember: GOD HAS ALREADY SPOKEN HIS WORD; IT IS YOUR TURN TO ACT IN FAITH.

105/ARE YOU BRUISED AND BROKEN

"There is a friend that sticketh closer than a brother" (Proverbs 18:24).

Also read: Is. 53:4-12

Once a little girl sang, "Jesus loves the little children...red and yellow, black and blue..."

She was right. Although her words came out wrong, Jesus does love every one of His children—especially the bruised and broken ones. Jesus said His mission in coming to earth was to "heal the brokenhearted" and "to set at liberty them that are bruised" (Luke 4:18).

Have you ever wondered why people often withhold themselves from the bruised and broken? I offer these reasons:

Many people, even Christians, are so bruised, broken or weary themselves they cannot help anyone else. Also, they may not realize others are hurting. Many hurting people force themselves to appear to be happy. Or, people's minds may be so preoccupied with their own lives they do not even notice others who need help.

If you have been bruised and broken by events in your life you need to see the Savior. He has the help you need. He understands because He was bruised and broken too, when His very own disciples forsook Him and fled, and when He had to die alone upon the cross—even forsaken by God.

* Jesus understands what's happened to your life. He is the same yesterday, today and forever. He was present at your bruising; He saw everything that happened and experienced the pain you felt.
* Jesus has the resources to help you recover. King David said in the 23rd Psalm, *"He restoreth my soul."* God has unlimited power to restore you by His Holy Spirit.

●

Remember: JESUS IS THE ANSWER TO YOUR BRUISED AND BROKEN LIFE.

MAKE SOMETHING HAPPEN!

"Why sit we here until we die?" (2 Kings 7:3).

Also read: Ps. 103:1-5; 107:9; 2 Cor. 9:8

Since Lee Iacocca saved the Chrysler Corporation from bankruptcy many have wished he would run for President of the United States. Iacocca says, "People say to me: 'You're a roaring success. How did you do it?' I go back to what my parents taught me. Apply yourself. Get all the education you can, but then, do something. Don't just stand there, MAKE SOMETHING HAPPEN!"

This is some of the best advice you could get anywhere, "Make something happen!" If you don't like your job, the place you live or the church you attend, make something happen!"

There is an interesting story in the Old Testament about four lepers who were sitting at the gate of a Jewish city that was surrounded by the Syrians. People were starving to death in the city because of the seige and the lepers realized that they must make something happen. Here's what they did:

> "Why sit here until we die?" they asked each other. "We will starve if we stay here and we will starve if we go back into the city; so we might as well go out and surrender to the Syrian army. If they let us live, so much the better; but if they kill us, we would have died anyway.
>
> "So that evening they went out to the camp of the Syrians, but there was no one there! (For the Lord had made the whole Syrian army hear the clatter of speeding chariots and a loud galloping of horses and the sound of a great army approaching. "The king of Israel has hired the Hittites and Egyptians to attach us," they cried out. So they panicked and fled into the night, abandoning their tents, horses, donkeys, and everything else.)
>
> "When the lepers arrived at the edge of the camp they went into one tent after another, eating, drinking wine, and carrying out silver, gold and clothing and hiding it (2 Kings 7:3-8, TLB).

If you're in a no-win situation why "sit there and die?" Make something happen!"

If you don't like your job, take some classes in a nearby college, study and prepare yourself for a better position or start looking for a different job.

If you don't like the place you live, start looking for a new home or maybe a new city. If you don't like your church, start looking around: "A church that's alive is worth the drive."

•

Remember: MAKE SOMETHING HAPPEN!

107/AIM HIGH!

"I press toward the mark for the prize of the high calling of God in Christ Jesus" (Philippians 3:14).

Also read: Prov. 23:7; Phil. 1:21

Before I became a Christian it was my goal to become a #1 country entertainer. I wanted to reach the top as a "Grand Ole Opry" star in Nashville, Tennessee.

This goal doesn't seem as great to me now as it did when I was in my darkened sinful condition—but even as a sinner I knew that I would only rise as high as my horizons. As a teenage entertainer I thought, "Even if I don't reach the top, my aiming high will lift me higher than I would be without a goal!"

What is your great goal in life? The problem with most people is not that they want too much, but that *they settle for too little.*

Paul the apostle believed in aiming high. He pressed toward the mark—for the prize of the high calling of God in Christ. He rejoiced that God had called him to be an apostle of the Christian faith.

Paul also believed in thinking high. A few verses later he writes, *"Whatsoever things are honest...just...pure... lovely...of good report: if there be any virtue, or if there be any praise, think on these things"* (Phil. 4:8).

If you will concentrate on good things it will empower you to do greater things. Have you ever noticed how positive-thinking people always seem to get things done?

Paul also believed in living high. He said, *"I can do all things through Christ which strengtheneth me"* (Phil. 4:13). I like to quote this verse by saying, "I can do *everything* through Christ who strengthens me."

This is the key for living victoriously. First, AIM HIGH. Second, THINK HIGH. Third, LIVE HIGH ON THE POWER OF GOD.

Meditate on these truths today. You'll find they'll make a difference in your life.

●

Remember: AIM HIGH!

108/MAKE WORK WORK FOR YOU!

"Now here is a command, dear brothers, given in the name of our Lord Jesus Christ by his authority: Stay away from any Christian who spends his days in laziness and does not follow the ideal of hard work"
(2 Thessalonians 3:6).

Also read: Job 14:15; Is. 65:22

It is shocking to realize that 70% of American workers do not love their jobs. Do you fall into this category? If so, there is a way you can make work work for you.

First, *Get into the rhythm of the job.*
When I shoveled snow with my teenage son recently, I realized there was a certain cadence to moving the shovel methodically. If I resented the job and refused to submit to the cadence required, I wouldn't accomplish much and the work would be much harder for me. So, get into the rhythm of your job!

Second, *Learn while you work!* Living life is like making a patchwork quilt. It's a little piece here, another piece there; you need to learn how to sew tiny portions of time together into a beautiful comforter. For instance:
   A. Listen to good educational or spiritual cassette tapes on your way to work.
   B. Do you have a book in your lunch box? Learn to read while eating. Let your mind dwell on something worthwhile.
   C. Learn how to ask questions of fellow workers. Everyone knows more about something than we do. So, I'm always asking questions, "How did you get into this?" "What's your hobby?" "What are the three most important things to know about this?" etc.

Third, *Plan while you work!* There may be no future in the job you have now. If so, use your free time to plan your escape—just like a prisoner plans his jailbreak. Remember that education and experience are the only ways you'll qualify for anything better, so plan to take all the extra courses at local colleges or technical schools you can.

You may not like the job you have now, but with study, work, and planning you will soon either find a job you'll love or you'll love the job you have!

•

Remember: GET THE RHYTHM: LEARN AND PLAN WHILE YOU'RE DOING YOUR JOB AND YOU'LL MAKE WORK WORK FOR YOU!

109/ARE YOU DRIFTING INTO ERROR?

"Ye do err, not knowing the scriptures, nor the power of God" (Matthew 22:29).

Also read: Ps. 32:8; Prov. 6:22 & 23; Jas. 1:5

The Sadducees came to Jesus one day and questioned Him about the resurrection (they didn't believe in it); they told Jesus a story of a woman who had had seven husbands. Their question was, "In the resurrection who's wife shall she be? For they all had her" (see verse 28).

Our Lord's reply to them is one you and I should take to heart. He said, "You are in error because you don't know the Scriptures or the power of God." If you and I fail to study the Word of God or if we fail to experience the power of God working miracles on our behalf, we will fall into error.

Are you spending enough time in the Scriptures studying God's Word? These two-minute devotionals are good but nothing takes the place of spending hours reading the Word, soaking it into your soul. Let me give you a tip on Bible reading. Don't read the Bible with a bias. By this I mean, don't read the Scriptures trying to fit them into your beliefs, but read the Scripture accepting what it says.

Remember, the Bible is the final authority on your Christian faith. This is why Paul wrote Timothy saying, *"Study to show yourself approved unto God, a workman that needs not to be ashamed, rightly dividing the Word of truth"* (2 Tim. 2:15).

1. Study, study, study so you will be approved of God; so you won't be ashamed of your life or works on Judgment Day.
2. Learn how to decide the truth rightly. In other words, don't divide it or apply it to fit your beliefs or prejudices. Have you ever stopped to realize that you may believe a lot of things that are not really scriptural?

If you do not study the power of God you will not see miracles on a daily basis and will eventually drift into a position where you don't think God works miracles at all. Then your God is merely a powerless deity in the sky.

•

Remember: DON'T DRIFT NTO ERROR; STUDY THE SCRIPTURES AND THE POWER OF GOD.

110/THE WAR WITHIN HEAVEN!

"And there was war in heaven: Michael and his angels fought against the dragon; and the dragon (the devil) fought and his angels" (Revelation 12:7).

Also read: 2 Cor. 10:3-5; 1 Jn. 3:8

If you've always pictured heaven as a peaceful place of harmony and happiness, you'd better take another look at today's text. The Bible says, *"And there was war in heaven."*

The struggle you and I have and the conflicts that are raging in the church have already reached into the heavenlies—and there was war in heaven.

I believe this battle was fought when Satan tried to cast God from His throne. The Bible describes the conflict this way, *"And there was war in heaven: Michael and his angels fought against the dragon; and the dragon fought and his angels, and prevailed not; neither was their place found any more in heaven. And the great dragon was cast out, that old serpent, called the Devil, and Satan, which deceived the whole world; he was cast out into the earth, and his angels were cast out with him"* (Rev. 12:7-9).

If you feel forces coming against you, know that these are the same forces that God felt coming against Him. God had created Michael, Gabriel and Lucifer—mighty archangels—and had given them authority and dominion. But sin got it's grip on Satan, who was deceived by his own beauty and power (see Ez. 28:13-17 and Is. 14:12-15). Satan forgot that God was his source of power and fulfillment and tried to usurp God's authority and position.

You can always tell when Satan is at work today because he is inspiring people to usurp God's authority and to question the ones whom God has set over His church.

The rebellions that rage within hearts today, that seek to usurp authority and position away from God and His appointed leaders, have already reached the throne of God.

●

Remember: THERE WAS WAR IN HEAVEN AND THE DEVIL AND HIS ANGELS WERE CAST OUT!

111/YOU'RE IN DEBT

"For I owe a great debt to you and to everyone else, both to civilized people and uncivilized alike; yes, to the educated and uneducated alike: ... to preach God's Good News" (Romans 1:14 & 15 TLB).

Also read: Matt. 9:38; Luke 18:1; 1 Thess. 5:17

The indebtedness Paul felt toward the lost made him a great preacher of the gospel. It compelled him to make the great sacrifices necessary to change the world.

Honestly, do you and I feel indebted to the lost? If we do we'll be praying for them. Samuel said, *"God forbid that I should sin against the Lord in ceasing to pray for you"* (1 Sam. 12:23).

Jesus said, *"The harvest truly is great, but the laborers are few; PRAY YE THEREFORE the LORD of the harvest, THAT HE WOULD SEND FORTH LABOURERS INTO HIS HARVEST"* (Luke 10:2, emphasis mine).

If you and I really feel indebted to the lost we will not sin against the Lord by failing to pray—we will seek God earnestly that He will send forth laborers into His harvest.

Here's how it works: as you and I pray, the Spirit of God moving in our lives will touch those around us and they will "catch the vision" and volunteer to minister. We'll also show our indebtedness by giving. The Bible says, *"How then shall they call on him in whom they have not believed? and how shall they believe in him of whom they have not heard? and how shall they hear without a preacher? "And how shall they preach, except they be sent?"* (Rom. 10:14 & 15).

It costs money to send men with the message. It also costs money to put the Gospel on T.V. and radio and print it in tracts and books and Bibles. If you really feel indebted to the lost you will rejoice in every opportunity to give. If you know a ministry that is sincerely getting the job done you will support it prayerfully and financially as much as you can.

•

Remember: YOU'RE A DEBTOR TO THE LOST TODAY; BE SURE TO PAY YOUR BILLS.

112/DON'T QUIT!

"God forbid that I should sin against the Lord in ceasing to pray for you" (1 Samuel 12:23).

Also read: Luke 18:1; Eph. 6:18; 1 Thess. 5:17

Persistance is the key to answered prayer. You must commit yourself to intercession if you want to get your prayers answered.

The Apostle Paul said, *"Moreover it is required in stewards, that a man be found faithful"* (1 Cor. 4:2).

There are many attributes of greatness, but persistance is surely one of them.

Wally Hilgenberg, former Minnesota Viking, tells the story of his early days at the University of Iowa. During his first football training season as a freshman he was intimidated by the many well-known players that had been recruited from all over the country. Finally after the discouragement and pain of the practices began to take its toll, Wally called his dad back in Wilton Junction, Iowa. He told his father that he thought he should just give up the whole idea of playing football for the University. His dad responded with great wisdom. He reminded his son of a talk they had when Wally went out for football in fifth grade. "Wally, you've never been a quitter. I want you to know that the first time you quit is the hardest; after that it gets easier every time." He told his son how proud he was of his many years of playing the game.

With the encouragement and affirmation of a loving father, Wally went on to have four successful years at the University of Iowa and then had a great career in the National Football League.

The prophet Samuel considered his persistent prayers so important that he said, *"God forbid that I should sin against the Lord in ceasing to pray for you"* (1 Sam. 12:23). Samuel never quit praying.

Never give up on God. He'll never give up on you!

•

Remember: THE FIRST TIME YOU QUIT IS THE HARDEST—AFTER THAT IT GETS EASIER EVERY TIME.

113/HOW TO BECOME A GREAT SPEAKER!

"Then said I, Ah, Lord God! behold, I cannot speak: for I am a child. But the Lord said unto me, Say not, I am a child: for thou shalt go to all that I shall send thee, and whatsoever I command thee thou shalt speak" (Jeremiah 1:6 & 7).

Also read: Pro. 3:26; Phil. 1:6; Heb. 13:6

The greatest fear of Americans is not death, but of standing up in front of a group of people and giving a speech.

If you get white knuckles and throat spasms whenever you stand before a group, today's devotion will help you become a great speaker.

1. USE HUMOR. Learn a few good jokes and practice them until they're perfect. Remember your punchline. Stop at the right moment. Timing is everything. Make your jokes short and sweet.
2. USE ANALOGY. Jesus was a master storyteller. He always compared the Kingdom of God to something the people understood. *"Unto what is the kingdom of God like? and whereunto shall I resemble it? It is like a grain of mustard seed, which a man took, and cast into his garden: and it grew, and waxed a great tree: and the fowls of the air lodged in the branches of it"* (Luke 13:18-19).

   Use your experiences to help you make your point; but don't look outside of yourself for something to say until you've looked within. Pray that the Holy Spirit will bring a story to your mind that will be the best illustration of your point.
3. QUOTE FAMOUS PEOPLE. If you feel inferior about your talk, beef it up with some powerful words of famous men and women. Great quotes give you credibility.
4. TOUCH THIER HEARTS! Paul said, *"The letter killeth but the spirit giveth life"* (2 Cor. 3:6). People are not moved by logic as much as emotion.

   The very best story is something that happened to you, that touches you—and then it will touch others. Be careful that you don't let your emotions carry you away, but remember, you haven't touched home plate until you've touched their hearts.
5. CLOSE WITH A DYNAMIC SENTENCE. The two most important parts are the beginning and ending; know how you want to end before you begin.

●

Remember: PREPARATION MAKES GREAT PRESENTATIONS!

114/THE PASSOVER

"When I see the blood, I will pass over you" (Exodus 12:13).

Also read: Ex. 12:26-51

Today is the High Holy Day of the Jewish people. Their celebration of the Passover goes back 3,433 years to the time when God delivered their ancesters out of Egypt.

Pharoah, king of Egypt, refused to let his Jewish slaves go free; so God, through His servant Moses, told the people He would send a death-angel to Egypt and kill the firstborn in every family—animal or human. The only way Jews could escape the judgment was to kill a perfect lamb and swab its blood on the doorposts of their homes.

The Lord said, *"For I will pass through the land of Egypt this night, and will smite all the first-born in the land of Egypt, both man and beast; and against all the gods of Egypt I will execute judgment: I am the Lord. And the blood shall be to you for a token* (sign) *upon the houses where ye are: AND WHEN I SEE THE BLOOD, I WILL PASS OVER YOU, and the plague shall not be upon you to destroy you, when I smite the land of Egypt"* (Ex. 12:12 & 13, emphasis mine).

We Christians can celebrate this Passover day in a special way because the Bible says, *"Christ our passover is sacrificed for us"* (1 Cor. 5:7). Jesus was the perfect Lamb of God, without spot or wrinkle, who was slain upon the cross so the angel of everlasting death would never come to our homes. Hallelujah!

Are you thankful for what Jesus has done for you? Have you applied His blood to your life and to your home? If so, you will never experience death in the true sense of the word (Jesus and the Apostle Paul refer to death as sleep). Christians never die.

Today is Passover; celebrate it with joy and thanksgiving.

•

Remember: CHRIST IS OUR PASSOVER.

115/WHAT ARE YOU STANDING FOR?

"I am ready to preach the gospel" (Romans 1:15).

Also read: Josh. 24:15; Prov. 11:24-25; Rom. 12:10-13

Doing something great for God doesn't depend on your ability or your inability—it depends on your availability.

Willingness is the key to being used of God. The book of Acts tells us about Stephen and Phillip. When the early church needed someone to help they chose these two men. The apostles said, *"It is not right for us to give up preaching the Word of God to serve* (wait on) *tables"* (Acts 6:2, RSV).

So they said, *"(Find among you) seven men of honest report, full of the Holy Ghost and wisdom, whom we may appoint over this business. But we will give ourselves continually to prayer, and to the ministry of the word.*

"And...they chose Stephen, a man full of faith and of the Holy Ghost, and Philip" (Acts 6:3-5).

So Stephen and Philip made themselves available as table waiters, serving food to needy people to whom the church ministered. When they made themselves available, God put them to work.

But the Bible says, *"He that is faithful in that which is least is faithful also in much"* (Luke 16:10). When Stephen and Philip were willing to do humble work, God exalted them.

A few verses later we read, *"And Stephen, full of faith and power, did great wonders and miracles among the people...and they were not able to resist the wisdom and the spirit by which he spake"* (verses 8, 10). When Stephen made himself available to God as a waiter, God soon began to use him to work wonders.

And Philip? The Bible says, *"Then Philip went down to the city of Samaria, and preached Christ unto them. And the people with one accord gave heed unto those things which Philip spake—hearing and seeing the miracles which he did"* (Acts 8:5-6).

God turned Philip and Stephen into miracle-workers—because they made themselves available.

•

Remember: IF YOU WANT GOD TO USE YOU AS A WONDER-WORKER, VOLUNTEER AS A TABLE-WAITER!

116/DON'T LEAVE THE WORD OF GOD!

"It is not reason (right) that we should leave the word of God, and serve tables" (Acts 6:2).

Also read : Deut. 13:4; Josh. 22:5; 1 Sam. 12:20-22

The early church faced a problem that you and I encounter every day: the problem of having enough time for the Word of God.

The Bible says, *"With the believers multiplying rapidly, there were rumblings of discontent. Those who spoke only Greek complained that their widows were being discriminated against, that they were not being given as much food in the daily distribution as the widows who spoke Hebrew. So the twelve called a meeting of all the believers.*

"We should spend our time preaching, and not administrating a feeding program" (Acts 6:1-2, TLB).

The apostles decided that the study of the Word of God and preaching was more important than anything else. They appointed seven honest men, full of the Holy Spirit, to take care of other things and said, *"But we will give ourselves continually to prayer, and to the ministry of the Word"* (verse 4).

The result? Verse 8 says, *"And the word of God increased: and the number of the disciples multiplied in Jerusalem greatly; and a great company of the priests were obedient to the faith and Stephen (one of the seven chosen to wait upon tables) FULL OF FAITH AND POWER, did great wonders and miracles among the people"* (emphasis mine).

Hallelujah! Stephen—chosen to be a waiter—became so supercharged as a result of the powerful sermons of the apostles that he did great wonders and miracles among the people.

You and I will have the same results if we make the same decision as the apostles did. Let's leave all the diversionary things and concentrate on the Word of God and prayer.

●

Remember: DON'T LEAVE THE WORD OF GOD!

117/THE "GALLUP-POLL" GOSPEL

"Speak unto us smooth things" (Isaiah 30:10).

Also read: John 16:29; Eph. 4:25; Heb. 12:25-29

Today we are drifting towards a "Gallup-Poll" Gospel. "Milque—toast" ministers find out what the people want to hear and then preach on these subjects. It's almost like a teacher asking her students what they want to learn. It leads to IGNORANCE.

Isaiah, the prophet, had the same problem in his day. He writes, *"They are stubborn rebels, they tell my prophets, "Shut up—we don't want any more of your reports,' or they say 'Don't tell us the truth; tell us NICE things; tell us lies. Forget all the gloom"*(Is. 30:9 & 10, TLB).

I hope you hear the true Gospel in your church and not a watered-down "Gallup-Poll" Gospel. When you're not living right you need a man of God, bold as a lion, to preach repentance both publicly and privately to you.

There are several "Gallup-Poll" messages being preached today. One is *"We're all God's Children."* This is a lie. Jesus told the religious leaders of his day, *"You are of your father the devil, and the lusts of our father you will do"*(John 8:44). While it is true that God created everyone it is a fact that many are following the devil and will end in everlasting Hell.

Another smooth message is *"All religions lead to Heaven"* Humbug! If this were true then Jesus died in vain. Many of today's religions were present at the time of Christ—and if they were sufficient God wouldn't have sent Christ to die for our sins. Jesus is truly the way! (see Jn. 14:6)

The power of positive thinking is also a deceitful trap. Man cannot save himself from sin by his own efforts (Rom. 7:14).

There are many "Gallup-Poll" Gospels galloping around today. Read God's Word and you won't be carried away.

●

Remember: READING GOD'S WORD FOR YOURSELF WILL KEEP YOU ON THE RIGHT TRACK!

THE GOD OF THE VALLEYS

"Their gods are gods of the hills" (1 Kings 20:23).

Also read: Psa. 18:2; 23:4-6; 27:1; Isa. 40:29; 41:10

Benhadad was a Syrian king who invaded Israel. His soldiers and chariots far outnumbered the Israelis', but God fought against the Syrians and they were smitten with a great slaughter (see verse 21).

The Syrian survivors failed to see the greatness of God as the cause of their defeat and said, "Israel's gods are the gods of the hills" (see 1 Kings 20:23). The Syrians believed that the Israelis' "god" had power only in the hills, so they decided to rebuild their armies and attack Israel again—this time in the valleys.

When the mighty Syrian army came against Israel the Bible says, *"The children of Israel (were like) two little flocks of kids (lambs); but the Syrians filled the country"* (verse 27).

The story continues, *"And there came a man of God and spake unto the king of Israel, and said, Thus saith the Lord, Because the Syrians have said, The Lord is God of the hills, but he is not God of the valleys, therefore will I deliver all this great multitude into thine hand, and ye shall know that I am the Lord"* (1 Kings 20:28).

During the battle the children of Israel killed one hundred thousand Syrian soldiers. The Syrians fled and wicked King Benhadad was captured.

Are you going through a valley experience in your life? If you feel today that you've reached the bottom—remember God is also a God of the valleys. God will deliver you if you'll hold steady and not despair.

Don't be afraid—the Lord is with you wherever you are. Jesus has promised, *"My sheep hear my voice, and I know them, and they follow me...*

"My father, which gave them (to) *me, is greater than all; and no man is able to pluck them out of my Father's hand"* (John 10:27-29).

●

Remember: YOUR GOD IS A GOD OF THE VALLEYS: HE WILL BE YOUR STRENGTH IN THE VALLEYS OF YOUR LIFE.

119/WHAT IS YOUR WORLD VIEW?

"Christ knows and Holy Spirit knows that it is no mere pretense when I say that I would be willing to be forever damned if that would save you" (Romans 9:3, TLB).

Also read: Mt. 25:35-40; Mk. 16:15; 1 Jn. 3:16-18

Today's text is worth our prayerful consideration. Paul the apostle said he would be willing to be damned to hell so that others could be saved and enjoy heaven.

This was the key to his life. Paul was willing to lay down his life for others. What is your world view? Why do you do what you do? Why do you exist? What propels you each day?

Do you really have a purpose in life? Whenever this question is asked people will respond by saying, "Yes, I want to be a school teacher or a nurse." But this is the way you will make a living. What's the purpose for which all other purposes exist?

You need a world view in order to see how your piece fits the puzzle.

The reason Jesus lived such an effective life is that His world view and God's were the same. One day Jesus' disciples said to Him, "Master, eat." But he said unto them, *"I have MEAT to eat that ye know not of....MY MEAT IS TO DO THE WILL OF HIM THAT SENT ME, AND TO FINISH HIS WORK.*

"Say not ye, There are yet four months, and then cometh harvest? behold, I say unto you, Lift up your eyes, and look on the fields; for they are white already to harvest" (Jn. 4:32-35, emphasis mine). (Wheat that should have been harvested, that is past due, turns white.)

Why get up this morning, go to work, or even attend church? These are all means to an end—but they are not an end in themselves. The end is that lost souls be won to Jesus Christ!

Are you living with the correct world view? Do you live and breathe soulwinning? If not, lift up your eyes!

●

Remember: PAUL WAS WILLING TO DIE SO OTHERS WOULD LIVE.

WHAT IS FAITH?

"What is faith? It is the confident assurance that something we want is going to happen. It is the certainty that what we hope for is waiting for us, even though we cannot see it ahead" (Hebrews 11:1 TLB).

Also read: Heb. 11

Because faith is an invisible reality, it is easy to think of it as some mystical thing without realizing how practical it really is. Faith is these things:

Faith is Personal Trust!

The Bible says, *"While God was testing him, Abraham still trusted God and his promises, and so he offered up his son Isaac, and was ready to slay him on the altar of sacrifice, yes, to slay even Isaac, through whom God had promised to give Abraham a whole nation of descendants! He believed that if Isaac died, God would bring him back to life again"* (Heb. 11:17-19, TLB).

Abraham had a *very personal trust* in God—even to the point of raising his son from the dead. This is faith.

Faith is Confidence!

The Bible says, *"By faith Moses, when he was come to years, refused to be called the son of Pharoah's daughter; choosing rather to suffer affliction with the people of God, than to enjoy the pleasures of sin for a season"* (Heb. 11:24 & 25).

Moses had more confidence in God than in Pharoah. This was faith in action.

Faith is Firm Reliance!

Can you say that God is reliable? The prostitute, Rahab, believed that God was reliable. She cast herself on God's mercy by hiding the Hebrew spies that came to Jericho. Rahab was saved because she trusted in the reliability of God.

Can you apply this to your situation? Do you have enough personal trust, confidence and reliance on God to meet your personal need—to give you a miracle?

Now, because you believe in God, act in faith! Do all you can in preparation for a miracle.

•

Remember: ACT UPON THE PERSONAL TRUST, CONFIDENCE AND RELIANCE YOU HAVE IN GOD!

121/ARE YOU AVAILABLE?

"Wherefore take unto you the whole armour of God, that ye may be able to withstand in the evil day, and having done all, to stand" (Ephesians 6:13).

Also read: Dan. 12:3; Matt. 5:13-16

Peter Marshall, who was once the chaplain of the U.S. Senate, prayed this prayer before the Senate on one occasion, "Lord, help us to stand for something, lest we fall for anything."

What do you stand for? Each political year candidates hit the trail trying to win votes. Sometimes they endorse so many positions you don't know where they stand. I heard the amusing story of one candidate who stood before a crowd and said, "Whatever you want—I'm for."

Where do you stand on the issues?

1. Abortion
2. Prayer in schools
3. Pornography
4. Homosexuality
5. Premarital sex
6. Social drinking
7. Gambling
8. Divorce
9. Communism
10. Disarmament

If you know where you stand on these issues, are you requiring the state and national candidates you vote for to represent your views in the House of Representatives, Senate and White House? I believe that Christians have been letting their representatives in government slip by without committing themselves. Also many representatives, after they are elected, betray their constituency. Before you vote next time, send a letter to the candidates asking for direct answers to these important questions and compare their responses.

Even more important, determine your own stand on these important subjects. Research these questions until you can speak clearly on your positions and vote knowledgeably. If you're not a registered voter, become one now so your choice can be heard.

•

Remember: KNOW WHERE YOU STAND SO YOU WON'T FALL FOR SLIPPERY WORDS.

122/HAVE YOU BECOME A SPIRITUAL PESSIMIST?

"And let us not be weary in well doing: for in due season we shall reap, if we faint not" (Galatians 6:9).

Also read: Ps. 51:12 & 13; 118:24; Rom. 14:17 & 18

Have you ever wondered why so many Christians are pessimistic and sullen? For twenty-eight years I've tried to figure out why Christians—who have been redeemed from sin and Satan, delivered from burning hell, are children of God, joint heirs with Christ, filled with the Spirit and headed for heaven—aren't happier.

I think I know how and I want to share my discovery with you. Read this carefully: "Pessimism comes not when we get tired of doing evil but when we get tired of doing good—which I suppose is the most serious sickness" (G.K. Chesterton).

Pessimism comes when you get tired of doing good. This is the truth. This is the sad sickness that has struck so many saints. They're tired of doing good.

I hate to say this, but in comparing the two lifestyles of the average Christian to the average sinner, I think the sinner's life appears to be more exciting. The sinner can dance, drink, cuss, gamble, commit adultery, and etc. It also destroys the mind, soul and body for time and eternity.

But this is not the way God planned it. The Christian life should be more exciting than any sinner's life. How?
1. WE COULD BE WINNING LOST SOULS TO JESUS CHRIST ON A DAILY BASIS. (Read Acts 2:47.)
2. WE COULD BE WORKING MIRACLES. (Read Mark 6:7, 12 & 13.)
3. WE COULD BE TEACHING OTHERS. (Read 1 Thess. 2:20.)

From these Scriptures and others it is easy to see that the only way you and I can keep from becoming tired of doing good is by teaching, preaching, and healing the sick. The miraculous will give us the godly excitement and joy our spirits crave.

•

Remember: TO GUARD AGAINST PESSIMISM BECOME A MIRACLE-WORKING SAINT.

123/IS PROSPERITY TEACHING SCRIPTURAL

"Give, and it shall be given unto you; good measure, pressed down, and shaken together, and running over, shall men give into your bosom. For with the same measure that ye mete withal it shall be measured to you again" (Luke 6:38).

Also read: 2 Cor. 9:6-7

A concerned partner wrote me recently saying, "It seems that encouraging people to give because they'll be blessed can be a real hindrance to those who are trying to learn about joyous, sacrificial discipleship. I'm sure it's important to teach people about giving, but why not teach them to do it because God wants them to, which is reason enough to delight in it?"

Reader, is it right to teach people to give to be blessed? I suppose a similar question would be, "Is it right to encourage people to get saved so they can go to heaven?"

If you boil it down to motives, one is as self-seeking as the other. Yet God urges us to come to Him and be saved, for it is better for a man to give up the pleasures of sin now—even with a selfish motive of "getting to heaven"—than to end up damned in hell.

After a man becomes a Christian he learns to love God for unselfish reasons. He begins to serve God just for *who* He is.

Paul wrote the Corinthians saying, *"I wanted to give you meat—but you were such spiritual babes I had to give you milk"* (see 1 Cor. 3:1).

The same is true when it comes to the lessons about giving. "Give and God will bless you" is a "milk" truth. (And remember—milk isn't bad.) The "meat" truths are:

1. We should give to God because we love Him. Giving is a way of acknowledging God's love.
2. We should give to God because God owns everything. We're really only giving back to God what is His in the first place.
3. We should give to help the lost and needy because we genuinely care.

Your giving reveals how much you love God and others. Why do *you* give?

•

Remember: GOD BLESSES THOSE WHO GIVE NO MATTER WHAT THE REASON.

124/BE CAREFUL NOT TO COUNT

"And Satan stood up against Israel, and provoked David to number Israel" (1 Chronicles 21:1).

Also read: Isa. 30:15; 2 Cor. 12:9; 3:5; Phil. 4:19

As I mentioned previously it was a sin for the kings of Israel to count their soldiers. God wanted Israel to trust in the Lord and not in the size of their armies.

But David was drifting from his faith in God. First, he took the gold crown and placed it on his head. Second, he began to treat his enemies revengefully. Third, he was anxious to know the numbers of his soldiers so he would not have to lean fully on the Lord.

Joab, David's military commander, cautioned David against such an action by saying, *"Why will my Lord the King cause Israel to sin?"* (verse 3, Literal).

But David was bullheaded and demanded that Joab obey. The Bible says, *"And God was displeased with this thing; therefore he smote Israel"* (verse 7). We're not told how God punished Israel; we only know that the punishment was so severe that David realized he had sinned. He cried out and said, *"I have sinned greatly in that I have done: and now, I beseech thee, O Lord, take away the iniquity of thy servant; for I have done very foolishly"* (2 Sam. 24:10).

You must be careful not to count the things you have. If you say, "Now I have a good job, a nice automobile, a good balance in my checking account and my health is good"—watch out. It's good to praise God for what you have, but don't trust in your riches, position or your health. They can all be swept away in a moment. Trust only in the Lord and live each day—even today—as a sacred gift.

•

Remember: BE CAREFUL NOT TO COUNT!

125/DON'T LET IT GO TO YOUR HEAD

"And David took the crown of their king from off his head, and found it to weigh a talent of gold, and there were precious stones in it; and it was set upon David's head" (1 Chronicles 20:2).

Also read: Psa. 36:11; Prov. 8:13; 11:2; 14:3; 29:23

One day King David and his armies attacked the pagan forces of Rabah and defeated them. God gave David a great victory and there were many treasures among the spoils.

One of the treasures was a solid gold crown studded with jewels. It was so beautiful that David decided to wear it rather than melting it down.

This was somewhat out of character for the shepherd-king who had always been a humble, unpretentious man of God. The desire to wear a crown reveals the pride that was creeping into David's heart.

The next verse makes me shudder. The Bible says of David that *"he brought out the people that were in it, and cut them with saws, and with harrows of iron, and with axes"* (1 Chron. 20:3). For David to torture his defeated foes so cruelly was also out of character for such a tenderhearted man.

But David was changing—his pride was causing him to wear a pagan crown and the desire for revenge was causing him to torture his enemies.

The very next chapter shows how David sinned against the Lord and provoked Him to anger by counting his soldiers. (God forbade Israeli kings to do this because He wanted them to always trust in His power alone.)

Victories can change your life for the worse. Many know how to serve God in adversity but few will serve God in times of prosperity. If God has been blessing your life, be careful that it doesn't go to your head. Be sure to treat your enemies graciously. If you become proud or revengeful, you're headed for disaster.

•

Remember: DON'T LET YOUR VICTORIES GO TO YOUR HEAD.

YOUR BURDENS CAN BLOCK THE BLESSING

"And Moses spoke so unto the children of Israel: but they hearkened not unto Moses for anguish of spirit, and for cruel bondage" (Exodus 6:9).

Also read: Pro. 3:5 & 6

It is possible that your burdens can block the blessing of God from coming into your life. When your spirit has been broken by heartache, you can plunge into such despair that you doubt that God is even there.

This is what happened when God sent Moses to the children of Israel. They had been slaves to Pharoah so long and had suffered so much that when Moses came with the message of hope and deliverance, he appeared to be mocking their misery. They were without hope and could not respond in faith.

But the Lord was patient with the children of Israel. He began to work His miracles of deliverance on stubborn Pharoah—and finally revived their faith.

I love God for this—because the Bible says, *"If we believe not, yet He abideth faithful: He cannot deny himself"* (2 Tim. 2:13).

This has to be one of the most powerful life-changing Scriptures in the Bible. It says that when we don't believe, God remains faithful, because He cannot deny Himself. God and His faithfulness doesn't depend on others. God does what is right, whether we believe He's going to do right or not.

If God, faith, prayer, miracles, etc, seem to be trite to your soul, it could be that you've allowed your burdens to block the blessing.

So don't get uptight about believing God. Relax—the Lord knows if you have been crushed by events beyond your control—and he doesn't expect you to "jump off your stretcher" and "snap to attention." God loves you. Believe that He does what is best for you.

•

Remember: TRUST GOD TO DO WHAT IS RIGHT.

127/HOW WOULD THE WORLD DESCRIBE US TODAY?

"Let your light so shine before men, that they may see your good works, and glorify your Father which is in heaven" (Matthew 5:16).
Also read: 1 Cor. 13; 1 Jn. 4:7 & 8

When the Emperor Hadrian of Rome wanted to know who Christians were, Aristides gave him this amazing description: *"They love one another. They never fail to help widows; they save orphans from those who would hurt them. If they have something they give freely to the man who has nothing; if they see a stranger they take him home, and are happy as though he were a real brother. They don't consider themselves brothers in the real sense, but brothers instead through the Spirit, in God."*

Would this be the way the world would see us today? I doubt it because we are all too busy to be brothers. We must slow down and discover again what it means to be a Christian. Let's use Aristides description as our outline.

1. THEY LOVE ONE ANOTHER. *"We know that we have passed from death unto life, because we love the brethren. He that loveth not his brother abideth in death...we ought to lay down our lives for the brethren"* (1 Jn. 3:14,16).
2. THEY NEVER FAIL TO HELP WIDOWS. *"Pure religion and undefiled before God and the Father is this, To visit the fatherless and widows in their affliction"* (James 1:27).
3. IF THEY HAVE SOMETHING THEY GIVE FREELY TO THE MAN WHO HAS NOTHING. *"But whoso hath this world's good, and seeth his brother have need, and shutteth up his bowels of compassion from him, how dwelleth the love of God in him?*
My little children, let us not love in word, neither in tongue; but in deed and in truth" (1 Jn. 3:17-18).
4. IF THEY SEE A STRANGER, THEY TAKE HIM HOME AND ARE HAPPY, AS THOUGH HE WERE A REAL BROTHER. *"Let brotherly love continue. Be not forgetful to entertain strangers: for thereby some have entertained angels unawares"* (Heb. 13:1-2).
5. THEY DON'T CONSIDER THEMSELVES BROTHERS IN THE USUAL SENSE, BUT BROTHERS INSTEAD THROUGH THE SPIRIT, IN GOD. *"Our bodies have many parts, but the many parts make up only one body when they are all put together. So it is with the "body" of Christ. Each of us is a part of one body of Christ..."* (1 Cor. 12:12).

Aristides' description has really challenged me to be more of what Jesus wants me to be. Do you feel the same challenge? •

Remember: THE WORLD SHOULD SEE ARISTIDES' DESCRIPTION OF CHRISTIANS IN US.

128/THE WAR WAS OF GOD

"For there fell down many slain, because the war was of God" (1 Chronicles 5:22).

Also read: Psa. 89:14; Isa. 9:7; John 5:30; Rom. 7:12

Many are confused when they read the Old Testament of how God directed wars the Israelis waged upon the inhabitants of Canaan. People cannot reconcile the thought of a peace-loving God directing His people to destroy the pagans.

What you must keep in mind is that God is also a just God who punishes sin. In fact, if God doesn't punish the wicked, who can? What if God had not moved against Adolph Hitler? This demonic dictator would have ruled the world and destroyed hundreds of millions of people.

I really believe God defeated Adolph Hitler in these ways:

First, by preserving the British forces who escaped the German forces at Dunkirk. (Remember how God sent rain and fog to cover the entire English channel until they could escape.)

Second, by prompting Hitler to overrule his generals and attack Russia. (His great advisors declared it was a mistake to wage war on two fronts.)

Third, by sending the terribly cold winter to Russia. (The German tanks and personnel carriers bogged down in the bitter cold.)

The reason God defeated Hitler was because of his sins. God used the allied forces to be His hand of judgment.

The same is true of the Canaanites, Ammorites, and others who sinned greatly. (Many of these pagans burned their children as offerings unto their pagan gods.) This grieved God greatly and He used Israel to be His instrument of justice.

If your view of God is one-sided and you see only His love and mercy, the Old Testament will be confusing. But if you also see that God is just and uses foreign nations to punish other nations for their sins, then you'll be at peace reading how the children of Israel made war.

•

Remember: THE BIBLE SAYS, "THE WAR WAS OF GOD."

129/HOW TO KEEP FROM CRUMBLING

"Study to shew thyself approved unto God, a workman that needeth not to be ashamed, rightly dividing the word of truth" (2 Timothy 2:15).

Also read: Isa. 34:16; Matt. 9:13; 11:29

You may be experiencing tremendous pressure at this time. The forces of hell are focused on you and your family. Maybe now you can feel them really pressing in. Here's how to keep from crumbling: *Make certain that you have established a personal relationship with God that doesn't depend on anyone else.*

In 2 Chronicles 24 you can read about Joash who was just seven years old when he began to reign as king of Israel.

Jehoiada was a priest who became King Joash's spiritual mentor and advisor. The Bible says, *"And Joash did that which was right in the sight of the Lord all the days of Jehoiada the priest"* (verse 2). During Jehoiada's lifetime Joash did many great things for God. The Bible says, *"But Jehoiada waxed old...and died"* (verse 15). After his death the leaders fo Judah came to King Joash and persuaded him to abandon the temple of God and to worship shame-idols instead! So the wrath of God came down upon Judah and Jerusalem again.

Are you making the same mistake as Joash? Is there someone who is a "pillar" in your life whom you lean on spiritually? A mom or dad, husband or wife, minister or Christian friend who supports you in spiritual things? If there is, what are you going to do when they're gone? Will you crumble?

I urge you to continue praying and reading God's Word and seeking truth as you are doing through this devotional. The more you build on the solid rock, Jesus Christ, the stronger you will be. Then you won't crumble under the pressure.

•

Remember: LEARN TO KNOW GOD FOR YOURSELF!

130/HOW PURITY OF HEART HELPS BALANCE IMPURITY OF DOCTRINE

"Blessed are the pure in heart: for they shall see God" (Matthew 5:8).

Also read: Phil. 4:8; Tit. 1:15; 2:15; Jas. 3:17

Through the Church Age there have been constant battles about Bible doctrine. Even in the days of Paul the apostle certain Judaizing teachers would follow him around teaching his new converts that they could not be saved without being circumcised (see Gal. 2:2-7).

I believe that you and I should know the truth, believe the truth and proclaim the truth to everyone we meet. However, there is another factor to consider. That is, a person with a *pure* heart is not as wrongly affected by wrong doctrine as we would like to believe. The reason why is that their purity of heart works to balance their doctrinal error.

For instance, I do not believe that God arbitrarily predestines certain people to heaven and others to hell as the Presbyterians do. (I believe we are predestined in Christ just like an airplane is predestined to fly from Minneapolis to Chicago—but it is "whosoever will" get on the plane.)

I read once where a famous evangelist in his seminary days asked his Presbyterian professor, "How can I preach evangelistic sermons if God has already predestined some to heaven and others to hell?"

The professor of a pure heart answered, "You go out and preach 'whosoever will can be saved' and let God predestinate whomever He will."

Wow! You see, the pure heart cancelled out the imbalance of doctrine.

As long as we are on earth, there will be different interpretations of the Bible by men. However, the important thing to remember is to stay pure in your heart. Let God work out the fine details!

•

Remember: PURITY OF HEART BALANCES IMPURITY OF DOCTRINE.

131/WHAT DO YOU LIKE

"*Set your affection on things above, not on things on the earth*" (Colossians 3:2).

Also read: Is. 26:3; Phil. 2:5; 4:8

The fact is you will become what you think most about. Or as one man said, "Tell me what you like and I'll tell you what you are!"

The Living Bible says, "*Since you became alive again, so to speak, when Christ arose from the dead, now set your sights on the rich treasures and joys of heaven where he sits beside God in the place of honor and power.*

"*Let heaven fill your thoughts; don't spend your time worrying about things down here. You should have as little desire for this world as a dead person does. Your real life is in heaven with Christ and God*" (Col. 3:1-3, TLB).

Someone has said, "You can tell what you love by what you think about when you're not thinking about anything else."

What do you like—food, sex, money, security, vacations, home, sports? There are a hundred different things that will press in on your mind until the thoughts of God will be choked out. Jesus said, "*He that received seed among the thorns is he that heareth the word; and the care of this world, and the deceitfulness of riches, choke the word, and he becometh unfruitful*" (Matt. 13:22).

So there really is a battle going on in your brain—between the thoughts of God and the thoughts of this world. And there is also a battle going on in your body between the desires of the Spirit and the passions of the flesh.

Which will you choose? Will you become like God or the devil? Will you resemble this world or the next? This is why you must set your affections on things above. Today resolve to look at things from heaven's perspective.

•

Remember: WHAT YOU LIKE IS WHAT YOU ARE.

132/DON'T MISUSE THE WELFARE SYSTEM

"We gave you this rule: 'He who does not work shall not eat" (2 Thessalonians 3:10).

Also read: Prov. 19:15; 1 Cor. 3:14

Today the United States and Canada are breaking down morally and financially under a growing welfare system. It is not working because it is contrary to the laws of God and nature.

Now, I am not hardhearted; if a man is sick or temporarily out of a job, he should have some help from the local or state government. The elderly, widows and orphans need a helping hand, too.

However, this is not the way the system is working. Recently I heard of an employee who was slow and somewhat lazy. His employer spoke with him often and for months tried to encourage him. Finally, when all else failed, he had to be let go. He immediately filed for unemployment benefits and has since not made efforts to support himself.

I can understand physically or mentally handicapped people needing a system such as this to depend on for survival, but why must we support laziness?

Such a system as this is immoral; not only is it costly in terms of taxing the working man, but it destroys personal initiative.

Paul the apostle wrote to the Christians living at Thessalonica and said, *"We hear that some of you are living in laziness, refusing to work, and wasting your time in gossiping. In the name of the Lord Jesus Christ ...we command them—to quiet down, get to work, and earn their own living"* (2 Thess. 3:11 & 12, TLB).

If God has blessed you with a clear mind, a strong body and a job, rejoice. If more people would assume their responsibility to go to work, you wouldn't be taxed *in part* from January - June 1st to pay the bill.

•

Remember: TO RECEIVE BENEFITS WITHOUT EFFORT DESTROYS YOU.

133/HE'S TOO BIG TO MISS!

"And David said to Saul, Let no man's heart fail because of him; thy servant will go and fight with this Philistine" (1 Samuel 17:32).

Also read: Deut. 33:27; Phil. 4:13; 1 Pet. 4:12 7 13

Goliath was an ungodly giant that had brought the army of Israel to shame. Everyone was afraid of him.

The Bible describes Goliath this way: *"Goliath...measured over nine feet tall! He wore a bronze helmet, a two-hundred pound coat of mail, bronze leggings, and carried a bronze javelin several inches thick, tipped with a twenty-five pound iron spearhead, and his armor bearer walked ahead of him with a huge shield"* (1 Sam. 7:4-7, TLB).

Everyone was afraid of him except the shepherd boy, David. Attitude made the difference. The fearful soldiers said, "He's too big to hit." But David said, "He's too big to miss!"

Where did young David get the courage to fight the giant? The answer will surprise you.

1. David was motivated by the reward he would receive.

   When he asked about the giant he was told, *"Have you heard about the huge reward the king has offered to anyone who kills him?...The king will give him one of his daughters for a wife, and his whole family will be exempted from paying taxes!"* (1 Sam. 17:25, TLB).

2. David was motivated by the honor it would bring to God.

   He said, *"Why should this heathen man bring dishonor to the armies of the living God? I'll go and fight for the Lord!"* (see 1 Sam. 17:26, TLB).

3. He was motivated by his past victories.

   When King Saul asked him how he thought he could kill the giant, David said, *"When I am taking care of my father's sheep, and a lion or a bear comes and grabs a lamb from the flock, I go after it with a club and take the lamb from its mouth...The Lord who saved me from the claws and teeth of the lion and the bear will save me from this Philistine!"* (see verse 34).

Wow! David was truly motivated by the material rewards offered, by the honor it would bring to God, and by the past victories the Lord had given him. These three will also motivate you to take on the giant that is threatening your life. Remember the reward, the honor it will bring to God, and the victories God has given you. Go fight a giant today.

•

Remember: HE'S TOO BIG TO MISS!

134/USE WHAT YOU'VE GOT!

"For my strength is made perfect in weakness"
(2 Corinthians 12:9).

Also read: Dan. 10:19; Psa. 27:1; Isa. 40:29; Eph. 3:16-17

I'll never forget the time when I was a young boy that I entered a talent contest in my tiny home town, Peever, South Dakota, population 200. Peever is located 10 miles south of Sisseton.

The contest was held at the local high school gymnasium where several people were competing for first place.

I had placed my guitar in the nearby furnace room until the contest started. When my turn came to play I stood up and soon discovered, to my horror, that someone had untuned one-half of my guitar strings. The lower three strings sounded terrible.

But I still had three strings in tune. So I played them as loudly as I could and sang my best—and won first prize!

I'll never forget the pride and joy I felt as I cashed the first prize check of $8 at the local restaurant. I had triumphed over my jealous enemies by using what little I had.

How about you? Are you living in defeat because you don't have all of the abilities you wished you had?

None of us do. We're all struggling with limitations and frustrations. But winners are people who try a little harder and use what they have to the maximum.

Once, several years ago, a disgruntled employee pointed out all of my weaknesses and said, "Lowell, what do you have?" I didn't answer him but I'd like to have said, "I have God's blessings and the anointing of His Spirit on my life, and I can communicate the Gospel message." I have all I need.

Count your strengths and build on them today. Don't forget Muhammed Ali, the greatest boxing champion in sports history, couldn't play the fiddle—but he didn't have to.

•

Remember: GOD'S STRENGTH IS MADE PERFECT IN WEAKNESS.

135/WHICH TAP BREAKS THE ROCK?

"Is not my Word like as a rock? saith the Lord; and like a hammer that breaketh the rock in pieces" (Jeremiah 23:29).

Also read: Rom. 1:16; Eph. 6:17; Heb. 4:12

A stone mason will tell you that it takes several blows of the hammer to split a rock. A rock has a grain in it much like a piece of wood and the mason keeps tapping on the rock with his hammer or chisel until it breaks open. He doesn't know how many hits it will take before it cracks, but he doesn't get discouraged because he's certain that every blow of his hammer moves him closer to victory.

God's Word and your prayers are much like the mason who keeps tapping on the rock; who knows which one will break open the difficult situation you are facing? And remember, the first tap is as important as the last—because it is the combined tapping that gets the job done.

If you're up against a rock-hard problem, start tapping (praying and using God's Word). Here's what to do.

First, *find a promise in God's Word that applies to your situation.* I've heard there are over 8,000 of them. As you read the Scripture that applies to your difficulty it will give you faith to pray. Imagine God's Word as the chisel and your prayers as the hammer—cutting in, breaking up the stoney situation.

Second, *look for the grain in your problem.* There's a weak spot in every person and every situation. Exploit it. Do everything you can to be sweet and tenderly persuasive (all the time, claiming God's promises and praying.)

Then keep tapping.

Sooner or later the situation is going to break open in your favor. God has never failed to fulfill one of His promises.

So keep on tapping and don't get discouraged. Your tough situation will soon crumble.

•

Remember: YOU MAY BE ONLY ONE TAP AWAY FROM VICTORY!

HOW TO KEEP HANGING ON!

"Looking unto Jesus the author and finisher of our faith; who for the joy that was set before him endured the cross, despising the shame, and is set down at the right hand of the throne of God" (Hebrews 12:2).

Also read: Ps. 27:1; Is. 40:31; Eph. 3:16 & 17; 6:10

Do you feel you've exhausted your strength? Is your faith weakening and you feel yourself slipping back into the hands of the enemy? Have you reached the point where you feel like giving up and hauling up the white flag of surrender?

If so, there's a way you can keep hanging on until your faith and strength are renewed. Today's text says that Jesus, the captain of our soul, won over the enemy by looking ahead. He looked past the suffering to the joy that was set before Him.

The religious leaders were about to crucify Jesus, His disciples were going to forsake Him. He would have to bear the excruciating pain of having 8 inch spikes driven into His hands and feet and He would be publicly disgraced and hung between two thieves on a cross on a dump heap outside of Jerusalem.

How did Jesus keep hanging on? What kept Him from crying out for the legions of angels to deliver Him? Why did He remain steady instead of scuttling the plan of our salvation?

Jesus kept His eyes on the reward set before Him—the joy of sitting down at the right hand of God with the redeemed. You'll find tremendous strength to go through your trials if you'll focus your eyes on what's ahead. Jesus said, *"To him that overcometh will I grant to sit with me in my throne, even as I also overcame, and am set down with my Father in his throne"* (Rev. 3:21).

Don't give up or give in—even when the pressure is overwhelming. Keep your eyes on Jesus and the promise of eternity. Let His strength be your strength. Remember, *"He giveth power to the faint; and to them that have no might he increaseth strength"* (Is. 40:29).

•

Remember: JESUS' STRENGTH IS ENOUGH TO KEEP YOU HANGING ON!

137/WE MUST PERSUADE MEN!

"And this is the condemnation, that light is come into the world, and men loved darkness rather than light, because their deeds were evil" (John 3:19).

Also read: Eph. 4:14-15; Col. 1:9-11; 1 Pet. 2:2-5

Someone has said, "God can heal blind eyes but He cannot open those that are shut." One of the most important lessons in living is to remain open to new ideas.

This is one of the problems of aging—your mind closes to new ideas. You become comfortable in what you believe so you shut out anything that upsets your tranquility.

I have picked up a lot of ideas in my 29 years of traveling but I must confess that I have seldom been able to transfer these ideas to anyone over 50 years of age. The reason why is probably two-fold. First, I am 46 and someone aged 50 resents a younger person teaching him. Second, new ideas are disturbing things that cause stress. Let me share this truth with you: "People resist change—even when they know it's for their own good."

How open are you to spiritual truths that are new and different from your present beliefs? How much do you hunger for knowledge? How many books do you read each month?

I commend you for reading this devotional. It reveals that you are hungry for new ideas. Jesus said, *"Everyone that doeth evil hateth the light, neither cometh to the light, lest his deeds should be reproved.*

"But he that doeth truth cometh to the light, that his deeds may be made manifest that they are wrought in God" (John 3:20-21).

Don't endorse every new idea that comes by, but don't reject something new just because it disturbs you. God has many new blessings for you. If you keep your eyes shut or are afraid of being disturbed, you'll miss His best.

•

Remember: GOD DOESN'T OPEN CLOSED EYES!

138/ARE YOU WISE ENOUGH TO GIVE?

"And every wise hearted among you shall come" (Exodus 35:10).

Also read: Ex. 35:21-22; Luke 6:38

What is there within us that wants to withhold from God? Why do people run from the Lord and refuse to get saved? Why do so many resist His Lordship and continue to "walk in the flesh" after they are saved? Why do so many find it difficult to give generously to the cause of the Savior?

The root of our rebellion is ignorance. The reason we resist God's plan is because we think our plan is better. It's as foolish as a car-buyer telling the manufacturer why he shouldn't spend money to put oil in his car.

When God instructed Moses to build a tabernacle in the wilderness, where God would dwell among the people, He said, *"Whosoever is of a willing heart, let him bring it an offering* (God doesn't want any grudge offerings)...*And every wise hearted among you shall come"* (Ex. 35:5, 10).

In other words, God said, "If you're wise enough to give you will come with your offering." Why is a wise man to allow God's Spirit to stir him up to give? Because *"God loveth a cheerful giver"* (2 Cor. 9:7). Can you imagine all the blessings God can pour upon a man whom He loves?

When I've seen my little boy, Lance, make a sacrificial gift of some of his pennies or candies to one of the members of our family, something rises up within me that immediately wants to restore what he has given away. I love to see a generous child. (I'm sure you feel the same way.)

Be wise enough to realize that if you respond to God generously, He will restore even more generously to you.

•

Remember: BE WISE ENOUGH TO GIVE.

139/THE PIT SYNDROME

"And he that sat upon the throne said, Behold I make all things new" (Revelation 21:5).

Also read: Ps. 103:1-5; 107:9; 2 Cor. 9:8

As president of Trinity Bible College in Ellendale, North Dakota, I've tried to make our 28-acre campus as beautiful as possible. One day, while driving along with a department head, I pointed out that one of the garbage cans needed painting. Then I asked, "Why didn't you see that?"

His response is a classic. He simply said, "I guess it's part of the Pit Syndrome. I've become so used to things as they are, I don't see the things that need changing."

How about you? Have you become a victim of the Pit Syndrome? Are you missing things around you that should be changed?

1. **Start with your Bible reading:** Would a new translation or paraphrased edition give the Scriptures new life to your heart and soul?
2. **What about your bed?** You spend 1/3 of your life—25 years—in the same spot. Maybe you need a new mattress. In my surveys nationwide, I find only one in three Christians think their mattress is the best they've slept on. Be good to yourself!
3. **Shuffle your furniture!** Why does everything have to be in the same place all the time? Try painting your rooms. A fresh color will perk things up.
4. **Dare I mention your closet?** These become catch-alls for junk. Clean them out and have a garage sale. You might even want to donate the money to God's work.
5. **How are your clothes?** Do you have anything fresh to wear? Connie and I have shopped in second-hand stores for years and found good-looking clothes for nearly nothing.
6. **Have you thought about making new friends?** People tend to get into boring cliques of friends that contribute nothing to their mental and spiritual growth.
7. **Try an unusual vacation!** Get away from the relatives. Go somewhere you've never been before. Call a travel agent and start looking at brochures. Maybe you won't be able to fly, but you can drive a long ways on the money from the garage sale you're going to have.
8. **And here's the unmentionable:** If you're married, try out some new romantic places and ways to make your love come alive.

Today's text says that God makes all things new—why don't you?

•

Remember: DON'T BE A VICTIM OF THE PIT SYN—DROME.

140/HOW THE TRUTH GETS TWISTED!

"For the wrath of God is revealed from heaven against all ungodliness and unrighteousness of men, who hold the truth in unrighteousness" (Romans 1:18).

Also read: Ps. 51:6; Pro. 3:3; 12:17; Rom. 2:8 & 9

Have you ever wondered how the truth gets twisted? The other night I watched a so-called minister on cable TV who's mind is in the twilight zone.

The sad thing is that he once preached the pure Gospel in a powerful way. God even used this man to lead a fellowship of hundreds of churches.

Where did he go wrong? The same place everyone does—he held the truth in unrighteousness. Today's text tells how God is angry with men and women who know the truth but fail to lead holy lives.

Truth is so pure that if you handle it with tainted hands it gets twisted. Then, once it's twisted, you are deceived and become reprobate. *"And even as they did not like to retain God in their knowledge, God gave them over to a reprobate mind"* (Rom. 1:28).

God's Word is like a compass, if you tamper with the needle you will alter it's ability to lead you to safety. Once you have ruined a compass, it's only time before you become lost.

I have found that God's Word teaches us tenderly and I must guard against the temptation to overrule it's directions. It's easy to give into sin and say, "The Bible doesn't say anything specific about this—so it can't be so bad." The fact is that the Bible addresses every area of your life and mine in principle.

I remember how my mother used to clean the containers that held the cream. She knew that the smallest amount of scum would harbor germs and fungus that would cause the cream to sour. You and I must keep the scum of sin out of our lives or the precious Word of God will sour in our souls—and the truth will get twisted.

How clean is your mind and soul today?

•

Remember: WE MUST KEEP OUR VESSELS CLEAN OR THE TRUTH WILL BECOME TWISTED.

141/PERSISTANCE PAYS!

"...I will not let thee go, except thou bless me" (Genesis 32:26).

Also read: Eph. 6:10; 1 Tim. 6:12

De Witt Talmage, the famous preacher, said, "If a man is right, all the bombardment of the world for five, ten, twenty, forty years will only strengthen him in his position. All you have to do is to keep yourself right. Never mind the world. Let it say what it will. It can do you no damage."

Jesus was a success because He wouldn't give up. When He was facing crucifixion, knowing He was going to die the Bible says He set his face as a flint (see Isaiah 50:7). Persistance pays—with it Jesus purchased our salvation.

Study these Scriptures:

"And ye shall be hated of all men for my name's sake: BUT HE THAT ENDURETH TO THE END SHALL BE SAVED" (Matt. 10:22, emphasis mine).

"Be strong in the grace that is in Christ Jesus...endure hardness, as a good soldier of Jesus Christ" (2 Tim. 2:1 & 3).

Sometimes when the going gets hard, it helps me to consider holding on for one more day. If I try to look at a week or a month or a year, I get too discouraged; but one more day is a parcel I can handle.

If you are going through a tough time, hang in there. If you've reached the end of your rope—tie a knot and hang on. It's when everyone and everything is against you that you develop the grit that makes you strong.

Don't let go—you can make it a while longer. If not a year, or a month, or a week, or a day or an hour—try a minute. Then invest the next minute praising God and reminding yourself of all the tough situations God has brought you through in the past.

●

Remember: PERSISTENCE PAYS!

142/THE WAR WITHIN THE CHURCH!

"But as then he that was born after the flesh persecuted him that was born after the Spirit, even so it is now" (Galatians 4:29).

Also read: 1 Cor. 6:15-20; Gal. 5:16-19; Eph. 4:22-27

Just as there is a struggle within you and me between the flesh and the Spirit of God, there is a struggle within the church between those who are "born after the flesh" and those who are "born after the Spirit." Today's text says that Ishmael, Abraham's son by Sarah's handmaid, Hagar, persecuted Isaac, who was Abraham's promised son by Sarah. (See Gen. 16-21.)

This is how conflict between the Arabs and Jews began —for the Arabs are Abraham's children by Ishmael, and the Jews are Abraham's children by Isaac. They have been fighting each other ever since the day Abraham celebrated Isaac's weaning (see Gen. 21:8-13).

Paul, the apostle, used this illustration of Ismael and Isaac to show the Galatian Christians what was happening in their midst. Certain teachers of the law had crept into the church and were corrupting the new converts with false doctrine.

Paul said, *"Cast out the bondwoman and her son: for the son of the bondwoman shall not be heir with the son of the freewoman. So then, brethren, we are not children of the bondwoman* (or slave), *but of the free. Stand fast therefore in the liberty wherewith Christ hath made us free, and be not entangled again with the yoke of bondage"* (Gal. 4:30 - 5:1 KJV).

The war within the church is between the carnally-minded Christians who prefer a religious system over the Spirit, and the spiritually-minded Christians who prefer the Spirit over the religious system. Whose side are you on?

●

Remember: THE WAR WITHIN THE CHURCH IS THE SAME AS THE WAR WITHIN OUR OWN HEARTS AND LIVES.

143/LISTEN FOR THE LORD

"And it shall be, when thou shalt hear a sound of going in the tops of the mulberry trees, that then thou shalt go out to battle: for God is gone forth before thee to smite the host of the Philistines" (1 Chronicles 14:15).

Also read: Deut. 5:1, 32-33; John 14:15, 21; Acts 5:29

David was about to go into battle against the Philistines and wondered if he was doing the right thing. The Bible says he inquired of God, and God said to him, *"Go not up after them; turn away from them, and come upon them over against the mulberry trees...And...when thou shalt hear a sound of going* (rustling) *in the tops of the mulberry trees, (you'll know I have) gone forth before thee"* (1 Chron. 14:14 & 15).

If you are anxious to know God's will for your life do these things:
1. *Enquire of the Lord.* Spend extra time in prayer and also in reading and studying the Scriptures.
2. *When you feel an impression in your inner spirit to do something, follow it*—even if it is opposite of what you had planned.
3. *Listen for the Lord.* Check the circumstances that start falling together. If you are really walking in God's will, you'll see signs that tell you you're on track. Unusual things will begin to "just happen" that will confirm your actions.

The Bible says, *"David therefore did as God commanded him: and they smote the host of the Philistines...and the fame of David went out into all lands: and the Lord brought the fear of him upon all nations"* (verses 16 & 17).

God gave David great success because he obeyed the Spirit's leading.

•

Remember: LISTEN FOR THE LORD!

HUNGRY FOR MORE

"I beseech thee, show me thy glory" (Exodus 33:18).

Also read: Deut. 5:24; Ps. 72:19; 97:6; Is. 60:2

Moses is one man who had seen it all. Raised in the court of the king of Egypt he had seen the pomp and glory of the Pharoah. Then fleeing to Midian he experienced the rural life of a sheep rancher for 40 years. After this, God appeared to Moses, calling him to be the deliverer of the Jews out of slavery.

Moses saw the mighty hand of God work nine great miracles in Egypt so that it humbled the pride of Pharoah. He also saw God open the Red Sea and provide miracle "manna," bread for the three million travellers on their way to Canaan.

One of the greatest experiences Moses had was when God called him to the top of Mount Sinai and gave him the Ten Commandments. God cut out stone and wrote on it the greatest moral code ever given to mankind.

Moses was a personal friend of the Living God (see Ex. 33:11). Yet Moses was hungry for even more. That day as God and Moses visited, Moses said, *"If I have found grace in your sight...I beg of you—show me your glory"* (Exodus 33:12 & 18).

This is what Moses hungered for more than anything else. He had experienced religion, miracles, victories, and more, but there was an overwhelming hunger to see God's glory, the innermost essence of God himself.

Are you hungry for more? Do you want more than just attending church, Bible studies and meetings? Is your soul crying out for a new dimension?

Then seek God's glory! Moses did and God showed him part of it. The effects were so great, a veil had to be put over Moses' face because of its great radiance from being with God.

•

Remember: IF YOU'RE HUNGRY FOR MORE, MAKE THE GLORY OF GOD YOUR GOAL!

145/WATCH YOUR WORDS!

"Set a watch, O Lord, before my mouth; keep the door of my lips" (Psalm 141:3).

Also read: Psa. 19:14; Prov. 15:26; Eph. 5:6

You have power in your tongue. The words you speak have power to build or destroy. This is why you must watch what you say.

Jesus said, *"Every idle word that men shall speak, they shall give account thereof in the day of judgment. For by thy words thou shalt be justified, and by thy words thou shalt be condemned"* (Matt. 12:36-37).

Your words will be your witness on Judgment Day. I used to think of this verse in the negative. I used to say to myself, "Lowell, you'd better watch what you say; your words will condemn you." But then I realized my idle words would justify me as well as condemn me. I began to recall the dozens of off-hand comments I made during the day that really show I love God and care about His work.

Today, watch what you say! Speak positive, upbuilding words. Say things that edify and lift your listeners. Your words of encouragement can lift the load many are bearing. Acknowledge the janitor; say, "I really appreciate how you keep this place so clean and comfortable." Thank the policeman saying, "If it weren't for men like you our community wouldn't be safe." Tell the clerk how her smile makes her whole department light up.

Say good things! And don't use this popular phrase when parting, "Take care." This phrase implies that there are dangerous forbidden forces "out there" and you'd better "take care" or you'll be the victim.

Instead say, "Have a great day!" God's Word says, *"Let your speech be alway with grace, seasoned with salt"* (Col. 4:6). Give your listeners a lift!

•

Remember: HEAVEN'S TAPE RECORDER IS RECORDING EVERYTHING YOU SAY—WATCH YOUR WORDS TODAY!

THE WAR WITHIN

"For the flesh lusteth against the Spirit, and the Spirit against the flesh: and these are contrary the one to the other: so that you cannot do the things that you would" (Galatians 5:17).

Also read: Rom. 8:6-8; Gal. 6:8; 1 Jn. 2:15-17

You and I are fighting a war within ourselves—between the flesh and the Spirit.

 The Spirit says, "Go!" but your flesh says, "No!"
 The Spirit says, "Share!" and your flesh, "Doesn't care!"
 The Spirit says, "Pray!" but the flesh, "Won't today!"
 The Spirit says, "Forgive!" but the flesh says, "Not as long as I live!"

The struggle is as old as Adam and Eve in the garden. God said they could enjoy everything in Paradise except the fruit from the forbidden tree but *"when the woman saw that the tree was good for food and that it was pleasant to the eyes, and a tree to be desired to make one wise, she took of the fruit there of, and did eat, and gave also unto her husband with her; and he did eat"* (Gen. 3:6).

Eve was tempted by the tree in three areas:
1. **Appetite:** She saw "it was good for food."
2. **Sight:** "It was pleasant to the eyes."
3. **Mind:** "A tree to be desired to make one wise."

The war within you involves these areas of your life:
1. **Appetite:** The desire for food, sex, liquor, drugs, tobacco, etc.
2. **Sight:** A craving to see pleasant things. A yearning for beautiful clothes, fancy cars, elegant homes, a desire to travel and "see" things. Also a lusting to read pornography and watch filthy movies, etc.
3. **Mind:** A hunger to "know" things that will make you wise without making you a better servant in God's eyes. Most of the world today is studying truth that is good—but Godless knowledge is power and men are craving this mental power today more than ever.

Who is winning the war: the flesh or the Spirit? You must make Jesus Christ Lord in each of these areas of your life:
1. He must be Lord of all you eat, drink, or do with your body.
2. Jesus must be Lord of all you see and hear.
3. Christ must be Lord of all you study and learn. He must be the reason why you want to know more and become a stronger person.

There is a war raging within you today. You can't avoid it, you must win it—by walking in the Spirit in complete obedience.

●

Remember: TO WIN THE WAR WITHIN, INVITE CHRIST INTO EVERY AREA OF YOUR LIFE!

147/THE UNPARDONABLE SIN

"Wherefore I say unto you, All manner of sin and blasphemy shall be forgiven unto men: but the blasphemy against the Holy Ghost shall not be forgiven unto men" (Matthew 12:31).

Also read: Matt. 12:22-37; Mark 3:22-30

Does today's verse surprise you? What is the unpardonable sin? People are so used to hearing that God will forgive everything, they are shocked to hear of a sin He will not forgive.

In Matthew 12, people brought a blind, dumb and demon-possessed man to Jesus Christ. Through the power of the Holy Spirit, Jesus healed the man; he could now both see and speak. But when the Pharisees heard about this great miracle, they said that Jesus cast out the devils by the power of the devil. Then Jesus answered them with the words of today's text.

> Please note: *The Pharisees gave Satan the credit for a miracle performed by the Holy Spirit. This is the unpardonable sin.*

Before I became a Christian, my life was very sinful. When I gave my life to Christ, it was a shock to our community. One minister said what happened to me was of the devil—that my conversion to Jesus Christ was an act of Satan. I believe if he meant what he said, this was the unpardonable sin, blasphemy against God's Spirit.

Don't confuse *blasphemy* against the Spirit with *resisting* the Spirit. Someone who resists the Spirit has not necessarily committed the unpardonable sin. Backsliders are often deceived by Satan into thinking that God is no longer dealing with them. But their concern over their spiritual condition proves the Holy Spirit is still with them.

You tread on dangerous territory when you get judgmental and critical of miracles and the power of God. Don't speak against an experience someone has had with God. Find out the truth for yourself and listen with an open mind.

•

Remember: THE UNPARDONABLE SIN IS GIVING SATAN CREDIT FOR A MIRACLE PERFORMED BY THE HOLY SPIRIT.

148/GOD DOESN'T OPEN CLOSED DOORS

"Knowing therefore the terror of the Lord, we persuade men" (2 Corinthians 5:11).

Also read: 1 Chron. 16:25; Mal. 3:16-17; Psa. 25:12-14

Paul the apostle was a fearful man. He knew God well enough to be afraid of facing Him with unconfessed sin on Judgment Day.

He writes, *"For we must all appear before the judgment seat of Christ; that every one may receive the things done in his body, according to that he hath done, whether it be good or bad.*

"Knowing therefore the terror of the Lord, we persuade men" (2 Cor. 5:10-11).

The Bible says, *"The fear of the Lord is the beginning of wisdom: a good understanding have all they that do his commandments"* (Psa. 111:10).

The reason why Paul preached with such converting fervor is he knew the nature of God. He was aware that God was totally against sin—just as a caring doctor hates cancer and disease.

Remember, God hates sin as strongly as He loves righteousness. The reason God hates sin so strongly is He has seen how it has destroyed the best of heaven. Sin turned Lucifer from one of God's greatest angels into a demon of unredeemable evil.

God hates sin because of the suffering it brings upon mankind. If you'll walk through any ghetto, hospital, prison or reformatory, you'll see the wages of sin is death. God loves life and sin is anti-life. It is an attack upon the essence of life itself.

God hates sin because of the price He paid to save us. Remember that God had to stand back and watch His only Son twist upon the nails crying out, *"My God, my God, why hast thou forsaken me?"* (Matt. 27:46).

If you had to give your only son in death to save someone from wrongdoing, you'd surely hate the evil that caused your son to die. This is why God hates sin.

•

Remember: IF YOU KNOW THE TERROR OF THE LORD YOU WILL PERSUADE MEN.

149/THE WAR WITHIN THE WORLD!

"I have given them thy word; and the world hath hated them, because they are not of the world, even as I am not of the world" (John 17:14).

Also read: Lk. 11:33; 12:8 & 9; Eph. 6:18-20; 1 Pet. 3:8-15

If you are wondering why there is a struggle within the world, it is because there is a battle between truth and falsehood, light and darkness and good and evil. These opposite forces are headed up by God and Satan.

Jesus said your non Christian friends will resent and even hate you because of the Word of God, the truth, the light, you have been given. The light of truth shines upon the darkness of their lying lives and as a result they hate you. *"And this is the condemnation* (or judgment), *that light is come into the world, and men loved darkness rather than light, because their deeds were evil.*

"For every one that doeth evil hateth the light, neither cometh to the light, lest his deeds should be reproved (examined or exposed).*"* (Jn. 3:19 & 20).

Jesus also said, *"Ye are the light of the world...Let your light so shine before men, that they may see your good works, and glorify your father which is in heaven"* (Matt. 5: 14 & 16).

So this may help you to see why you're not accepted by your non Christian friends. The light of your life is shining on their darkness and is exposing their wicked deeds. And frankly, most people would rather put out the light than clean up their lives. This is why the Apostle John wrote, *"Marvel not, my brethren, if the world hate you"* (1 Jn. 3:13).

But don't let that stop you from speaking the truth. Failure to speak up will only allow darkness to dominate. Today, determine you will let your light shine on whatever discussions come up with your friends. Don't curse the darkness; light your candle of truth and let it tenderly flicker forth for the glory of God.

•

Remember: THE WAR WITHIN THE WORLD CAN BE WON BY SHINING YOUR LIGHT!

150/ARE YOU A PHILIPPIAN GIVER?

"When I first brought the Gospel to you and then went on my way, leaving Macedonia, only you Philippians became my partners in giving and receiving. No other church did this" (Philippians 4:15, TLB).

Also read: Acts 20:35; 2 Cor. 9:7

Don't miss the impact of this amazing statement: Paul said, "The only church that became my partners in giving and receiving were you Philippians. No other church did this." Why didn't the other churches Paul established become partners in "giving and receiving?" It is because they did not understand the laws of God regarding sowing and reaping.

The Corinthians were a rough, carnal lot, and Paul said more to them about giving than any other church. Because of their lack of spirituality they needed the most encouragement to give.

But the Philippians were different. They knew the truths of "giving and receiving." This freed them to be liberal with their gifts. This is why they became Paul's partners: they knew when they gave, God would give back to them *"pressed down, shaken together, full and running over"* (Luke 6:38).

Are you a Philippian giver? Do you really believe that when you give you will receive? I've heard some people say, "I don't want to give to God expecting a return—I just want to give because I love Him."

This is a great attitude but it breaks down under the pressure of everyday living. When you have bills pressing and you're asked to give, your reason will press in and say, "I love God, but just can't afford to give."

Philippian givers know that when they give they will receive. In fact, they'll say, "I really can't afford not to give."

More than anything, you want to be the kind of person of whom God says, "Of all the Christians in your area, you're the one I could really count on to be my partner."

If you are running short on finances, check your heart and see if you're a Corinthian Christian who needs to be pushed into giving or a Philippian Christian who delights in it.

•

Remember: BE A PHILIPPIAN GIVER!

151/WHY YOUR PRAYERS ARE NOT ANSWERED!

"For this thing I sought the Lord three times, that it would depart from me" (2 Corinthians 12:8, Literal).

Also read: Psa. 6:9; 39:12; 37:7-9; 40:1-3; 1 Tim. 2:8

Have you been praying about a situation and not receiving an answer? If you've been discouraged about the lack of answered prayer consider these reasons:

1. *God may will differently.* Paul begged God three times to take away the thorn in his flesh but God answered, *"My grace is sufficient for thee"* (verse 9). God may have a plan that's different from the one you've laid out.

2. *You may not be ready to receive the answer.* The Bible says of young John the Baptist, *"The child grew, and waxed strong in spirit, and was in the deserts til the day of his shewing unto Israel"* (Luke 1:80). What if young John the Baptist had tried to start his ministry earlier? He would have been frustrated because God wouldn't have blessed him.

3. *You may have wrong motives in your prayers!* Jeremiah the prophet said, *"The heart is deceitful above all things, and desperately wicked: who can know it?"* (Jer. 17:9). The Apostle James says, *"Ye ask, and receive not, because ye ask amiss, that ye may consume it upon your own lusts"* (Jas. 4:3).

4. *You may have sin in your life.* The psalmist David said, *"If I regard iniquity in my heart, the Lord will not hear me"* (Psa. 66:18).

5. *You may have a division between yourself and another.* Jesus said, *"If you bring your gift to the altar, and there remember that your brother has (hard feelings) against you, leave your gift there before the altar, and go your way. First be reconciled to your brother, and then come and offer your gift"* (Matt. 5:23 & 24, NKJ).

6. *It may be that you haven't prayed fervently enough.* Jesus said, "Ask, seek, knock" (see Matt. 7:7). The varied degrees of seeking show that increased intensity is needed to penetrate the strongholds of hell.

●

Remember: THERE ARE REASONS WHY YOUR PRAYERS ARE NOT ANSWERED: BE PATIENT WITH THE LORD AND ASK HIM TO SHOW YOU HIS REASONS.

152/THE KEYS TO SUCCESS!

"This book of the law shall not depart out of thy mouth; but thou shalt meditate therein day and night, that thou mayest observe to do according to all that is written therein; for then thou shalt make thy way prosperous, and then thou shalt have good success" (Joshua 1:8).

Also read: 1 Ch. 22:13; Ps. 1:1-3; Is. 48:17; Mt. 6:33

If you ever go into business, small or large, there are four key rules to success.

1. **Product**
   Whatever you make must be something that people want. You'd have a hard time selling iceboxes today because electric refrigerators have taken over the market.
   You can sell anything if it's something people want. In other words, "Find a need and fill it."
2. **Price**
   People will pay only so much for something. Some people say the quickest way to make a million dollars is to invent something that sells for less than $10.00 that everyone has to have.
3. **Place**
   You won't succeed selling Mercedes Benz automobiles in the jungles of Equador. Market your product in the region where people can buy it. Study surveys to find the best place to market your product.
4. **Promotion**
   He who has a thing to sell and goes and whispers in a well is not so apt to get the dollars as he who climbs a tree and hollers.

Just as there are natural laws to success in business, there are laws to success in the spiritual world.

1. **Keep the Word of God in your mouth.** *This book of the law shall not depart out of they mouth."* This means you should memorize Scriptures and quote them throughout the day.
2. **Keep the Word of God in your mind.** *"But thou shalt meditate therein day and night."* The actions of your life are a result of the meditations of your mind. If you think right, you'll live right. If you think wrong, you'll live wrong.
3. **Make certain you obey God's laws.** *"Observe to do according to all that is written therein."* Learning about God is not as difficult as learning to obey Him. Being able to say, "No! I will not yield to temptation" is the key to spiritual success. Note: You'll never be able to stand in such a way unless you have been meditating on God's Word and quoting it.

The best part about God's laws of success is that they are guaranteed to make you a winner: *"For then thou shalt make thy way prosperous and then thou shalt have good success."*

●

Remember: THE KEYS TO SUCCESS REALLY WORK!

153/WE'RE ALL THE SAME

"And lead us not into temptation" (Matthew 6:13).

Also read: Jas. 1:12; 2 Pet. 2:9

Here's a probing observation: "Superficially we're different, but inside we're all the same" (Becky Manley Pippert).

This is true. Often the struggling soul looks at an overcoming Christian with despair, feeling that somehow it's easier for others to win over sin than it is for him. False!

One famous preacher said, "You may think the Christian life is easy for me, but you'll never know how many dark nights I've fought back the demon forces that threatened and the lusts that raged in my body."

The will to withstand temptation and discouragement is the real test of your commitment to God. Champions have a determination to overcome in spite of the obstacles.

Muhammed Ali will always be remembered as one of the all-time great boxing champions. When he was old (for a boxer) he had to face Larry Holmes. Ali said, "All I could think of after the first round was, 'O God, I've still got 14 rounds to go.' I had nothing. Nothing. I knew it was hopeless. I knew I couldn't win, and I knew I'd never quit. I knew Holmes would win, but he was going to have to kill me to get me out of the ring."

We're all the same. The Bible says, *"There hath no temptation taken you but such as is COMMON TO MAN:* (we're all tempted by the same things) *but God is faithful, who will not suffer* (permit or allow) *you to be tempted above that ye are able; but will with the temptation also make a way to escape, that you may be able to bear it"* (1 Cor. 10:13, emphasis mine).

If you're being tempted, look for the way to escape which God is providing for you. Flee from the presence of evil. God will help you if you'll do what He says.

•

Remember: WE'RE ALL THE SAME—THE WINNERS JUST TRY HARDER.

DO YOU HAVE A GRIPE AGAINST GOD?

"Produce your cause, saith the Lord; bring forth your strong reasons, saith the King" (Isaiah 41:21).

Also read: Ps. 55:22; Is. 55:8; Jer. 33:3

Your Christianity is more of a personal relationship than anything else. It is important that your relationship with God remain open. The key to loving God is living honest enough to admit your truest feelings to Him.

Do you have a gripe against God? Has something happened where it appears He has let you down? I'm not trying to create a problem, but I'm asking you to admit it if it's there. The writer to the Hebrews said, *"Look after each other so that not one of you will fail to find God's best blessings. Watch out that no bitterness takes root among you, for as it springs up it causes deep trouble, hurting many in their spiritual lives"* (Heb. 12:15, TLB).

The most bitter hurt of my life was when our daughter Lisa abandoned the Christian faith to live a sinful life in the world. I was crushed because I felt God had let me down. I had served Him with all my heart and truly believed that if I sought His Kingdom first, all other things would be added to me, including the welfare of my family.

I wept hot tears, but the only way my faith survived was by constantly reading the Bible and discovering how God felt. Verses like this one helped me, *"I will seek that which was lost, and bring again that which was driven away, and will bind up that which was broken"* (Ex. 34:16).

Do you have a gripe against God? Have you felt that He let you down when your loved one died or you weren't healed, or you struggled financially, or your marriage failed? The way to get the gripe out of your soul is to:
1. Admit it's there.
2. Search the Scriptures.
3. Pray and give God time to reveal His plan.

●

Remember: GOD LOVES YOU ENOUGH TO BEAR YOUR GRIPES.

155/DON'T LOSE HEART

"And he spake a parable unto them to this end, that men ought always pray, and not to faint" (Luke 18:1).

Also read: Psa. 55:17; Matt. 1:9-11; Jas. 5:16-18

Are you struggling over why God doesn't answer your prayers? Jesus said you should always pray and not faint (or lose heart). If you've been disheartened over unanswered prayer, consider the determined widow: She went before the wicked judge and pleaded with him continually until he said, *"Though I fear not God, nor regard man: Yet because this widow woman troubleth me, I will avenge her, lest by her continual coming she weary me"* (verses 4 & 5).

Notice the words, "trouble me." The woman made such a fuss that it drove the judge mad. This is the way you need to get on God's case about your request.

Jesus said, *"And shall not God avenge his own elect, which cry day and night unto him though he bear long with them?"*

"I tell you that he will avenge them speedily" (verses 7-8).

Jesus used the story of the unjust judge to show you that even a wicked man will move if you bother him long enough. How much more will your loving Father in heaven answer your prayers!

But Jesus added one more phrase, *"Nevertheless when the Son of man cometh, shall he find faith on the earth?"* In other words, Jesus doubted that Christians living in the last days would have this kind of "I-won't-take-no-for-an-answer" prayer.

How about you? Have you given up praying for someone or something? Don't! You may only be one prayer away from victory.

•

Remember: PRAY AND DON'T LOSE HEART.

THE SUBTILITY OF SIN!

"For sin ... deceived me, and by it slew me" (Romans 7:11).

Also read: Luke 21:8; Eph. 4:14; Rev. 20:10

One of the great mysteries of life is how sin can deceive so many wise people into doing wrong. Consider Solomon, one of the wisest men who has ever lived, a man whose collection of Proverbs is part of our Bible today—yet he was deceived by sin. Solomon ended up with 700 wives and 300 combines (I call them combines instead of concubines because they really threshed him). This very wise man ended up worshipping pagan idols made of stone (see 1 Kings 11).

If sin is so subtle it can deceive the wisest man, imagine what it can do to you and me!

Look how Satan beguiled Eve with his subtlety.

He misquoted the commandment of God saying, *"Hasn't God said that you can eat of all of the trees in the garden? If you eat the forbidden fruit you shall not surely die"* (see Gen. 3:1-4). Satan twisted God's Word. Don't let him deceive you. God wrote what He meant and meant what He wrote. Don't mess with the Scriptures or you'll be deceived.

Second, Satan was able to persuade Eve to look at the tree. The Bible says, *"And when the woman saw that the tree was good for food, AND THAT IT WAS PLEASANT TO THE EYES, AND A TREE TO BE DESIRED to make one wise, she took of the fruit thereof, and did eat, and gave also unto her husband with her: and he did eat"* (Gen. 3:6, emphasis mine).

Sin worked its subtlety on Eve through her eyes. The longer she looked—the more she desired the forbidden. Have you been looking at forbidden things? Don't let Satan use *your* eyes to tempt you!

•

Remember: SIN IS SUBTLE. TO ESCAPE SATAN, OBEY GOD'S WORD—YOU'LL SAVE YOURSELF ETERNAL GRIEF.

157/OUR LIGHT AFFLICATION

"For our light affliction, which is but for a moment worketh for us a far more exceeding and eternal weight of glory" (2 Corinthians 4:17).

Also read: Rom. 8:17 & 18; 2 Cor. 4:8-18; 1 Pet. 2:20 & 21

Are you in the fire? Are you having a difficult time? Before you have a pity party for yourself, take a look at all the Apostle Paul went through: false teachers in the Corinthian church were suggesting that Paul was not truly serving Christ so he wrote:

> "They say they serve Christ? But I have served him far more! (Have I gone mad to boast like this?) I have worked harder, been put in jail oftener, been whipped times without number, and faced death again and again.
>
> "Five different times the Jews gave me their terrible thirty-nine lashes. Three times I was beaten with rods. Once I was stoned. Three times I was shipwrecked. Once I was in the open sea all night and the whole next day...
>
> "I have lived with weariness and pain and sleepless nights. Often I have been hungry and thirsty and have gone without food; often I have shivered with cold, without enough clothing to keep me warm.
>
> "Then, besides all this, I have the constant worry of how the churches are getting along" (2 Cor. 11:23-28, TLB).

It would be hard to compare the great struggles of Paul with the small trials you and I are often called to bear. But how did Paul view his sufferings? He called his sufferings "light." This is truly remarkable.

How could he refer to his crushing afflictions as light? Paul realized the worst can only last for a little while. (Even the ax that severed his head from his body was but for a moment.)

He knew that God uses the fires of affliction to refine our souls and develop the character that is pleasing in His sight. Pain is the process by which God produces saints.

> Paul said, "Compared with the eternal reward we will receive for our suffering, the few trials we have here are almost insignificant."

What if you received a million dollars for every tear you shed? Or a billion dollars for every time your heart ached? Or a trillion dollars for every pain in your body? Would that ease the pain? Paul said, "The light affliction you have will only last a moment; then you'll be rewarded beyond measure forever."

•

Remember: REJOICE—YOUR LIGHT AFFLICTION WILL WORK WONDERS FOR YOU.

158/HOW TO MAKE YOUR WALLET FAT!

"The liberal soul shall be made fat: and he that watereth shall be watered also himself" (Proverbs 11:25).

Also read: Deut. 28:2-8; Psa. 37:25; Matt. 6:31-33

If you are struggling financially there is a way you can do yourself a favor—by becoming liberal in showing appreciation to others. The more you help others the more they will help you.

Art Linkletter, a very successful entertainer and multi-millionaire entrepreneur, says that each morning he sends cards of thanks to people he has met the day before—thanking them for the small favors they have done. He says the small postcards build such good will that many who receive them return the favor by giving him tips on deals that literally pour money into his pockets. They say, "Let's tell Art about this terrific deal. He's such a good guy we want him to get in on making some of this money."

Are you liberal in your appreciation of others? If you're a married man, the Bible says, *"He that loveth his wife loveth himself"* (Eph. 5:28). Your kindness returns to you multiplied.

Are you liberal with God? Do you give the Lord the first tenth of everything you earn? If you have been cutting God short of His share, correct the situation today. Write a check for a soulwinning ministry today.

The prophet Malachi said, *"Will a man rob God? Yet ye have robbed me. But ye say, Wherein have we robbed thee? In tithes and offerings.*

"Ye are cursed with a curse: for ye have robbed me, even this whole nation.

"Bring ye all the tithes into the storehouse, that there may be meat in my house, and prove me now herewith, saith the Lord of hosts, if I will not open you the windows of heaven, and pour you out a blessing, that there shall not be room enough to receive it.

"And I will rebuke the devourer for your sakes...saith the Lord of hosts" (Mal. 3:8-11).

•

Remember: BE LIBERAL WITH YOUR FAMILY, FRIENDS, AND GOD. THIS IS THE WAY TO MAKE YOUR LIFE AND WALLET FAT!

159/GOD, WHO MADE THE STARS, IS WITH YOU!

"If I ascend up into heaven, thou art there: if I make my bed in hell, behold, thou art there" (Psalm 139:8).

Also read: Ps. 8:3-9; 147:4 & 5

David said that God is everywhere; God's presence reaches to the very end of the universe.

If God is everywhere, this entire universe is within God. He looks down upon this universe much the same as you would look down at your stomach.

Consider the size of this universe. The distance in space is so great the miles are counted in light years. A light year is the distance light travels in one year. The speed of light is 186,000 miles per second or about 6 trillion miles in one year.

There are also quasars (hot burning masses of stars), shooting outward that are 12 billion light years distant and still moving away. Multiply 12 billion by 6 trillion and you have a number beyond comprehension!

If this is the size of the universe and the entire universe is within God (for there is no place where God is not), then we have a God so great that no human mind can comprehend His dimensions.

This should help build your faith when facing a problem. Your heart may tremble when facing a crisis, but how could any problem be outside of such a great God's control?

It's almost ridiculous to doubt such a great Creator. But just like a small penny can blot out the blazing sun simply because we are holding it too close to our eye, so our small problems can blot out the greatness of God if we cling too tightly to our troubles.

Back away from your problem when it threatens to overwhelm you. Take a new look at God. Read the Bible and review what He has done for others in conditions similar to yours. Then pray until you get a fresh touch from the Holy Spirit to make these truths real.

•

Remember: GOD IS WITH YOU!

160/HEAVEN WILL BE NOISY

"And I beheld, and I heard the voice of many angels round about the throne...saying with a loud voice, Worthy is the Lamb that was slain to receive power, and riches, and wisdom, and strength, and honour, and glory, and blessing" (Revelation 5:11 & 12).

Also read: 1 Chron. 15:16; Psa. 31:22; 47:1; 77:1

I hope you won't be shocked to find that when you get to heaven you will discover it to be a noisy place! John the apostle saw heaven and wrote, *"I beheld, and, lo, a great multitude, which no man could number, of all nations, and kindreds, and people, and tongues* (By God's grace you and I will be among this number. This is the assembly of saints from all ages past and present.) *stood, before the... Lamb, clothed with white robes, and palms in their hands;*

"And cried WITH A LOUD VOICE, saying, Salvation to our God which sitteth upon the throne, and unto the Lamb" (Rev. 7:9 & 10, emphasis mine).

I felt impressed by the Holy Spirit to write this devotional on the subject of worshipping loudly. Do you lift up your voice loudly when you pray?

The early Christians prayed loudly. The Scripture says, *"They lifted up their voice to God with one accord...And when they had prayed, the place was shaken where they were assembled together; and they were all filled with the Holy Ghost, and they spoke the word of God with boldness"* (Acts 4:24, 31).

If you want God to start shaking the place where you pray, and if you want to receive Holy Ghost boldness to win others to Christ, then start praying louder. Don't be afraid of your own voice. Lift it up, cry unto God, and you will reach heaven with your prayers.

•

Remember: HEAVEN IS A NOISY PLACE WHERE THE SAINTS PRAY LOUDLY. START PRAYING LOUDLY NOW AND HEAVEN WILL COME INTO YOUR HEART!

161/HAVE YOU HARDENED?

"Harden not your hearts, as in the provocation, in the day of temptation in the wilderness: When your fathers tempted me, proved me, and saw my works forty years" (Hebrews 3:8-9).

Also read: Phil. 1:6-10; Col. 1:9-11; 3:16

Lee Iacocca, the chairman of the Chrysler Corporation has become a national hero. He saved Chrysler after it was so far gone that most financial experts had buried it. As soon as he was elected chairman he made sweeping changes in the leadership of almost every department of management and planning.

He quotes his friend Charlie Beachorn, who used to say, "Once a guy is over twenty-one, you'll never change his style or his habits. You may think you can, but his self-image is locked in. Nobody is ever humble enough to learn anything after he is grown up."

The question is, have you become hardened? You can become inflexible and set in your ways until neither God nor man can do anything with you.

How can you keep from getting hardened?

1. Stay aggressive with your faith! Don't bog down. Believe God for more, claim more of His promises, press forward into new realms of responsibility each day.

    I don't know what you are facing today, but don't stop at the border of impossibility. Press on! If you're facing a rough situation that takes faith, God is pleased to be your God!

2. Continue to repent! To keep your heart soft requires constant repenting. The Pharisee in the temple thanked God he was righteous and not as other men, even as the publican beat his chest and cried for God's mercy. Jesus said the sinner received God's blessing, but the Pharisee got the cold-shoulder (see Lk. 18:10). I don't care how good a person you are, you have enough suppressed sinful urges that it would be embarrassing for you to see your heart and and mind and deeds projected over your local T.V. station and transmitted into the homes of your neighbors.

So stay humble. You and I haven't arrived, we've barely begun our journey. Keep yourself open to new thoughts and ideas. Don't let your heart become so hardened you can't change.

•

Remember: HARDEN NOT YOUR HEART!

162/DO YOU KNOW ANY PRISONERS?

"I was in prison and ye came unto me" (Matthew 25:36).

Also read: Jas. 1:27; 1 Jn. 4:7

Connie answered the telephone. I could hear the operator instructing the party on the other end of the line to put her money in the pay phone.

The clinking sound of the coins seemed to go on forever.

Connie looked over at me and said,"It's Pearl" (a lady from Minnesota who has lived the past nineteen years in a rest home).

As they talked the desperate situation of Pearl's condition touched Connie so deeply that tears were streaming down her cheeks. You see, the only reason Pearl calls our home is that she hardly has anyone else who really cares. She earns a few cents from the little things she sews at the rest home. When she has saved enough money, she makes a call to Connie. This has continued for years. Each time Pearl calls, Connie and I are deeply touched.

Pearl is in prison—not a prison made with bars, but a pretty prison, a convalecent home, where she is waiting for death; and no one seems to care.

Would you take a moment today to visit one shut-in, wherever he might be? Nurses who work at rest homes say the greatest suffering of old people is that they are nearly forgotten. Hardly anyone cares enough to visit them, including their own loved ones and family.

Jesus said that every visit you make to a prisoner or shut-in will be recorded and reviewed on Judgment Day. He also said that visiting a "prisoner" is just like visiting Him.

Visit someone today; bring him a home-made meal, a book, record, or cassette. Hold that person's hand, hug him, share your love in a personal way.

By doing this you will show God that you really love Him, too.

•

Remember: VISIT A PRISONER TODAY!

163/HONOR THE ELDERLY!

"You shall give due honor and respect to the elderly, in the fear of God. I am Jehovah" (Leviticus 19:32, TLB).

Also read: Ps. 90:10-14; 2 Cor. 4:16-18; 5:1

My parents are 70 years old. My mother has Parkinson's disease and my father was just informed that only 10% of his heart is working.

We are praying for Mom and Dad's healing, but in the meantime they are seeing doctors who try to help them the best they can.

Growing old is tough. It's hard to see my parents aging. I remember Mom at harvest time, working 100 miles per hour, feeding a threshing crew of 25 men, and Dad, wet with sweat and strong as a lion, helping to haul the sacks of grain in a bundle wagon to the threshing machine. Now, Mom needs help to get out of her chair and Dad wheezes a bit when he talks.

I don't write these things to depress you, but to remind us that, should the Lord tarry, the last years of our lives may be a great struggle—similar or worse than what my parents are going through. In fact, you may be going through your own aging agony, or suffering from a physical struggle, as you read these words.

This is why God tells us to honor the elderly. We owe our heritage, as well as our lives, to them. Paul, the apostle, wrote Timothy, *"Let the elders that rule well be counted worthy of double honour, especially they who labour in the word and doctrine"* (1 Tim. 5:17).

Should the Lord tarry, you will get old soon—and people will walk by you as if you don't exist. It will hurt, more than you can even imagine. So, take time today to appreciate one of God's silver saints. Write a letter, call, and better yet, visit someone who needs and deserves the double honor.

•

Remember: GOD WILL REWARD YOU FOR HONORING THE ELDERLY.

164/WHAT IS YOUR EPITAPH?

"And he did that which was right in the sight of the Lord" (2 Chronicles 29:2).

Also read: Isa. 26:3; Rom. 8:2-13, 37; Gal. 5:13-25; Phil. 4:8

It is interesting to read the Old Testament books of Chronicles. In describing the kings of Israel the writer usually says, *"He did that which was right in the sight of the Lord"* or *"He did that which was evil in the sight of the Lord"* (2 Chron. 33:2).

It is usually black or white. The epitaph of the kings of Israel is that they did good or evil *"in the sight of the Lord."*

This is the deciding difference: you can live your life by the principles of people, or by the principles of God. You'll find there is a great chasm between the two—often as big as the Grand Canyon.

The difference between men and God is that *"The Lord seeth not as man seeth; for man looketh on the outward appearance, but the Lord looketh on the heart"* (1 Sam. 16:7). Your outward actions often disguise what is going on in the secret chambers of your heart. If you want to live a righteous life it must begin in your thoughts. As you think, you will be (see Prov. 23:7).

Thoughts are baby deeds. The only way you will ever have it said that you "did that which was right in the sight of the Lord" is if you *think* that which is right in the sight of the Lord.

So, guard the musings of your mind. When it wanders into a lustful, vengeful, jealous, unChristlike thought, rebuke it in the name of Jesus. *"Let this mind be in you, which was also in Christ Jesus"* (Phil. 2:5).

I have found that my greatest battles rage in my mind. That is when I must turn my heart and mind over to the Lordship of Jesus Christ and allow Him to drive the evil thoughts away.

•

Remember: IF YOU WANT YOUR EPITAPH TO SAY THAT YOU DID RIGHT, THEN YOU MUST THINK RIGHT, STARTING TODAY!

165/WHY GOD FEELS FAR AWAY!

"Beloved, think it not strange concerning the fiery trial which is to try you ... " (1 Peter 4:12).

Also read: Jud. 2:23; Job 7:17-21; 1 Pet. 4:12-19

There will be times in your Christian life when God will feel far away. He withdraws for a reason—that He might test your heart to see if you really love Him enough to keep His commandments. God withdrew from the Garden to allow Adam and Eve to be tempted. You know the results—they failed.

There is a life-changing verse of Scripture that tells us that this happened to King Hezekiah, *"GOD LEFT HIM TO TRY HIM, THAT HE MIGHT KNOW ALL THAT WAS IN HIS HEART"* (2 Chron. 32:31, emphasis mine).

Does God feel far away from you today? Then rejoice, because He may have withdrawn His annointing from your life to test you. If so, this is a very important time for you. The way you respond to this "dry time" will determine your future. If you feel God is far away, I encourage you to be extra cautious. Temptation is near and you need to walk carefully lest you fall.

Once, years ago, I was talking with a minister about preaching when he said, "Anyone can preach when the anointing is there. It takes a real preacher to preach when it's bone dry." I've never forgotten what he said. It's also true of your Christian life. Anyone can live for God when they feel the Lord very near. But when the Lord feels far away that's another matter.

When I was growing up on the farm I used to take the bridle off my horse and ride her, just to see if she would respond to my gentle nudges without the bit in her mouth. I was testing my mare's obedience.

Does God feel far away? If so, He's probably testing your obedience and willingness to "hang in there." When He finds you're faithful to Him, He'll soon be close to you again.

•

Remember: GOD MAY FEEL FAR AWAY, BUT HE'S NEAR ENOUGH TO SEE HOW YOU'LL RESPOND TO TEMPTATION.

MY FAVORITE PSALM

"This poor man cried, and the Lord heard him, and saved him out of all his troubles" (Psalm 34:6).

Also read: Psa. 86:5; Isa. 50:7; Rom. 10:9-10

If you were to ask me what Psalm is my favorite, I'd probably say, "The 34th!" David expresses the principles that I have found so helpful in my walk with God.

1. YOU MUST SPEAK POSITIVELY. *"I will bless the Lord at all times: his praise shall continually be in my mouth"* (verse 1). No matter how tough things are going, you need to live with an attitude of gratitude. You dare not mumble or complain.

2. YOU MUST NOT BE AFRAID. *"I sought the Lord, and he heard me, and delivered me from all my fears"* (verse 4). Fear is a force that will make a prisoner out of you. It will wrap its icy fingers around your mind and strangle your faith. You must live aggressively—and press, press, press forward. Cast out all fear or it will paralyze you.

3. GOD WILL DELIVER YOU FROM ALL YOUR PROBLEMS. *"This poor man cried, and the Lord heard him, and saved him out of all his troubles"* (verse 6). I believe God is going to save you from the problems plaguing you today. God does answer prayer; you will be saved.

4. ANGELS ARE GUARDING YOUR LIFE. *"The angel of the Lord encampeth round about them that fear him, and delivereth them"* (verse 7). You are not alone; angelic watchmen are guarding each step you take. The Bible says about angels, *"Are they not all ministering spirits, sent forth to minister for them who shall be heirs of salvation?"* (Heb. 1:14).

5. GOD WILL ANSWER YOUR PRAYER. *"The eyes of the Lord are upon the righteous, and his ears are open unto their cry...The righteous cry, and the Lord heareth, and delivereth them out of all their troubles"* (verses 15, 17). Thank God, He guarantees to deliver you and me from all our troubles. Cry out today and the Lord will help you!

•

Remember: MY FAVORITE PSALM (34) GUARANTEES THAT GOD WILL DELIVER ME WHEN I CRY OUT TO HIM!

167/FREELY GIVE!

"Freely you have received, freely give" (Matthew 10:8).

Also read: Mt. 16:18 & 19; Mk. 16:15-20; Lk. 4:18

Have you ever wondered why God wants us to give freely? Does He know something about charity that you and I have missed?

The setting in today's text is found in Matthew where Jesus commissioned His disciples to become missionaries. He said, *"Go, preach, saying the Kingdom of heaven is at hand. Heal the sick, cleanse the lepers, raise the dead, cast out devils: freely ye have received, freely give"* (Matt. 10:7-8).

So this concept of giving freely involves much more than money. Jesus said because you've freely received: healing, cleansing, resurrection from the dead and deliverence, you should freely pass on these helps to others.

Are you?

It is your God-given ministry to heal the sick and to cast out demons. Jesus said, *"The harvest truly is great, but the labourers are few: pray ye therefore the Lord of the harvest, that he would send forth labourers into his harvest...and heal the sick that are therein, and say unto them, The kingdom of God is come nigh unto you"* (Lk. 10:2, 9).

You should also know how to cast out demons. If this makes you gulp, it should, because this pushes you out of the comfortable Christian setting into the frontline battle zone.

But these miracle deeds are not as difficult as they sound. They are wrought by Christians who are walking in the Spirit and who take the word of God literally.

What we all need to do is to fast and pray. We need to get a greater hold of God's power so we can freely give of the things God has freely given to us.

•

Remember: FREELY GIVE, AS YOU HAVE BEEN GIVEN!

DON'T BARTER YOUR BIRTHRIGHT

"And Jacob said, 'Sell me this day thy birthright'" (Genesis 25:3).

Also read: Deut. 21:16; 2 Chr. 21:3; Heb. 12:16

Billions of dollars of goods are traded by barter each year in the U.S and Canada. Many say it is the fastest growing form of exchange. Say you are a building contractor and needed a computer; you could trade your skills as a builder for the machine you needed. You'd build the salesman a new building in exchange for a computer and no cash would change hands, only merchandise. This is what they call the barter system.

Esau bartered his birthright for a bucket of beans and angered God. In the Bible God says, *"Jacob have I loved but Esau have I hated"* (Romans 9:13). God hated Esau's passions that overruled his reason.

Have you allowed your flesh to overrule your spirit? How are you handling food, sex, sleep and drink? If you are "giving in" to the desires of your body you are bartering the eternal for the temporal. You are trading the long-range peace of God for fleeting pleasures.

Philippians 3:19 sounds a stern warning, describing the enemies of Christ saying, *"Whose end is destruction, whose God is their belly, and whose glory is their shame, who mind earthly things."* If you are living to eat instead of eating to live—then your god is your belly. I'm not against eating, but the high point of your day should not be bread or bed—it should be the time you meet with God.

Are you an Esau, bartering the blessing for beans in your belly? If so, then decide that you will begin this moment to make God the Lord of your appetites! I know you'll hurt—but when you really mean business your flesh will give up and say, "Oh well, I can't win so I'd better do what I'm told."

•

Remember: DON'T BARTER AWAY YOUR BLESSING!

169/GOD LIKES TO SAY "YES"!

"Delight thyself also in the Lord; and he shall give thee the desires of thine heart" (Psalm 37:4).

Also read: Psa. 68:19; Matt. 21:22; Mark 11:24; John 15:7

Do you realize that God likes to say "yes"? That's right! God likes to do good things for you.

One of the most difficult things I have to do is say "no" to one of my four children. I love them so much I want to say "yes" to every one of their requests.

However, there are many times when I must say "no" to keep them from hurting themselves. Recently, my son, Lowell Jr., wanted to stay home from school for a week. Even though it hurt him deeply, I could not allow him to break the rules.

If you believe God likes to say "yes," why don't you make a list of all the things you'd really like to receive from Him and then begin praying about them? Keep track of your prayer requests in a little notebook, and then record the date God answers them. You'll be surprised how many of your prayers will be answered in a 12-month period. Jesus says, *"If ye abide in me, and my words abide in you, ye shall ask what ye will, and it shall be done unto you"* (Jn. 15:7).

Today's text is a blank check to receive God's very best. The only stipulation is that you abide in Christ and make certain His words abide in you.

As you walk in the Spirit in the light of God's Word, you will pray according to the will of God. And when you know God wants you to have something—even as badly as you want it for yourself—it will fire up your prayers to the greatest degree of efficiency.

•

Remember: GOD LIKES TO SAY "YES!"

GOD'S GLORIOUS DREAM FOR YOU!

"And God came to Laban the Syrian in a dream by night, and said unto him" (Genesis 31:24).

Also read: Jn. 5:24; 6:27; 11:25 & 26

God has big plans for you, far beyond your wildest imagination. It is written, *"Eye hath not seen nor ear heard, neither have entered into the heart of man, the things which God hath prepared for them that love him"* (1 Cor. 2:9).

1. **God wants you to be like Himself—perfect!** Jesus said, *"Be ye therefore perfect, even as your Father which is in heaven is perfect"* (Matt. 5:48).

   Have you considered that you were created to become like God—perfect and powerful? The thought is so revolutionary it stuns the senses.

   Are you like God? I feel foolish asking the question, but I ask it only to lead you to the next, "How can you become like God?"

   The answer is through testing. This is why the Bible says, *"My brethren, count it all joy when you fall into various trials, knowing that the testing of your faith produces patience. But let patience have its perfect work, that you may be perfect and complete, lacking nothing"* (Ja. 1:2-4, NKJ).

   If you're serious about becoming like God, you must let trials and patience do their perfect work. Don't panic over the events taking place in your life. God is watching over every move.

2. **You were created to do the works of God.** *"Go, preach, saying, The kingdom of heaven is at hand. Heal the sick, cleanse the lepers, raise the dead, cast out devils: freely ye have received freely give"* (Matt. 10:7,8).

   You have been called by Jesus Christ to declare His gospel, to announce that the Kingdom of God has come. To demonstrate this fact you are to heal the sick, cleanse lepers, raise the dead and cast out devils; the works that only God can do."

   If you are going to do God's works, you'll need to know God's Word. Be filled with God's Spirit and fellowship with God's people.

3. **You were created to rule and reign with God!** The Bible says, *"To him that overcometh will I grant to sit with me in my throne, even as I also overcame, and am set down with my Father in his throne"* (Rev. 3:21).

What a glorious dream! To be like God, to do the works of God and to rule and reign with God. It's beyond anything we could imagine.

•

Remember: GOD WANTS TO PREPARE YOU FOR MUCH MORE THAN JUST ENTERING HEAVEN.

171/THREE KEYS TO SUCCESS!

"Ask, and it shall be given you; seek, and ye shall find; knock, and it shall be opened unto you" (Luke 11:9).

Also read: Luke 18:1; 1 Tim. 2:8

I like simple formulas. It is difficult for me to remember complicated things. So here are three easy things you need to succeed:

1. *You need to be positive!* D. L. Moody said that God never uses a negative person. How positive a person are you? Do people come to you regularly for encouragement? Do they call you to share your testimony? How many letters and phone calls do you share with your friends each week? Positivism begins when you believe down deep in your spirit that you will succeed in life because of your relationship with God. Remember, God is a success; if you're created in His image, it is God's will for you to succeed, too.
2. *You must be prayerful!* Jesus was the most successful man who ever lived. His success was a result of His prayer life. Prayer enables you to saturate your spirit with God's. This energizes your soul and gives you the will to win, to sacrifice and make whatever dedication that is necessary to succeed. This is why Jesus said, *"Pray always"* (Luke 21:36).
3. *You must be persistent.* You can't give up. Every successful athlete learns how to push past the pain barrier. When their bodies are crying out for rest, they push on—and on—and on. The person who gives in too easily never wins.

Do you want to succeed? To be positive in a negative world is difficult. To pray when you don't feel like it is work, and to be persistent in the face of pain is not easy. But think of it this way: you're going to suffer one way or the other. You'll either suffer as a success or suffer as a failure. Remember, failures suffer, too. They suffer from low self-esteem, regret, and fear of their accountability to God for a wasted life.

These thoughts spur me on! If I'm going to suffer I want to do it on my own terms—as a winner; don't you? Whatever it takes, I'll do, because the alternative (failure) is more painful.

●

Remember: TO SUCCEED BE POSITIVE, BE PRAYER—FUL, BE PERSISTENT.

IT AIN'T OVER TILL IT'S OVER

"Fight the good fight of faith, lay hold on eternal life" (1 Timothy 6:12).

Also read: Ps. 25:3-5; 27:14; Is. 40:31

Yogi Berra, the famous catcher and manager of the New York Yankees, noticed how many baseball games are won in the last of the 9th inning. His maxim became a byword in the sports world, "It ain't over till it's over."

This morning I called a friend who's wife has left him. He is crushed. Besides the emotional trauma of being rejected he is struggling with his future. My friend is the leader of a department in one of the largest Christian denominations in America. He is wondering how he can continue his leadership role if his home is hurting.

I simply told him. "It ain't over till it's over! Don't quit until you have swung the last strike of the 9th inning."

When our daughter Lisa abandoned the Christian faith and our family, I thought that I couldn't go any further with the ministry. I was going to quit and get a job doing something else.

But I couldn't find a release in my spirit to let go. God had used me to help others and, in spite of conditions, I felt He would continue to make me a blessing.

So I continued, and as a result several great things have happened.

1. The Lord used my leadership and ministry to help save Trinity Bible College from closing it's doors. Today the college has nearly doubled in number and we're training over 500 young men and women to be soulwinning pastors, evangelists, missionaries and Christian leaders. It is reported that as of this writing we are the fastest growing accredited Bible College in America.
2. During the past 3 years, through our crusades and rallies, over 25,000 people have given their lives to Jesus Christ. And this does not count those who have been won to Christ through our literature, records and cassettes and teaching tapes.
3. My ministry to hurting people has deepened. One lady came up to me recently and said, "Lowell, now you're hurting like the rest of us and you're a better preacher as a result of it." I believe she's right.

Are you going through a difficult time? Does it appear the odds are against you? Don't be discouraged beyond measure because God often works His greatest miracles when you and I have exhausted our options.

•

Remember: USE EVERY MOMENT OF A TRYING TIME IN YOUR LIFE FOR GOD'S GLORY!

173/WHY GOD DOESN'T PUNISH SINNERS PROMPTLY

"Thine own wickedness shall correct thee, and thy backslidings shall reprove thee: know therefore and see that it is an evil thing and bitter, that thou hast forsaken the Lord thy God" (Jeremiah 2:19).

Also read: John 3:3; Rom. 1:18-20; 3:23; 5:8, 12; 6:23

Asaph, the psalmist, was having a struggle with the question of why God doesn't punish sinners more promptly. In Psalm 73 he says, *"My steps had well nigh slipped. For I was envious at the foolish, when I saw the prosperity of the wicked...They are not in trouble as other men; neither are they plagued like other men...Behold, these are the ungodly, who prosper in the world; they increase in riches."*

Asaph is so depressed by the prosperity of the wicked he finally cries out, *"Verily I have cleansed my heart in vain, and washed my hands in innocency. For all day long have I been plagued, and chastened every morning... When I thought to know this, it was too painful for me"* (see verses 2-16).

He says, "Why do wicked people get blessed and I suffer?" But then Asaph makes a great discovery. He writes, *"Until I went into the sanctuary of God; then understood I their end. Surely thou didst set them in slippery places: thou castedst them down into destruction"* (verses 17 & 18).

Asaph realized, when he was in the house of God, that at death sinners will be judged suddenly for their sins—no matter how much they prospered in life. He realized that it would be a fearful thing to fall into the hands of a living God.

Jeremiah the prophet said that the *"wickedness of sinners will correct them"*—that sooner or later they will reap the evil seeds they have sown.

Then Asaph said, *"Thus my heart was grieved, and I was pricked in my reins* (conscience). *So foolish was I, and ignorant: I was as a beast before thee"* (verses 21 & 22).

"Thou shalt guide me with thy counsel, and afterward receive me to glory" (verse 24).

•

Remember: GOD DOESN'T NEED TO PUNISH SINNERS PROMPTLY BECAUSE THEIR OWN SINS WILL PUNISH THEM, AND THEY WILL FACE THE WRATH OF GOD AT DEATH.

174/IF YOU CAN'T FLEE - FLOW!

"...I have learned how to get along happily whether I have much or little. I know how to live on almost nothing or with everything. I have learned the secret of contentment in every situation" (Philippians 4:11 & 12).

Also read: Heb. 13:5

How contented are you? There is so much unrest and tension today that the vitamin companies are making a mint selling pills for "stress."

The next time you're in a tight spot remember this advice: "If you can't flee—flow!"

One of the greatest forces on this planet are the ocean tides. Scientists and engineers are working on ways to harness the mighty forces of these tides. Their plan is to create large underground caverns that will fill with water when the tides roll in; then, when the tides go out they will have millions of gallons of water to release through generators creating electricity. I think the idea is terrific.

Are there tides rolling in against you? Then learn how to harness these forces for the glory of God. Paul learned this secret when he was imprisoned. He could have become discouraged, but he used his time well and invested his hours writing the Epistles that bless us today.

If you are in such a condition that you cannot fight or flee—then flow. Enter into the realm of the Holy Spirit and you'll plug into the Mighty River of God that has been flowing since the day of Pentecost.

Today is your chance to rise on the tide that is flowing against you. Lift up your voice and praise God. Don't fight the forces that overwhelm you. Don't flee what you cannot—but begin flowing with the strength of the Lord.

●

Remember: IF YOU CAN'T FIGHT OR FLEE—FLOW IN THE POWER OF HIS HOLY SPIRIT.

175/GOD HAS OTHER SHEEP

"And other sheep I have, which are not of this fold: them also must I bring, and they shall hear my voice; and there shall be one fold, and one shepherd" (John 10:16).

Also read: Psa. 133:1; Acts 2:41-47; Rom. 12:4-5

Denominational pride is one of the worst enemies of the Christian church. If you belong to a church of respectable denomination, it's good, but don't make it your god.

For 27 years I have evangelized among many denominations and found there are wonderful people of God in every church.

I would not go so far as to say that all the churches are right in all points of their doctrines, but people who love God dearly seem to grow in God in spite of the errors—much in the same way families continue to grow in spite of an alcoholic father or uncle.

The Bible says, *"And the disciples were called Christians first in Antioch"* (Acts 11:26). This is what you and I should call ourselves, "Christians first." Then if someone presses us for details, we'll give the name of the church or organization we belong to.

Jesus said, *"I have other sheep who are not of this fold. I must go bring them in too. Then in the end there will be one fold and one shepherd"* (see John 10:16).

Now, the answer is not to dismantle all the denominations and build one super-church, but we should de-emphasize our differences and seek our oneness in Christ. Jesus said, *"By this shall all men know that ye are my disciples, if ye have love one to another"* (John 13:35).

Today, make a special effort to show you are truly one of the Lord's disciples—by showing love to one of His sheep who may not be of your fold.

•

Remember: GOD HAS MANY SHEEP OF DIFFERENT BACKGROUNDS, EXPERIENCES, AND UNDERSTANDINGS, BUT THEY ARE ALL HIS—YOU AND I SHOULD LOVE THEM.

176/THE POWER OF YOUR THOUGHTS

"Solomon, my son, know the God of your father, and serve him with a perfect heart and with a willing mind: for the Lord searches all hearts, and understands all the imaginations of the thoughts" (1 Chronicles 28:9).

Also read: Psa. 10:4; 139:23; Isa. 55:7-9; Gal 6:3

What is the true essence of anything? Don't let the next question puzzle you, but consider it carefully: Before this devotional book was created, what was it?

It was a thought in my mind.

Thoughts are the true essence of reality. In fact, thought is part of the true essence of God. The Bible says, *"In the beginning was the Word (the idea, the energy of thought), and the Word was with God, and the Word was God"* (John 1:1).

Thoughts are the true essence of what you are. Your life is an expression of your thoughts. The reason you work where you work, live where you live, worship where you worship and say what you say is a result of what you think.

This is why you must always be conscious of the power of your thoughts. Whatever you think is what you're going to be. If you sow thoughts of righteousness you will be like God. If you sow evil thoughts you will become like Satan.

So the real battlefield of your destiny is in your mind. This is why Paul wrote the Philippians, *"Finally, brethren, whatsoever things are TRUE, whatsoever things are HONEST, whatsoever things are JUST, whatsoever things are PURE, whatsoever things are LOVELY, whatsoever things are of GOOD REPORT: if there be any virtue, and if there be any praise, THINK on these things"* (Phil. 4:8, emphasis mine).

You must guard your thoughts today. Don't allow secular songs, sensual TV shows, trashy romance novels, filthy jokes, or unclean things to corrupt your mind—for if you sow an evil thought you will reap a dirty deed (see Gal. 6:7). Remember, thoughts are baby deeds.

In order to live right—think right!

•

Remember: THERE IS POWER IN YOUR THOUGHTS!

177/YOU NEED A DREAM!

"For a dream cometh through the multitude of business" (Ecclesiastes 5:3).

Also read: Gal. 5:16

Now that God has given you this New Year, what do you hope to achieve with it? I found these life changing lines recently, "It is not easy to find balance, for if one does not have wild dreams of achievement, there is no spur, even to get the dishes washed. One must think like a hero to behave like merely a decent human being" (from the *Journal of Solitude* by May Sarton).

Have you ever noticed how things begin to slide when your dreams die? When you're depressed you don't feel like cleaning your room or even combing your hair. You may feel animosity towards others when you're the victim rather than the victor.

> Robert Browning said in his poem, *Andrea Del Sarto,* "A man's reach should exceed his grasp, or what's a heaven for?" We should always be striving to become just a little more than we already are. This does not mean we should not be happy with what we are right now, but there's always room for improvement!

Where do you find a realistic dream?—By walking in the Spirit. The Bible says, " ... *Eye hath not seen, nor ear heard, neither have entered into the heart of man, the things which God hath prepared for them that love him. BUT GOD HATH REVEALED THEM UNTO US BY HIS SPIRIT"* (1 Cor. 2:9-10, emphasis mine).

God has prepared a lot of wonderful things for you this year. But you will never discover what they are unless you decide to "walk in the Spirit."

I commend you for taking time to read this devotional. Now, as you pray, enter into the Spirit. Pray until you touch God. Then as God's Spirit moves within your spirit, dreams of great achievement will come forth. This will help you put up with the "nicky-nacky" things that come with daily living. A true dream will put the steam in your life.

•

Remember: YOU NEED A DREAM TO STAY MOTIVATED; WALK IN THE SPIRIT TODAY. AS YOU DO, GOD'S PLANS FOR YOUR LIFE WILL BEGIN TO UNFOLD.

178/DRY UP THE SWAMP

"Neither give place to the devil" (Ephesians 4:27).

Also read: Matt. 7:15-17, 20-23; Luke 21:34; Rom. 13:11-14

Acommunity in Connecticut recently banned the sale of alcoholic beverages during the early evening hours after a notable citizen was killed by a drunken driver. They'll no longer allow bars to serve liquor during the "Happy Hour" because of the the extra intoxicated drivers it places on the highway.

The mayor said, "Liquor is like malaria. You can deal with it mosquito by mosquito or dry up the swamp." His town decided to dry up the swamp.

This decision needs to be made in every city in America today. When drunken drivers kill over 25,000 each year and maim 800,000, it's time to dry up the swamp.

During the Vietnam war, when America was losing 5,000 men each year, (because of the fighting), there were demonstrations on college campuses and in the streets and before the White House in Washington to end the war to save the lives (and rightly so). However, we destroy 25,000 each year because of drunken drivers and hardly anyone says anything—because they want to drink!

Let's dry up the swamp! And while we're drying up the abusive sale of alcoholic beverages (why must we sell liquor at all hours of the day? Is it necessary to sell liquor at food stores next to the milk counter?) Let's also dry up:

*The pornographic swamps
*The prostitution swamps
*The gambling swamps
*The homosexual bath-house
*The drug dealer swamps
*The X-rated movie swamps

And also any other life-degrading, soul-damaging, body-killing swamps.

Paul the apostle said, *"Neither give place to the devil."* It could also be translated, "Don't give the devil a chance!"

•

Remember: DRY UP THE SWAMPS!!

179/BE CAREFUL NOT TO POINT!

"Judge not, that ye be not judged" (Matthew 7:1).

Also read: Rom. 6:11-12; Heb. 11:25-27; 1 John 2:15-17

Once a little girl walked up to her older brother and hit him on the head with a hammer. When he reacted by pulling her hair, the little girl ran crying to her mother. Pointing an accusing finger at her brother, she complained, "He hurt me! It's all HIS fault!" The mother, who had witnessed the scene, wisely said, "Never point your finger at someone else. When you do, THREE fingers on your hand are pointing back at YOU. Look at your hand." The daughter, looking at the fingers pointing at herself, guiltily stopped accusing her brother.

While it's easy to blame others for our problems and unhappiness, we seldom realize that by blaming others we are also accusing ourselves. It is vital to dry up the swamps of degeneration listed in yesterday's devotional, but it is also important to dry up the swamps of evil in our personal lives. Rather than dealing with each temptation—one problem at a time—let's work on drying up the source:
1. Dry up the materialism, lust and violence that comes into your life by refusing to watch worldly TV programs.
2. Dry up the unclean thoughts that come into your mind by refusing to listen to secular music or reading trashy novels.
3. Dry up the unclean influence in your life by refusing to be close friends with wicked people. (We would try to win them, but not join them; this requires a delicate balance.)

Don't be so quick to point an accusing finger at others. Don't forget, there are THREE fingers pointing back at you!

•

Remember: IT'S NOT "POLITE" TO POINT!

180/HOW IS YOUR INVESTMENT PORTFOLIO?

"But lay up for yourselves treasures in heaven, where neither moth nor rust doth corrupt and where thieves do not break through nor steal" (Matthew 6:20).

Also read: Matt. 19:21; Luke 12:33; I Tim. 6:19

Most wealthy men have a portfolio of investments; they divide their holdings into blue chip stocks, real estate, and high interest treasury notes and bonds. You and I may not have much going in this category (I know I don't), but we can have heavenly portfolio of investments that will return eternal dividends. Jesus said you'll get a 100%, 60%, or 30% return on your investment in God's work. *"But he that received seed into the good ground is he that heareth the word, and understandeth it; which also beareth fruit, and bringeth forth, some an hundredfold, some sixty, some thirty"* (Matt. 13:23). Do you view your giving as an investment? If so there are several things that wise investors do.

First, they search for proven, up and coming companies. Don't ever "dump" your tithes and offerings—look for the best investment for your giving. Your careful investment will be fruitful. (How I thank God for the many partners like you who have invested in this soul-winning work! Because of your dedication we are reaching millions with the Gospel.)

Second, a wise investor watches his return. He wants to know how much he is receiving on his investment. (This is the reason we give reports of the numbers won to Christ in our crusades. It is not to brag but to report to the wise investors who are backing this effort.)

If you are investing in God's work, wherever it may be, ask "How many souls were saved?" Remember, you're the investor, and you have a right to know.

Finally, a wise investor in God's work looks for a blessing because of his giving. You don't give to get, but you're wise enough to know that when you give you will receive (See Luke 6:38).

If you follow these principles, you can be sure *you* are a wise investor of your giving.

•

Remember: A WISE INVESTOR BUILDS A STRONG PORTFOLIO OF INVESTMENTS. BE SURE TO ADD TO YOURS TODAY!

181/JESUS—A FULL-TIME INTERCESSOR

"But this man (Jesus), because he continueth ever, hath an unchangeable priesthood, Wherefore he is able also to save them to the uttermost that come unto God by him, seeing he ever liveth to make intercession for them" (Hebrews 7:24 & 25).

Also read: Isa. 53:12; 1 Tim. 2:1-6

My attitude towards prayer changed greatly the day I realized that prayer has been our Savior's full-time ministry for nearly 2,000 years.

When Jesus returned to heaven He became our full-time priest and intercessor. Because He lives forever He has an unchangeable priesthood. The prayers of Jesus keep us protected from Satan and energized by the Holy Spirit.

This should encourage you to also become an intercessor. Your prayers cannot save the lost, but your petitions will give God reasons to work in extra special ways on their behalf.

Your prayers also strengthen your spiritual muscles so that you become more than you are.

Our spirits are willing but our flesh is weak (see Matt. 26:41). One sure way to strengthen your flesh is to allow the Holy Spirit to draw you into the role of an intercessor. As you battle hell's forces, as you lay hold of God, as you plead, beg, and cry out to Him, you are stretching yourself. Prayer helps you to grow in God.

So don't get discouraged about the problems that are thrown your way. God is allowing your difficult situation to drive you to your knees so you will arise greater than you are. Don't forget—God wants to make you just like Jesus, and Jesus is an intercessor, praying now, this very moment, on your behalf in heaven.

•

Remember: TO BECOME LIKE JESUS YOU NEED TO BE AN INTERCESSOR. PRAYER IS OUR SAVIOR'S FULL-TIME MINISTRY.

182/YOUR PROBLEM MAY BE PART OF GOD'S PLAN

"O, the depth of the riches both of the wisdom and knowledge of God! How unsearchable are his judgments, and his ways past finding out!" (Romans 11:33).

Also read: Rom. 12:12; Deut. 4:30, 31; Jn. 16:33

If you have a problem that is perlexing you, have you ever stopped to realize that your problem may be part of God's plan?

One of the greatest crises the Jews faced was when they came out of Egypt and were trapped between the mountain and the Red Sea. Pharoah had changed his mind about letting them leave and sent 600 of his best chariots and soldiers to capture them and kill their leaders.

The Bible says, *"As the Egyptian army approached, the people of Israel saw them far in the distance, speeding after them, and they were terribly frightened, and cried out to the Lord to help them"* (Ex. 14:10, TLB).

Their lives were on the line. Within minutes Pharoah's chariots would be cutting them to pieces. Their blood would stain the desert sands, and it would be all over.

How did they get into such a fix? God had planned it! The Bible says, God told Moses, *"Pharoah will think those Israelites are trapped now, between the desert and the sea! And once again I will harden Pharoah's heart and he will chase after you. I have planned this to gain great honor, power, and glory over Pharoah, and all his armies, and the Egyptians shall know that I am the Lord."*

So they camped where they were told.

So you can see from God's Word, HE PLANNED THE PROBLEM!

Have you done your best to obey God's word and do His will? If so, then you can be assured that what has happened to you is part of God's plan—even your problems! God wants to receive the glory from delivering you from an impossible situation. He wants to show his greatness on YOUR behalf.

•

Remember: RECOGNIZE YOUR PROBLEMS MAY BE PART OF GOD'S PLAN.

183/HOW TO KEEP FROM FEELING OLD!

"But ye shall receive power, after that the Holy Ghost is come upon you" (Acts 1:8).

Also read: Is. 40:29; Mic. 3:8; Matt. 9:8

I've just turned 46 years and I feel as young as I did when I was 20! But this youthful feeling of energy depends upon resources outside of my body.

When people ask me where I find my energy I say there are three sources:

First, I depend on the *inspiration of the Scriptures.* When I start reading all that God has planned for His people, I get excited. Or when I consider the horrible fate of the wicked—to be cast into hell forever—this motivates me to do everything I can to help them.

As you read the Bible, suddenly you realize the realities of angels, devils, heavenly witnesses, Jesus, the throne of God, etc. Keep yourself inspired; read the Bible until you come across something that makes your heart leap—soon you'll feel it in your feet!

Second, I depend on *adrenalin.* Your body is made to react to stress, danger, and excitement. Your glands will excrete a shot of adrenalin into your blood system that works like pumping high-test Ethyl alcohol into your gas tank. ZOOOOOM! And away you go!

You must force yourself to see the great challenge of winning others to Christ. Take a new step of faith every day. Force yourself to stay in step with the leading of the Holy Spirit. This will keep your adrenalin pumping.

Third, I depend on the *anointing of the Holy Spirit.* God has promised, *"They that wait upon the Lord shall renew their strength; they shall mount up with wings as eagles; they shall run, and not be weary; and they shall walk, and not faint"* (Isaiah 40:31).

If you want to keep from feeling old, get into God's Word until your spirit "tingles." Commit yourself by faith to a project that gets your adrenalin moving. Then pray until the anointing of the Holy Spirit comes upon you. When these three are working for you, you'll feel like leaping over a wall!

•

Remember: FEELING OLD IS UNNECESSARY IF YOU PROGRAM YOUR BODY RIGHT.

184/BE ENTHUSIASTIC!

"It is good to be zealously affected always in a good thing" (Galatians 4:18).

Also read: Psa. 47:1, 7; 107:8; 147:1; 1 Pet. 2:9

God's Word says it's right to get excited about good things. But I've met so many people who have put their emotions on ice and live dull, drab lives. They never shout, laugh or cry, because they take pride in themselves that they are "steady."

So is a corpse!

Have you lost contact with your truest feelings? Are you a walking "Mt. Rushmore"—solid, but seldom experiencing the full joy of living?

Sometime ago I attended a Gospel music concert in Nashville, Tennessee, and sat next to a man who was as stoic as a stump. God was blessing the songs of the singers and musicians on stage until I was crying, laughing, and at times, standing and praising God with the rest of the crowd.

But not the stranger next to me. He sat alone—silent, with a bemused detachment from the rest of us who were "carrying on."

But I pitied the man. He had blocked off the moving of God's Spirit in his life. He had quenched the Holy Ghost. He may have been a Christian, but he was emotionally dead.

Don't commit emotional suicide. Allow God's Spirit to thrill and chill you. Open up and laugh and cry, however the Spirit moves you. God didn't give you emotions for only worldly and sensual pleasure—He gave them to you so He could bless you and enjoy your fellowship.

Look at it from God's point of view. If you were God, would you want to hang around a dead stick?

Have a great time living life to it's fullest.

•

Remember: IT'S A GOOD THING TO GET EXCITED ABOUT GOD!

185/LEARN TO USE YOUR IMAGINATION!

"Now nothing will be restrained from them, which they have imagined to do" (Genesis 11:6).

Also read: Jere. 23:17

Today's text is a powerful statement. God says if you will use your imagination, what you can do is unlimited. The Living Bible says *Nothing will be UNATTAINABLE!*

God spoke this verse when the people of the early world joined together to build the Tower of Babel. *"And the whole earth was of one language, and of one speech...And they said...let us build us a city and a tower, whose top may reach unto heaven; and let us make us a name, lest we be scattered abroad upon the face of the whole earth"* (Gen. 11: 1,4).

However their desire to build a super-city and a high tower was in direct rebellion to God's command to *"Be fruitful, and multiply, and replenish the earth"* (Gen. 9:1).

"But when God came down to see the city and the tower mankind was making, he said, 'Look! If they are able to accomplish all this when they have just begun to exploit their linguistic and political unity, just think of what they will do later! Nothing will be unattainable for them!" (Gen 11:5-6, TLB).

God thwarted their plans for a metro-center and tower by giving them different languages. *"Come, let us go down and give them different languages, so that they won't understand each others words!"* So, in that way, God scattered them all over the earth; and that ended the building of the city. That is why the city was called Babel, (meaning "confusion"), *"because it was there that Jehovah confused them by giving them many languages, thus widely scattering them across the face of the earth."* (Gen.11:7-9, TLB).

There is a life-changing principle in this story. If you will stay closely related to others, communicate carefully, and use your imagination, what you can accomplish for God with your life is unlimited.

•

Remember: YOUR IMAGINATION IS THE CREATIVE POWER OF GOD!

186/HOW YOU CAN BE GLAD ON YOUR SAD DAYS!

". . . and rejoice in hope of the glory of God" (Romans 5:2).

Also read: Rom. 8:26; Phil. 4:4

My mother, GG, is struggling with Parkinson's disease. She was the strong force directing the office staff of the Lundstrom Ministry for many years, and it hurts me to see her suffering. Please pray for her.

I visited with a neighbor yesterday who is 72 and so crippled with arthritis that he can barely move—yet he forces himself to do his chores. He says if he stops moving his hands and feet, they will lock and he'll be bedridden. His goal is to farm one more year before he dies.

Some days are so sad and the news is so bad, the question is—how can one be glad in such a sorrowful world?

The answer is to look beyond time into eternity. Someday soon my mother will be young and strong again. This is also true of my farmer-neighbor. Thank God this earth is not all there is to life—or who could bear the pain.

If the pain of living has reached an unbearable level, you can diffuse your sorrow by looking ahead. See the deliverance awaiting you. Imagine the joy of seeing Jesus and your loved ones once again. Visualize yourself walking and talking and laughing without pain ever again.

How do you get a fresh vision of the future? Through the Holy Spirit of God. The Bible says, *"Eye hath not seen, nor ear heard, neither have entered into the heart of man, the things which God hath prepared for them that love him.*

". . . But God hath revealed unto us by his Spirit: for the Spirit (revealeth) *all things, yea the deep things of God"* (1 Cor. 2:9-10).

•

Remember: YOU CAN BE GLAD EVEN ON YOUR SAD DAYS IF YOU'LL LOOK FAR ENOUGH AHEAD TO THE HOLY SPIRIT.

187/WHAT YOU SHOULDN'T WEAR TODAY

"I will clothe you with change of raiment" (Zechariah 3:4).

Also read: Rom. 6:11, 12; 12:2; 1 Cor. 10:13; Heb. 11:25-27

The question you face each morning is, "What will I wear today?" But there is a spiritual equivalent to this question that is answered in the book of Colossians, chapter three.

Paul begins by saying, *"If (you) then be risen with Christ, seek those things which are above, where Christ sitteth on the right hand of God. Set your affection on things above, not on things on the earth"* (Col. 3:1, 2).

Then Paul tells you what *not* to wear. He tells us to mortify (or put to death) our members which are on earth, such as:

1. Fornication (Sexual activity before or outside of marriage.)
2. Uncleanness (Impure thoughts, stories or actions.)
3. Inordinate affection (Feelings toward others that are not proper or natural, such as a desire to commit adultery or engage in homsexual behavior.)
4. Evil concupiscence (Inflamed sexual desire; an unnaturally strong desire to have sexual fulfillment. Married couples have to guard against this, because while sex in marriage is natural, concupiscence can cause problems.)
5. Covetousness (Idolatry; the desire to want for yourself something that belongs to someone else.)

Then Paul says in verse 8, *"Put off all these."* In other words, don't "wear" these actions:

*Anger (the mean, resentful type)
*Wrath (the explosive, hair-trigger type)
*Blasphemy (cursing)
*Filthy communications (dirty words or jokes)
*Lies (deceiving people), *"Seeing you have put off the old man with his deeds"* (see verse 9).

As you look in your mirror today, what do you see?

•

Remember: IF YOU'RE "WEARING" ANYTHING LISTED ABOVE, YOU STILL HAVE TIME TO "CHANGE YOUR CLOTHES."

188/WHAT YOU SHOULD WEAR TODAY

"I counsel thee to buy of me...white raiment, that thou mayest be clothed" (Revelation 3:18).

Also read: Matt. 6:25-34; Isa. 61:10; Rev. 3:4-5

Many people today are going through the process of having their "colors" analyzed. This means an expert will study your hair color and skin tone and help you decide which colors of clothing you should wear to help you look your best. People today have a horror of wearing the wrong thing.

Yesterday we read about what Paul tells NOT to wear. Today we're going to look at what he tells us we SHOULD wear (see Col. 3:10-14): *"And (you) have put on the new man, which is renewed in knowledge.*

Put on, therefore, as the elect of God, holy and beloved:
1. *Bowels of mercies* (a forgiving and compassionate nature)
2. *Kindness* (being courteous and thoughtful of others)
3. *Humbleness of mind* (don't think too highly of yourself)
4. *Meekness* (a gentle, self-effacing personality)
5. *Longsuffering* (patience)
6. *Forebearing one another* (putting up with the foibles and quirks of others)
7. *Forgiving one another* (offering forgiveness to those who offend you)

And above all these things—
8. *Put on charity"* (strive to love one another)

When you have put on the above "clothing," you will be at peace in your heart and have the confidence you need to see you through your day. Just as a well-dressed, well-groomed person can relax and forget about his appearance and move forward with confidence to tackle the day's business, so will YOU be able to relax and forget about your own problems and concentrate on ministering to others.

•

Remember: THANKS TO PAUL, YOU KNOW WHAT TO WEAR TODAY!

189/SAYS VS. DOES

"Not everyone who SAYS to me, 'Lord, Lord,' will enter the kingdom of heaven, but only he who DOES the will of my Father who is in heaven" (Matthew 7:21, NIV, emphasis mine).

Also read: Matt. 12:50; Rom. 2:13; James 1:22

Profession of a spiritual life does not automatically mean possession of it. Just because a person can talk the talk does not necessarily mean he can walk the walk.

God is looking for those who will obey His Word, being doers rather than just talkers. It's easy for many people to read the Bible and talk about what God wants them to do, but actually *doing* it is a different story!

There is a good test in Scripture to help you determine whether or not a person has these two dimensions of his spiritual life working together. Matthew 7:15-16 instructs us to, *"Watch out for false prophets. They come to you in sheep's clothing, but inwardly they are ferocious wolves. By their fruit you will recognize them"* (NIV). Find out what a person's reputation is before embarking in relationships.

The wisdom of Proverbs 11:14 states, *"In the multitude of counselors there is wisdom"* (NIV).

I like to have personal recommendations from people I know and trust before I launch out on a project or work with new people.

We all have blind spots in our evaluations; the protection we can gain from trusted godly friends is a blessing from God.

Associate with those who not only TALK about the Christian life but who are actively LIVING it.

You will be known by those with whom you associate.

•

Remember: OUR WALK SHOULD MATCH OUR TALK.

190/KICK OUT THE GRUMPY GOAT!

"(These curses shall come upon you) because thou servest not the Lord thy God with joyfulness, and with gladness of heart, for the abundance of all things" (Deuteronomy 28:47).

Also read: 1 Pet. 1:7; Lk. 8:15; 1 Tim. 6:11

God doesn't like grumps. In fact today's text tells us He will curse those who refuse to serve Him joyfully.

My wife, Connie, and I have always encouraged our children to have a positive mental attitude. Whenever we're traveling down the road in our bus, and one of the children becomes out of sorts, we say, "Let's stop the bus and kick out the Grumpy Goat!"

Sometimes, to illustrate it graphically, we have stopped the bus until the child decided to change his or her attitude. When the child agrees we've kicked the imaginary bad attitude out the door, it's usually accompanied by laughter and a great release of tension.

Abraham Lincoln said that, "People are about as happy as they want to be." He recognized that a joyful disposition is the result of a personal decision. Psalm 100 tells us to *"Serve the Lord with gladness: come before his presence with singing. Enter into his gates with thanksgiving and into his courts with praise: be thankful unto him and bless his name. For the Lord is good; his mercy is everlasting; and his truth endureth to all generations"* (verses 2, 4, & 5).

If you're going through a difficult time, you might say, "How can I be joyful when I'm going through such a trial?"

I love the way The Living Bible renders James 1:2 & 3. It says, *"Dear brothers, is your life full of difficulties and temptations? Then be happy, for when the way is rough, your patience has a chance to grow. So let it grow, and don't try to squirm out of your problems. For when your patience is finally in full bloom, then you will be ready for anything, strong in character, full and complete."*

Difficulties develop patience, and patience develops godliness. So rejoice when things go wrong, knowing that God will work your problems for his praise.

•

Remember: KICK OUT THE GRUMPY GOAT. DECIDE TODAY TO BECOME AN "UP" PERSON IN A DOWN WORLD!

191/WORK FOR THE LORD!

"And whatsoever you do, do it heartily, as to the Lord, and not unto men" (Colossians 3:23).

Also read: Mark 19:43-45; John 13:14, 15; Rom. 15:5-7

Do you love your job? If work is a drudgery to you, it is probably because you're working for the wrong boss. Maybe you've made the mistake of trying to please the company instead of trying to please Christ.

God's Word says you should do your work heartily, or with joyful effort, as unto the Lord and not unto men. This is the only way you can love a boring job.

Your work may consist of:

1. *Manual Labor.* As you move about your tasks, begin to thank God for your body that responds to your commands. Think about the many sick who are lying in hospital beds helpless and without strength, who cannot move, lift, clean or do any of the things your job consists of. Thank God for your strong body and make each move a sacrifice of praise.

2. *Meeting the Public.* This is especially difficult because you can get burned out with people until you become glazed and insensitive. It's easy to become mechanical and thoughtless in your daily work.

If you're meeting the public, serve each person as you would serve the Lord himself. Think of God, who sends loving rain upon the just and the unjust. When people get nasty or difficult to deal with, send a shower of blessing upon them. In so doing, you will be like your loving Father in heaven.

3. *Managing Others.* If you're not careful, you'll only see problems, problems, problems. You need to concentrate on the promises of God to give you wisdom. One manager said, "Business is a combination of sport and warfare." He found the challenge of competition exciting.

As you manage, think of God in heaven, managing this whole universe. If He can keep things going, so can you, because, *"Greater is he that is in you than he that is in the world"* (1 John 4:4).

•

Remember: WORK AS UNTO THE LORD—HE'LL HELP YOU TO LOVE YOUR JOB.

192/JESUS WANTS TO HEAL YOU

"And behold, there came a leper and worshipped him, saying, Lord, if thou wilt, thou canst make me clean" (Matthew 8:2).

Also read: Luke 7:1-10

If you want to be healed it is critically important, it is *imperative* that you believe it is God's will to heal you.

The leper asked the question you may be asking, "Lord if it is your will, you can heal me." Jesus responded by saying, *"I WILL, be thou clean"* (Matt. 8:3 emphasis mine). When Jesus reached forth His hand and touched him, while saying these words, *"Immediately his leprosy was cleansed"* (Matt. 8:3).

Do you believe that if Jesus came into your room, right now, and if you asked Him to heal you—that He'd say, "No, I'm sorry—maybe some other day?"

Never.

Jesus would heal you immediately. He never turned away one person that needed healing. Peter declared that, *"God anointed Jesus of Nazareth with the Holy Ghost and with power; who went about doing good, and HEALING ALL that were oppressed of the devil; for God was with him"* (Acts 10:38 emphasis mine).

So settle in your heart and mind—Jesus wants to heal you.

Here are two more facts that will inspire your faith. When you pray the Lord's prayer, *"Thy will be done in earth as it is in heaven"* (Matt. 6:10), you are confessing that Jesus wants to heal you now, here upon the earth, just as you will be healed in heaven.

Also, because you can honestly believe that Jesus will **heal** you in heaven, why don't you just move up the date of your deliverance? Believe now, this very moment, that Jesus will heal you.

•

Remember: JESUS WANTS TO HEAL YOU NOW!

193/YOUR MISTAKE CAN BECOME A MASTERPIECE

"And we know that all things work together for good to them that love God, to them who are the called according to his purpose" (Romans 8:28).

Also read: 1 John 1:9; 2 Cor. 5:17; Eph. 1:6, 7

One day in the late afternoon, some fishermen in the highlands of Scotland came into a small Scottish inn for a cup of tea. They were laughing and talking and having a good time. One fellow was describing the "one that got away" to his friends and threw out his hands in the typical fisherman's gesture. At that very moment the waitress was setting down his cup of tea. The collision left a huge tea stain running down on the whitewashed wall. The fisherman apologized profusely.

Another gentleman seated nearby said, "Never mind," and rising from his chair he took a crayon from his pocket and began to sketch around the ugly brown stain. Slowly there emerged the head of a magnificent royal stag with antlers spread. This talented stranger was Landseer, England's foremost painter of animals.

If an artist can do that with an ugly brown stain, imagine what God can do with your sins and mistakes if you will give them to Him.

Recently a young woman I know, who was raised in a Christian home but went astray, felt regret for her wayward life. A mature Christian woman said, "I believe her life of sin will become the basis of her new relationship with God." She's right. Jesus said of the sinful woman who knelt at His feet, bathing them with tears of repentance, *"Her sins, which are many, are forgiven; for she loved much; but to whom little is forgiven, the same loveth little"* (Luke 7:47).

Jesus said in effect, "If you are forgiven much, you will love much." So don't worry about the stains of your life. Just give your love and appreciation to God, the great Artist who is sketching your mistakes into a masterpiece today.

•

Remember: ALL THINGS WORK TOGETHER FOR GOOD—EVEN YOUR BLUNDERS!

194/THE PILLARS OF PROSPERITY!

"Therefore whosoever heareth these sayings of mine, and doeth them, I will liken him unto a wise man, which built his house upon a rock" (Matthew 7:24).

Also read: Deut. 31:6; Ps. 27:1, 14

Imagine how much you and I would learn if we could spend a few minutes with Moses and David, the two most powerful leaders in the Old Testament. What makes the following words so significant is that they were spoken by these two men near the end of their illustrious lives. They are worth framing and reading aloud each day.

Moses said to Joshua, *"Be strong and of a good courage; fear not, nor be afraid...for the Lord your God, he is the one who is going to be with you: He will never fail you, nor forsake you"* (Deut. 31:6, paraphrased).

Then David said to Solomon, *"Be strong and show yourself a man: and keep the charge of the Lord your God, to walk in his ways, to keep his statues, and his commandments and his judgments, and his testimonies, as it is written in the law of Moses, that you may prosper in all you do, wherever you go"* (1 Kings 2:2 & 3, paraphrased).

It's amazing how similar these two last messages are. Each begins with saying *"Be strong"*, because both Moses and David knew how easy it is to be weak under the pressures of life. BE STRONG! is the first pillar of prosperity.

Then Moses says *"Be of a good courage"*, and David says, *"Show yourself a man."* In other words, BE COURAGEOUS! This is the second pillar of prosperity.

Moses urges the people to keep God's covenant. And David says, *"If you'll keep God's commandments, you'll prosper in everything you do no matter where you go."* KEEP GOD'S COMMANDMENTS! This is the third pillar of prosperity.

Your success is dependent on these three pillars. Is there an area where you have given into the enemy? *BE STRONG!* Has the spirit of fear kept you from taking an aggressive step forward in that project or that relationship? *BE COURAGEOUS!* Have you been compromising these principles in an attempt to find happiness or success. *KEEP GOD'S COMMANDMENTS!*

•

Remember: THESE THREE PILLARS OF PROSPERITY ARE THE FOUNDATION OF LIFE!

195/YOU MUST SHARE CHRIST

"Woe is unto me, if I preach not the gospel" (1 Corinthians 9:16).

Also read: Luke 24:44-48

You don't have any choice in your decision to witness to your friends. Jesus Christ has appointed you as His personal representative in your community. You are called to share the gospel with your works and your words (preferably in that order).

Jesus says, *"Ye are the light of the world. A city that is set on a hill cannot be hid. Neither do men light a candle, and put it under a bushel, but on a candlestick; and it giveth light unto all that are in the house. Let your light so shine before men that they may see your good works, and glorify your Father which is in heaven"* (Matt. 5:14-16).

Jesus also said, *"Ye have not chosen me, but I have chosen you, and ordained you, that you should go and bring forth fruit, and that your fruit should remain"* (John 15:16).

Now we see that you are not only the light of the world, you have been chosen and ordained by Jesus Christ to go and bring forth fruit—and that the souls you win to Christ should last forever.

Jesus said, *"But ye shall receive power, after that the Holy Ghost is come upon you; and ye shall be witnesses unto me"* (Acts 1:8).

If you have not been sharing Christ with your friends it is the surest sign that the Holy Spirit has not been flowing in your life.

When you're filled with the Holy Spirit, you will forget your fears—the Holy Spirit will give you the right things to say (see John 16:15).

There are 2 billion lost souls in the world today who have never heard the name of Jesus as Savior. What should you do? I've given my whole life to the great task of witnessing—I hope you will, too.

●

Remember: WE SHOULD CRY "WOE ARE WE IF WE PREACH NOT THE GOSPEL." WITNESS TO SOMEONE TODAY!

196/WHY ARE YOU JEALOUS?

"(If) the spirit of jealousy (came) upon him, and he be jealous of his wife...Then shall the man bring his wife unto the priest" (Numbers 5:14 & 15).

Also read: Prov. 6:34; Song of Sol. 8:6; 2 Cor. 11:2

Are you jealous of other people? If so, I believe it is because you have a low opinion of yourself—or maybe too much pride. (Surprisingly, both attitudes can abide in the same heart).

I was visiting with a dentist recently, on a flight from Phoenix to Omaha, when he told me about the struggle his brother is having with jealousy. He said, "My brother hates me because he thinks that people love me and they don't love him. But it's only that I love myself—which results in people loving me; he doesn't love himself, and that results in people not loving him."

If you are struggling with jealousy, remember: the root of your problem is your own lack of self-love, your pride, or both. You may think that God and people prefer others over you. But this is not true. It's just that others may be doing more things right than you are.

In my early days, before becoming a Christian, I owned and managed a dance band. We were doing well. One day we received an invitation to appear on a popular TV show in the region. I invited a singer-friend to appear on the show as my special guest.

After the show, I discovered that everyone raved about my friend's performance but they didn't say a word about mine.

I was stung. I felt a surge of jealousy burn through me. I asked myself, "Why did they notice him and not me?"

Finally, I asked, "Why do you think my friend went over so well?" One guy answered, "Because he kept smiling all throughout the show. Even when he wasn't singing we could see him grinning from ear to ear, having a great time."

That was it! He smiled more than me. He wasn't better than me, he just did more things right than I did. Since then I have tried to smile as often as I can. And now, when I smile, people like me too. How silly jealousy is!

●

Remember: IF YOU ARE JEALOUS OF OTHERS, FIND OUT WHY. THEN DO THE RIGHT THING AND THINGS WILL WORK GREAT FOR YOU TOO.

197/WHY GOD DOESN'T ALWAYS PUNISH THOSE WHO REFUSE TO SERVE THE LORD!

"The goodness of God leads you to repentence" (Romans 2:4, NKJV).

Also read: Ex. 34:6; Ps. 27:13; Rom. 2:4

If you have a loved one who is not living for the Lord, you may have prayed that God would chastise him until he repents.

This method is not always successful. There are certain types of people who will not repent no matter how hard God smites them. Here's what God said through his prophet Isaiah: *"The children I raised and cared for so long and tenderly have turned against me. Even the animals—the donkey and the ox—know their owner and appreciate his care for them, but not my people Israel. NO MATTER WHAT I DO FOR THEM, THEY STILL DON'T CARE.*

"Oh, what a sinful nation they are! They walk bent-backed beneath their load of guilt. Their fathers before them were evil too. Born to be bad, they have turned their backs upon the Lord, and have despised the Holy One of Israel. They have cut themselves off from my help.

"Oh, my people, haven't you had enough punishment? Why will you force me to whip you again and again? Must you forever rebel? From head to foot you are sick and weak and faint, covered with bruises and welts and infected wounds, unanointed and unbound" (Is. 1:2-6, TLB, emphasis mine).

God said he had whipped the people to the point of death and there was still no desire within them to give up their sins. The time will come during the great tribulation when God will pour out His judgments upon the world, but it will have very little effect on bringing men to repentence.

The reason why God doesn't smite rebels who refuse to repent is that it doesn't always work. The greatest force that moves men and women to Christ is the goodness of God.

•

Remember: GOD IS DOING EVERYTHING HE CAN TO LEAD PEOPLE TO SALVATION, AND SMITING DOESN'T ALWAYS WORK!

198/PORPOISES WITH A PURPOSE

"One God and Father of all, who is above all, and through all, and in you all" (Ephesians 4:6).

Also read: John 17:11; Eph. 4:4-6

Once I read a story of how 3 porpoises located the body of a drowned teenager and nudged it to shore at the feet of the amazed but grief-stricken father.

It happened in Corolla, North Carolina. Marshall Cherry was watching from shore when the small raft his son was paddling capsized going through the breakers off the Currituck Outer banks.

He said, "There were three big porpoises in the shallow water right behind the body. We all saw them."

The father said the porpoises worked themselves right up to the beach behind the body and pushed it to shore.

That story really made me wonder, because if fish can get together to help "save" a dead man from the sea, why can't Christians get together to save the lost from hell?

Many people are prejudiced against any message except one that comes from the pulpit of their own church. Why?

First, people are biased because *many have never seen the "big picture" of God's Kingdom.* If you only attend your own church and seldom work with others in united crusades, etc. you will never see how God works through so many different people.

Second, *it's comfortable to be opinionated.* Once you place everyone in a pigeonhole you don't have to think anymore. Prejudice allows you to lay aside your heart and your brain.

Third, *religious leaders often use bigotry to control their followers.* They'll teach their people that "Ours is the true church—the others are in error." This keeps everyone in line; followers are never allowed to open their minds. They simply do what they are told.

The porpoises teach us a lesson: they all had one purpose. Jesus prayed that we would become one in love for God, for each other and for lost souls.

•

Remember: LET'S LEARN TO WORK TOGETHER FOR GOD'S PURPOSE.

199/HALF-BREED BELIEVERS

"And I, brethren, could not speak unto you as unto spiritual, but as unto carnal, even as unto babes in Christ" (1 Corinthians 3:1).

Also read: Rom. 7:14-25; 8:5-8

Are you a half-breed believer? A spiritual half-breed is someone whose soul is saved but is yet controlled by the passions of the flesh. "Carnal" is the word used to describe these people.

You may be in the Kingdom but not under the control of the King. You may be on your way to heaven but not close enough to God to enjoy the journey.

Many in the Corinthian church were carnal. They are a good case study of carnality.

First, THEY LOVED TO ARGUE AND DEBATE. *"For ye are yet carnal: for whereas there is among you envying, and strife, and divisions, are you not carnal, and walk as men?"*

Second, THEY HAD THEIR FAVORITE PREACHERS. *"For while one saith I am of Paul; and another, I am of Apollos; are ye not carnal?"* (1 Cor. 3:3 & 4).

Carnal Christians follow men more than Jesus Christ. (Don't become an exclusive follower of any preacher—whether he be Billy Graham, Oral Roberts, Robert Schuller, Jerry Falwell or Lowell Lundstrom.)

Third, THE CORINTHIANS ALLOWED OPEN SIN TO BE PRACTICED IN THEIR MIDST. Paul says, *"It is reported commonly that there is fornication among you...and you are puffed up* (proud) *and have not rather mourned, that he that hath done this deed might be taken away from among you"* (1 Cor. 5:1 & 2).

Fourth, THE CORINTHIANS WERE POOR GIVERS. In 1 Corinthians 9, Paul has to remind them of their obligations to support God's work.

If you have a struggle giving generously to God, chances are you are a carnal Christian.

Don't be a half-breed believer; give yourself totally to God and you will be blessed!

●

Remember: A HALF-BREED BELIEVER IS A POOR WITNESS!

200/THREE WAYS TO CHANGE YOUR LIFE

"If you want favor with both God and man, and a reputation for good judgment and common sense, then trust the Lord completely; don't ever trust yourself" (Proverbs 3:4 & 5, TLB).

Also read: Ps. 36:3; 40:3; 71:5

One psychiatrist who has studied human nature said the only lasting way to change your life is by doing something different with your ears, hands, and eyes.

Keeping this rule in mind, notice how God is willing to help you in these three areas of your life.

"And thou shalt love the Lord thy God with all thine heart, and with all thy soul, and with all thy might, and these words, which I command thee this day, shall be in thine heart" (Deut. 6:5-6).

NOTICE THE EARS! *"And you shall teach them diligently unto thy children, and shalt TALK of them when thou sittest in thine house and when thou walkest by the way, and when thou liest down, and when thou risest up"* (verse 7) In other words, talk about the Word of God from the time you get up in the morning until you go to bed in the evening. Rehearse God's Word in your ears. When you think God's thoughts it won't be long until you begin to live God's way.

NOTICE THE HANDS! *"And thou shalt bind them for a sign upon thine hand"* (verse 8).

I try to keep Christian books and magazines in the kitchen, living room, bedroom, bathroom, and even in the family car and 4 wheel drive. If I have a good article close by, it helps my hands to pick up a portion of God's Word.

NOTICE THE EYES! *"And they shall be as frontlets (decorations on your forehead), between thine eyes* (verse 8).

It's always good to keep scripture verses taped to your mirror, refrigerator door or dashboard of your car. The more you keep the Word of God before you, the more change it will make in your life.

•

Remember: USE YOUR EARS, HANDS, AND EYES AS CONDUITS OF GOD'S WORD!

201/CONSIDER THE FORCE-CHILL FACTOR

"All night they lie naked in the cold, without clothing or covering" (Job 24:7).

Also read: Ps. 147:17 & 18

There are times when South Dakota gets bitterly cold in the winter. The other night it dropped to 35 below; with winds gusting to 40 miles an hour and more, the wind-chill factor plunged to a frightening 90 degrees below zero!

Burrrrrrrrrrrrrrrrr, that's cold! A friend of mine said he went to kick his cat out the door and froze his foot! Another said he threw out a pail of water and it was so cold that it froze so quickly the ice was hot!

Seriously, when I was young, weathermen didn't report the wind-chill factor—only the temperature. But they have become wiser today—and by doing so, have saved many lives.

Just as weathermen consider the wind-chill factor, Christians should consider *the force* of the temptations and trials that come against them.

The cruel thing about life is that trouble is merciless. The only thing you can do when everything goes wrong is to draw near to God and wait out the storm. Don't venture out into the storm, because the "force-chill" can kill you.

Job recognized this. When he lost all of his children and all of his possessions he fell down upon the ground and worshiped God (see Job 1:20).

When you are faced with a strong "force-chill" factor—when things are going bad for you—do as Job did: worship God and lean on His protection.

•

Remember: STAY WITHIN THE WARMTH OF GOD'S PROTECTION.

202/HE CANNOT DENY HIMSELF

"If we believe not, yet he abideth faithful: he cannot deny himself" (2 Timothy 2:13).

Also read: Deut. 7:8, 9; Josh. 23:4; Isa. 54:9, 10

This is one of the greatest statements in the Bible. You must meditate upon it reverently to assimilate its fullness.

God's Word says that even during the times when your faith falters, when you do things that deny the Lord, yet God remains faithful—because He cannot deny himself.

You are so linked to Jesus Christ—that as a believer you are part of His very body. Even when you're rotting with the poison of sin, God doesn't deny you. He remains faithful and tries to help you recover.

Think of it this way: If you contracted an infection in your arm and large boils appeared, would you go to the doctor and ask him to amputate it? No, you would ask the doctor to do everything possible to heal the boils.

Only when every possible measure failed would you cut your arm off. The same is true of God's relationship to you. You are an arm of God. Even when unbelief and sin infect your spirit, God remains committed to you. He works hard to rid you of the poison of evil.

Or think of it this way: If you have a son or daughter that does something wrong, are you going to expel them from your family? Not until you've done everything humanly possible to redeem them. Your children are part of your own body. This is why the Scripture says, *"HE CANNOT DENY HIMSELF"* (emphasis mine).

But understand this truth: Through Jesus Christ you have become part of God. *"Your life is hid with Christ in God"* (Col. 3:3). God cannot easily deny you because you are part of Himself. While amputation is a real possibility, it is surely a "court of last resort." This doesn't give you license to sin, but it does give you the assurance that during seasons of unbelief God will not throw you out of His Kingdom.

•

Remember: GOD CANNOT DENY HIMSELF—AND YOU ARE PART OF GOD.

203/HOW TO HANDLE A POOR PREACHER!

"And he gave some, apostles; and some, prophets; and some, evangelists; and some, pastors and teachers; for the perfecting of the saints, for the work of the ministry" (Ephesians 4:11 & 12).

Also read: Col. 1:9; 2:8-10

I cannot tell you how many poor sermons I have suffered through during my Christian life. It frustrates me to listen to well-meaning, but empty men sharing cold hearted religious theories.

Even the truth kills unless it is set ablaze by the Holy Spirit. *"For the letter killeth but the spirit giveth life"* (2 Cor. 3:6). The sad fact is that very few ministers study to be practical in their approach on fiery in their delivery. Very few pray their sermons hot. One survey shows that the average minister prays less than seven minutes a day; whereas, Jesus often prayed all night. *"And it came to pass in those days, that (Jesus) went out into a mountain to pray, and continued all night in prayer to God"* (Luke 6:12). The apostles also emphasized prayer, *"These all continued with one accord in prayer and supplication"* (Acts 1:14).

How do you handle a poor preacher?

1. Pray for him, that God will enlighten him to his spiritual need.
2. You can invite him to come along with you to hear fiery soulwinning preachers at crusades or conferences.
3. Give him red-hot practical books and cassette tapes on soulwinning and ways to minister to people's needs.
4. At the proper moment (if you become friends and he is humble and open enough to listen), express your concern over his spoken ministry. Don't be afraid to speak up. Preachers are an isolated lot. Very few really tell them what they need to hear.
5. Remain faithful. Do not talk about the man of God behind his back. If you say anything constructive or critical say it to the man himself—face to face.
6. You can choose a different church. Sometimes the only message a cold man hears is an empty pew. You wouldn't eat food at a restaurant that feeds you cold food. Neither should you attend a church where the sermons are consistently cold.

•

Remember: THE PREACHER YOU CHOOSE TO LISTEN TO IS THE MOST IMPORTANT PERSON IN YOUR LIFE NEXT TO JESUS CHRIST!

204/ARE YOU SPEAKING UP?

"I am not ashamed of the gospel of Christ: for it is the power of God unto salvation to every one that believeth" (Romans 1:16).

Also read: Ps. 25:2; 119:46; 2 Tim. 2:15

Are you really speaking up for your Lord and Savior Jesus Christ? Consider this quotation carefully:

"History will have to record that the greatest tragedy of this period of social transition was not the strident clamor of bad people, but the appalling silence of the good people."

Martin Luther King Jr.

There are an estimated 50 million born-again Christians in America—why is it, then, that our country continues to slide into ruin? It's because of the many who could speak up and don't.

Jesus said, *"Ye are the salt of the earth"* (Matt. 5:13). You CAN help change your world.

There are many ways you can exert a "salting" influence on those around you:

*First, speak up by helping to elect good people to public office. Get involved with the political process.

*Also, when someone starts to tell a shady story, you can smile and say, "Come on, Tom, is this a clean joke I can laugh at?"

*Or when someone says, "Ministers should never have anything to do with politics," you could ask, "Why is it when liberals speak up for their causes, even supporting Marxist guerillas in Central America, no one says a word, but when conservative ministers speak up for righteousness everyone cries, 'Separation of church and state—preachers stay out of politics?"

It takes courage to speak up for the Lord in the presence of the ungodly, but trust God to help you today.

•

Remember: HISTORY WILL WONDER WHY YOU AND I DID NOT SAY MORE.

205/THE TOUCH OF FAITH!

"For she said, 'If I may touch but his clothes, I shall be whole" (Mark 5:28).

Also read: Mk. 11:22; Gal. 2:20; 2 Cor. 5:7

This is truly an amazing story. A great crowd was following Jesus. Among them was a woman who obviously had cancer. *"She had an issue of blood twelve years, and had suffered many things of many physicians, and had spent all that she had, and was nothing bettered, but rather grew worse"* (verses 25, 26)

Doesn't this verse tell the tale of so many who have an incurable disease? In the middle of her depressing situation, the woman heard that Jesus was coming to her area and she said within herself (and this is where true faith is always born), *"If I may touch but his garment, I shall be whole"* (Matt. 9:21).

If you are needing healing, it is what you say within yourself that makes it happen. Don't say, "This runs in our family," or, "I deserve to suffer; God is punishing me," or, "It's my fault; I should have gone to the doctor quicker," etc. Not a single one of those phrases will build faith in your heart. You must say, "If I touch Him, I will be healed."

How can you touch Jesus today? YOU CAN TOUCH JESUS BY YOUR FAITH! *"We have access by faith into this grace wherein we stand, and rejoice in hope of the glory of God"* (Rom. 5:2). When you really believe that God is willing and wants to heal you, it opens heaven to your request.

Many people rubbed shoulders with Jesus that day and received nothing. What made the woman's touch different? Realizing that healing had gone out of Him, Jesus asked, *"Who touched my clothes?"* The disciples said, *"All this crowd pressing about you, and you ask who touched you?"* (verse 31, TLB). They were annoyed that Jesus would ask such a question.

But the question was not foolish. Whereas the crowd touched Jesus in the natural, the woman touched him in faith. And that one touch healed her completely!

•

Remember: THE TOUCH OF FAITH WORK MIRACLES!

206/YOUR FLESH IS WEAK!

"Watch and pray, that you enter not into temptation: the spirit indeed is willing, but the flesh is weak" (Matthew 26:41).

Also read: Prov. 28:13; Eph. 6:10-11, 16; Jas. 4:7

We know our flesh is weak—but there are times when our flesh is weaker than usual. Recently I was visiting with a government auditor. He investigates federal courts so they will do an accurate job accounting for the money they receive from bail bonds, fines and penalties.

This auditor said that most stealing occurs whenever an employee is going through a personal crisis. For instance, a man in the accounting department needs money to put his son through college so he decides to "borrow" money from the general fund. Or a woman working in the payroll department desperately needs money to pay for her husband's doctor bills so she begins to write checks to people of assumed identities and cashes the checks herself.

This government inspector said that most dishonesty begins during a traumatic period in a person's personal life when they're weaker than usual.

Are you going through a tough time? If your mate has been treating you unkindly you might be tempted to "get even" by having an affair. Or if your family doesn't appreciate you, it might be easy to do something wrong because "If no one cares about me, why should I struggle?"

The fact is that God cares! And regardless of what your loved ones or others do—you are important to God!

If you have been weakened by a traumatic event in your life (death, sickness, divorce, discouragement, the loss of your job, etc.)—watch out! Just like wolves chasing a herd of deer through deep snow, Satan is waiting for you to drop back (weaken) so he can destroy you.

But Jesus, the great Shepherd of your soul, is urging you to get closer to Himself. He will protect you from the destroyer during your weak moments.

●

Remember: YOUR FLESH IS WEAK, BUT THE LORD IS STRONG!

207/OUTNUMBERED?

"Be strong and courageous, be not afraid nor dismayed... for there be more with us than with him: with him is an arm of flesh; but with us is the Lord our God to help us, and to fight our battles" (2 Chronicles 32:7-8).

Also read: Ex. 14:13; Isa. 41:13; Matt. 14:27

Have you ever felt outnumbered? Today's text is a great encouragement assuring you of God's mighty hand on your behalf. God is for you, the devil is against you; *you* cast the deciding vote. *You* plus *God* make a majority.

Remember when Lucifer was thrown out of heaven? The Bible says that one-third of the angelic hosts switched sides and aligned with Satan. The important thing to remember is that God's angels have Satan's demons outnumbered 2 to 1. So who do you think is going to win?

First John 4:4 tells us, " *...greater is he that is in you, than he that is in the world."*

You can take the attitude of the military field general who radioed this report to war headquarters: "We have a great position; the enemy has us surrounded—we will attack."

If you feel so outnumbered that you are in peril, just hold your ground and God will come to your help. Jesus said *"I will never leave thee nor forsake thee"* (Heb. 13:5). So this is all the confidence you need to win.

Remember, you are God's child and He has almost as much at stake as you do. If you fail, the non-Christian will say your God is powerless. So remind God in your prayers how important it is for you to win.

•

Remember: YOU ARE NOT OUTNUMBERED NO MATTER HOW STRONG YOUR ENEMIES MAY APPEAR TO BE.

"This book of the law shall not depart out of your mouth; but you shall meditate on it...to do everything that is written in it; for then you shall make your way prosperous, and then you shall have good success" (Joshua 1:8, Literal).

Also read: Psa. 1:2; Matt. 12:32-37; John 3:34; Jas. 1:22-25

Can you imagine what it would be like to sit down with God and discuss your future with Him in person? Just think of the many ideas the two of you could come up with that would guarantee your success and security.

There is a way you can succeed and be prosperous. It is far different from the advice given to you in the worldly books you'll find in bookstores. Napoleon Hill's great book, *Think and Grow Rich*, Dale Carnegie's classic, *How to Win Friends and Influence People*, and the recent bestseller by Thomas J. Peters and Robert H. Waterman, Jr., *In Search of Excellence*. All have one flaw—they are missing the God-factor.

I recommend you read these books and use the information to change your life, but don't forget the principles God has set forth in Joshua 1:8.

First, SPEAK GOD'S WORD. *"This book of the law shall not depart out of your mouth."* The more Scriptures you memorize and share, the more you are talking just like God.

Second, MEDITATE ON GOD'S WORD. Psychiatrists say you can tell what you love the most by what you think about when you're not thinking about anything. What does your mind drift to when you relax? Money, sex, power, pleasures or God?

Learn to discipline your mind to think about His Word constantly, so you can have His thoughts in your head.

Third, DO GOD'S WORD. As Marilyn Hickey says, "Advice heard but unheeded is useless." Jesus said, *"He that hath my commandments, and keepeth them, he it is that loveth me...and I will love him, and will manifest myself to him"* (John 14:21).

•

Remember: IF YOU THINK GOD'S THOUGHTS, SPEAK GOD'S WORDS AND DO GOD'S DEEDS— YOU ARE A SUCCESS!

209/HEALING—THE DANCING HAND OF GOD!

"Though he slay me, yet will I trust in him" (Job 3:15).

Also read: Deut. 32:39; Acts 14:9

Someone has said that "healing is the dancing hand of God." It has always been a mystery why God will heal one and pass over another; why one dies and the next lives!

I personally know the leader of one super-faith movement, whose grandson suffered a brain tumor. No amount of prayer brought deliverance. He had to be operated on by a surgeon. I know a famous faith healer who was unable to see his son delivered from drugs. I know another miracle worker who died on the operating table. The greatest miracle worker of the Old Testament was Elisha, but the Bible says, *"Now Elisha was fallen sick of his sickness whereof he died"* (2 Kings 13:14).

Here's what will blow your logical circuit breaker. The Bible says, *"So Elisha died and was buried. (and later) In those days bandit gangs of Moabites used to invade the land each spring. Once some men who were burying a friend spied these marauders so they hastily threw his body into the tomb of Elisha. And as soon as the body touched Elisha's bones, the dead man revived and jumped to his feet!* (2 Kings 13:20 & 21, TLB).

It appeared there wasn't enough power of God to heal Elisha of his sickness, but there was enough power of God to raise a dead man who touched his bones.

These inconsistencies cannot be explained. So we have the statement, "Healing is the dancing hand of God."

How then can we face sickness, believing it is God's will to heal, and yet knowing that he might not heal? The answer is found in the reply the three young Hebrews gave to King Nebuchadnezzar, who threatened to burn them in the fiery furnace unless they bowed down to his pagen idol.

They simply said, "God is able to deliver us. But if He doesn't, it's okay. We still believe!" (See Daniel 3:17 & 18.)

●

Remember: THIS KIND OF FAITH ENABLES YOU TO COPE WITH THE DANCING HAND OF GOD!

210/HOW TROUBLE WORKS FOR YOUR GOOD!

"Dear brothers, is your life full of difficulties and temptations? Then be happy, for when the way is rough, your patience has a chance to grow." (James 1:2-3, TLB).

Also read: Rom. 5:3-8; Jas. 1:4-8

One thing is common among us: we all have problems. We're all facing difficult situations in one or more areas of our lives. But the difference between the succumbers and the overcomers is that winners know that troubles work for good.

>The Bible says, *"For our light affliction, which is but for a moment, worketh for us a far more exceeding and eternal weight of glory"* (I Cor. 4:17). The Bible says your afflictions work for your good. You are not the victim but the victor when trouble comes your way. This is why Paul said, *" ... We glory in tribulations also: knowing that TRIBULATION WORKETH PATIENCE..."* (Rom. 5:3, emphasis mine). The Holy Spirit also inspired Paul to write, *"For we know that ALL things WORK together for good to them that love God"* (Rom. 8:28, emphasis mine).

What problem are you facing today? It surely qualifies under the category of all things—so say this out loud, "All things work together for good. My problem is working for my benefit."

Peter writes to believers saying, *"Who are kept by the power of God through faith ... Wherein ye greatly rejoice, though now for a season, if need be, ye are in heaviness through manifold temptations: That the trial of your faith, being much more precious than of gold that perisheth ... "* (1 Pet. 1:5-7).

Peter said your problems are like the fire that burns the impurities out of gold. Don't despise the heat; the hotter things get, the more you are going to pray; and the greater pressures bear upon you, the more like Jesus Christ you will become if you keep the right attitude.

If you know everything is going to turn out right, it doesn't make much difference what happens—because God is working all things for your benefit. So, rejoice in your problems!

●

Remember: TROUBLES WORK FOR YOUR GOOD WHEN YOU'RE SERVING GOD!

211/GET IN THE RIGHT LANE

"Master, we have toiled all the night, and have taken nothing" (Luke 5:5).

Also read: Josh. 1:8; Psa. 119:105; Prov. 3:5, 6; Isa. 30:21

Do you have the feeling that you're not going anywhere or accomplishing anything?

You may be right. Recently when I was in Tulsa, Oklahoma I drove up to a stoplight and waited and waited for the light to turn green.

After five minutes I was about to run the stop light, thinking it was out of order, when I discovered my mistake—I was waiting in the wrong lane. The road was very wide and I'd gotten too far to the left (to make a left-hand turn). The wheels of my car had not tripped the mechanical device that changed the lights.

Maybe you're in the wrong lane of life. Maybe you should be working at a different job, attending a different church or maybe living in a different part of the country.

The disciples had fished all night without getting a thing when Jesus appeared and gave them new directions. The Bible says, *"(Jesus) said unto Simon (Peter), Launch out into the deep, and let down your nets* (to catch fish).

"And Simon answering said unto him, Master, we have toiled all the night; and have taken nothing: nevertheless at thy word I will let down the net.

"And when they had done this they (caught) a great multitude of fishes: and their net brake" (Luke 5:4-6).

The reason the disciples hadn't caught anything was they were fishing in the wrong spot. But Jesus knew where the action was and urged them to launch out into the deep.

I believe that Jesus will help direct you, too, to the right place. But be sure to get close enough to Him to hear His voice!

•

Remember: YOU MUST GET IN THE RIGHT LANE!

212/HOW TO GET THE MOST OUR OF YOUR BIBLE READING!

"So they read in the book in the law of God distinctly, and gave the sense, and caused them to understand the reading" (Nehemiah 8:8).

Also read: Ps. 119: 8-12, 18, & 33

If the Bible gets boring to read, there are ways you can arouse your spiritual desire so you'll enjoy the Scriptures and receive the maximum impact of God's Word.

When my soul is dry; when I approach the Word of God, one way I prime myself is to reread the passages I have underlined during previous reading. I often make a mark in the margin of my Bible beside the passages where God gave me an illumination or an anointing. Rereading these passages often sparks my soul.

I have also enjoyed using different translations. It keeps me from thinking that I've read this before.

One of the best tips is to pray for a fresh anointing of the Spirit so that you can read the Scripture with the same moving of the Spirit that the writer felt when he was moved by the Holy Ghost. *"For the prophesy came not in old time by the will of man: but holy men of God spake as they were moved by the Holy Ghost"* (2 Pet. 1:21).

This is why Ezra had the Scripture read carefully and clearly to the people, so they would understand the sense and the spirit by which God was speaking to them. The Bible says, *"As Ezra read from the scroll...the Levites went among the people and explained the meaning of the passage that was being read. All the people began sobbing when they heard the commands of the law"* (Neh. 8:7-9, TLB).

When you really get the sense and the meaning of God's Word, it will touch your heart. There will be an emotional, life-changing response.

•

Remember: IF YOU'LL PRAY FOR A SOFT TOUCH OF THE HOLY SPIRIT UPON YOU AS YOU READ THE WORD OF GOD, IT WILL TRANSFORM YOUR LIFE.

213/YOU MAY FEEL TIRED

"And let us not be weary in well doing: for in due season we shall reap, if we faint not" (Galatians 6:9).

Also read: 1 Cor. 6:19 & 20; Heb. 12:11

Did you know that your blood travels 168 million miles in one day? One health magazine says that the average adult, weighing 175 pounds, will probably, in one day, speak 5,000 words, move 750 muscles, exercise 7 million brain cells, perspire over 1 pint of water, breathe 23,040 times, and eat nearly 4 pounds of food.

Maybe this explains why you may feel weary at times!

God is going to help you today, and every day of your life. Actually, your body is a miracle. King David said, *"I will praise thee; for I am fearfully and wonderfully made; marvellous are thy works"* (Ps. 139:14).

If you are lacking the energy you need to live vibrantly take this quick check-up:

1. Are you getting enough exercise, so that your heart and body get a good workout each day? (Note: you need to check with your doctor before launching out on any strenuous exercise program.)
2. How is your diet? Are you eating nutritious foods? If you're taking in too much sugar and soft drinks, coffee and alcohol or, if you smoke, you're placing your body under too much strain.
3. Is something bothering you? I experience my worst fatigue when going through an unresolved spiritual conflict, praying for a lost loved one, or interceeding for a need. That's when I must apply the verse, *"Casting all your care upon Him; for He careth for you"* (1 Pet. 5:7).

If you're feeling tired, take care of yourself; claim God's promise for strength and cast all your care upon Him.

•

Remember: YOUR BODY IS A MIRACLE MACHINE THAT DESERVES GOOD CARE.

KNOWING CHRIST THROUGH SUFFERING

"That I may know him, and the power of his resurrection, and the fellowship of his sufferings, being made conformable unto his death" (Philippians 3:10).

Also read: Rom. 5:3, 4; 2 Cor. 4:8-10, 17, 18; 2 Tim. 2:11, 12

One of the most difficult problems facing Christians today is that many want to know Christ in the power of His resurrection—but not in the fellowship of His sufferings.

Their basic philosophical (they will say theological) position is that Jesus Christ suffered so that we would not have to suffer, that He was made poor so that we could be made rich.

And while I agree this is true and proclaim it everywhere, this is not the total truth. If it were, Paul would not have said, *"That I might know Him...and the fellowship of his sufferings."* The only way you can know Jesus Christ in the fellowship of His sufferings is to go through similar sufferings—rejection, physical pain, scorn, abuse, sorrow, the pain of intercession, etc.

Surprisingly, Paul said the great objective of his life was not to win lost souls to Christ, nor to enjoy a life of prosperity and blessings, but to truly know Jesus Christ intimately—in His power and in His pain. Paul wanted the total knowledge of God—including His sufferings.

It is a fact that people who have never suffered find it difficult to comfort others who are hurting. If you have never known the pain of losing a loved one, you simply cannot console the bereaved.

The fact is that God is hurting today. Jesus wept over Jerusalem—and imagine how much He is weeping over the large cities of today.

If you're going through a time of suffering, use your pain to draw near to the heart of God. He is well aware of your agony.

●

Remember: YOU'LL KNOW CHRIST BETTER IF YOU'LL DRAW NEAR HIM DURING YOUR SUFFERING.

215/WHEN YOUR WHY FILLS THE SKY!

"Lord, why are you standing aloof and far away? Why do you hide when I need you the most?" (Psalm 10:1, TLB).

Also read: Matt. 6:33; 7:11; Ja. 1:5

Someone has said, "When trouble strikes, from our hearts comes a cry of *'Why?'* that fills the sky." In this psalm, David asks two major questions that often rise within us when adversity comes. First, Lord, why are You standing aloof and far away? Why are You hiding when I need You most?

I think the reason the Lord stands back is to test us, to see what is really in us. The Bible says of Hezekiah that *"God left him, to try him, that he might know all that was in his heart"* (2 Chr. 32:31).

As a father, I want my sons to grow up and be strong Christian men. As much as I would protect them against mortal danger, I would not escort them to the school playground and fight their battles. There's a time when they need to stand on their own to become strong. I think God does the same thing. Whenever trouble strikes, we cry out and want His immediate assistance. Then, when He fails to appear instantly, we think He has forgotten us!

Actually, you and I have power delegated to us, so we can act on our own. We have power to bind the enemy. Jesus said, *"I give unto you power...over all the power of the enemy and nothing by any means shall hurt you"* (Luke 10:19).

We are guaranteed answers to our prayers. Jesus said, *"Whatsoever ye shall ask in my name, that will I do, that the Father may be glorified in the Son. If ye shall ask anything in my name, I will do it"* (Jn. 14:13 & 14).

So if things are tough, before you cry out, "Where are You God? Why are You hiding from me?" Begin to use the power and authority God has given you. Act in His power. Exercise your divine mandate.

•

Remember: WHEN YOU'RE TEMPTED TO CRY "WHY?" ACT BOLDLY IN FAITH!

216/YOU'RE NOT ALONE!

"Thus saith the Lord ... Fear not; for I have redeemed thee, I have called thee by thy name, thou art mine. When thou passest through the waters I will be with thee: and through the rivers, they shall not overflow thee: when thou walkest through the fire, thou shalt not be burned; neither shall the flame kindle upon thee" (Isaiah 43:1-2).

Also read: Deut. 4:31; Isa. 41:17; Heb. 15:5

The wonderful thing about being a Christian is that you're not alone. God is always with you. The Lord assures you that when you pass through deep waters He will be by your side; you won't be washed away with the flood and that fire won't burn you. You won't be *isolated* from the flames—but you'll be *insulated*.

You may know these truths as a theory, but there's a way you can experience them: turn your eyes away from your conditions to Christ.

I enjoy going hunting with my boys, Lowell Jr., 16, and little Lance, 7. Lance does fine in the wilderness until evening comes. As the shadows lengthen and the birds and animals start making night sounds Lance will say, "I want to go home to Mother." There have been times he cried because he was afraid. That's when I've said, "Why are you afraid? I'm here. Everything will be O.K." But that seldom quiets him. As long as his mind is on the unknown his heart trembles.

If you're going through deep waters, if you're in the fire, turn your heart and mind toward the Lord. Read God's Word more than ever. I find real comfort from reading how God has delivered others from their problems. *"These things were written for our learning, that we through patience and comfort of the scriptures might have hope"* (Romans 15:4).

Then be sure to pray. Praise and worship will open up your inner spirit so you will become conscious of God.

God is with you; you are not alone. Say these words out loud: *"God is with me now; Jesus will never leave me nor forsake me."*

●

Remember: YOU'RE NOT ALONE!

217/ARE YOU A PARTICIPANT OR A PARASITE?

"I exhort therefore, that, first of all, supplications, prayers, intercessions, and giving of thanks, be made for all men; For kings, and for all that are in authority; that we may lead a quiet and peaceable life in all godliness and honesty" (1 Tim. 2:1 & 2).

Also read: Matt. 5:14-16; Heb. 11:1-3, 33, 34; 1 John 5:4, 5

Paul urges us to pray for our leaders. In fact he says we should intercede for those in authority. They need our prayers to help them make the right decisions in running the state and nation so we will be able to live a quiet and peaceable life.

Are you involved in helping to turn this country around for God? Are you praying and working to get honest and reputable men elected to office? The sad thing I have noticed is that most Christians are parasites instead of participants in the electoral process.

Do you know there are an estimated 15 million born-again Christians in America who are not even registered to vote? THIS GREAT BLOCK OF UNCOMMITTED CHRISTIANS COULD TURN THIS NATION AROUND FOR GOD! But the apathy of the righteous is pathetic.

I hope you'll get involved in the coming election—and in every local and state election that is held. The Communists claim they can control a country by having only 5% of the populace committed to their cause.

What can you do?

Recently a Christian man in Minneapolis decided to attend his precinct that was electing delegates of his party to the state convention. He stood up and said, "I'm angry at all the pornography being shoved at us in stores and theatres. I'm sick of the alcohol being peddled everywhere—and I'm upset by the divorce rate and numbers of abortions in our state." He mentioned several other things and concluded by saying, "If you elect me as a delegate I'll speak out against these issues." He won on the next ballot.

•

Remember: BE A PARTICIPANT—NOT A PARASITE. ELECT GOOD MEN TO OFFICE.

218/WHY YOU SHOULD ATTEND CHURCH!

"Let us not neglect our church meetings, as some people do, but encourage and warn each other, especially now that the day of his coming back again is drawing near" (Hebrews 10:25, TLB).

Also read: 1 Jn. 1:7; Phil 1:5 & 6

A Gallup Survey shows there are literally millions of people who do not attend church and yet claim to be "born-again" believers in Jesus Christ. I'm sure they are saved, but they have failed to see the importance of attending church. This problem is not new. Even in Bible days, the writer to the Hebrews said some were neglecting to attend church.

Whenever the subject of church attendance is brought up, someone will say, "I don't have to go to church to be a Christian. God knows I love Him with all my heart, and that's all that matters." But there are two facts today's text emphasizes that you may have overlooked. You need encouragement when you're feeling down, and you need warning when you're slipping spiritually. If you're not part of a body of believers, you won't receive either one, and this increases your risk of falling away because of discouragement or compromise with sin.

Remember, the devil with his demons are lurking in the darkness waiting to trip you up. Don't be so presumptuous as to think you don't need anyone—because you do! The Bible says, *"Two are better than one; because they have a good reward for their labor. For if they fall, the one will lift up his fellow: BUT WOE TO HIM THAT IS ALONE WHEN HE FALLETH: FOR HE HATH NOT ANOTHER TO HELP HIM UP"* (Eccles. 4:9 & 10).

Fellowship with believers is also good because it helps to round off your rough edges. I've known a few hermits in my life, and they are always a little weird. Living alone brought out their eccentric ways until they became a little odd. Be sure this doesn't happen to you!

•

Remember: YOU NEED THE CHURCH!

219/DON'T WITHHOLD YOUR WITNESS

"...and ye shall be witnesses unto me" (Acts 1:8).

Also read: Prov. 14:5, 25

In 1915 a Jewish merchant, Leo Frank, was lynched after being convicted of murdering a teenage girl.

But apparently he was innocent.

Alonzo Mann, 14 years old, who worked at Frank's pencil factory in Atlanta, Georgia saw a fellow worker—not Frank—carrying the girl's body. She was beaten and strangled and dumped in the factory basement.

The man Alonzo saw carrying the girl's body was Jim Conley—who threatened to kill Alonzo if he told anyone about it. Alonzo's family, fearing for his life, also advised him to remain silent.

As a result, Leo Frank was led to the gallows and hanged for a crime he probably never committed.

Day after day, Alonzo's conscience troubled him for withholding his witness. Months went by, years, and even decades as he struggled over the secret that could clear Frank's name.

Recently newspapers and T.V. carried the story of how Alonzo Mann, 84, went before the Georgia State Parole board, asking them to pardon Leo Frank. He finally gave his witness—but 70 years too late. He said, "I have had to live with this for 70 years."

Just think of the regrets many people will have when they get to heaven and look back at the many chances they had to speak up for Jesus—and didn't. Don't withhold your witness today. Use taste and tact, but don't be afraid. The eternal destinies of men and women are in the balance.

•

Remember: DON'T LIVE IN MISERY THE REST OF YOUR LIFE—DON'T WITHHOLD YOUR WITNESS!

220/THE DEVIL'S MONUMENT

"For God hath not given us the spirit of fear; but of power, and of love, and of a sound mind" (2 Timothy 1:7).

Also read: Ps. 27:1; 31:24; 56:11; Prov. 3:25, 26

On the outskirts of San Jose, California is a rambling mansion that is a monument to fear and superstition. It was built by a lady whose husband was the son of the man who invented the Winchester rifle.

This mysterious house is called the Winchester Mansion. The reason it is so large is that a spiritualist-medium told the woman she would not die as long as she was building on the house.

So being very rich, she continued to build on the house for 38 years. It has 130 rooms. It was remodeled dozens of times. It has stairs that lead to nowhere, doors that open into blank walls, secret passageways, and steps only two inches high.

Thousands of people tour this mansion each year to view the strange sights and learn of the torments of this fear-filled woman.

Are you unnecessarily afraid of things? If so, you may be building your own monument to fear. Did you know that fear is a spirit? And Jesus said a spirit is like the wind (see John 4:24 first and then John 3:8). God and demons exist in spirit form—like the wind. (We can't see the wind, but we know it's there, because we can see its effect.) Wind will blow in wherever you let it.

Don't allow a single crack in your stand against fear. If you're a little afraid of traveling on the highway, force yourself to take a 20-mile trip. If you're uneasy in the dark, take a walk tonight. In other words, do the very thing you are afraid of. Maybe you won't be able to do it with ease, but each time you take a step toward conquering your fear you are minimizing its strength.

Don't run away from your fears because they will only grow worse. Remember that *God* doesn't send us fear—He gives us His power, love and a sound mind to conquer it!

•

Remember: FEAR IS A SPIRIT-WIND TRYING TO BLOW INTO YOUR LIFE. DON'T YIELD ONE INCH OR YOU'LL BUILD A MONUMENT TO THE DEVIL.

221/WHY GOD ALLOWS TRAGEDIES!

"The secret things belong unto the Lord our God: but those things which are revealed belong unto us and to our children for ever, that we may do all the words of this law" (Deuteronomy 29:29).

Also read: 2 Tim. 2:12; 1 Pet. 5:10; Matt. 17:17

The news today was tragic. Several Palestinian terrorists walked into a Rome airport and fired machine guns and threw hand grenades among the innocent passengers that were waiting to board their Israeli flights. Many were killed and over 100 were wounded. At the same moment, Palestinian terrorists attacked unarmed passengers in Vienna, Austria, repeating their senseless slaughter of civilians.

The questions are, "Where is God? Why does He allow such needless suffering? Has He forgotten to manage the world He created?"

Today's text says the secret things belong unto God, but the things that are revealed belong unto us and our children. While it's hard to understand many of the things that are happening around us, we have confidence that God is a good God.

Think of the terrible holocaust the Jews went through in World War II. Hitler sent more than six million to his furnaces in Dachau, Buchenwald, Auschwitz and others.

Why, would God allow so many millions of innocent people to suffer? I do not know, but I do know as a result of those millions dying, the sympathy of the world moved in favor of establishing Palestine as a homeland for the Jews. The United Nations voted in 1947 to make the Holy Land a homeland for the Jews. So in international terms the evil worked for good. Their suffering helped to create the State of Israel.

So, in comparison, the good far outweighs what appears to be evil. God is ever able to work the evil for good if we let Him.

•

Remember: WHAT APPEARS TO BE TRAGEDIES TO US WILL EVENTUALLY BECOME TRIUMPHS FOR GOD!

222/HOW GOD "SETTLES UP"

"Should you be angry because I am kind?" (Matthew 20:15, TLB).

Also read: Matt. 16:27; 20:1-17

Jesus told an interesting parable in Matthew 20 about the owner of an estate who hired a number of men to work in his fields.

He hired several workers early in the morning (about 6 or 7 a.m.) who agreed to work that day for what would be about $20 in today's wages. Then later he hired more men about 9 a.m. and even more at 5 p.m. When he settled up with all of the men that night, he paid each one $20.

That created a howl of protest from those who were hired in the morning. The estate owner responded by saying, *"I did you no wrong! Didn't you agree to work all day for $20? Take it and go. It is my desire to pay all the same; is it against the law to give away my money if I want to? Should you be angry because I am kind?"* (vs. 13-15).

This parable was to teach how God settles up with everyone who serves Him. For instance: one man hears the Gospel when he's five, repents and serves God faithfully until he's 70 and dies. Another man doesn't hear the Gospel until he's 65; then he repents, serves God faithfully until he's 70 and dies.

Jesus taught us that both men will get to heaven. The man who came into the Kingdom at age 65 will receive the same salvation as the one who was converted at age 5.

The key to this teaching is based on their knowledge of the opportunity. Just be certain you have not INTENTIONALLY waited until you are 65 or so to serve the Lord—that's like giving leftovers to God!

Jesus also taught that we will be rewarded for our works (see 1 Cor. 3:11-15; Matt. 25:14-30 and Rev. 22:12). Actually we are saved by grace and rewarded for our works. Salvation is a gift—rewards are given for effort.

•

Remember: WHEN GOD SETTLES UP HE'LL BE GENEROUS AND FAIR.

223/YOU ARE A WATCHMAN!

"O son of man, I have set thee (as) a watchman unto the house of Israel; therefore thou shalt hear the word at my mouth, and warn them from me" (Ezekiel 33:7).

Also read: 1 Jn. 5:10; Prov. 14:25

It is a sobering thought to realize that you and I are God's watchmen. We have been placed in our communities to speak up for the Lord's cause, to warn sinners of their awful end.

The Bible says, if we fail to warn the sinner and he dies in his sins, God will hold us responsible, (see Ezek. 33: 8 & 9).

Has God been speaking to you about sharing Christ with someone and you have been putting it off? Don't!

Recently, an unsaved friend of mine dropped by my house. We laughed and talked, and I thought, *golly, this is the first time he's ever been so friendly. I should try to win him to Christ. No, maybe he'll think I'm pushing him. I shouldn't take advantage of his openness to lay the gospel on him the first time he's open. I'll do it next time.*

My friend died of a heart attack a few days later. I never got a second chance. Needless to say, I was troubled by my failure. I went to his widow and led her to Christ, the first time I got home off the road.

I've driven to the cemetery and prayer, "O God, don't ever let me fail a friend again!"

I know he watched me on television and heard me share the Gospel via the tube. But, I think if I had really spoken up for Christ, instead of being so sociable and overly sensitive as to how he might react, I could have led him to a personal relationship with Jesus Christ. Now, I'll live with my failure for the rest of my life.

It's not a good feeling. Lest you make the same mistake, speak up. Even admit you're afraid of how your friend will react. Anything is better than knowing your friend may have gone to hell because of you.

●

Remember: YOU ARE A WATCHMAN!

224/CONSIDER THE SOURCE OF YOUR SUFFERING

"So I returned, and considered all the oppressions that are done under the sun..." (Ecclesiastes 4:1).

Also read: Psa. 34:19; Rom. 5:3, 4; 1 Pet. 3:14; 4:12, 13

When trouble comes your way it's important to know where it comes from. I believe suffering has 5 sources:

1. *Ignorance.* When the deformed thalidomide babies were born without arms and legs people first thought it was God's fault—but when the truth was revealed, the medical laboratories had not adequately researched the sedative that was given to pregnant women. As a result of their ignorance the thalidomide babies were born.

    This suffering, and others like it (smoking, alcohol, drugs, etc.) is a result of ignorance—both willful and innocent.
2. *Misdirected Self-will.* What about the teenager who insists on speeding and crashes his car? His passengers are maimed and broken for life. This suffering was not an act of God, but a result of misdirected self-will. Anyone who stubbornly refuses to obey God's laws or man's will suffer.
3. *Nature.* We enjoy the rain, but rain is a result of cold fronts meeting warm fronts and the result is often tornadoes as well as rain. When a tornado rips through a town, leaving a trail of death, many people call the disaster an act of God. How foolish!

    Now in one sense God made the earth and has all power to interrupt the course of nature—but generally nature will run its course. You must learn to accept the laws of nature.
4. *Satan.* The Bible clearly says Satan walks about as a roaring lion, seeking whom he may destroy (see 1 Pet. 5:8 & 9).
5. *God.* The Bible says, *"For whom the Lord loveth he chasteneth, and scourgeth every son whom he receiveth"* (Heb. 12:6).

The next time you're going through a tough time, be careful as to where you place the blame.

•

Remember: CONSIDER THE SOURCE OF YOUR SUFFERING.

225/THE BATTLE IS BIGGER THAN YOU THINK!

"From the first day you set your heart to understand, and to chasten yourself before God, your (prayers) *were heard, and I am come* (as a result of your prayers). *But the* (demon) *prince of the kingdom of Persia* (resisted) *me for* (twenty-one) *days"* (Daniel 10:12 & 13, Literal).

Also read: 2 Cor. 10:3-5; 1 Pet. 5:8-9; 1 John 4:1-4

The prophet Daniel was aware that God's people (Jews) were in bondage and needed deliverance. He decided to fast and pray for their release. Finally, after 21 days of earnest prayer, the Lord appeared to Daniel and said in effect "I left from heaven with your answer on the first day of your prayer. But as I neared earth, the demonic prince of Persia resisted me and fought with me. Finally Michael (one of God's archangels) came to help me break through and now I've come with your answer."

This passage of Scripture was an eye-opener to me. It revealed that the spiritual battle you and I are fighting is much bigger than we have imagined. Even the Lord ran into resistance from Satan and needed help to break through to reach earth.

I believe Jesus has all power in heaven and earth, as He declared in Matthew 28:18, but this doesn't mean His power is exercised without resistance. The police in the U.S. and Canada have all power, but evil men can give the police a battle.

If you understand the scope of this struggle, that you are truly fighting *"against principalities, against powers, against the rulers of the darkness of this world, against spiritual wickedness in high places"* (Eph. 6:12) then you will take all prayer and supplication in the Spirit as outlined in Ephesians, chapter 6. Don't stop praying. Hang on like Daniel did—even if it takes 21 days!

•

Remember: THE BATTLE IS BIGGER THAN YOU THINK!

226/HOW TO SOLVE YOUR PROBLEMS!

"And it came to pass in those days, that (Jesus) went out into a mountain to pray, and continued all night in prayer to God" (Luke 6:12).

Also read: Psa. 46:1-3; Jn. 14:27; Phil. 4:6 & 7; Heb. 4:3, 9

Jesus was building the Kingdom of God and needed disciples—but whom should He choose? The scribes and Pharisees and chief priests and Levites were so hardened by their cast-iron opinions they would never accept the new concepts Jesus was trying to teach.

This left the common people: the fishermen, tax gatherers and other "now qualified" men. As the pressure mounted and Jesus knew He'd have to select twelve, He decided to solve His problem by spending an entire night in prayer.

Jesus knew He would have to get into the Spirit before He would know what to do in the natural. This is also the key to solving your problems.

It's good to get advice. The Bible says, *"Where no counsel is, the people fall; but in the multitude of counsellors there is safety"* (Prov. 11:14). If you are having problems it's wise to get good advice from qualified people, because there's sense in re-inventing the wheel.

However, when the experts disagree, there is one Mighty Counsellor, the Lord of Glory, who can advise you how to act.

This is when you need to get away from everything and spend special time in prayer and communion with God. The Holy Spirit will give you special directions on how to solve your problems.

Jesus spent many nights in prayer. This was one of the reasons for the great results of His ministry.

So if you're facing serious problems, do these 3 things:
1. Seek counsel from the wisest people you can find.
2. Seek advice from the Scriptures. Maybe your particular problem will not be described, but the principles of God's Kingdom will apply.
3. Seek God in prayer. Enter into the Spirit and you will find answers to the problems you are wrestling with in this material world.

•

Remember: WHEN YOU'RE REALLY CLOSE TO GOD, YOU'LL KNOW HOW TO SOLVE YOUR PROBLEMS.

227/PRAY LOUDER!

"They shall lift up their voice" (Isaiah 24:14).

Also read: 1 Pet. 5:7; Ja. 1:2-4, 12

One of my pet peeves is Christians who pray so quietly that hardly anyone can hear them. The quiet murmur creates a lonely silence that is restricting to the Spirit of God. This doesn't mean that every prayer should be bombastic, but I've found that most believers pray too meekly and quietly. We need to turn up the volume!

The Bible says the early Christians prayed loudly. *"And being let go, they went to their own company, and reported all that the chief priests and elders had said unto them. And when they heard that, THEY LIFTED UP THEIR VOICE TO GOD WITH ONE ACCORD....and when they had prayed the place was shaken where they were assembled together; and they were all filled with the Holy Ghost, and they spake the word of God with boldness"* (Acts 4:23,24,31, emphasis mine).

There is a humorous story of what happened at the White House when Lyndon Johnson was president. As a group sat down for a Sunday meal, he asked Bill Moyers, his press secretary and former Baptist minister, to lead in prayer. Bill prayed so quietly the President was annoyed and asked him why he didn't pray louder. Moyers replied, "I wasn't speaking to you."

I think the reason most people do not pray louder is they are coming humbly to the throne of grace. But the Bible says to *"come boldly unto the throne of grace, that we may obtain mercy, and find grace to help in time of need"* (Heb. 4:16).

I think some pray quietly because they think God prefers quiet prayers. The truth is quite the contrary. When blind Bartimaeus cried out, *"Jesus, thou son of David, have mercy on me,"* the Bible says, *"Jesus stood still"* (Mark 10:47,49).

•

Remember: PRAYER IS MORE THAN SOUNDS AND VOLUME. BUT TRUE PRAYER SHOULD HAVE ENOUGH FERVENCY TO REACH HEAVEN.

228/FUN WILL KEEP YOUR FIRES BURNING

"Rejoice in the Lord always; and again I say, Rejoice" (Philippians 4:4).

Also read: Psa. 32:11; 89:16; 106:5

When George Burns was 89 years old, he signed a 5-year contract with Caesar's Palace in Las Vegas. That's *faith!* He says he's so old he remembers playing Caesar's when Julius was there.

Why is George going to Caesar's while most of his contemporaries are going to the undertakers? I believe it's because he's having fun. Fun keeps your fires burning.

This is why Paul said to the Thessalonians, *"Always be joyful!"* (I Thess. 5:16, TLB). To the Philippians he wrote, *"Whatever happens, dear friends, be glad in the Lord. I never get tired of telling you this and it is good for you to hear it again and again"* (Phil. 3:1, TLB).

Are you rejoicing? You may be saying, "How can I rejoice in my condition?" The truth is that many people with much less than you are rejoicing. Songwriter Fanny Crosby was blind. However, she kept her heart filled with praises of God. Her gratitude overflowed into her songs like, "Blessed assurance, Jesus is mine, Oh, what a foretaste of glory divine."

When Fanny was only 9 years old she wrote:
Oh what a happy soul am I although I cannot see
I am resolved that in the world contented I will be.
So many pleasures I enjoy that other people don't
To weep and sigh because I'm blind I cannot and I won't.

At age 25 Fanny Crosby received her sight—but not in this world. She died and went home to heaven where she saw Jesus for the first time.

Have the fires of your joy been burning low? If so, ask God to forgive you for being ungrateful. Then begin to thank Him for all the great things He has done for you. Soon your heart will be so full you will begin to burn with joy.

•

Remember: REJOICE IN THE LORD; HAVING FUN WILL KEEP YOUR FIRES BURNING.

229/IT WASN'T WORK

"Do all things without murmurings" (Philippians 2:14).

Also read: Eph. 6:6-7; 1 John 2:17; 5:14-15

Recently I attended an awards ceremony where a certificate of appreciation was given to a man who had labored for many years at a thankless task.

The gesture touched his heart. He shed a few tears and then said, "I loved what I was doing; and even though it wasn't easy—it wasn't work."

I love that line. It should be the theme of every worker. Do you love your job enough to say, "It wasn't easy—but it wasn't work"?

The key to enjoying your job is to know that it is God's will. If it's in His will, then you're not working for the man or the money—but you're working for the Master—glorifying Him in everything you do.

It is very important that you love your job. Why? Because you'll only be good at the thing you like to do. Otherwise, you're just putting in time—trading your time and life for money. That is a poor exchange.

Keep this fact in mind—*work is not a curse.* When God created Adam he placed him in Paradise *"to dress it and to keep it"* (Gen. 2:15). God knew that Paradise wouldn't be Paradise without something worthwhile to do.

If you're not in love with your work, take some time each day to decide what you really want to do with your life. There are so many colleges, correspondence courses and books available that whatever your interest is you can soon develop your abilities to the point where you could earn your living at it.

The Chinese say, "A journey of a thousand miles begins with just one step." Take that first step towards happiness today by deciding what God wants you to do, and then start preparing yourself for a change. Soon you'll be able to say, "It wasn't easy—but it wasn't work."

•

Remember: IF YOU LOVE WHAT YOU'RE DOING, IT'S NOT WORK.

230/GOD IS WEAVING!

"And we know that all that happens to us is working for good if we love God and are fitting into his plans" (Romans 8:28, TLB).

Also read: 2 Cor. 12:9 & 10; Rom. 5:3 & 4; Matt. 11:28

LIFE'S WEAVING

My life is but a weaving
    Between my God and me;
I may not choose the colors,
    He knows what they should be.
For He can view the pattern
    Upon the upper side,
While I can see it only
    On this, the under side.

Sometimes He weaveth sorrow,
    Which seemeth strange to me;
But I will trust His judgment,
    And work on faithfully;
'Tis He who fills the shuttle,
    He knows just what is best;
So I shall weave in earnest
    And leave with Him the rest.

At last, when life is ended,
    With Him I shall abide,
Then I may view the pattern
    Upon the upper side;
Then I shall know the reason
    Why pain with joy entwined,
Was woven in the fabric
    Of life that God designed.

— Author Unknown

●

Remember: EVERYTHING WORKS FOR GOOD EVEN IF IT APPEARS TO BE BAD!

231/WHY SIN?

"There is a way which seemeth right unto a man, but the end thereof are the ways of death" (Proverbs 4:12).

Also read: Prov. 10:16; 14:34; Rom. 6:12

An evangelist is reported to have announced that there are 577 different sins people can commit. He received thousands of letters from people who wanted the list; possibly they were afraid they were missing out on some.

If you think about it, sinning is an art of stupidity. Why should anyone sin? What has sin ever done for you?

It destroys your relationship with God; it ruins your relationships with friends, family and associates; it costs money, and it weakens your mind and impairs your body.

The list could go on, but you pay a price for sinning—so why sin?

First, *there is momentary pleasure.* Moses chose to suffer affliction with the people of God rather than to enjoy *"the pleasure of sin for a season"* (Heb. 11:25). But you have to decide if the short term joy is worth the long term pain.

Second, *sin allows you to have your own way—at least for awhile.* The Bible says, *"all we like sheep have gone astray, we have turned each one—'to his own way"* (Isa. 53:6). The problem with a life of sin is that you can only have your own way as long as your body lasts. When your body breaks down, you'll still have the desire to sin but you won't have the machinery. (As one old man said, "I'd sin more but I don't have the strength.")

Sin is the easy way to ruin. Jesus said, *"Enter by the narrow gate; for the gate is wide and the way is easy, that leads to destruction, and those who enter by it are many"* (Matt. 7:13, RSV).

So, the choice is yours; as far as I'm concerned, sin is a bad bargain.

•

Remember: WHY SIN? IT'S NOT WORTH THE CONSEQUENCES.

232/FORGIVE FROM YOUR HEART!

"And his lord was (angry), and delivered him to the tormentors, till he should pay all that was due unto him. So likewise shall my heavenly Father do also unto you, if (you) from your hearts forgive not every one his brother their trespasses" (Matthew 18:34 & 35).

Also read: Matt. 6:14 & 15; Mk. 11:25; Col. 3:13

This may be the most important devotional you will read because it touches the very heart of your relationships with others. Jesus said, *"It (is unavoidable) that offenses come"* (Matt. 18:7). But Jesus also says that when these unavoidable offenses come you should forgive your brother from your heart.

Forgiving from your heart is much different from forgiving from your head or lips. You can mechanically say, "I forgive you"—but to truly *release* that forgiveness from your heart is another matter.

I'm sure you know the story that preceeds today's text. The apostle Peter came to Jesus and said, *"How often shall my brother sin against me, and I forgive him?...seven times?"* Jesus responded by saying, *"Not...seven times, but...seventy times seven"* (verses 21 & 22).

Then Jesus told the story of a servant who owed a king over 55 million dollars. Because the servant could not pay, the king was going to sell the servant, his wife and children on the market as slaves. The man begged for mercy and the king forgave his debt. But then the servant went out to another of his fellow servants (who owed him a mere 44 dollars) and demanded his money. When the fellow servant begged for mercy, the man would not forgive him his debt and cast him into prison. Then the king heard about his servant's heartlessness and *"delivered him to the tormentors until his debt was paid"* (see verse 34).

The truth is, if you don't forgive others who have hurt you, you will be tormented by inner conflict until you say from your heart, "I forgive you!"

Are you in torment today? If so, forgive your brother or that one who has hurt you so deeply.

•

Remember: YOU MUST FORGIVE FROM YOUR HEART IF YOU WANT GOD TO FORGIVE YOU FROM HIS HEART.

233/WHY CHURCHES ARE NOT MORE EVANGELISTIC!

"Go and make disciples in all the nations, baptizing them in the name of the Father and of the Son and of the Holy Spirit, and then teach these new disciples to obey all the commands I have given you; and be sure of this— that I am with you always, even to the end of the world" (Matthew 28:18-20, TLB).

Also read: 2 Tim. 4:5

The greatest percentage of evangelical churches are small. Most have under 100 attending. The question is, "Why aren't these Bible-believing churches more evangelistic? Why aren't they experiencing greater growth?"

There are many reasons, but the main one is *the pastor is not a soulwinning man.* In my 29 years of ministry, working with thousands of ministers, I can count on two hands the number of true soulwinning pastors I have met.

Many men become religious machines that turn out sermons and administrate committees, but very few have a fiery passion for lost souls.

Tommy Barnett is one of the great soulwinners of our day. He has built two churches from just a few hundred into thousands within short periods of time. Tommy says, "Someone asked me the other day, 'Pastor Barnett, is there anything wrong with a church being small?' I said, 'No, not for a week. But if you've got a soulwinning church, that church can't stay small.' The Bible says that *'the Lord added to the church daily'* (Acts 2:47). If we will do what we ought to do, we will spread the Word wherever we go and you can't keep a church small. The minimum number of people that ought to be saved in one year in a church is 365!"

Another reason churches are not winning souls is that laymen, as well as ministers, have a tendency to forget that the fires of hell await the wicked that we fail to win. If we remember this we'll become more evangelistic in soulwinning, and the church will grow.

•

Remember: YOU AND I CAN MAKE THE CHURCH MORE EVANGELISTIC!

234/WHY THE ANIMALS WENT WILD!

"Righteousness exalteth a nation: but sin is a reproach to any people" (Proverbs 14:34).

Also read: Psa. 9:15-20; Prov. 29:2; Gal. 6:17

One night several years ago there was a great electrical failure in New York; the city was plunged into darkness. The world was shocked at reports of the looting and pillaging that took place as thousands of New Yorkers went berserk in a billion dollar orgy of greed.

Notice, I said *greed*—not *need*! They didn't steal necessities; only luxuries. The greatest loss from the New York blackout was not money but the loss of faith in mankind. One overseas newspaper called the looting, "The night of the animals." Why did they do it? Columnist William Safire cut to the heart of the problem when he said, "The looters looted because of the spreading non-ethic that stealing is okay if you can get away with it; that only a jerk passes up the opportunity to rip off his neighbor; that society not only owes you a living, but the good life as well."

Much of North America is adopting this animalistic philosophy. Shoplifting is common; major crimes take place every 10 seconds. What happened in New York is just a warning of things to come—unless there is a genuine spiritual awakening.

You and I must do everything we can to help promote the teachings of God everywhere. George Washington, the father of our country, said, "The basis of all freedom is law, the basis of law is morality, the basis of morality is religion and the basis of religion is the Bible." A study of early American textbooks showed that 67 percent of the material taught moral lessons of right from wrong. Today, less than 6 percent of school materials are doing this. Is it any wonder our young people have lost their sense of right and wrong?

Do everything you can to fill your mind with God's Word; then promote it wherever you can.

•

Remember: JESUS TAKES THE "ANIMAL" OUT OF PEOPLE!

235/WHAT JESUS LOOKS LIKE!

"Then I lifted up mine eyes, and looked, and behold a certain man..." (Daniel 10:5).

Also read: John 6:40; 1 Pet. 1:7-9; 1 John 4:14

Have you ever wondered what Jesus looks like? The modern day paintings hardly do Him justice. But some people have seen Jesus as He really is.

There are two descriptive passages of Scripture that describe our Savior in His glory. The first is found in Daniel, chapter 10. The prophet Daniel had been fasting and praying for three weeks when Jesus appeared unto him. Now the Bible doesn't say it was Jesus but the descriptions of Christ in the first chapter of the Revelation and in Daniel match perfectly.

Daniel says, *"I looked up and suddenly there before me stood a person robed in linen garments, with a belt of purest gold around his waist, and glowing, lustrous skin! From his face came blinding flashes like lightning, and his eyes were pools of fire; his arms and feet shone like polished brass, and his voice was like the roaring of a vast multitude of people. I, Daniel, alone saw this great vision; the men with me saw nothing, but they were suddenly filled with unreasoning terror and ran to hide, and I was left alone. When I saw this frightening vision my strength left me, and I grew pale and weak with fright"* (Dan. 10:5-8, TLB).

The Apostle John also saw Jesus: *"When I turned to see who was speaking, there behind me...was one who looked like Jesus who called himself the Son of Man, wearing a long robe circled with a golden band across his chest. His hair was white as wool or snow, and his eyes penetrated like flames of fire. His feet gleamed like burnished bronze, and his voice thundered like the waves against the shore. He held...a sharp, double-bladed sword in his mouth, and his face shone like the power of the sun in unclouded brilliance. When I saw him, I fell at his feet as dead"* (Rev. 1:12-17, TLB).

●

Remember: THIS IS WHAT JESUS REALLY LOOKS LIKE. BE READY TO STAND BEFORE HIM WHEN HE RETURNS.

236/THE HOTLINE TO HAPPINESS

"For the kingdom of God is not meat and drink; but righteousness, and peace, and joy in the Holy Ghost" (Romans 14:17).

Also read: Prov. 17:22; Ps. 34:14; Matt. 25:21

Your desire to be happy is as fundamental as breathing. But the mistake most of us make is seeking happiness in the wrong place. Jesus told us to seek the Kingdom of God first because it would be the hotline to happiness (see Matt. 6:33).

Notice the three things the Kingdom of God is:

First, *It is Righteousness*, This means it is an upright standing before God and your fellowman. When you know God is pleased with your life—when you can approach Him without fear or reservation—you have taken a giant step in the direction of real happiness.

Second, *It is Peace*. This word in the original Greek means, "The absence of turmoil." Can you imagine living in a world that was free from stress and turmoil? This will be your life in the Spirit.

I know many get upset over the daily news, the price of food and clothing, etc., but all of this fear will vanish when you begin to understand how much you mean to God. King David said he had never seen the righteous forsaken or his seed begging bread (see Ps. 37:25).

You can have this turmoil-free life when you enter into a personal walk with God through the Holy Spirit.

Third, *It is Joy in the Holy Ghost*. This word, joy, in the original Hebrew means "to leap or to spin around in pleasure." Have you ever become so happy you felt like leaping and spinning around? This is the joy that awaits you when you enter into the realm of the Spirit.

Does all this sound exciting? The way to make this work is to soak your soul in the Scriptures and to share this message with others.

•

Remember: EXPERIENCING THE KINGDOM OF GOD IS THE HOTLINE TO HAPPINESS.

237/GOD'S SIMPLE PLAN OF SALVATION

"Believe on the Lord Jesus Christ, and thou shall be saved" (Acts 16:31).

Also read: Jn. 20:21; Acts 13:39

If you are a Christian the most difficult task you have is making salvation clear and plain to your non-Christian relatives and friends. If you are fuzzy about your faith and wonder if you will go to heaven at death, the most difficult task you have is understanding how simple God's plan of salvation really is.

Let me review it for you:

First, *You are a sinner.*

> The Bible says, *"For all have sinned, and come short of the glory of God"* (Rom. 3:23) I know how much I've failed God, and I'm sure you've failed Him, too.

Second, *You will die for your sins.*

> The Bible says, *"For the wages of sin is death"* (Rom. 6:23). Because you and I have sinned, we are separated from God just as death will one day separate us from our bodies.

Third, *Jesus Christ died for our sins!*

> The Bible says, *"But God commends his love toward us, in that while we were yet sinners, Christ died for us"* (Rom. 5:8).

God, our Father in Heaven, loved us so much that He sent Jesus Christ, His only begotten Son (the true physical manifestation of Himself) to die on the cross for our sins against God.

Fourth, *You need to receive Jesus Christ into your heart and life if you want to be saved. "For whosoever shall call upon the name of the Lord (Jesus Christ) shall be saved"* (Rom. 10:13).

We have sinned, but God who is rich in mercy sent Jesus, His Son, to die in our place. If we receive the Risen Savior into our hearts as Lord and Savior, He will save us from our sins.

Salvation isn't complicated. Just learn these four steps and you'll be able to share it with confidence to anyone!

•

Remember: SALVATION IS SIMPLE.

238/DON'T SAY YOU'VE FAILED!

"For God is not unmindful to forget your work and labor of love, which you have showed toward his name, in that you have ministered to the saints" (Hebrews 6:10).

Also read: Ps. 37:18; John 5:24; 1 Cor. 2:9-11; 15:54-55

Late in the last century an old man died in New York, considering himself a failure. He had lived in New York for 28 years, working as a customs inspector. His death received only 3 lines of notice in the newspaper.

Today his name is one of the most famous in American literature: Herman Melville, author of the classic novel, *Moby Dick.* His book has sold millions of copies. It was first published in 1851. In 10 years it had sold only 123 copies; during the next 25 years it only sold 22—less than one a year.

Herman, desiring to be a great writer, went to his grave defeated—thinking he had failed. Some thirty years later a noted critic was persuaded to read the book and later said, "Having done so, I hereby declare that since letters began (the writing of stories), there never was such a book, and that the mind of man is not so constructed so as to produce another; that I put its author with Robelair, Swift, and Shakespeare."

Today his book appears on the list of the ten greatest novels in the world.

Do you feel you've failed in life? Don't! Only God knows the people you have helped and encouraged, the prayers you have prayed, the money you have given, and the people who have been touched as a result.

One of the glories of heaven is to be rewarded for all you have done. Even a glass of water given in Jesus' name will be rewarded (see Matt. 10:42).

•

Remember: DON'T SAY YOU'VE FAILED. YOUR LIFE IS A BOOK AND ONLY GOD KNOWS ALL THE WONDERFUL THINGS WRITTEN IN IT.

239/UNMOVED!

"Those who trust in the Lord are steady as Mount Zion, unmoved by any circumstance" (Psalm 125:1).

Also read: Ps. 47:1; 98:4-6; 150:1-6

One day as I was going through a great trial, one of my dedicated staff handed me this verse. It settled my spirit immediately. What a gem!

Those who trust in the Lord are steady as Mount Zion. I have visited Jerusalem and the city is really built on a rock. There appears to be very little soil—just granite.

Jerusalem is also a high city. The elevation is 2,400 feet above sea level. So when you read in the Scriptures of "going up to Jerusalem" this is really the truth.

Whatever problems you have today, picture yourself sitting upon the high Holy Mountain of Jerusalem—a city built upon a rock. You will be steady—unmoved by any circumstance.

Are you under attack? If so, this gives you an opportunity to express your faith in God. Do these things:

First, find a Scripture from God's Word that applies to your situation. Today's text is terrific.

Second, say *out loud* "I am trusting in the Lord, I shall remain steady, unmoved by any circumstance."

Third, tell yourself God has never failed you before and He will not fail you now.

Fourth, enter into the Spirit. As Paul says in Galatians, *"Walk in the Spirit, and ye shall not fulfill the lust of the flesh"* (Gal. 5:16). Fear is a force of the flesh. The way to break its hold is to enter into God's presence. When the Spirit of the Lord is moving on your body, fear will vanish like darkness flees the light.

Tuck away these truths in your heart. When you go through a trial, the Holy Spirit will bring them to your remembrance.

•

Remember: TRUSTING IN THE LORD WILL KEEP YOU STEADY AS A ROCK.

240/HAVE YOURSELF A LAUGH

"A happy face means a glad heart: a sad face means a breaking heart" (Proverbs 15:13, TLB).

Also read: Psa. 146:5; Prov. 16:20; Jas. 5:11

Larry Hagman, who plays the role of "J.R." on the television series, "Dallas," has a most unusual way of cheering himself up. I've read that when he awakens he forces himself to laugh for 4 minutes. Each morning after his 4-minute self-therapy of laughter he feels he is better prepared to meet the day.

How about you? Do you enjoy laughing? Believe it or not it's really good for you. The Bible says, *"A merry heart doeth good like medicine: but a broken spirit drieth the bones"* (Prov. 17:22).

Amazingly, there are many people who haven't learned how to laugh. They have always been taught that life is a serious business and that laughter is not in good taste. The truth is that laughter is a great therapy. A good joke will keep you from going out of your mind. You've probably seen the sign hanging in many businesses that says, "You don't have to be crazy to work here—but it helps."

The Bible says, *"When a man is gloomy, everything seems to go wrong; when he is cheerful, everything seems right!"* (Prov. 15:15, TLB).

If things haven't been going right for you, try laughter. Put a smile on your face. Paul Little, a great soulwinner, said, "Every Christian should have 3 or 4 sure-fire jokes." He pointed out that it helps to get the conversation rolling.

How about you? Would you like to have yourself a laugh? If you do, here are some tips:

1. *Memorize* the punch line of your joke.
2. *Tell your joke quickly.* Cut out all but the most important words.
3. *Quote the jokes of famous comedians.* They are masters of merriment and they'll save you from groping for words.

Join me in the ministry of helping others laugh.

•

Remember: DON'T FORGET TO MAKE LAUGHTER A PART OF YOUR LIFE.

241/WE MUST PULL TOGETHER!

"(I pray)...that they also may be one in us: that the world may believe that you have sent me (Jesus) (see John 17:21).

Also read: Mark 9:38-40; 1 Cor. 1:9-10; 12:18-27

On March 2, 1944 the most unusual train tragedy in history took place near Salerno, Italy.

On that rain-soaked night, two engines were pulling a long passenger train when they entered a long tunnel called Galleria-dele-armi. There were over 600 passengers on board when they entered the tunnel—but only 100 came out.

But these are the facts investigators put together:
* It was a rainy night and the tracks were slippery.
* The two engines were carrying a heavy load of passengers on an incline.
* There was no collision.
* The train did not derail.
* But 500 passengers were asphyxiated to death from the engine fumes—the worst train tragedy in history.

What happened on that black rainy night is filled with speculation, but investigators found the first engine did not have its brakes on and was set in reverse. The second engine had brakes on but was set in forward gear.

It appears that when the train began the incline and entered the tunnel the wheels began to slip. But just then the two engineers had fatally different ideas of what to do: the first decided to back up and start again; the second decided to go forward by sanding the slippery tracks.

Because of their mixed signals the train stalled. Carbon monoxide fumes killed 500 passengers—including the two engineers.

Jesus prayed that you and I would become one so that the world would believe, that we all have our signals right, so the Gospel train won't stall and cause many to die.

Don't say negative things or withhold fellowshipping with Christians from denominations different from yours. This could result in many people dying without Jesus Christ.

•

Remember: WE MUST PULL TOGETHER!

242/HOW DOES GOD SPEAK TO YOU?

"...and the Lord said to them, even with a prophet, I would communicate by visions and dreams; but that is not how I communicate with my servant Moses. He is completely at home in my house! With him I speak face to face! And he shall see the very form of God!" (Numbers 12:6-8 TLB).

Also read: Ex. 20:19; Acts 8:29; Rom. 1:20

Here is a heavy question: "How does God speak to you?" Moses was one man of whom God said, *"With him I speak face to face."*

In these last days when the Bible says, *"Iniquity shall abound and the love of many shall wax cold"* (Matt. 24:12), a great number of people are content to communicate with God on a remote basis.

*Some are content to hear God's message through nature. They seldom attend church or read the Bible—but the great outdoors is their cathedral.

*Others are content to hear God's message through men. Many are not afraid of God but they're content to hear God through a minister. A sermon a week is as close to God as they really care to come.

*A growing number of people are hearing God by reading the Bible! The Scriptures, of course, are the final authority in knowing God. If you really want to know how God thinks, acts, and feels about things, you should study the Scriptures. You'll never know God until you do.

*You can also hear God speak through the Holy Spirit. The Bible says, *"While Peter thought on the vision, the Spirit said unto him, Behold, three men seek thee"* (Acts 10:19).

*God also said that people will hear from Him through visions and dreams: "I saw the vision of God" (Ez. 1:1).

But the greatest way God ever speaks is face to face as He has done with Moses and others.

•

Remember: GOD SPEAKS TO YOU IN MANY WAYS; ARE YOU LISTENING?

243/DRIVE AWAY THE BUZZARDS!

". . . fear not, neither be discouraged" (Deuteronomy 1:21).

Also read: Is. 43:1-7; Luke 12:32; 1 Cor. 10:13

A buzzard is one of the most dreaded creatures of the desert. It always attacks a man or animal who is about to die. It preys on weakness.

In Genesis you can read about Abraham, who journeyed into the wilderness and made a sacrifice to God. He built an altar to the Lord and offered a heifer, goat, ram, turtle dove, and a young pigeon. But that's not all. The Bible says, *"when the fowls came down upon the carcasses, Abram drove them away"* (Genesis 15:11). Abraham felt a responsibility not only to make his sacrifice but to protect it from the buzzards.

You have given your life to God as a living sacrifice, but if God is to receive it, you must also drive away these buzzards:

First, the *Buzzard of Discouragement.* This bird will attack you when you are physically and spiritually weak. This is why you must get your rest and spend time in God's Word. Drive that bird away today!

Second, watch out for the *Buzzard of Fear!* This bird will scare you to death if he can. He'll tell you that you're finished, that you'd better just give up and die. Drive him away!

And then there's the *Buzzard of Temptation.* He says you're not strong enough to endure the trials—that it's unfair for God to expect you to go on against such odds. This buzzard will start picking on your body before you're even dead. Cry out against him!

You may have some buzzards moving in on you today that I haven't mentioned. Whatever they are, say, "In the Name of Jesus Christ of Nazareth, the Lord, I rebuke you and all the devils and demons. I'm not going to be defeated. I am going to triumph in Jesus' Name. Amen."

●

Remember: DRIVE AWAY THE BUZZARDS!

244/STIR UP THE GIFT

"Wherefore I put thee in remembrance that thou stir up the gift of God, which is in thee" (2 Timothy 1:6).

Also read: Psa. 5:3; 55:17; 95:2; 142:1, 2; Heb. 11:6

How do you feel in your spirit today? Are things really happening for you? Do you feel the mighty rivers of God flowing out of your soul? Or do you feel flat and in a slump?

If you are not experiencing life in the way you would like to today, then you need to stir up the gift of God. This is what Paul encouraged Timothy to do. The Holy Spirit will move in you to the measure that you stir up your soul. How can you stir up your soul? Read more of God's Word, pray louder, longer and more fervently. Clap your hands and raise your voice to God—whatever it takes to get your soul moving in God's direction.

I know this may not appeal to your natural reasonings, but it is important to your growth and spiritual development. You must be willing to do whatever it takes to get ahold of God—and for God to get ahold of you.

Do you know how to shake yourself out of the dull habits of praying half-heartedly? Try these suggestions:

1. *Pray standing up.* When you pray as you're kneeling it's too easy to fall asleep.
2. *Pray out loud.* Lift up your voice until it shakes the room!
3. *Pray while walking around.* The more action, the better. You can stir yourself with movement.
4. *Pray with your hands raised heavenward.* Paul said, "I will therefore that men pray every where, lifting up holy hands" (1 Tim. 2:8).
5. *Pray boldly.* "For we have not a high priest which cannot be touched with the feeling of our infirmities; but was in all points tempted like as we are, yet without sin. Let us therefore come BOLDLY unto the throne of grace, that we may obtain mercy, and find grace to help in time of need" (Heb. 4:15 & 16, emphasis mine).

•

Remember: STIR UP THE GIFT OF GOD.

245/GOOD MORNING, FATHER!

"O God, thou art my God: early will I seek thee: my soul thirsteth for thee, my flesh longeth for thee in a dry and thirsty land, where no water is" (Psalm 63:1).

Also read: Ps. 5:3; 88:13; 92:1 & 2

An Indian girl, Carol One-Chance Black Hawk, found this special prayer two years ago and says that she prays it aloud each morning. By doing this, she puts on her spiritual armor and receives victory throughout the day. She adds her own prayers in between the major points. There is much more to her prayer than space allows me to show you, but here's a little to give you a taste of it!

"Good morning, Father!
Good morning, Jesus!
Good morning, Holy Spirit!
You are my Great and Mighty God, and I love ya!

Romans 12:1 - Heavenly Father, according to your Word, I present my body a living sacrifice, holy, acceptable in your spirit.

1 John 1:9 - I confess all sin that you show me in my heart, and by Your Power within me, I turn from those sins. Thank you for forgiving me of all my sin and cleansing me of all unrighteousness. Fill me to overflowing with Your Holy Spirit.

Eph. 6:14-17 - Now, Father, I put on the belt of Truth. I put on the breastplate of righteousness. I put on my feet the preparation of the Gospel of peace. Above all, I take the shield of faith wherewith I shall be able to quench all the fiery darts of the wicked one. I put on the helmet of salvation and pick up the sword of the Spirit, which is the Word of God."

Then she prays: "Let others see Jesus in me today; let me shine as Your light wherever I may be.

"I pray in the Name of Jesus, my risen Savior, who is LORD OF MY LIFE! Amen."

•

Remember: PUT ON YOUR SPIRITUAL ARMOR AND RECEIVE VICTORY THROUGHOUT YOUR DAY!

246/ENTER INTO HIS PRESENCE!

"Let us come before his presence with thanksgiving, and make a joyful noise unto him with psalms" (Psalm 95:2).

Also read: Psa. 51:11; 140:13

How fulfilling is your prayer life? Do you feel you're really making contact with God in heaven or do you feel disconnected?

One of the greatest Psalms in the Bible declares, *"Serve the Lord with gladness: come before his presence with singing ... Enter into His gates with thanksgiving, and into his courts with praise: be thankful unto him, and bless his name"* (Psalm 100:2,4).

You can see the steps you should take when entering into God's presence.

1. *Serve the Lord with gladness!* Be joyous when you approach God. Imagine how boring it must be for God to listen to people mumbling their prayers. Lift up your voice, bless the Lord, encourage Him! Serve Him with gladness.

2. *Come before His presence with singing!* Try singing a special love song to the Lord "in the spirit." God created you to sing and your song will touch God as much when praying alone as when you sing with a congregation—maybe even more.

3. *Enter into His gates with thanksgiving!* Learn how to thank God. Pray out loud; raise your hands heavenward (see 1 Tim. 2:8). Express your thanksgiving without inhibitions. Don't say, "Our church or family doesn't pray this way." Do as the Bible says and you'll find your prayers getting through.

4. *Enter into His courts with praise!* Tell God how wonderful He really is. Articulate your feelings with your lips. Praise has power to bring you into God's presence.

5. *Bless His name!* You have a lot of things to thank God for—so bless Him! Encourage God for His grace and patience. When you sincerely follow these steps it will help you to enter into His presence when you pray. These steps may be new to your prayer life, but you'll find them very effective.

•

Remember: ENTER HIS PRESENCE WHEN YOU PRAY— IT WILL BRING YOU THE FULFILLMENT AND JOY YOU ARE SEARCHING FOR.

247/OLD SERMONS

"Therefore every (scholar) which is instructed into the kingdom of heaven is like unto a man that is an householder, which bringeth forth out of his treasure things new and old" (Matthew 13:52).

Also read: Prov. 8:34; Matt. 7:24-27; John 5:24; Jas. 1:22-25

Have you ever heard a preacher repeat himself? If so don't think less of the man. Jesus said a true scholar brings forth truths out of his treasure house—both OLD and new.

I know some pastors and evangelists who are afraid to repeat their best sermons. This is foolishness. D. L. Moody, the famous evangelist, said, "A man doesn't preach a sermon good until he preaches it twenty-five times." It takes that long to knock the "schlock" out of it. (Schlock is a popular expression referring to unnecessary words.)

You might say, "Isn't it boring to hear a preacher retell a story?" Not if you will listen constructively. Whenever a minister repeats a story or sermon, listen to see how he uses different phrases, observe the ways he abbreviates it. By listening carefully I've been able to learn something new every time.

Did you know that people only remember 7% of what they hear the first time? Ninety-three percent is lost—as if it had never been. This means you could listen to the same sermon at least 14 times before it really sinks in. This is why Jesus said every scholar brings forth out of his treasure things both old and new.

You probably heard the story of the congregation who complained to the pastor that he was repeating the same sermon week after week. To this he replied, "When you start living up to this sermon I'll give you another."

Be patient. You can hear the same sermon over and over again, and as long as it is anointed by the Spirit of God, you'll learn something new each time. If you're listening to a minister repeat himself, don't turn off your mind. Jesus said, *"He that hath an ear, let him hear what the Spirit saith"* (Rev. 2:7).

•

Remember: OLD SERMONS ARE LIKE SOLID GOLD—KEEP MINING THEM UNDER THE ANOINTING OF THE SPIRIT.

248/GOD LOOKS AT YOUR PROBLEM DIFFERENTLY!

"For as the heavens are higher than the earth; so are my ways higher than your ways, and my thoughts than your thoughts" (Isaiah 55:9).

Also read: Lam. 3:37; Jer. 29:11 & 12; Ecc. 3:1

One of the greatest sorrows a Christian parent can experience is to see your child turn away from the Lord. Everything within you cries out, "Where did I fail?" or, "Why didn't I do things differently?" You feel you've failed God as well as your child.

I'm sure this is what the parents of Samson felt when he came home and announced that he was going to marry a Philistine girl. Remember, Samson was a miracle child. His mother was barren until the time the angel of the Lord appeared unto her and announced his birth. Samson grew up in a godly home and as a teenager experienced the moving of the Spirit.

The Bible says, Samson's parents *"objected strenuously"* (Judges 14:3, TLB). But he wouldn't change his mind.

However, God was working behind the scenes. Even though it is not His general will that Christians marry unbelievers, the Scripture says, *"HIS FATHER AND MOTHER DIDN'T REALIZE THAT THE LORD WAS BEHIND THE REQUEST, for God was setting a trap for the Philistines, who...were rulers of Israel"* (verse 4).

This is the verse of scripture I am holding on to for our daughter, Lisa. We raised her to serve the Lord. Today she is not serving Him, but we're praying for her salvation. The Lord will then use her compromise to win a great victory against the devil.

Later on Samson did win a great victory against the Philistines. God worked the evil for good because His ways are above our ways.

If you're really in a fiery trial, memorize today's text. Repeat it over and over until the truth becomes alive in your soul.

•

Remember: GOD LOOKS AT YOUR PROBLEM DIFFERENTLY. YOU MAY SEE DEFEAT. HE SEE'S THE VICTORY COMPLETE!

249/"PURR" YOUR PRAISES!

"Let every thing that hath breath praise the Lord" (Psalm 150:6).

Also read: Ps. 150

Did you hear about the tomcat who lives in luxury? His owner says, "All this cat has is a meow, a motor and a leg rub, and he gets everything he wants out of life."

The man went on to say that the first thing the tomcat does when he lets him in early in the morning is rub against his leg. "Now this is a very clever cat, because he knows I will get him some cat "crunchies." But he's not satisfied with just crunchies; he wants milk—preferably warm. So he's learned how to make his requests known with thanksgiving.

"The other morning I let him in and counted the number of times he rubbed against my leg. He went back and forth 17 times. How can you resist a cat that says 'I love you!' 17 times *before* you give him anything?"

The man was right; with a meow, a purring motor vibrator and a leg rub, that clever cat had the run of the place.

The Bible says that wisdom is the principal thing and we should seek it with all our strength.

You and I would be wise to know that gratitude is the key to getting anywhere with God or men. The Bible says, *"with thanksgiving let your requests be made known unto God"* (Phil. 4:6). The Psalmist says, *"Oh that men would praise the Lord for his goodness, and for his wonderful works to the children of men!"* (Psalm 107:21).

Praise also works with men. Paul said, *"(I) cease not to give thanks for you, making mention of you in my prayers"* (Eph. 1:16). The Living Bible says it this way, *"I have never stopped thanking God for you. I pray for you constantly."* Praise and appreciation of others helped Paul to build many missionary churches in the pagan world.

So let's learn from the apostle (or the cat); it doesn't hurt to "purr."

•

Remember: IT'S WISE TO "PURR" YOUR PRAISES!

250/BE A COMFORTER!

"God, that comforteth those that are cast down, comforted us by the coming of Titus" (2 Corinthians 7:6).

Also read: Job 2:11; Isa. 40:1; John 11:19; 2 Cor. 1:3-7

Nearly everyone you meet today has problems; each one is struggling with a situation that appears to be beyond his strength or ability to handle.

This is why you should be a comforter. When the Apostle Paul was going through a rough time he was comforted by the coming of Titus.

Do you make an effort to comfort others? Even leaders like your pastor, your boss, your banker, or your doctor need to know how much you care. The best way to encourage others is to stay "prayed up" and full of the Holy Spirit. Jesus said, *"But when the Comforter is come, whom I will send unto you from the Father, even the spirit of truth...he shall testify of me"* (John 15:26).

When you are full of God, people will feel His presence in your life. The Holy Spirit will also give you encouraging things to say. Titus shared the good news of what God was doing in the Corinthian church: *"He told us your earnest desire, your mourning* (repentence), *your fervent mind* (warm affection) *toward me; so that I rejoiced the more"* (2 Cor. 7:7).

If you want to be a comfort to others, you need to share good news—especially since nearly everything they hear is bad.

Each day I try to find an uplifting verse of Scripture, an exciting spiritual truth, a good report of something God is doing or a hilarious joke to share with friends. This is the way I try to comfort others throughout the day.

So, be like Titus—stay "prayed up" full of the Holy Ghost and make an effort to say something good to those you visit today.

•

Remember: YOU ONLY PASS THIS WAY BUT ONCE— COMFORT OTHERS ALONG YOUR WAY.

251/WILL YOU BE GOOD ENOUGH TO KEEP?

"For we must all appear before the judgment seat of Christ; that every one may receive the things done in his body...whether it be good or bad. Knowing therefore the terror of the Lord, we persuade men" (2 Corinthians 5:10 & 11).

Also read: Heb. 4:13; Prov. 15:3

I love to fish and was lucky enough to catch a 22 pound muskie in Canada last summer. Recently I ran across this poem:

> THE FISHERMAN'S PRAYER
> God grant that I may live to fish
> Until my dying day.
> And when my final cast is made,
> I very humbly pray,
> When in the Lord's own landing net
> I'm peacefully asleep,
> His mercy then will judge me
> "As good enough to keep!"

Paul the apostle was very concerned that you and I be prepared to stand before the judgment seat of Christ. Knowing it would be a fearful thing to give account for every thought and deed, Paul said he worked hard to win people to Christ. The question arises then, "What will God be looking for on Judgment Day?"

1. PURITY. Jesus said, *"Blessed are the pure in heart: for they shall see God"* (Matt. 5:8). John the apostle said, *"Every man that hath this hope in him purifieth himself, even as he is pure."* (1 John 3:3).
    You must purify yourself. God is pure. So, when you appear before him, he will look for His own character in you!
2. FAITHFULNESS. Paul said, *"It is required in stewards that a man be found faithful"* (1 Cor. 4:2).
3. GENUINE LOVE. In Revelation, Jesus wrote to the Ephesian Christians who were hard working, holy, and helpful; but they had lost their first love. That burning love and zeal for Christ. He said, *"Remember therefore from whence thou art fallen, and repent, and do the first works: or else I will come unto thee quickly, and will remove thy candlestick...except thou repent"* (Rev. 2:5).

•

Remember: IF YOU WANT GOD TO KEEP YOU, BE A GOOD FISH.

252/WHO OWNS WHAT?

"The earth is the Lord's, and the fulness thereof; the world, and they that dwell therein" (Psalm 24:1).

Also read: Gen. 1:1 - 2:3; Hag. 2:6-9

The first law of supernatural prosperity is this: *God owns everything. You do not own anything. You only manage what God loans to you.* A billionaire died recently and someone asked how much he left; a wise man answered, "He left everything."

You don't own your children—they are *"an heritage of the Lord"* (Psa. 127:3). You don't even own your body; it returns to dust at death. You don't own your spirit, for it also returns to God. The Bible says in Ezekiel 18:4, *"All souls are mine".* The only possession you have is your will. You can say "Yes" or "No." This is why the greatest decision you will ever make is to say "Yes" to God.

What if you used your will against Him? Let's say you were walking down the street one day and a tiny ant crawled up out of a crack. You said, "Let me walk by!" And the ant piped up, "No!" What would you do? Whammm! You would stomp your foot down and that would be the last of the ant. You and I are ants in comparison to God; the stupidest thing we can do is refuse to do our Father's will.

Don't say "No" to God by insisting that everything He has entrusted you with is *yours.* It's not. However, God has given you the privilege of managing His possessions. What an honor! A song says, "If all I have belongs to Him, then all He has is mine!" That's the truth! The Bible says we are *"heirs of God and joint-heirs with Christ!"* (Rom. 8:17). God has placed you here on earth to see how you are going to manage your inheritance.

Say "Yes" to God. Trust Him completely with anything He has given you. If you have not done so already, acknowledge His total Lordship over everything that is "yours."

•

Remember: GOD OWNS EVERYTHING—HE HAS GIVEN YOU EVERYTHING. WHAT WILL YOU DO WITH IT?

253/AFRAID—BUT MOVING FORWARD

"And I was with you in weakness, and in fear, and in much trembling" (1 Corinthians 2:3).

Also read: Ps. 27:1, 3; 91:4-7; Prov. 3:25, 26; 2 Tim. 1:7

Are you facing a fearful situation? If you're afraid—welcome to the company of faith-heroes! If you think the Apostle Paul was a superman read today's text along with this verse, *"For, when we were come into Macedonia, our flesh had no rest, but we were troubled on every side; without were fightings, within were fears"* (2 Cor. 7:5).

Paul was afraid, but not in a cowardly, retreating sort of way. He said, *"We are troubled on every side, yet not distressed; we are perplexed, but not in despair; persecuted, but not forsaken; cast down, but not destroyed"* (2 Cor. 4:8 & 9).

Fear can propel you toward victory as well as defeat. The outcome depends on your decision at the moment you confront a dangerous situation. Psychologists say that the same force that causes you to flee can prompt you to conquer if you will be aggressive.

Fear triggers the release of adrenalin into the bloodstream—so you're potentially stronger when you're afraid. But with this energy you must decide whether to run or to fight.

I remember, as a boy, how I hated to walk to Grandma's house in the dark. Every bush had shadows and the night sounds were so eerie that they sent shivers down my spine. As long as I walked slowly and kept "cool" I was all right. But if I once yielded to my fears and started to run, my heart would leap into my throat and waves of terror would sweep over my body.

You must learn to face your fears. If you're afraid of water—go swimming; if you're afraid of flying—go by air on your next trip. Are you afraid of Satan? Then rebuke him saying, "Evil one, the Lord rebuke you for what you're doing in my life."

What is it you fear? God will give you the power to conquer it.

•

Remember: USE THE POWER OF FEAR TO KEEP YOU MOVING FORWARD.

"Who is it that overcomes the world? Only he who believes that Jesus is the Son of God" (1 John 5:5, NIV).

Also read: Lk. 11:28; Jam. 4:7; 2 Chron. 16:9

Connie and I were in a restaurant one day when we noticed a man sitting at the next table who kept watching us. Finally, he came over and said, "I watch you on television. You have the greatest Christmas specials. I admire what you're doing even though your philosophy is different than mine."

I said, "Thank you. What is your philosophy?"

He said, "I'm one of the heads of the Communist Party. We watch you very carefully because you communicate so well. In fact, we video taped your last special and showed it to the heads of the Communist Party in my country. We all admired how well you express your Christian values.

"Of course," he added, "you understand, Mr. Lundstrom, ultimately you and your Christian philosophy are going to lose. We are going to take over the world, and we are soon going to take over this country. If you were wise, you would join us. We need a communicator like you, someone who can articulate what we feel. Why don't you join us?"

I said, "Sir, do you know much about Bible prophecy? The Bible refers to Russia in Ezekiel 38 as 'the land of Magog.' It says you guys are going to lose. Now, I don't want to join up with losers, but I would like for you to invite me to talk with your leaders. I'll show you that you're going to lose in your plan to gain the world. The One who is going to win is the Lord God Jehovah. Jesus is going to rule the world."

He suddenly had to leave in a hurry.

No one wants to be a loser, and the best way you can be sure you are going to win is to accept Jesus as your Lord and Savior, and live for Him. With Christ, you will not only win in the end, but you will win in your everyday life.

•

Remember: WITH JESUS, YOU ARE ON THE WINNING SIDE!

255/PRAISE GOD WITH WHAT YOU HAVE!

"I will bless thee while I live: I will lift up my hands in thy name" (Psalm 63:4).

Also read: Ps. 146:2; 1 Peter 1:7; 4:11

Do you wish you had more to offer God? Sometimes the few talents we have seem so insignificant compared with God's blessings.

Our smallness always seems exaggerated when we are sick, but that's when we need to learn to praise God with what we have. Several years ago Evangelist Dwight Thompson called upon a pastor friend in the hospital. The man had served God faithfully for years but was now suffering from great depression; both of his legs were amputated.

As Dwight walked down the hospital corridor toward the man's room, the devil said, "I've almost got Brother Taylor. I've taken away his health, his wealth, and his will to live. It won't be long before he'll be cursing God and I'll have his soul." When the evangelist walked in, the pastor began crying and said, "Why me? I've served God all these years and now this, why me?"

The pastor was so depressed that the evangelist could do very little to encourage him. Finally he prayed for him and started to leave.

Just then he turned and said, "Brother Taylor, as I was on my way to see you today, the devil said, "I've almost got Brother Taylor. I've taken away his health, and his wealth and his will to live and it won't be long before he'll be cursing God and I'll have his soul."

Hearing this, a fire lit up in the eyes of the bedridden pastor, and he replied, "Oh, the devil told you that, did he? Well you tell him this: I've still got two good hands; and as long as I have them, I'll lift them up to praise the Lord! And I've still got a tongue; and as long as I have it I'll use it to praise the Lord. You tell the devil he hasn't heard the last from me yet!"

•

Remember: DON'T LET THE DEVIL DISCOURAGE YOU; KEEP PRAISING GOD WITH WHAT YOU HAVE.

256/WHY PAIN IS IMPORTANT

"And God shall wipe away all tears from their eyes; and there shall be no more death, neither sorrow, nor crying, NEITHER SHALL THERE BE ANY MORE PAIN: for the former things are passed away" (Revelation 21:4, emphasis mine).

Also read: Rom. 5:3, 4; 1 Pet. 2:20, 21; 5:10

If you are in pain, today's text describes heaven in a way that only a sufferer could understand: Praise God, heaven will be pain-free!

One of the great questions of life is, "If God is loving and all-powerful, why doesn't He rid the world of pain? Why does He allow people to suffer so?"

One of my friends, a godly Christian leader, experienced terrible pain before he died from cancer. The tumor on his back was the size of a basketball. I'll never forget how he cried the day I prayed with him. After his funeral his son said, "Dad fought death and died an inch at a time."

When your body screams for mercy, when each breath is torture and death seems more merciful than life, it is very difficult to believe that a loving God would ever allow pain to exist.

However, pain is important. *Pain protects your body.* There are many cases where people have lost their sensitivity to pain. Each day they must check over every inch of their bodies to see if they have contacted infection from an undetected wound. Leprosy (called Hansen's disease) desensitizes fingers and toes to the point where victims literally wear them off—because they don't feel anything when they are hurt. Because of a lack of pain, some lepers have foolishly lifted live coals out of fires and burned off their fingers.

It is impossible to live a normal life without pain—it protects you from destroying yourself.

Yet, for the one who suffers continually, God gives His promise that one day He will abolish pain—and this will surely be heaven for everyone.

•

Remember: PAIN IS IMPORTANT—BUT GOD IS MAKING ALL THINGS NEW IN A PAIN-FREE WORLD!

257/ALL YOU HAVE TO DO IS ASK!

"Jesus answered and said unto her, If thou knewest the gift of God, and who it is that saith to thee, Give me a drink; thou wouldest have asked of him, and he would have given thee living water" (John 4:10).

Also read: Is. 12:3; Ps. 126:5 & 6

There are times when I get down. Everyone does. There are times when you need to be lifted up, to be comforted, to be strengthened.

In John 4, Jesus met a woman at the well of Samaria who was having a difficult time. Five marriages had ended in failure and now she was living with a man who wasn't her husband. Jesus, perceiving the woman's lonely heart, looked at her and said—

"whosoever drinketh of this water—referring to the well of Jacob and to life in general—*shall thirst again: but whosoever drinketh of the water that I shall give him shall never thirst; but the water springing up into everlasting life"* (verses 13 & 14).

Can you imagine how depressed in spirit this woman must have been? No doubt, she felt that her life was empty, meaningless, and hopeless. Jesus told her, "The way to come out of your depression is to drink of the satisfying water I can give you."

Before I became a Christian, I had a rock 'n roll dance band, and we played in nightclubs. I smiled and put on a happy front, but inside I felt empty and sad—like the woman at the well. I said, "There's got to be something more for me."

Then Jesus came into my heart. I was born again. Thank God, the well of living water He gave me has been springing up in my heart ever since. Jesus told the woman at the well all she had to do to have this life-giving water was ask Him for it. That's all you have to do also. And you'll never be the same!

•

Remember: ASK JESUS TO FILL YOUR EMPTINESS AND HE WILL!

"Let everything that hath breath praise the Lord. Praise ye the Lord" (Psalm 150:6).

Also read: Psa. 135:1-3; 138; 142; 147:1; 149:1-6

My 7½ year old son, Lance, is one of the great loves of my life. I was 38 when Lance was born. Someone said when you have a son at this age you love him twice as much: first as a father and secondly as a grandfather.

Anyway, I love to do things for and with Lance. There's really nothing I want from him except his love. He can't afford to buy me anything and I wouldn't really want him to spend his money on me even if he had some.

All I want is to see his eyes twinkle with love and to hear him say, "Dad, I love you."

I'm sure this is true of God. He owns the cattle on a thousand hills and the earth and its fullness belong to Him (see Ps. 50:10). God already owns everything, so there really isn't anything we can give to Him except our love.

If our love and praises are what nourishes God—then we should be careful not to withhold what He desires most.

David exhorts all of creation to praise God in Psalm 148:1-4, *"Praise ye the Lord. Praise ye the Lord from the heavens: praise him in the heights. Praise ye him, all his angels: praise ye him all ye hosts. Praise ye him, sun and moon: praise him, all ye stars of light. Praise him, ye heavens of heavens, and ye waters that be above the heavens."*

If all creation is to praise the Lord, don't you think that you and I, who were created in God's own image, should praise Him, too?

Is God starving for expressions of your love? Learn to pray out loud. Verbalize your feelings. The Lord wants to know how you feel about Him (See Psalm 50:23, TLB).

•

Remember: LET GOD KNOW YOU REALLY LOVE HIM.

259/SPEAK YOUR WORLD INTO BEING

"...God, who quickeneth the dead...calleth those things which be not as though they were" (Romans 4:17).

Also read: Prov. 18:4, 7; Matt. 12:34-37; Mark 11:23

Think on this: God calls things that are not, as though they were. When Abram was a childless old man God changed his name to Abraham, *"...a father of many nations"* (Gen. 17:5) even though at that time Abram didn't have an heir. In the book of Revelation the Lord shows the Apostle John the glories of heaven and says, *"It is done"* (Rev. 21:6), even though it was centuries away.

Do you want to be like God? Then begin speaking your world into existence. Be careful. The words you say either build up your world or tear it down.

Faith and unbelief are invisible forces and remain unseen until you give substance to them. The moment you speak words of either faith or doubt, you have given substance to invisible feelings.

Thought is powerful.

Words are more powerful.

Words in print are most powerful of all.

The Bible says, *"Death and life are in the power of the tongue"* (Prov. 18:21).

This is why gossip is so deadly. Gossip is usually a rehash of someone's failures. The moment you participate in it you have spoken your own defeat into existence. The Bible says, *"A wholesome tongue is a tree of life"* (Prov. 15:4).

What kind of world have you built with your words? Do you like what you've built? Are you proud of your job, family, and spiritual life?

More importantly—what kind of world are you going to build with your words? Are you speaking words of praise and appreciation, words of hope and promise, words of success and accomplishment? It's never too late to change your world of words.

●

Remember: YOU ARE SPEAKING A WORLD INTO BEING WITH YOUR WORDS—MAKE SURE IT IS THE BEAUTIFUL WORLD YOU WANT IT TO BE.

260/THREE WAYS WE COMMUNICATE WITH GOD

"God is a Spirit: and they that worship him must worship him in spirit and in truth" (John 4:24).

Also read: Jn. 16:7; 1 Cor. 2:12; Prov. 1:23

There are three ways to communicate with God.

First, through prayer—when you ask God for things.

Second, through praise—when you thank God for what He's already done. This is a deeper form of prayer.

And third, through worship—when you worship God for who He is. You don't ask Him for anything. You just love and adore Him. This is pure worship, the most uplifting of all communication with God. It will lift you out of your emptiness. It will quicken you and re-energize your life.

So many times we come to God with our list of wants and needs. Or we thank Him for doing this, this, and this, hoping He will do more, more, and more. But real communication with God is when you worship Him for who He is.

True worship is through the Spirit. There is within every one of us an insatiable hunger to worship God. You have this hunger. I have it. We all have it. Nothing else will satisfy this desire, and nothing pleases God more than for us to worship Him from deep down within our inner spirit.

Jesus told the Samaritan woman at Jacob's well, *"The hour cometh, and now is, when the true worshippers shall worship the Father in spirit and in truth: for the Father seeketh such to worship him"* (John 4:24).

The Bible says we don't know how to pray as we ought. But the Spirit *"Helpeth our infirmities...and maketh intercession for us with groanings which cannot be uttered"* (Rom. 8:26). The Holy Spirit, who understands the deep mysteries of God and who knows all about you and your problems, intercedes directly with God for you. So learn to communicate with God from your inner being through the Spirit.

•

Remember: WORSHIPING IN THE SPIRIT REACHES GOD!

261/WATCH OUT FOR THE LITTLE THINGS

"The little foxes...spoil the vines" (Song of Solomon 2:15).

Also read: Jas. 3:5-8

Little things can really mess up your life. Robert Romano of Staten Island, New York, was driving home from work early one day when he came to a deserted intersection.

His car ran over a small nail in the road and his tire blew. Romano lost control and hit a street lamp. The impact bent over the pole and the car careened towards a fire hydrant, snapping it off and causing flooding under the street.

The deluge undermined the intersection which collapsed, leaving a 50-foot crater in the street. The cave-in ruptured a gas main and police in hip boots had to evacuate 17 nearby residents to safety.

One little nail in the wrong place caused this awesome series of events.

There is an unusual verse in the Bible that says, *"Dead flies will cause even a bottle of perfume to stink! Yes, a small mistake can outweigh much wisdom and honor"* (Ecc. 10:1 TLB).

If you want to be a success you have to constantly be on guard about the little things.

Here are some little things to watch:

1. *Beware of hard feelings.* If someone has a grudge against you or refuses to respond warmly to you it's best to be sincere and forthright in asking why they appear to be offended.
2. *Beware of bad habits.* Ask your close friends and loved ones what annoys them most about you; they'll tell you. Then try your best to change.
3. *Beware of unfinished business.* The best time to do something is when you think of it. If you can't do it then, jot it down on a pad of paper so you won't forget. Unfinished business has a way of finishing you off as far as credibility is concerned.

•

Remember: IT'S THE LITTLE THINGS THAT REALLY MESS UP YOUR LIFE.

JESUS HAS ABOLISHED DEATH

"...Jesus Christ, who hath abolished death...hath brought life and immorality to light through the gospel" (2 Timothy 1:10).

Also read: Ps. 23:4; 1 Cor. 15:55-57; 1 Thess. 4:13-14

You and I are speeding towards death at the rate of 60 minutes per hour. Each heartbeat is a countdown to "boxing-day," when we're boxed up in a coffin and buried.

Longfellow said, "Our hearts, though stout and brave like muffled drums, are beating funeral marches to the grave."

Death is knocking at our door. We can see the signs of decay with every gray hair, every wrinkle and with every visit to the cemetery.

Into this horrible blackness shines a light so brightly it destroys the darkness. Jesus Christ says, *"I am the resurrection, and the life: he that believeth in me, though he were dead, yet shall he live; And whosoever liveth and believeth in me shall never die"* (John 11:25, 26).

Jesus declares that He has power over death—can He prove it?

1. He proved it by raising Lazarus from the dead, four days after his death (see John 11).
2. He proved it by raising the widow of Nain's son from the dead (see Luke 7:11-18).
3. Jesus proved it by His own resurrection from the dead (see John 20).

These exhibits of power prove that Jesus Christ has abolished death. Those who trust in Him are transported to Paradise in the presence of God. Paul says, *"We are confident...and willing...to be absent from the body, and to be present with the Lord"* (2 Cor. 5:8).

Death is really only a breath you take between this world and the next. Please do this: Hold your breath for the count of ten. (Did you do it? If not, please go back and do what I said.)

Now, for that moment you did not breath; were you dead? Not at all. That is all dying is: Death is like holding your breath while your life goes on.

•

Remember: JESUS HAS ABOLISHED DEATH!

263/HELPING GOD WORK A MIRACLE

"Whatsoever thou shalt bind on earth shall be bound in heaven: and whatsoever thou shalt loose on earth shall be loosed in heaven" (Matthew 16:19).

Also read: Jam. 2:18; Jn. 14:12; Matt. 17:20

God wants you to be an overcomer. The Scripture says He *"always causeth us to triumph in Christ"* (2 Cor. 2:14). To be an overcomer, there are times when you need a miracle. And the Bible tells you the principles to follow to help God work a miracle when you need one.

Miracles must be made to happen. That surprises some people, because they think a miracle is something that happens to someone else...something that happened in the Bible...something they have nothing to do with. But Jesus taught us that we make miracles happen by acting on His word.

A miracle is the result of you and God working together as a team. You do your part and God does His part. The result is a wonder of God—a miracle.

The Lord reminded me of this wonderful truth recently. In a meeting one night, a farmer who had received Christ in one of our crusades said, "Lowell, God worked a miracle for me today. He stopped the rain."

Knowing how wet it had been in Western Minnesota at that time, I knew that for the Lord to stop the rain for this man, it was a miracle.

"I helped God work the miracle," he said.

"What do you mean, you helped God work the miracle?" I asked.

He said, "I took authority over the rain. I told the rain to stop in the name of Jesus, and it did."

Has the devil been attacking you lately? I want you to realize that you, too, can take authority over him in the name of Jesus. Begin acting on God's Word. Speak your faith in Jesus' name. Then watch God begin to act on your behalf!

●

Remember: YOU CAN HELP GOD WORK A MIRACLE!

264/THERE WILL BE A LOT OF GOOD PEOPLE IN HELL

"And whosoever was not found written in the book of life was cast into the lake of fire" (Revelation 20:15).

Also read: Dan. 12:1; Luke 10:20; Rev. 20:12; 21:27

It's shocking but true—there will be a lot of "good" people in hell. Have you ever wondered how you can be sure you're going to heaven? Jesus said *"I am the way, the truth, and the life: no man cometh unto the Father but by me"* (John 14:6).

The reason there will be a lot of good people in hell is because they failed to see the necessity of a personal relationship with Jesus Christ.

Today's text says that your name must be written down in the Lamb's book of life if you're going to make it to heaven. Have you repented of your sins and received Jesus Christ as your personal Savior? When you do, the Lord writes your name down in His heavenly book.

The most important question I can ask you is "Do you belong fully to Jesus Christ?" If you are confused about this question, then you should examine your personal relationship with the Lord. *"The Spirit itself beareth witness with our spirit that we are the sons of God"* (Romans 8:16).

If you want to be saved, do this:
1. Repent of *ALL* your sins.
2. Believe Jesus Christ died for *ALL* your sins and arose again from the dead.
3. Receive Jesus Christ into your heart as your *personal Savior.*
4. As a sign of your obedience to Jesus Christ, be baptized in water, receive communion and join in fellowship with other truly committed believers.

•

Remember: THERE WILL BE A LOT OF GOOD PEOPLE IN HELL. BE SURE *YOU* ARE SERVING JESUS CHRIST ON A PERSONAL BASIS.

265/YOU NEED A REVELATION OF CHRIST!

"I, (Paul)...cease not to give thanks for you, making mention of you in my prayers...That...God...may give unto you the...revelation in the knowledge of him" (Ephesians 1:16 & 17).

Also read: John 5:39; 2 Tim. 3:16; 1 Pet. 1:24-25

There are two ways you can know something: 1) head knowledge and 2) by encountering—through revelation or actual experience—the truth you believe.

For instance: You may believe in Hawaii, but it's another thing to experience it: walking down Waikiki beach with the sun setting in the west, hearing the splash of the waves and feeling the beautiful breezes blowing on your exhilarated body.

The same is true of Jesus Christ! Your knowledge of Him needs to be more than theological. You need to experience Him to really know Him.

This is why Paul the apostle wrote, *"That I might know him, and the power of his resurrection"* (Phil. 3:10).

Are you content to know Jesus only as a *historical fact*, that He was a spiritual superman who lived and died 2,000 years ago? But then you only know him as a historical character, like you know George Washington or Abraham Lincoln.

Are you content to know Jesus only in the *theological way?* You can quote the Scriptures declaring who He is and why He is the way.

Or do you desire to know Jesus Christ by experiencing Him? Do you want to know Him in the power of His resurrection?

If so, then you'll have to be like Peter, James and John, who saw Jesus transfigured on the mountain. You'll have to get away from all the hubbub and activities of your schedule and go up alone with Jesus to the mountain.

Then as you pray, you'll see Him as He really is, full of power and great glory. And you, too, will be transfigured and changed into His likeness.

•

Remember: SEARCH FOR THE FULLEST REVELATION OF JESUS CHRIST!

THERE'S A DIFFERENCE

"With joy shall ye draw water out of the wells of salvation" (Isaiah 12:3).

Also read: Jn. 14:16 & 17; 15:26; Acts 2:38

The 'well' experience of salvation is wonderful. But God has even more for us—a 'river' experience!

John 7:37-39 (TLB) says, *"Jesus shouted to the crowds, 'If anyone is thirsty let him come to me and drink. For the Scriptures declare that rivers of living water shall flow from the inmost being of anyone who believes in me.' (He was speaking of the Holy Spirit, who would be given to everyone believing in him: but the Spirit had not yet been given, because Jesus had not yet returned to his glory in heaven.)"*

Jesus said you can have more than a well of living water. You can have a river flowing right out of your innermost being. This is something even greater than what you receive when you become a born-again Christian. It's the same water, but is a greater dimension.

Peter and John prayed for the new converts of Samaria to receive the Holy Spirit *"(For as yet he was fallen upon none of them: only they were baptized in the name of the Lord Jesus.) Then laid they their hands on them, and they received the Holy Ghost"* (Acts 8:16 & 17).

These new believers had the well, but they also needed the river. The well was good, but the river was "expedient"—needful, necessary—as Jesus said in John 16:7, because it was more of Him.

You see, God has provided an answer for our weaknesses, our frustrations, our heartaches, and our depressions. The Holy Spirit is the very power and presence of Christ himself. Today Jesus is not with you in His physical body, but He can be in you through the power of the Holy Spirit.

Open you heart and yield your will to God's will. Begin to worship Him, and the river of God's Spirit will begin to flow through your being.

●

Remember: THE HOLY SPIRIT IS MORE OF JESUS!

267/THREE WAYS OF WINNING

"Thanks be unto God, which always causeth us to triumph in Christ" (2 Corinthians 2:14).

Also read: Phil. 1:6; 4:13

There are three ways of winning in life: first by luck, second by leverage and third by the Lord. If you want to win big in life, you'll learn the ways of all three.

Let's look at *Luck*: Soloman wrote, *"I returned, and saw under the sun, that the race is not to the swift, nor the battle to the strong, neither yet bread to the wise, nor yet riches to men of understanding, nor yet favour to men of skill; BUT TIME AND CHANCE HAPPENETH TO THEM ALL"* (Ecc. 9:11, emphasis mine).

He's right! There is an element of luck in life—being at the right place at the right time, meeting the right person, etc. Most of us need to depend on something more reliable.

Leverage. When you live life, giving it all you've got, it gives you leverage, or as the famous homerun-hitter, Ted Williams said, "The harder I try, the luckier I get."

Are you trying to better yourself mentally, spiritually, socially and financially?

Today: Try learning something extra by reading a book or learning from someone you meet.

Today: Get something more from God. Dig a new truth out from the Bible—believe for at least one small miracle.

Then: *Look at the Lord!* Today's text says we triumph in Christ. When my luck lets me down, and my leverage is weak, the Lord makes up the difference!

•

Remember: THERE ARE 3 WAYS OF WINNING IN LIFE—AND THE LORD'S WAY IS THE BEST.

WHY YOU NEED TO BE HOLY

"Follow peace with all men, and holiness, without which no man shall see the Lord" (Hebrews 12:14).

Also read: Lev. 20:7-8; Eph. 1:4; 5:25-27; 1 Thess. 3:13; 4:3

I believe, without a doubt, that these are the last days. Jesus said that many would wax cold in their spirit (see Matt. 24:12) and fall away from the faith (see 1 Tim. 4:1). This is why it is so important that we see the importance of holiness.

Today's text says that without holiness we will never see the Lord. I believe that sin blinds us to God's loving character in this life, and it separates us from God in the world to come.

How can you tell if you are a holy person? Compare your life with the 10 commandments (see Ex. 20:1-17)—and remember Jesus added one in John 13:34.

Do you always put God first?
Do you refrain from giving attention to materialistic things?
Do you refrain from using God's name in vain?
Do you honor your parents?
Do you reverence the Lord's day, refraining from work and pleasure so you can be spiritually restored?
Do you keep from harboring hatred in your heart?
Do you protect your mind from lustful thoughts?
Do you refrain from stealing?
Do you try not to deceive people?
Do you make certain that you do not covet what belongs to others?
Do you love fellow believers?

Another test is to check your life against the works of the flesh listed in Galatians 5:19-21. There is not enough space to print it here, but I hope you will take the time to look it up now.

I don't intend for you to become depressed by reading these Scriptures, but in these last days—when many are throwing away their faith for "easy religion"—it's good to examine ourselves to see how we measure up.

•

Remember: WITHOUT HOLINESS NO MAN WILL SEE GOD.

269/GIVE GOD NO REST!

"Take no rest, all you who pray, and give God no rest until he establishes Jerusalem" (Isaiah 62:7, TLB).

Also read: 1 Jn. 3:22; Matt. 18:19; Mk. 11:24

What an encouraging word that is for us to pray for the lost—especially our unsaved loved ones! God says, "Don't give me any rest. Pray day and night until I establish your loved ones for Christ!"

The number one prayer request I receive is for loved ones who are not living for God. People's hearts are broken because their children, their husband or wife, or their parents, or brothers' and sisters are not Christians. And I share that same hurt with you.

My favorite Scripture that encourages me to pray for my lost loved ones is found in Luke 18:1-8 (TLB), where Jesus gave this parable:

One day Jesus told His disciples a story to illustrate their need for constant prayer and to show them that they must keep praying until the answer comes.

"There was a city judge," he said, "a very godless man who had great contempt for everyone. A widow of that city came to him frequently to appeal for justice against a man who had harmed her. The judge ignored her for a while, but eventually she got on his nerves.

"I fear neither God nor man,' he said to himself, 'but this woman bothers me. I'm going to see that she gets justice, for she is wearing me out with her constant coming!"

Then the Lord said, "If even an evil judge can be worn down like that, don't you think that God will surely give justice to his people who plead with him day and night? Yes! He will answer them quickly!

So be encouraged. God has given you power and authority through the name of Jesus. He said, *"Whatsoever ye shall ask in prayer, believing, ye shall receive"* (Matt. 21:22).

•

Remember: DON'T GIVE GOD ANY REST. KEEP PRAYING FOR YOUR LOVED ONES, AND HE WILL ANSWER!

THE WEIGHTIER MATTERS!

"Ye...have omitted the weightier matters of the law, judgment, mercy and faith" (Matthew 23:23).

Also read: Ps. 139:23; 2 Cor. 13:5

I'm sure you've heard that the danger of life is to major in minors and minor in majors. We all know the story of a money-hungry man who worked overtime and lost his family.

The same danger is true of religion. The scribes and Pharisees meticulously tithed all of their possessions, right down to the smallest spices from plants—but they failed to manifest justice, mercy and faith.

The Sadducees were the religious liberals. They did not believe in spirits, angels or the resurrection (see Acts 23:8).

The Pharisees believed in miracles but they had developed such a rock-hard legalistic system of religion that when Jesus began to cut through the religious red tape to help sinners, they were shocked and offended.

Let's be careful that we don't make the same mistake. If we count ourselves holy because we don't drink, dance, cuss, commit adultery, read smut, or because we attend church, tithe, work on committees, etc.—then we are only in the shallows of spiritual depths. We have chosen the lighter and forsaken the weightier matters of the law. Consider the following:

First, *Judgment.* Only a person filled with God's Spirit can truly judge righteously, otherwise we are only making our decisions from what appears to be the truth instead of what really is true.

Second, *Mercy.* There is very little mercy among fundamentalist Christians today. As one man noted, "Christians are the only soldiers who kill their wounded."

Third, *Faith.* We need to increase our faith in the Lord. We need to draw closer to Him in Bible study and prayer and learn to depend on Him for all our needs.

Don't be guilty of majoring in the minors!

•

Remember: THE WEIGHTIER MATTERS ARE JUDG—MENT, MERCY AND FAITH. PRACTICE THEM TODAY!

271/STAND UP TO YOUR MOTHER!

"Asa... removed (his mother Maachah) from being queen, because she had made an idol in a grove: and Asa cut down her idol, and stamped it, and burnt it at the brook Kidron" (2 Chronicles 15:16).

Also read: Isa. 50:10; Mark 12:30; Rom. 6:13-16; 12:1-2

It takes courage to stand up for God—especially when you must stand up to your own mother. This is what Asa did when he discovered his mother was an idol worshipper. He removed her from the throne and destroyed her idol.

If you are determined to serve God, the time may come when you'll have to stand against your own family. This is why Jesus said, *"If any man come to me, and hate not his father, and mother, and wife, and children, and brethren, and sisters, yea, and his own life also, he cannot be my disciple"* (Luke 14:26).

Jesus was not trying to destroy family relationships but he was trying to draw the line as to how much your mother, father and family should influence you. Jesus was saying, "No one except God is to be first in your life—no matter what they say or do!"

This is very difficult to understand, because as children we are taught to obey our parents. But there comes a time in your life and mine when we must decide who will control us—our Lord and Savior Jesus Christ or the ones we love.

I'll never forget what my mother said after I became a committed Christian. She did not know the Lord, and in her state of spiritual darkness, she turned to me and said, "Lowell, I'd rather see you dead than see what's happened to you."

But I held my ground and within a few weeks, Mom, Dad, and my brothers Larry and Leon were all converted.

If you have a loved one who is influencing you to forsake the Lord or compromise your principles, do what Asa did: stand up for right and obey God—even if it offends your own mother.

•

Remember: EITHER CHRIST IS LORD OF ALL OR HE'S NOT LORD AT ALL.

272/GRIT FOR GOD!

"I press toward the mark for the prize of the high calling of God in Christ Jesus" (Philippians 3:14).

Also read: Is. 41:10; 1 Thess. 5:24; Ps. 112:7

Sometime ago, we had a young man speak in chapel at Trinity Bible College who was on his way to Thailand to become a missionary. This is one of the toughest mission fields today. On his card, the missionary had written these words: "To choose ease rather than effort is to choose decay." This young man had the grit it takes to do things for God!

Grit comes from within. Napoleon once said that in every battle there is a ten-minute period when the army wins or fails depending upon the will of the soldiers. It's in your spirit that you win or lose in life.

The Apostle Paul had grit—an indomitable spirit for God. Some people think if you're a Christian, life is going to be gentle with you. But it was not so with Paul. Read his description of experiences where he had to have bulldog courage and endurance.

"Of the Jews five times received I forty stripes save one. Thrice was I beaten with rods, once was I stoned, thrice I suffered shipwreck, a night and a day I have been in the deep; in journeyings often, in perils of waters...of robbers...by mine own countrymen...by the heathen...in the city...in the wilderness...in the sea...among false brethren; in weariness and painfulness, in watchings often, in hunger and thirst, in fastings often, in cold and nakedness" (2 Cor. 11:24-27).

Paul put everything he had into serving God.

Maybe you've been in a battle lately, and the devil has been throwing his best shots at you. God knows the fears you face. He also knows the temptation you might have to just chuck it all and give up. That's why the Scripture says, *"Having done all, to stand"* (Eph. 6:13). Stand up inside with your faith!

•

Remember: YOU CAN CONQUER ANYTHING THE DEVIL THROWS AT YOU IF YOU FACE IT WITH YOUR FAITH AND REFUSE TO GIVE UP!

273/WHEN GOD SOUGHT TO KILL MOSES

"And it came to pass by the way in the inn, that the Lord met him and sought to kill him" (Exodus 4:24).

Also read: Num. 22:22; Gen. 17:14

Do you realize there was a time when God sought to kill Moses? That's right! It's shocking but true.

God had called Moses from the burning bush to go down to Egypt to deliver the Hebrew slaves from the cruel hand of Pharoah. Moses was on his way when God sought to kill him.

Why? Because Moses was apparently having a difficult time putting his house in order. It appears that he and his wife Zipporah were not in agreement about circumcising their son.

Read this passage carefully, *"And it came to pass by the way in the inn, that the Lord met him, and sought to kill him.*

"Then Zipporah took a sharp stone, and cut off the foreskin of her son, and cast it at his feet, and said, 'Surely a bloody husband art thou to me."

"So he let him go."

God was angry with Moses because he had not fulfilled the circumcision covenant that God had first established with Abraham (see Gen. 17:11, 14).

Moses could not hope to be a representative of the Living God without his son being circumcised. It angered God that Moses thought he could be an agent of God without fulfilling the covenant rites.

The lesson for you and me is that God has called us to a new covenant, a covenant of heart circumcision. *"For we are the circumcision, which worship God in the Spirit"* (Phil. 3:3).

If you want to please God and not make Him angry with you, fulfill your faith covenant with Him—circumcise your heart by cleansing it from all sin.

●

Remember: YOU HAVE A HEART COVENANT WITH GOD.

274/DON'T BE MODEST ABOUT MIGHTY THINGS!

"For if thou shalt confess with thy mouth the Lord Jesus, and shalt believe in thine heart that God hath raised him from the dead, thou shalt be saved" (Romans 10:9).

Also read: Matt. 5:14-16; Luke 11:33; 12:8, 9; 2 Tim. 2:15

Do you have a problem confessing your faith in Jesus Christ? Don't be modest about mighty matters. You need to speak up for Jesus Christ if you hope to be saved.

Isn't it strange that sinners feel free to curse Christ while Christians are afraid to confess Him?

Here are some thoughts that may encourage you:

First, if your friend was walking down a road and didn't see a truck coming toward him, you'd yell at him to save his life. So, speak up to save his soul!

Second, when you withhold your witness you are confessing your own insecurity. You are saying, "I must conform or he will not like me; I'm afraid to be disliked."

The Bible says, *"Greater is he that is in you, than he that is in the world"* (1 John 4:4).

Third, don't forget that your friends want your approval as badly as you want theirs. Why live under the pressure of their standards while they should be living under the standards God has given *you?* In other words, think of the old joke, "I don't have ulcers, I give them." Don't purposely give people ulcers, but don't be afraid of people when they should be afraid (or have a holy reverence) for the God within you.

Fourth, learn to say, "I don't know." There are many Christians who are afraid that when they get into a deep discussion about Bible matters they'll be asked a question they cannot answer. Don't let this fear put you into bondage. Just be ready to say, "I don't know the answer to your question, but I'll try to find it for you later." Then move on with the discussion.

Salvation is a mighty matter—don't be modest about it. Speak up! Your salvation and that of your friends depends on it!

•

Remember: THE BIBLE SAYS, *"THE FEAR OF A MAN BRINGETH A SNARE"* (Prov. 29:25). DON'T BE MODEST ABOUT MIGHTY MATTERS.

275/SAY YES TO JESUS

"Since the creation of the world God's invisible qualities—his eternal power and divine nature—have been clearly seen, being understood from what has been made, so that men are without excuse" (Romans 1:21, NIV).

Also read: Jn. 5:24; 10:27 & 28; 2 Tim. 1:10

Some people say it's hard to believe in God. I disagree. It's the easiest thing you'll ever do.

My family and I visited the various museums of the Smithsonian Institute in Washington, D.C., one summer. The Museum of Natural History was my favorite. I noticed there were scientific explanations on all the exhibits. As I read the explanations I began to notice the vocabulary: 'perhaps,' 'maybe,' 'scientists suppose.' The most used phrase was, 'It is believed.'

Of course, science would never stoop so low as to acknowledge the possibility of a God who created the universe. It's theories are filled with uncertainty. Yet people believe science. But if the Bible says, "For God possibly so loved the world that He might have given His only begotten Son, that maybe if you believe in Him you might not perish, but it is believed you will have everlasting life," would you believe it? I'm not the brightest guy who ever lived, but I wouldn't. If I am expected to make an intelligent choice between 'perhaps,' 'maybe,' and 'it is believed,' and the great *I Am* who spoke the universe into existence, set the planets in their courses, and established the boundaries of the sea, the choice is an easy one for me.

Believing in God and committing your life to Him is the most intelligent thing you'll ever do. Not to do so is tragically foolish. The most awesome moment in all eternity will be when those untold numbers of unbelievers stand before God, lost forever and ever. In this little breath of life on earth they never took one tiny moment to say, "Yes, Jesus." To know the truth in your heart and not respond to it is the greatest tragedy of life.

•

Remember: GOD IS REAL. HE LOVES YOU, DIED FOR YOU, AND IS ALIVE TODAY, READY TO LIVE IN YOUR HEART.

276/WHEN GOD'S GONE

"If Christ be not raised, your faith is in vain; (and) ye are yet in your sins" (I Corinthians 15:17).

Also read: Acts 17:3; Rom. 11:3; Eph. 1:10-14

What happens if God is dead? Michael Harrington has written a new book entitled, *The Politics at God's Funeral: The Spiritual Crisis of Western Civilization.*

The gist of this book is that centuries ago God was in His heaven and the social, political and economic structures on earth were in order. Each person had his station in life and from that station he served his family, his master and his God.

Capitalism, according to Harrington, separated man's function and goals. You did well for yourself and you did well for God, but the two were no longer closely related. The secular and the sacred had moved far apart.

Harrington wants men and women "of faith and anti-faith" to work together to introduce "moral dimensions."

This is where he falls off the cliff. Whenever you mention "moral dimensions" the question is, which moral dimensions? How can atheistic communists and believing Christians find accord? It's like asking the devil and Jesus to come up with a united plan.

But at least Harrington is wise enough to realize this world is on the wrong track and we need moral and spiritual values to bring us back.

This is what happens when faith dies. If God is dead in your heart and mind, you will fill the empty hours with sensual hedonistic pleasures.

Thank God, He is not dead in our hearts today.

* We have the true guide for living—the Bible and the Ten Commandments.
* We have the living Resurrected Christ abiding within us by the Holy Spirit.
* We have a transcendent hope that is real. Jesus said, *"I go to prepare a place for you"* (John 14:2).

Come to think of it, you and I have everything the atheists wish they had!

•

Remember: WHEN GOD IS GONE, YOU'VE LOST YOUR SONG: WHEN GOD'S ALIVE, THERE'S HOPE INSIDE.

277/THE DANGER OF OUR DAY!

"Watch out! Don't let my sudden coming catch you unawares; don't let me find you living in careless ease, carousing and drinking, and occupied with the problems of this life, like all the rest of the world" (Luke 21:34 & 35, TLB).

Also read: 1 Cor. 3:9-15; 1 Jn. 2:15-17

One of the great dangers of our day is that only half of the gospel is being declared and that many Christians have only a portion of the true faith preached to them.

Of course, I know many dedicated men of God, both pastors and evangelists, who are crying out against the spirit of compromise and the "easy religion" being preached today. Thank God for them! But I know others who have given in to what I call "the comfort zone" of Christianity.

Today, in evangelical circles we hear a lot about receiving Christ, but very little about repentance; believing in Christ, but very little about obeying Him.

What I see missing in the Church today is the compelling burden to win the lost. There is such a casualness about commitment that it is frightening. Christians seem to think if they are saved, it is enough. But Paul wrote in 2 Cor. 5:10 that all Christians will appear before the judgment seat of Christ to be judged for their works—good or bad.

Paul went on to say that some saints will have a reward, whereas others will have their works burned up. Don't confuse the gift of salvation and rewards. Salvation is the gift of God, but the reward you will receive in heaven depends upon your works.

God help us to shun the comfort zone and enter the combat zone of personal evangelism, where we are willing to pray and make personal financial sacrifices to underwrite soulwinning efforts!

•

Remember: CHRISTIANS WHO ENTER THE COMBAT ZONE FOR SOULS WILL BE REWARDED!

THE FOUR SEASONS OF LIFE

"To every thing there is a season, and a time to every purpose under the heaven" (Ecclesiastes 3:1).

Also read: Psa. 90:10-14; 92:12-15; 2 Cor. 5:1; Tit. 2:2-4

There are four seasons in each year and four seasons in your life. Each life's season is unique and richly blessed of God; each stands for a different era:

SPRING—REBIRTH   FALL—HARVEST
SUMMER—ABUNDANCE   WINTER—REST

Spring. The years between 0-25—REBIRTH. Statistics show that most people receive Jesus Christ as their personal Savior during their youth. They are "born-again" by the Spirit of God; this is the beginning of their spiritual lives.

Summer. The years between 25 and 50—ABUNDANCE. In this season you make the greatest strides forward in your life. You learn the principles that make you blossom and grow tall and strong in your faith and your career. You should reach your abundance during this period because your energy level will never be as high again.

Fall. The years between 50 and 70—HARVEST. This is the harvest season of your life. The maturation of your faith and spiritual walk now results in many people coming to Jesus Christ. In your career, you have risen to the point where you can reap the harvest of your labors. This should be the most productive period in your life—reaping the harvest of investments both spiritual and material.

WINTER. The ages between 70 and 90—REST. These are the years you can rest and count the blessings God has given you. But be careful that you don't relax to the point that you stop living. You need a challenge to keep you going for God, but the pressure isn't on you to achieve the way it was in your earlier years. You can "rest" in the fact that you have done your best and will continue to do the same until you go to meet the Lord.

•

Remember: EACH SEASON OF YOUR LIFE WILL BE BLESSED WHEN YOU LIVE IT FOR GOD.

279/SOUR GRAPES

"And what do you mean, using this proverb saying, our fathers have eaten sour grapes and so the children's teeth are set on edge" (Ezekiel 18:2, Literal).

Also read: Jer. 31:29-34

Are you a victim of the sour grape mentality? Do you feel you're a victim of what your parents have done; that you're the product of a poor environment?

This is what the children of Israel were saying. The Living Bible describes it more literally, *"Why do people use this* (sour grape) *proverb about the land of Israel: the children are punished for their father's sins? As I live, says the Lord God, you will not use this proverb any more...for all souls are mine to judge...and my rule is this: It is for a man's own sins that he will die"* (Ez. 18:2-4).

Many people were complaining to the prophet Ezekiel that they were being punished for their parents' sins, that they were victims of circumstances. But the Lord set them straight. He said, "Forget about your sour-grape philosophy—it's not worth anything."

Be careful that you don't make the same mistake.
* *Don't blame your folks for your present condition.
* *Your church, school, friends, place of work, relatives, town, or other things are not to be blamed for your downfall or present condition.

Take responsibility for your own situation. If you don't like your life the way it is, remember these things:
1. Your personal committment to God will change you spiritually.
2. Your personal committment to study will change you intellectually.
3. Your personal committment to work and study will change your situation financially.
4. Your personal committment to others will change you socially.

●

Remember: DON'T CRY "SOUR GRAPES"—YOU'VE GOT WHAT IT TAKES TO BE A WINNER!

280/THREE STEPS YOU CAN TAKE TO RECEIVE HEALING

"Is any sick among you? Let him call for the elders of the church; and let them pray over him, anointing him with oil in the name of the Lord: and the prayer of faith shall save the sick, and the Lord shall raise him up" (James 5:14 & 15).

Also read: Heb. 11:6; Eph. 2:8 & 9

Believe the journey to your personal healing begins by asking yourself the question Jesus asked the crippled man who had lain at the Pool of Bethseda 38 long years: *"Wilt thou be made whole?"* (Jn. 5:6). In other words, do you really want to be healed?

Now that might sound like a dumb question, but it's not. Jesus asked this question because it's possible that even though you are sick, you can make peace with your problem. You can get used to it. And the Lord asked the straightforward question—"DO YOU WANT TO BE HEALED?"

If you want to be healed, take these three steps:

Step 1: Find and associate with people who believe in the miracle-working power of God to heal. They will strengthen your faith.

Step 2: Begin to study the Word of God. Romans 10:17 says, *"Faith cometh by hearing, and hearing by the Word of God."* If you study the miracles that have taken place in the lives of people, you will discover they happened where the Word of God was proclaimed and lifted up and studied and believed. Miracles take place when you get the Word into your mind, your heart, and your spirit.

Step 3: Now act upon your faith. You can believe in healing as a theory, but that's what it is—theory—until you act upon the faith you have. Jesus said you don't need a lot of faith. As much as a grain of mustard seed can move a mountain (see Matt. 17:20). Use the faith you have and claim your deliverance.

•

Remember: ANY AMOUNT OF FAITH WILL WORK WHEN YOU PUT IT TO WORK.

281/LIFE ISN'T FAIR

"Whom have I in heaven but thee? and there is none upon earth that I desire beside thee" (Psalm 73:25).

Also read: Isa. 40:29-31; Phil. 4:12, 13; Heb. 13:5, 6

"Life isn't fair!" is a cry you hear over and over again. "Why have I been hurt the way I have?"

You're right; life isn't fair, and no one ever said it was. If you protest when something bad happens to you (either at your own hand or that of others) you are actually appealing to a higher power to put some equality back into life. This is why the Psalmist David said of the Lord, *"Whom have I in heaven but You?"* David knew that life wasn't fair—and without God's help he'd never make it.

Don't lament your hurts and mistakes—just move on. When you demand that people and situations be fair you're asking more than life can offer. Only God is fair. Beyond that, nothing should be expected to be fair. Don't waste your efforts appealing to a rule that life should treat you fairly. It never has and chances are it never will.

But God is fair—and this is what matters most.

* God hears and answers prayers (John 14:14).
* God takes vengeance upon evildoers (Rom. 12:19).
* God cares deeply about you and can work even the evil things done against you for good (see Rom. 8:28).

When things go wrong say, "Lord, You're fair. You see this evil that has befallen me and I'm trusting You to work this thing for good. You have all power in heaven and in earth and You will take vengeance on all whom You will. I rest my case with You, Lord."

Only then will you be free from the terrible burden of trying to figure out why people and circumstances have hurt you.

Life isn't fair. When you were born you simply began life with a scream of complaint. Unless you change your attitude you might die the same way.

God is in charge. He'll work all things well on your behalf if you love him and trust Him.

•

Remember: LIFE ISN'T FAIR—BUT GOD IS.

282/TAKE AUTHORITY OVER SATAN

"And the seventy returned again with joy, saying, Lord, even the devils are subject unto us through thy name" (Luke 10:17).

Also read: Mark 16:17; Luke 9:1; Jas. 2:19

Satan is your enemy, but you have authority over him, in the name of Jesus. Our Master said, *"Behold, I give unto you power to tread on serpents and scorpions, AND OVER ALL THE POWER OF THE ENEMY; and nothing shall by any means hurt you"* (Luke 10:19 emphasis mine).

In Matthew the Bible says, *"And when he had called unto him, his twelve disciples, he gave them power against unclean spirits (demons) to cast them out and to heal all manner of sickness and all manner of disease.*

"These twelve Jesus sent forth and commanded them, saying...preach...The kingdom of heaven is at hand...Heal the sick, cleanse the lepers, raise the dead, cast out devils" (Matt. 10:1-7).

You can see by these Scriptures that you should be in control over the situations you face. You have the power, in the name of Jesus, and the authority, to put the devil on the run. But authority and power that is unused is worthless. A police officer can stand in busy traffic all day long but until he raises his hand of authority not one car will stop.

You can see what it took for Jesus to take authority over Satan in the wilderness temptation. Note: *Prayer was not enough. Jesus had been praying for 40 days and nights. *Fasting was not enough. He had gone over 40 days without food. *Quoting the Scriptures was not enough—Jesus did this three times and the devil came back. The only thing that worked is when Jesus used His authority and ordered Satan to depart. *"Then Satan went away..."* (Matt. 4:10) but not one second sooner.

•

Remember: GOD HAS GIVEN YOU GREAT AUTHORITY IN THE NAME OF JESUS. START USING HIS NAME, AND REBUKE SATAN OUT LOUD.

283/THE KEY TO BEING USED OF GOD

"In a great house there are not only vessels of gold and of silver, but also of wood and of earth; and some to honour and some to dishonour. If a man therefore purge himself from these (sins), he shall be a vessel unto honour, sanctified, and prepared unto every good work" (2 Timothy 2:20 & 21).

Also read: Jam. 1:21 & 22; Rom. 12:1 & 2; 2 Cor. 6:17 & 18

For 20 years of my life, the devil misquoted these verses to me. He made me feel like I would never do much for God. I have always wanted the Lord to be proud of me and to do great things for Him. But I looked around and saw great men of God who were doing so much more for the Lord than I was, and I had to fight my feelings of inferiority.

The devil would bring verse 20 to me. And I would think, some vessels are made to be great for God—some for honor, and some for dishonor. I'm just a smalltown boy. I can't expect to be able to do everything. I guess God just wants me to be one of the lesser vessels.

Have you ever felt like that?

One day I heard a man of God preach on verse 21. He brought out that God's Word says if a man will purge himself from sin and depart from iniquity, he will be a sanctified vessel, useful and ready for any good work. I realized then that lesser vessels can become great vessels in God's kingdom—not to gratify their own egos but to honor Christ—if they will cleanse, sanctify, and consecrate their lives to God.

Do you want God to use you? Do you want to accomplish things for God that will honor His name? The key is purging: purging out thoughts you shouldn't have, friends who pull you down, music that doesn't edify you, TV programs that have a negative influence, habits that are not good for you. Then God can use you.

●

Remember: A VESSEL GOD USES FOR HIS HIGHEST PURPOSES HAS TO BE CLEAN!

284/YOU NEED FRIENDS

"Two are better than one...for if they fall, the one will lift up his fellow: but woe to him that is alone when he falleth; for he hath not another to help him up" (Ecclesiastes 4:9 & 10).

Also read: Psa. 119:63; Prov. 18:24; John 15:12-14

Lone Rangers are lonely. If you are what hunters call a "lone wolf" you may get by during your times of strength—but how will you make it when you weaken? This is why you need a friend.

Some people are afraid to make friends because they have a poor self-image. They say, "No one would like me if they got to know me as I really am." This is not true. There is something wonderfully different about you that someone needs to complete his own inadequacies. Imagine a blind, 300-pound 7-foot giant of a man carrying a 3-foot high dwarf who has good eyesight. They both need each other. The dwarf needs the giant for his strength and the giant needs the dwarf for his sight.

You also need friends to tell you the truth about yourself. Most of the people you meet will tell you what you want to hear—not what you need to hear. It's good for you, spiritually, to have friends who will level with you.

A true spiritual friend can double the fire of God in your life. If you put one log on a fire the fire will die out, but putting two together will create a draft that sends the fire blazing upward. This is probably why Jesus sent His disciples forth in pairs, *"And he called unto him the twelve, and began to send them forth by two and two; and gave them power over unclean spirits* (Mark 6:7).

Don't forget that Jesus is the best friend you'll ever have. He knows you better than you know yourself. He accepts you as you are and loves you with a perfect love.

Don't neglect your friends—both Jesus and your earthly friends need to hear from you. Write a letter or make a telephone call to someone today—and don't forget to spend time with Jesus, your best friend.

•

Remember: YOU NEED FRIENDS—MAKE AN EFFORT TO COMMUNICATE WITH THEM TODAY.

285/GOD'S PROTECTION

"Because he loves me,' says the Lord, 'I will rescue him; I will protect him, for he acknowledges my name" (Psalm 91:14, NIV).

Also read: Ps. 91:1-16

We need to understand our position, promise and privilege of protection.

Our position is that of children of God (see Rom. 8:16). Like any loving Father, God wants to protect His children from harm. Have you ever observed a father watching his son going through a very painful medical treatment? The father flinches and may actually wince as his son experiences great pain. You can see by the look on the father's face that he is wishing *he* could take the pain upon himself to save his beloved son much anguish.

That's exactly what our Father, God, has done. He took the pain of our sin upon Himself (through Jesus Christ) to spare us the excruciating consequences of our sin.

The promise of God's protection is a marvelous thing! Psalm 91:4 states, *"He will cover you with his feathers, and under his wings you will find refuge"* (NIV).

I am so thankful for the Lord's hand helping us in this ministry these many years. You need to know that God is watching over you too. Psalm 34:7 tells us, *"The angel of the Lord encamps around those who fear him, and he delivers them"* (NIV).

What a privilege to know, *"The Lord will rescue me from every evil attack and will bring me safely to his heavenly kingdom"* (2 Tim. 4:18).

•

Remember: WE ARE SEATED WITH CHRIST IN THE HEAVENLIES—WE ARE PROTECTED!

WHEN GOD TURNS YOU DOWN

"I had in mine heart to build an house...for the ark...but God said, Thou shalt not build an house for my name" (1 Chronicles 28:2 & 3).

Also read: Deut. 31:8; Rom. 8:28; Phil. 4:12-13

David loved the Lord and wanted to build a magnificent temple as a house for the ark of God.

The idea was so terrific that when David first proposed it, the prophet Nathan agreed and said, *"Go, do all that is in thine heart; for the Lord is with thee"* (2 Sam. 7:3).

But that night God awakened the prophet and told him that He didn't want David building the temple because he had been a man of war and had shed too much blood (see 2 Sam. 7:4 and 1 Chron. 28:3).

God turned David down.

God squelched David's dream.

At this moment David could have become very bitter. Hadn't he fought many wars for the Lord? Hadn't he been faithful to serve God?

But David had such an excellent spirit that it didn't stop him from doing everything possible towards completing the temple.

First, he gave Solomon, his son, the plans for the temple that he had received by the spirit (see 1 Chron. 28:11).

Second, he provided all of the materials (including gold and silver) that were needed to complete the project (see verses 14:18).

Third, he gave Solomon encouragement to complete the building of the temple. *"And David said to Solomon his son, Be strong and of good courage, and do it"* (verse 20).

Have you desired to do something great for God but the Lord has turned you down? If so, don't sulk around about it—do what you can. For example, if God doesn't allow you to preach, then support a soulwinning minister who has the calling.

If God turns you down, don't be discouraged—be encouraged that there are many things you can still do to build His Kingdom.

•

Remember: IF GOD TURNS YOU DOWN, DON'T LET IT GET YOU DOWN—JUST LOOK AROUND TO SEE ALL THE GOOD THINGS YOU CAN DO.

287/DO IT!

"And David said to Solomon his son, Be strong and of good courage and do it" (1 Chronicles 28:20).

Also read: Deut. 10:12; Psa. 138:8; Jer. 29:11

Yesterday I shared with you what David did when God turned him down. Today I want you to be encouraged by what David told Solomon just before he died:

1. *"Be strong."* If you're going to go anywhere in life you must prepare yourself for a struggle. Life isn't easy. Rather than whining and complaining, you must be strong.

2. *"Be...of good courage."* Courage is the ability to tackle the impossible. Don Schula, the winning coach for the Miami Dolphins football squad, is called "Chisel Chin" because of his determination.

3. *"Do it."* There are complainers and explainers, but it's a minority of men and women who simply do it. Determine to be one of them.

4. *"Fear not, nor be dismayed."* Fear is a choice. Psychologists say the same fear that drives you to flee from something will drive you towards conquering it—if you will make the decision to *win*.

5. *"God will be with you."* *"If God be for us, who can be against us?"* (Rom. 8:31). God and you make a majority. Don't be afraid of your tasks today.

6. *"He will not fail you nor forsake you."* When is the last time God ever failed to come through for you? (Before you answer, think: can you be sure that what appeared to you to be a failure really was?) God doesn't forsake His people. He will keep you by His power.

7. *"...Until you have finished all the work for the Lord."* If you continue in the will of God, I believe God will be with you in all that you do until your work for Him here on earth is complete. If you believe this it will give you peace.

Remember David's advice to Solomon. If you desire to do something that is consistant with the will of God, go ahead and do it!

•

Remember: GOD'S WILL IS TO SIMPLY "DO IT!"

"It is Christ that died, yea rather, that is risen again, who is even at the right hand of God, who also maketh intercession for us" (Romans 8:34).

Also read: Ps. 86:7; Jn. 14:14; 1 Jn. 5:14

Many people don't understand how important prayer is. They think it is some kind of vocal exercise to vent their frustrations. It's not. When you pray you are moving the hand of God. You are giving God the opportunity to do something miraculous.

You see, God is a just God. He is Judge of all the earth. And His righteousness will allow Him to only do so much for a person until special intercessary prayer is made for that one. It's like a state governor. Suppose a man is found guilty of murder and sentenced to die. The governor must uphold the law of the land. That is his duty.

But suppose this convicted man's friends and community pass a petition and bring hundreds of names to the governor. They say, "We appeal to you, Governor, for pardon and clemency. Grant this man mercy." Then the governor, because he has the petition in his hand, can act beyond the law. He can give this man a pardon or change his sentence.

That's what prayer does. When you petition the Father in Jesus' name, all of heaven opens up to you. You don't need hundreds of names—you only need one, the name of Jesus.

Right now Jesus is standing at His Father's right hand, making intercession for you. When you pray in His name, He turns to the Father and says, "Father, You have heard this petition. I ask You now to grant this request on the basis of the blood I shed for this one."

By praying, you are loosing God's hand to act in spite of His righteous judgment. You allow Him to act in mercy.

•

Remember: YOU ARE NOT OVERCOMING GOD'S RELUCTANCE WHEN YOU PRAY. YOU ARE TAKING HOLD OF GOD'S WILLINGNESS.

289/THE POWER OF YOUR TONGUE!

"God...quickeneth the dead, and calleth those things which are not as though they were" (Romans 4:17).

Also read: Psa. 34:13; 141:3; Prov. 18:21; Jas. 1:26; 3:5-13

You have tremendous power in your tongue. You can speak things into existence—good or bad.

For instance, when you forget something and you say, "That's the way I always am—always forgetting things!", you will only reinforce your belief that you are a "forgetter." You have to watch what you say!

There are many invisible thoughts, beliefs and feelings in your heart and mind. When you speak you are giving substance to the invisible. (I'm sure you'll agree that a spoken thought is a more powerful influence than an unspoken one.)

So use your tongue as carefully as God does. When the world was in chaos, the Bible in Genesis 1 tells us, *"And God said, Let there be light...And God said, Let there be a firmament...And God said, Let the waters under the heaven be gathered together"* (see Gen. 1:3-9). The phrase, "And God said" was used nine times. God used the power of His words to turn the world into Paradise.

You can do the same thing with your tongue; call *what is, not as if it is.* Say to yourself, "I am a friendly person, I am kind, I am helpful, I am liked." And, believe it or not, you *will* become as you have spoken yourself to be.

It's a fact that if you talk as if you were sick, you will feel sick. If you allow every pain, cramp or nausea to dictate how you feel, you'll always feel badly. But if you talk as if you were healthy, you'll feel better and actually be better. Train your tongue so it will command your brain. Don't follow your feelings—follow your faith.

•

Remember: YOU HAVE THE POWER OF LIFE OR DEATH IN YOUR TONGUE—USE YOURS TO LIVE!

290/HOW PAIN PREACHES

"It is good for me that I have been afflicted; that I might learn thy statutes" (Psalms 119:71).

Also read: Psa. 34:19; 2 Cor. 6:4-10; 2 Tim. 4:5

Pain is the most powerful preacher on earth. It converts more people than Billy Graham, Oral Roberts, Robert Schuller, Jimmy Swaggart, Lowell Lundstrom and all other preachers combined.

Pain tells you this is an imperfect world. It causes you to ask, "How did things get this way?" The Bible says, *"For we know that the whole creation groaneth and travaileth in pain together until now. And not only they, but ourselves also, which have the firstfruits of the Spirit, even we ourselves groan within ourselves, waiting for the adoption, to wit, the redemption of our body"* (Rom. 8:22, 23).

What Paul is saying is that even we Christians groan within, awaiting the time when God will deliver us from this painful world.

When people hurt it reminds them that this is an imperfect world and that God must have something better in mind. It also causes them to ask, "Why am I hurting now?"

Remember it wasn't until the prodigal son's body was wracked with pain that he remembered his father's goodness and returned home (see Luke 15:11-32).

If God took away all pain from this world He would eliminate the greatest converting force on this planet. We should not curse God for pain but thank Him for using it to bring us to our senses and to the altar of repentence. David said, *"It is good...that I have been afflicted; that I might learn thy statutes"* (Psa. 119:71).

Pain will even help you to pray. The Bible says of Jesus, *"And being in...agony he prayed more earnestly"* (Luke 22:44).

When your soul is in great pain your prayers are propelled heavenward with an intensity that you need to move God.

●

Remember: PAIN IS A PREACHER, TELLING US THIS IS AN IMPERFECT WORLD, URGING US TO REPENT AND PRAY FERVENTLY.

291/WHY JESUS WON

"This is the word of the Lord . . . (It is) Not by might, nor by power, but by my spirit, saith the Lord of hosts" (Zechariah 4:6).

Also read: Lk. 4:18; Jn. 14:12, 16 & 17

Would you like to win victories over Satan as Jesus did? Recently I was reading Luke chapter 4 and these phrases jumped out at me:

"And Jesus BEING FULL OF THE HOLY GHOST returned from Jordan" (verse 1, emphasis mine).

"And Jesus returned in the power of the spirit into Galilee" (verse 14).

"And they were all amazed saying, what a word is this! for with authority and power he commands the unclean spirits, and they came out" (verse 36).

These verses make it clear that the reason Jesus won such great victories over Satan was because of the great measure of the Holy Spirit that flowed through His life.

Do you realize you can have the same measure of the Holy Spirit flowing in your life? And with the same results? Jesus said, *"And WHATSOEVER YOU SHALL ASK in my name, THAT WILL I DO, that the Father may be glorified in the Son. IF YOU SHALL ASK ANYTHING IN MY NAME, I will do it"* (John 14:13 & 14, emphasis mine).

These are powerful Scriptures! Once you see that you can actually do the works of Jesus you will ask, "Why am I not doing these things?"

Ask yourself these questions:

1. Am I filled with the Holy Spirit to the measure I should be?

2. Have I been asking God to do these great things that are available to me?

If you want to have victory over Satan, ask God to fill you with His Holy Spirit and to use you to do great things.

●

Remember: "(IT IS) NOT BY MIGHT, NOR BY POWER, BUT BY MY SPIRIT, SAITH THE LORD."

292/TRUE BEAUTY

"He (Jesus) shall grow up before him as a tender plant, and as a root out of a dry ground: he hath no form nor comeliness; and when we shall see him, there is no beauty that we should desire him. He is despised and rejected of men; a man of sorrows, and acquainted with grief; and we hid as it were our faces from him; he was despised, and we esteemed him not" (Isaiah 53:2,3).

Also read: Matt. 5:44 & 45; Ps. 103:6; Jn. 16:33

Have you ever felt ugly? You see the good-looking faces on television or in magazines and feel like you just don't have what it takes in the looks department. A lot of people's self-esteem suffers because they feel ugly. They think no one really understands how they feel, especially God. But the Bible says of Jesus, *"There was no attractiveness at all, nothing to make us want him"* (Isa. 53:2, TLB). It was not the beauty of Christ's outward appearance, but the beauty of His spirit, that drew the multitudes to Him.

We place so much emphasis on physical beauty in our society. Everyone wants to be young, good looking, and tanned. We spend billions of dollars every year on improving our outward appearance, and there is nothing wrong with that if we keep it in perspective. But nothing—no diet, hair cut, clothes, make-up—can remove the hurt of rejection and make us feel beautiful inside. Only Jesus can do that.

The Bible says Jesus was despised and rejected, a man of sorrows and grief. People turned away from Him. That is why He understands your hurt. He knows what it is like to have people make fun of you, to put you down, to make jokes about you. To God, you are beautiful because you are His child. He loves you and wants to heal you hurts.

When Jesus lives in your heart, you have His spiritual beauty within you. You have His love, power, and grace. That is everlasting beauty that nothing can ever take away.

•

Remember: THE ONLY REAL LASTING BEAUTY IS THE BEAUTY THAT COMES FROM JESUS LIVING IN YOUR HEART.

293/CAN YOU MARCH IN STEP?

"All these men of war, that could keep rank, came with a perfect heart to Hebron, to make David king over all Israel" (1 Chron. 12:38).

Also read: Deut. 10:12; 1 Kings 3:14; Josh. 22:5

One of the difficult things to learn in the army is how to march in perfect step. Once, several years ago, the Lundstroms appeared at a Job Corps Camp in Wisconsin where hundreds of inner-city youth were being trained in factory skills. We came to sing and preach and invite them to receive Christ.

While I was in the bus preparing for my sermon, outside I heard a commanding voice barking out a cadence, "Hup! one—two—three—four!" The commander's voice was so demanding in tone that I opened the curtain and looked out, expecting to see a unit of soldiers marching in perfect file.

Instead I saw something that made me burst out with laughter. About 50 guys, with broomhandles instead of guns, were moving along out of step, out of line, in total disorder, while the commander of the troop boomed out official cadence.

If you really want to do something great for God, if you want to get close to the commander-in-chief and win His respect, you must get in step. Are you doing today exactly what God wants you to do?

    Are you working where God wants you to work?
    Are you attending the church God wants you to attend?
    Are you living where God wants you to live?
    Is there anything in your life that is not in harmony with God's will?

If you are out of step with what the Lord would have you do, get in line. Spend time in His Word, and earnest prayer. Make David's prayer yours, *"Search me, O God, and know my heart: try me, and know my thoughts: And see if there be any wicked way in me, and lead me in the way everlasting"* (Psa. 139:23-24).

•

Remember: IF YOU WANT TO MOVE FORWARD IN THE RANKS, YOU MUST LISTEN TO GOD'S VOICE AND GET IN STEP WITH HIS COMMANDS.

294/FOOTPRINTS IN THE SAND

"And, lo, I am with you alway, even unto the end of the world" (Matthew 28:20).

Also read: Is. 63:9; Heb. 13:5

The following is a popular poem that has been making the rounds in recent years. Even if you've seen it before, you'll enjoy reading it again—especially the way the sentences are arranged.

Footprints in the Sand

One night I had a dream -
I dreamed I was walking along the beach with the Lord, and
Across the sky flashed scenes from my life.
For each scene I noticed two sets of footprints in the sand;
One belonged to me, and the other to the Lord.
When the last scene of my life flashed before us,
I looked back at the footprints in the sand.
I noticed that many times along the path of my life,
There was only one set of footprints.
I also noticed that it happened at the very lowest and saddest times in my life.
This really bothered me, and I questioned the Lord about it.
"Lord, you said that once I decided to follow you,
You would walk with me all the way;
But I have noticed that during the most troublesome times in my life,
There is only one set of footprints.
I don't understand why in times when I needed you most, you should leave me."
The Lord replied, "My precious, precious child. I love you, and I would never, never leave you during your times of trial and suffering.
When you saw only one set of footprints,
It was then that I carried you."

—Author Unknown

•

Remember: JESUS SAID HE WOULD BE WITH YOU ALWAYS. BE SURE TO TALK WITH HIM AS HE WALKS WITH YOU TODAY.

295/TIRED OF SITTING ON THE SIDELINES?

"The harvest truly is plenteous, but the labourers are few" (Matthew 9:37).

Also read: Heb. 6:10; 1 Tim. 4:16

I've been an evangelist almost 29 years, and I've discovered that most Christians are living dull, unexciting lives. The average Christian feels he is living on the sidelines. He knows that God is doing great things through "superstars" of the gospel—men and women who are leading thousands to Christ. But the average Christian feels that he is left out of the action.

Very few Christians consider themselves to be truly partners with God. Most are "spectators" instead of participants in what God is trying to accomplish in people's lives. They are saved enough to get to heaven, but not blessed enough to enjoy it. Church attendance is a drag and they are void of the joy of Jesus Christ that should be theirs.

I'll never forget the concern of a businessman, a deacon in his church, who approached me at the end of one of our crusades. He said, "Lowell, it's going to kill me to go back to my church after this crusade. It's the same old boring ritual week after week. I'll just sit on the bench for another five years, and nothing really exciting is going to happen."

This man was crushed to think the excitement of the crusade had passed. He had seen families brought together, couples reunited, and individual lives healed and changed dramatically by God's Spirit and power. Now what was he to do?

If, like this deacon, your enthusiasm for life has waned and you're searching for a new dimension in your relationship with God, find out what God is doing and get in the middle of the action! Become a partner with God in His great redemptive plan to reach the lost.

•

Remember: A PARTNERSHIP RELATIONSHIP WITH GOD ENABLES YOU TO EXPERIENCE LIFE TO THE FULLEST!

HOW IS YOUR BOOK DOING?

"And the rest of the acts of Solomon, and all that he did, and his wisdom, are they not written in the book of the acts of Solomon?" (1 Kings 11:41).

Also read: 2 Chron. 20:34; Est. 10:2; Phil. 4:3; Rev. 3:5

It's easy for us to study the lives of Bible characters and pick them apart, but I've often wondered what would happen if your life and mine were recorded in print so others could study our deeds?

I'm afraid I'd have many embarrassing chapters.

This helps me be merciful when I read of David's adultery, Noah's drunkenness, Peter's cursing, Thomas' doubts, etc. I know the potential for these evils dwell in me and this is why I should not be critical of others.

How about you? Do you realize that God is keeping a book of the acts of your life? The Bible says, *"For we must all appear before the judgment seat of Christ; that every one may receive the things done in his body, according to that he hath done, whether it be good or bad"* (2 Cor. 5:10). John the apostle saw a vision of judgment day in heaven and wrote, *"...and the books were opened"* (Rev. 20:12).

How is your book doing? If you will live each day, knowing that it is being recorded in heaven, it will change a lot of your actions. You'll pray more, witness more, give more, love more, etc. You'll also stand more firmly against the lusts of your flesh that would seduce you into doing wrong.

If there are some chapters and paragraphs in your life that you'd like to change, remember what the Bible says: *"If we walk in the light, as he is in the light, we have fellowship one with another, and the blood of Jesus Christ his Son cleanseth us from all sin"* (1 John 1:7).

I saw a bumper sticker recently that said, "Just for the record, God's writing everything down."

•

Remember: IF YOU DON'T LIKE WHAT'S BEING WRITTEN IN YOUR BOOK—EDIT OUT THE WRONGS BY REPENTING OF THEM TODAY.

297/LISTEN WITH YOUR OTHER EARS!

"He that hath an ear, let him hear what the Spirit saith unto the churches" (Revelation 2:7).

Also read: Prov. 18:15; 22:17

One week I was feeling low in spirits and needed a lift. I visited a church, hoping the pastor would minister to my needs.

But his message was a letdown. The longer he talked the more I wished I had stayed home. Then I began to condemn myself for feeling resentful. But his words were empty and the Holy Spirit had nothing to work with, so the service was FLAT.

As I was sitting there, I said to myself "Lowell, you need to get something from God—now." So I opened my Bible and located the text from which the pastor was speaking and began to read all the verses of Scripture in that chapter. Soon the Holy Spirit began to quicken different verses to my heart and I dug out my own message—while the pastor rambled on.

I listened with my other ears. What do you do in church when the pastor has a meaningless sermon? Rather than smolder, Tim Sims and Dan Pegoda have written a book entitled, *101 Things To Do During A Dull Sermon.* Some of their amusing suggestions are:

Sharpen the pencils in the racks on the back of the pews. A pen knife will help you accomplish this vital but often overlooked task in the life of the church.

The Bible says the hairs on your head are numbered. "Yes", the authors say. "but do you know the number? If there are too many to count on one Sunday, divide up your head and count only those hairs on one side of the part."

I think my idea is better than theirs. The next time you're in church and the pastor doesn't hit oil, pray for him; then begin to read your Bible and mark the verses meaningful to you. Let God speak to your heart through His Word.

•

Remember: LISTEN WITH YOUR OTHER EARS.

INVEST WITH ETERNITY IN MIND!

"Seek ye first the kingdom of God, and his righteousness; and all these things (your desires and necessities of life) *shall be added unto you"* (Matthew 6:33).

Also read: Rev. 2:10; Matt. 16:27; 25:34

Financial planning is big business today. Courses in personal finance and investment management have soared in popularity among college students. Leading magazines carry articles by financial experts advising you how to invest to get the highest yield on the dollar.

Good stewardship demands that Christians take good care of their financial affairs, because they have been commissioned by the Lord Himself to manage those affairs for Him. The Word tells us to begin by putting our priorities in proper order.

Life is a trade off. We trade our energy, time, talent, abilities, and money for things we believe are of value. One man works on cars, another on bookkeeping. One woman gives herself to motherhood and keeping the house, and another works in an office.

There are a million ways to invest your life, and just as many to waste it. One fact should never be forgotten. You only have one life to spend, and only what you do for Christ will last.

Jesus tried to focus the attention of His disciples on the lasting values of the kingdom. In our text, Jesus was saying that your eyes should not be on your bank account or the Dow Jones stock averages as much as on the treasures you are laying up in heaven.

The business world says profit is the bottom line. While this may be true for a non-Christian, a kingdom Christian does not live for personal profit, but to be of service to God and, consequently, is rewarded with immeasurable benefits that last forever.

•

Remember: YOU HAVE ONLY ONE LIFE TO SPEND. ONLY WHAT'S DONE FOR CHRIST WILL LAST!

299/THE ROAD TO RUIN

"Who changed the truth of God into a lie, and worshipped and served the creature more than the Creator" (Romans 1:25).

Also read: Psa. 1:1-6; Prov. 16:27

Have you ever wondered how people turn away from God and become homosexuals or atheists? How can such a thing happen?

Paul the apostle wrote to the Romans in chapter 1, verses 21 to 24, explaining how the ungodly found themselves on the road to ruin:

1. *When they knew God they glorified Him not as God.* (The first thing that happens when people backslide is they fail to worship God as openly and freely as they should.)
2. *Neither were they thankful.* (They begin to take God's blessings for granted.)
3. *Became vain in their imaginations.* (As people drift away from God they begin to concentrate on the wrong things. This world with its pleasures and philosophies becomes more important than God and His righteousness.)
4. *Their foolish hearts were darkened.* (Gradually a cloud of darkness settles over people's minds and hearts until they cannot see the truth.)
5. *Professing to be wise, they become fools.* (An arrogant spirit takes hold and they begin to think they are superior to the foolish believers who humbly follow Christ.)
6. *Changed the glory of the incorruptible God into an image made like to corruptible man.* (Soon people think that God thinks the same way they do, that if they don't see sin as doing wrong, God must surely think the same.)
7. *Wherefore God also gave them up to uncleanness.* (Once God is no longer a living reality in people's hearts and lives, the lusts of the flesh take over until they cannot resist the urge to sin.)

The tragic end of a man or woman who departs from God is this:

They are given over to a reprobate mind (verse 28).

Paul continues to say, *"Their lives became full of every kind of wickedness and sin... They were fully aware of God's death penalty for these crimes, yet they went right ahead and did them anyway, and encouraged others to do them too"* (Rom. 1:29-32, TLB).

●

Remember: THE ROAD TO RUIN BEGINS BY FAILING TO GLORIFY GOD. GIVE HIM PRAISE AND GLORY TODAY!

300/WHO WATERED DOWN THE WINE?

"...every one of us shall give account of himself to God" (Romans 14:12).

Also read: Matt. 12:36-37

There is a legend of a king who invited his people to a great feast; he also requested that each bring a bottle of wine for the festivities.

The wine from each guest's bottle was poured into a great vat. But when pitchers of the liquid were drawn off—each contained only water.

What had happened? Was this the miracle of Cana in reverse? NO! What happened was that each guest felt that his wine wouldn't be missed, so everyone had poured water into the vat.

This legend has a lesson for the church: whenever Christians are challenged to get involved in God's work they say, "They won't miss me!" The larger the church, the quicker people are inclined to feel they won't be needed.

The Bible says, *"Our bodies have many parts, but the many parts make up only one body when they are all put together. So it is with the 'body' of Christ...Some of us are Jews, some are Gentiles, some are slaves and some are free. But the Holy Spirit has fit us all together into one body. We have been baptized into Christ's body by the one Spirit, and have all been given that same Holy Spirit"* (1 Cor. 12:12 & 13, TLB).

Are you holding up your part in the body of Christ? What are you doing to press the body forward? If your eye dimmed you could not read this devotional; if your mind went blank you could not comprehend these words—and your body would be the loser. ALL parts are needed.

So hold up YOUR part. Each of us will give account of HIMSELF to God. On that day you don't want to be embarrassed over your poor performance.

•

Remember: DON'T WATER DOWN THE WINE.

301/HOW ARE YOU HANDLING CONFLICT?

"Whatsoever things are true, whatsoever things are honest, whatsoever things are just, whatsoever things are pure, whatsoever things are lovely, whatsoever things are of good report; if there be any virtue, and if there be any praise, think on these things" (Philippians 4:8).

Also read: 1 Cor. 10:13; 15:58; Jam. 1:12

Every day of our lives, most of us encounter conflict, and most of the time we don't like it. But conflict is part of God's plan for us. He made it part of His creation.

When God put Adam and Eve in the Garden of Eden, He also put conflict there. He told them they could have the fruit of any of the trees in the garden except one, and that tree was forbidden. Why did God do that? He wanted to test Adam and Eve's obedience to Him through conflict.

No matter where you are today, you will encounter conflict. Whether or not you win or lose depends on your attitude of gratitude. If Adam and Eve had been grateful for the wonderful things God had provided; they wouldn't have cared that one tree was forbidden to them. Instead, they began to focus on the one forbidden tree and to feel resentful because God wouldn't let them have its fruit. They disobeyed God and lost the conflict.

How are you handling conflict? Is there a war going on inside you? Only you determine if you win or lose. Instead of concentrating on negative things, focus on the positive things. If you have an attitude of gratitude in your heart and say, "Look at all the great things I have to be grateful for," you will win. If you look at the bad things, you will lose.

Someone said, "Criticism is like a fly. It passes over the good parts of the body to feast on the sore." There will always be things about life you don't like. There is no perfect spouse, job, or situation in this world. We all have faults as well as strengths, burdens as well as blessings. It's what we focus on that counts.

•

Remember: CONFLICT PRESENTS OPPORTUNITIES FOR US TO CHOOSE THE RIGHT OVER THE WRONG, THE GOOD OVER THE BAD. IT ALLOWS US TO DEMONSTRATE OUR FAITH, LOVE, AND OBEDIENCE TO GOD.

302/YOU MUST BIND THE DEVIL!

"No man can enter into a strong man's house, and spoil (take away) *his goods, except he will first bind the strong man: and then he will spoil his house"* (Mark 3:27).

Also read: Matt. 18:18; Rom. 8:37; Jas. 4:7-8

If you as a Christian are going to live victoriously in this life, you must learn to bind the devil. You can't avoid Satan or tiptoe around him. He is set on your defeat and destruction and you must learn how to bind him so you can move forward.

Men accused Jesus of casting out demons by the power of the devil. Jesus responded by saying, *"How can Satan cast out Satan? And if a kingdom be divided against itself, that kingdom cannot stand. And if a house be divided against itself, that house cannot stand. And if Satan rise up against himself, and be divided, he cannot stand, but hath an end* (he will fall apart)" (Mark 3:24-26).

Then Jesus said, "(Satan must be bound before his demons are cast out), *just as a strong man must be tied up before his house can be ransacked and his property robbed"* (Mark 3:27).

Have you ever been binding Satan? If he has been moving against you or your loved ones, you must take authority over him. The Bible says, *"Then he called his twelve disciples together, and gave them power and authority over ALL devils, and to cure diseases. And he sent them to preach the kingdom of God, and to heal the sick"* (Luke 9:1, 2, emphasis mine).

Jesus has given this same authority to you. He said, *"Whatsoever you shall bind on earth shall be bound in heaven: and whatsoever you shall loose on earth shall be loosed in heaven"* (see Matt. 16:19).

This promise was not only for Peter—this same authority is given to all of God's children. Remember that Jesus said, *"If ye shall ask any thing in my name, I will do it"* (John 14:14).

•

Remember: IF YOU WANT TO WIN YOU MUST BIND THE DEVIL. BIND HIM IN JESUS' NAME TODAY!

303/CLEAN UP THE CLUTTER

"You shall eat in a clean place" (Leviticus 10:14).

Also read: Neh. 13:9

I never cease to be amazed how clutter creeps into my life. Messes multiply and before I know it, my closet is jammed, my drawers are filled with junk and even the night stand by my bed is running over.

I have to fight the messes that move against me; and if it weren't for my wife, Connie, I would be inundated with the clutter.

The best way I've found to attack the clutter is to have periodical rummage sales (someone told Connie and me if you don't use something twice a year, it should go.) A garage sale helps eliminate a lot of clutter.

Another way is to declare a cleaning day. This works best for me. I make up my mind to go through every box and drawer. I don't allow a thing to stop me until I'm finished. (It's surprising how much you can go through in one day of determined effort.)

God told the Levites and the priests to "eat in a clean place." How clean is your home? Have you kept things up or have you let things go? Today is a great day to get rid of your clutter.

Would you like some motivation? The average garage sale of junk collected from the attic, closets, garage and basement amounts to over $200.00. Isn't that something you could use?

Maybe there is a good mission work or evangelistic endeavor that needs the money from your junk. Just think how your mess can bless if you use the money for God!

Could you be suffering from a mild depression because of the messy house, dirty car and cluttered life you live in? Then start cleaning up today!

•

Remember: WHEN YOU PRAY THAT GOD'S KINGDOM COME, THIS IMPLIES ORDER. LET GOD'S KINGDOM CONQUER YOUR CLUTTER.

304/A TRIBUTE TO A WINNER

"Because the Lord God helps me, I will not be dismayed; therefore, I have set my face like flint to do his will, and I know that I will triumph!" (Isaiah 50:7, TLB).

Also read: Phil. 4:13; Eph. 3:12

Determination is the key to your success with both God and man. Keep this in mind as you meditate on this special tribute to a winner that I found on a high school coach's office door.

Tribute To A Winner

A winner is a man who can persevere in the face of all adversity. He walks quietly with true humility and maintains his dignity with calm pride. He boasts not of his victories, yet accepts readily his defeats. He has tenacity of purpose, devotion to his God and his family. He never believes he can be beaten, yet never seeks an excuse if he fails.

A winner never loses sight of his goals, never stops striving, no matter how large the task might be. He's quick with praise, yet not fickle with his compliments. He inspires, he leads, he works, he sweats, he bleeds and cries—but never quits.

A winner will attempt the impossible, challenge the odds, and achieve the improbable—never underestimating his opponent but always expecting him to do what he himself would do in similar circumstances.

A winner may never achieve his ultimate purpose, but he will never give up! Whatever pinnacle a winner may reach, he will never be satisfied nor will he lose sight of those who helped him get to where he is.

And so—He lives and dies—winning!

Author unknown—tribute was personally edited for this devotional.

•

Remember: IF YOU WILL REMIND YOURSELF THAT THE LORD IS WITH YOU AND IF YOU WILL SET YOUR FACE AS A FLINT AND DRIVE FEAR FROM YOU HEART—YOU WILL SURELY TRIUMPH!

305/WAYS TO ELIMINATE PAIN

"I will bless the Lord at all times: his praise shall continually be in my mouth" (Psalms 34:1).

Also read: Jer. 17:14; 33:6; Matt. 9:35; Jas. 5:14, 15

Researchers are trying to discover the source of pain. They are baffled by it—because in order for them to eliminate pain they must also eliminate pleasure. The same nerves that respond to excitement-producing pleasure, when alarmed, produce pain.

They have come this far in their research: that pain sufferers can reduce their pain by interrupting the signals to the brain. If a patient will think strongly on something other than pain he can cancel out the sting of it.

A dentist told me that a doctor who specialized in pain said, "Whenever you have a pain, just consider it to be an itch on the top of your head. Then just scratch your head (think new ideas) and the pain will go away."

If you're hurting, the idea of pain being referred to as an itch may be trite and even insulting, but the concept is correct. In fact, with severe sufferers, doctors have connected electric prods to their spinal columns to interrupt the signals. When the pain becomes unbearable, the patient simply turns on the current for relief.

There is a spiritual way to do much the same thing. Today's text says, *"I will bless the Lord at all times: his praise shall continually be in my mouth."*

The words "all times" and "continually" include the times when you are suffering from pain.

If you are hurting, my heart goes out to you. Pray this prayer with me, "Father in heaven, in Jesus' name I come before You, asking You to heal my body, deliver me from sickness and loose me from this pain. In Jesus' name. Amen."

•

Remember: CANCEL OUT YOUR PAIN WITH PRAISE!

LEARN TO WALK WITH GOD

"Enoch walked with God" (Genesis 5:24).

Also read: Is. 2:5; 30:21; Col. 2:6

This is one of the greatest biographies ever written of a man. *"...he walked with God."* But Enoch had dynamic results. The Bible says *"Enoch walked with God; and he was not; for God took him."*

This means he was caught up into heaven. Day after day Enoch visited with God and became such good friends that one day I think God said, "There's no sense in waiting until you die, Enoch, you could just as well come on up today."

The greatest need in the church today is men and women who enjoy walking with God. Tell me, if you were locked in a room for ten hours a day—could you have a good time just visiting with God?

You see, what's happened is that everyone is busy learning facts about God, but so few are walking with Him. It's like a man forever studying about women, but failing to talk to his wife. She'll soon become frustrated and angry.

Until you can feel comfortable talking with God for hours, you've not yet learned how to walk with Him. This doesn't mean that each day you must spend hours on your knees doing nothing else but praying, but you should awaken with a prayer in your heart and continue in an attitude of prayer all day long while you work, visit, shop and so on.

Walking with God like this doesn't make you into some kind of "Religious Weirdo." Enoch was a family man—his son was Methuselah. He lived a normal, busy life—but he still walked with God.

Will you walk with God today? Do as the Bible says, *"Walk in the Spirit"* (Gal. 5:16). You'll experience phenomenal results!

•

Remember: WALK WITH GOD!

307/THE MEASURE OF A MAN

"I consider everything a loss compared to the surpassing greatness of knowing Christ Jesus my Lord, for whose sake I have lost all things. I consider them rubbish, that I may gain Christ and be found in him"
(Philippians 3:8 & 9, NIV).

Also read: Is. 26:4; 41:10; Ps. 37:39

A man once said, "The measure of a man is not his wealth or his achievements as much as it is what it takes to make him quit." That's a big line. How much does it take to make you quit? That's the measure of what you are.

Life is like a combine. It cuts off the stalks of grain. Then it separates the straw and the grain through a series of grates that get smaller and smaller. At the end, the grate is just big enough for the wheat to go through. The combine repeatedly shakes the grain down. That's like life. From the top to the bottom, it is shaking all of us. What size are you? What does it take to shake you out?

Mohammed Ali once had a fight in Las Vegas when he was past his prime. He wasn't in good physical shape, and he later said that by the end of the first round all his strength was gone. "But," he said, "I determined that I was going to make it through that fight and that my opponent wasn't going to punch me out. I wasn't going to quit." That attitude made Mohammed Ali a great fighter, a champion.

The making and breaking of your life is in the things that are coming against you. Do you give up easily when trouble comes or do you determine to fight and win? Sometimes we face difficulties and they threaten to overwhelm us. Do you hang in there and fight or do you throw in the towel? What you do determines your measure.

The Apostle Paul went through a lot to serve Christ, but he said that he considered everything a loss just to know Him. That is truly the measure of greatness.

•

Remember: THE MEASURE OF WHO YOU ARE IS DETERMINED BY THE SIZE OF THE BATTLES THAT CANNOT DEFEAT YOU.

HELP SOMEONE IN CHAINS

"The Lord give mercy unto the house of Onesiphorus; for he often refreshed me, and was not ashamed of my chain; But, when he was in Rome, he sought me out very diligently, and found me. The Lord grant unto him that he may find mercy of the Lord in that day; and in how many things he ministered unto me at Ephesus, you know very well" (see 2 Timothy 1:16-18).

Also read: Mark 8:34-37; Luke 3:10-11; 10:33-34

Our text today is a long one because Onesiphorus did so many encouraging things for Paul that it would be unfair to cut him short of his mention in Holy Scripture.

*He was not ashamed to associate himself with Paul, a prisoner in chains.

*He often refreshed Paul during his preaching tours in Ephesus.

Paul proved that Onesiphorus would find mercy from the Lord on Judgment Day.

Are you ministering to those around you who are also in chains?

1. *What about those who are in chains of sickness?* Have you visited them in the hospital or their homes?

2. *What about those in chains of prison?* How long has it been since you've taken some cakes and pastries to those in your local jail?

3. *What about those in chains of loneliness?* Are you visiting shut-ins and nursing home residents? Do you invite strangers (non-family) into your home?

4. *What about those in chains of poverty?* How many boxes of groceries do you give to the poor? How much clothing?

The list could go on and on. My purpose is not to make you feel guilty, but to prompt you to take time to fulfill your mission as a disciple of Jesus Christ. I know you're busy, but what if Onesiphorus had been too busy to visit Paul?

Today God is writing a book of your life in heaven. *"For we must all appear before the judgment seat of Christ; that every one may receive the things done in his body, according to that he hath done, whether it be good or bad"* (2 Cor. 5:10).

If you want the mercy of God on Judgment Day, take time to minister to others today.

•

Remember: HELP SOMEONE IN CHAINS TODAY!

309/WITHOUT HOPE

"At that time you were without Christ...aliens...strangers...having no hope...and without God" (Ephesians 2:12).

Also read: Rom. 5:2; 15:13; Heb. 6:11

Do you realize the despair of the nonchristian people you will meet today? You must look past their smiles, masking their inner feelings of hopelessness.

Here is a poem that was written by an unsaved man.

WHAT'S IT ALL ABOUT?

Why was I born, I wonder why.
    Was it just to plant my sperm and years later—die?
How can I understand the infinite with only a finite mind?
    It's like trying to explain the sunrise to someone born blind.
I'm just a speck in the universe—for that my ego is bitter,
    'cause I've got feelings and dignity but to the universe I'm
    just litter.

There's a happy ending to this despairing story. The man who wrote these words later became a Christian, but his poem expresses the hopelessness many people feel before they come to Christ.

Today as you go about your daily duties, recognize the emptiness in the lives of the people you meet; this will help you to witness more effectively.

When speaking—express hope. Say, "I'm glad God has everything under control." Or mention, "If I wasn't a Christian I'd get depressed." Or, "I'm sure glad I know how everything is going to turn out."

These phrases and others that you can think up will prompt the nonchristian to say, "What did you mean by that?" Then you have a great opportunity to share your testimony!

•

Remember: ENCOURAGE THE HOPELESS YOU WILL MEET TODAY.

"Beware of covetousness: for a man's life consisteth not in the abundance of the things which he possesseth" (Luke 12:15).

Also read: Matt. 4:4; 6:20; Rev. 22:5

Many people are buying the devil's great lie that what will make them happy is comfort and security—things!

I often ask Christian couples in our seminars what they want most out of life. They usually say, "Oh, we don't want to be rich. All we want is to have things nice for us and the kids."

Have you ever visited a mortuary? Everything is nice. The flowers are nice, the music is nice, the undertaker is nice, the corpse is nice. Everything is nice and dead!

Jesus clearly considered money and our material needs to be important. That's why He dealt with these matters at length. However, our Lord pointed out that it takes more than money and things to satisfy the human heart. You can go through the motions of living and never truly live.

In His Sermon on the Mount, Jesus acknowledged man's search for security and comfort, and He made this incredible offer:

"Your heavenly Father knoweth that ye have need of all things (food, shelter, clothing, transportation). *But seek ye first the kingdom of God, and his righteousness; and all these things shall be added unto you"* (Matt. 6:32 & 33, emphasis mine).

To be fulfilled, you have to be a part of something that is bigger than you and that lasts longer than you do—something that will give you drive, energy, and enthusiasm. The greatest thing going, now and for all eternity, is the kingdom of God'

•

Remember: GOD HAS CHOSEN YOU TO BE HIS PARTNER IN TAKING THE GOSPEL TO THE LOST, AND THROUGH THAT RELATIONSHIP WITH HIM TO HAVE YOUR PERSONAL NEEDS MET ABUNDANTLY!

311/HANG ON IN PRAYER!

"From the first day you set your heart to chasten yourself before God, your words were heard, and I am come as a result of your prayers—but the Prince of Persia resisted me for 21 days!" (Daniel 10:12 & 13, Literal).

Also read: Psa. 27:14; 33:20; 130:5; Isa. 25:9; 40:31

Have you been praying about a situation without receiving an answer? Then today's text will greatly encourage you.

Daniel was a man of God who set his heart to seek God for the deliverance of his people. Here's what Daniel did:

First, *he had a genuine burden to pray.* "*In those days I Daniel was mourning three full weeks*"(Dan. 10:2). The Holy Spirit laid such a great burden upon him that he prayed for 21 days.

Second, *he fasted while he prayed.* "*I ate no pleasant bread, neither came flesh nor wine in my mouth...till three whole weeks were fulfilled*" (verse 3).

If you will refrain from food and sex (see 1 Cor. 7:5) during an intensive period of prayer, it will help you to become more sensitive to the Spirit's leading. You'll know how to pray more effectively.

Third, *Daniel held on until he received an answer to his prayers.* It must have been most discouraging to pray for 21 days and nights without receiving an answer—but Daniel held on.

When the Lord arrived, he explained to Daniel why his prayers were not answered immediately. He had fought a battle in the heavenlies with the demonic prince of Persia. This demon prince withstood the Lord until the Archangel Michael came to the Lord's aid.

If you have been praying earnestly about something, don't give up. Don't quit praying now! Chances are there is a spiritual struggle going on in the heavenlies and you may be close to a breakthrough.

●

Remember: HANG ON IN PRAYER—THE LORD IS ON HIS WAY.

312/YOU'RE NEVER TOO OLD!

"And Moses was an hundred and twenty years old when he died: his eye was not dim, nor his natural force abated" (Deuteronomy 34:7).

Also read: Gen. 5:5, 27; 9:29; Ps. 39:5

Your mind can deceive you. Society and public opinion can brainwash you into thinking that you're old when you're not.

Billy Graham is nearly 65 and preaches constantly. He says he needs a nap in the afternoon to keep up his strength, but what's a little nap, compared to a full day of activity?

Moses was 120 years old when he died and he still had clear vision and was physically strong. You're God's child. Claim your inheritance. Push yourself along and don't give up the ship when you've barely gotten out of the harbor. Here's what others in history have accomplished in their golden years:

* Socrates gave the world his wisest philosophy at 70.
* Plato did his best teaching after 60.
* Francis Bacon was 60 before he wrote his greatest works.
* Phillips Brooks, one of the world's greatest preachers, was a powerful figure at 84.
* Emerson wrote *Conduct of Life* at 60.
* Gladstone was still a prominent figure in political and intellectual circles when he was 80.
* Goethe wrote a part of *Faust* at 60 and finished it at 82.
* Victor Hugo wrote *Les Miserables* at 62.
* John Milton completed *Paradise Lost* at 56 and *Paradise Regained* at 63.
* Jules Verne wrote wonderful stories at 70.
* Noah Webster wrote his monumental dictionary at 70.

Don't let your age prevent you from accomplishing the great things God has planned for you.

•

Remember: YOU'RE ONLY AS OLD AS YOU THINK.

313/HOW GIVING TO GOD WORKS!

"If you give, you will get! Your gift will return to you in full and overflowing measure, pressed down, shaken together to make room for more, and running over" (Luke 6:38, TLB).

Also read: Mal. 3:10; 2 Cor. 9:16; Prov. 19:17

When you give, it starts a chain reaction that influences man to give back to you what you've given to God in faith.

Two of our longtime Faith Partners, Mr. and Mrs. Bernard Smith, discovered this spiritual truth several years ago when they gave a sizeable gift to help us get our television program on the air.

"We didn't have $10 when we gave that gift," they said. "We wrote out a check by faith. And before it cleared the bank, the money was there. We had more than a thousand dollars come in that we didn't expect.

"We had started a recreational canoe rental and service business. By normal standards, a six percent yearly increase in business is phenomenal, but that year we increased our gross income 110 percent!

The Smiths are retired now, but they continue to give faithfully and with joy. "Giving to God is not a sacrifice," says Mr. Smith. "It's a two-way street. When we give, God just showers His blessings down."

A while back the Smiths gave to help us pull out of a financial crisis. Afterwards, a man called Mr. Smith and said, "Would you care if I paid $1,200 on that longtime note I owe you? You'll get it in the mail tomorrow."

Mr. Smith said, "He asked would I care! Can you imagine? But that's how giving to God works. I firmly believe there's no way you can out give our Savior!"

•

Remember: ONLY WHAT YOU GIVE CAN BE MULTIPLIED BACK TO YOU!

314/ARE YOU A CHRISTIAN CRANK?

"And walk in love, as Christ also hath loved us, and hath given himself for us an offering and a sacrifice to God for a sweet-smelling savour" (Ephesians 5:2).

Also read: 1 Cor. 13:13; Col. 3:14; 1 John 4:16

Recently I heard someone describe a believing woman this way: "She was a Christian, but she sure was a crank." Wise King Solomon said, *"A constant dripping on a rainy day and a cranky woman are much alike!"* (Prov. 27:15, TLB).

The thought of being a Christian "crank" really hit me. I began to think of the kind of impression I make on other people. If you and I claim to be Christians we need to have visible examples of the fruits of the Spirit in our lives: *"...love, joy, peace, longsuffering* (patience), *gentleness, goodness, faith, meekness and temperance"* (see Gal. 5:22 & 23).

Your behavior is noticed by other people—it reflects what you believe and what is important in your life. You are the only "Bible" some people will ever read. You must make a good impression on those you meet today. If you want people to enjoy being around you, you must be positive in your thinking. The way to be a positive thinker is to spend time saturating your mind with God's Word and good Christian literature and music.

Everything we learn primarily comes through our eyes and our ears. The way you can change your personality is to change your listening, watching and reading patterns.

Don't allow immoral TV programs, obscene books, dirty jokes, worldly songs or titillating gossip to come into your mind. The Bible tells us, *"Whatsoever things are TRUE, whatsoever things are HONEST, whatsoever things are JUST, whatsoever things are PURE, whatsoever things are LOVELY, whatsoever things are of GOOD REPORT; if there be any VIRTUE, and if there be any PRAISE, think on these things"* (Phil. 4:8, emphasis mine). Let's not only *think* about these things, let's *act* on them.

•

Remember: DON'T BE A CHRISTIAN CRANK.

315/LET GOD DECIDE

"And the Lord came, and stood, and called as at other times, Samuel, Samuel. Then Samuel answered, Speak; for thy servant heareth" (1 Samuel 3:10).

Also read: Jn. 14:15; 1 Jn. 3:22-24

When you're praying about a decision, the important thing is to allow God to make it for you.

Recently I talked with a man who said, "Lowell, I've always dreamed of using my talents for the Lord."

I felt an inner prompting to ask him to come to work with us. Suddenly, the conversation shifted. He began to explain how his company was going to promote him, how he had salary security, etc.

Finally I said, "Dear Brother, you need to read where Paul wrote the Galatian Christians saying, *'Are ye so foolish? having begun in the Spirit, are ye now made perfect by the flesh?'* (Gal. 3:3). If you had the prompting of the Lord to work for Him, why are you considering anything else when you're given the opportunity?"

If you want to know the will of God, you need to be willing to do *whatever* He says. We often want to know God's will and *then* decide if we want to do it. We want to decide if we want to agree with what God has said. God will not be interested in revealing His perfect will to you under those circumstances.

When you join the armed forces, you don't choose whether or not you will obey your orders—you simply join and then you are expected to obey the orders given you.

So decide now—
1. Do you really want to know God's will?
2. Do you trust God enough that you will obey Him regardless of what He says?

My friend Jim Kirby, shared this poem with me recently:
>He knows, He loves, He cares
>Nothing this truth can dim;
>God always gives His best to those
>Who leave the choice with Him.

•

Remember: "TRUST AND OBEY—FOR THERE'S NO OTHER WAY TO BE HAPPY IN JESUS"—John H. Sammis.

316/UNDERSTAND YOUR POWER IN CHRIST

"I pray that you will begin to understand how incredibly great his power is to help those who believe him. It is that same mighty power that raised Christ from the dead" (Ephesians 1:19, TLB).

Also read: 1 Jn. 5:18; Ps. 32:7; 138:7

Many times Christians let the devil defeat them simply because they do not understand the power that is available to them through Jesus Christ.

Jesus said, *"All power is given unto me in heaven and in earth"* (Matt. 28:18). ALL POWER! Now if Jesus has all power, how much power does that leave the devil? NONE! The devil doesn't have any power except the power that we give him. Christ is in you, and He's given you power and authority over the devil.

The Apostle Paul prayed for the eyes of Christians to be opened to Christ's power dwelling in them. He said, "Oh, if your eyes could be opened to understand the power you have, you would not be discouraged or defeated!"

Paul went on to say that Christ was exalted *"far above all principality, and power, and might, and dominion, and every name that is named, not only in this world, but also in that which is to come: and hath put all things under his feet"* (Eph. 1:21 & 22).

Anything that comes against you or your family spiritually, physically, emotionally, or financially—anything!—Jesus' name is above it. Your victory is not in yourself, but in the Lord Jesus. When you meet trouble, you can get behind Him to fight.

Have you ever seen war movies where soldiers in the infantry followed behind tanks, crouching low so the tank with its great power and armor could protect them as they fought? That's what you and I can do—get behind Jesus and let Him lead the way, because He has all power to win the battles we face.

•

Remember: CHRIST IS IN YOU, AND HE'S GIVEN YOU POWER OVER THE DEVIL!

317/IF YOU LOVE—YOU WILL GIVE!

"For God so loved... that he gave" (John 3:16).

Also read: 1 Chron. 16:29; 29:9; Prov. 11:24-25

Do you love to give to God's work? I believe your financial response at offering time is one of the truest indicators of your love for God.

*If you love God—you'll give to make Him happy, just as loving parents enjoy giving gifts to their children.

*If you love God—you'll give to help others find Him. When you give to a soulwinning ministry you also are helping to win souls.

*If you love God—you'll give because the Spirit of God dwelling within will prompt you to be as generous to God as He has been to you.

*If you love God—you'll give because of the great debt you owe to Him.

*If you love God—you'll give because you know He will give you more in return than you gave in the first place.

Recently I met a young couple who were going through a financial crisis. They asked me to pray about their problem. As I encouraged them I felt a prompting of the Holy Spirit to give them a gift. When my flesh resisted, these Scriptures came to mind, *"What does it profit, my brethren, though a man say he hath faith, and have not works? can faith save him?*

"If a brother or sister be naked, and without food, And one of you say unto them, Depart in peace, be warmed and filled; notwithstanding ye give them not those things which are needful to the body; what doth it profit?

"Even so faith, if it hath not works, is dead, being alone" (Jas. 2:14-17).

After remembering these verses I went to my checkbook and wrote my "letter" of love to them and God.

●

Remember: IF YOU LOVE—YOU WILL GIVE!

318/JESUS IS GREATER THAN WORDS DESCRIBE

"For unto us a child is born, unto us a son is given: and the government shall be upon his shoulder: and his name shall be called Wonderful, Counsellor, The mighty God, The everlasting Father, The Prince of Peace. Of the increase of His government...there shall be no end" (Isaiah 0:6 & 7).

Also read: Prov. 24:5; Mic. 4:5; Zep. 3:12; Acts 21:13

The prophet Isaiah saw Jesus in superlative terms. The same is true of the Apostle John. The beloved disciple said of Jesus, *"And there are also many other things which Jesus did ... I suppose (if they should be written) that even the world itself could not contain the books that should be written"* (John 21:25).

In Matthew, Jesus is the Messiah; in Mark, He is the Miracle-Worker; in Luke, He is the Son of Man; in John, He is the Son of God; in Acts, He is the Holy Spirit; in Romans, He is the Justifier; in 1 & 2 Corinthians, He is the Gifts and Fruit of the Spirit; in Galatians, He is the Redeemer from the curse of the Lord; in Ephesians, He is the Christ of Eternal riches; in Phillipians, He is the supplier of every need; in Colossians, He is the fullness of the Godhead; in 1 & 2 Thessalonians, He is the Coming King; in 1 & 2 Timothy, He is the Mediator between God and Man; in Titus, He is the faithful Shepherd; in Philemon, He is a Friend closer than a brother; in Hebrews, He is the Blood of the covenant; in James, He is the mighty Physician; in 1 & 2 Peter, He is the Supreme Shepherd; in 1, 2 & 3 John, He is Everlasting love; in Jude, He is the Lord returning with 10,000 of His saints; and in Revelation, He is the King of Kings and Lord of Lords and He reigns forever and ever, and ever and ever, and of His dominion there shall be no end.

This is Jesus, the Name above all Names!

•

Remember: JESUS IS GREATER THAN ALL THE WORDS THE ENGLISH LANGUAGE COULD EVER DESCRIBE. TELL HIM WITH YOUR OWN WORDS HOW MUCH YOU LOVE HIM TODAY!

319/WHAT ARE YOUR WAGES?

"Remember, the Lord will pay you for each good thing you do, whether you are slave or free" (Ephesians 6:8, TLB).

Also read: Eph. 6:5-7; 2 Chron. 15:7

Do you love your job? Paul Harvey says, "If you're working on a job you wouldn't do if you weren't paid for it—you need to look for a new profession."

Would you work at your job if you were rich enough to quit? If not, then you need to re-examine your work ethic.

According to God's Word, you are not working for the man (your boss) or the money—you are working for The Master, our Lord and Savior, Jesus Christ.

If you work to make money you are missing the true motive of working—you are selling yourself for dollars instead of serving God.

Here is a life-changing poem:

My Wage

I bargained with life for a penny
And life would pay no more
However I begged at evening
When I counted my scanty store;

For life is just an employer,
He gives you what you ask,
But once you have set the wages,
Why, you must bear the task.

I worked for a menial's hire
Only to learn, dismayed,
That any wage I had asked of life,
Life would have gladly paid.

— Jessie B. Rittenhouse

Are you selling out for money when you should be serving God?

What will happen if you give your job your best and your employer doesn't pay you sufficiently?

●

Remember: "THE LORD WILL PAY YOU FOR EACH GOOD THING YOU DO."

320/THE TEN COMMANDMENTS ARE NOT MULTIPLE CHOICE

"If you shall hearken diligently unto the voice of the Lord thy God, to observe and to do ALL his commandments...the Lord thy God will set you on high above all nations of the earth (see Deuteronomy 28:1, emphasis mine).

Also read: Ex. 20:1-17; Deut. 5:1, 32-33; 11:26-28

The further a person drifts from God the less confidence he has in what God says. He begins to think the Ten Commandments are multiple choice.

Dolly Parton, a popular country-pop singer and actress, has recently been quoted in *Redbook* magazine as saying that it's okay if her husband has his girlfriends and she has her lovers, "as long as he don't love somebody more than me. I think I would be hurt if he fell in love with someone else, but I like the fact that he's got friends. He takes his girlfriends to dinner and to lunch. Now whether he goes to bed with them or not, I don't care as long as it don't hurt me."

She said her husband, Carl Dean, doesn't care what she does either. "He'd rather I have friends—male friends—because he feels they would protect me. He knows I'm always coming home."

The Bible says, *"Thou shalt not commit adultery"* (Ex. 20:14).

One youth pastor observed, "Today many would rather yield to the temptations of sin and enjoy its fleeting pleasures—with plans to repent later—than to resist temptation and remain pure."

Don't be deceived. God's grace is not a license to sin. *"For if we sin wilfully or by design after that we have received the knowledge of the truth, there remaineth NO more sacrifice for sins"* (Heb. 10:26, emphasis mine).

Now it's true that God forgives every repentant soul, but you can only repent so many times before your heart becomes hardened—then you don't really feel sorry about your sin anymore.

•

Remember: BEWARE! THE TEN COMMANDMENTS ARE NOT MULTIPLE CHOICE.

321/NO MATTER WHAT!

"If ye continue in my word, then are ye my disciples indeed" (John 8:31).

Also read: John 15:10; Acts 14:22

I could tell the pastor's spirit was crushed. His face twitched nervously as he spoke. The words that came from his lips expressed the wounds of his soul.

A devil-inspired church board member had persuaded the other members of the official board to fire him. The congregation was so shocked and angered by the board's conspiracy they walked out on the church, pledging to remain loyal to the pastor if he would remain in their city and begin a new church. Board members were threatening to sue him, and the leaders of his denomination recommended that he leave town.

This pastor was torn by the injustice done to him. He was a humble man who didn't want to hurt God's work by causing further turmoil.

As he shared the story, the Holy Spirit led me to say, "Did God call you to your city?" He said, "Yes!" "Has God told you to leave?" "No." "Then stay! Start another church. If you turn your back and run away from the problem, you won't be able to live with yourself because you'll know you were a coward." Then the Holy Spirit spoke through me and said, "Don't leave town—no matter what!"

I spoke with that pastor later and he was praising the Lord. He said, "Lowell, God really spoke through you. When you said, 'Don't leave town—*no matter what!*', I was changed. I determined I wasn't going to run away from my problem.

"When the leaders of my denomination saw I wasn't going to run they decided to support me. Our new church is growing rapidly and I'm really happy."

Are you facing a difficult situation? Then don't run away—NO MATTER WHAT! If you'll hold your ground, you'll win—because God will help you.

•

Remember: DON'T GIVE UP—NO MATTER WHAT!

322/ARE YOU WINNING?

"He that winneth souls is wise" (Proverbs 11:30).

Also read: 1 Cor. 9:24-27; 1 Tim. 4:16; Gal. 6:9

Vince Lombardi was a football coach who believed in winning. He transformed the Greenbay Packers from a mediocre team into Superbowl Winners. His philosophy was:

"Winning is not a some time thing; it's an all time thing. You don't win once in a while. You don't do things right once in a while. You do them right all the time. Winning is a habit. Unfortunately so is losing."

Paul the apostle also thought that winning was an all time thing. In 1 Cor. 9:24-27 he wrote that it's easy to give up and give unto the flesh because we like to be comfortable. But the fact is that winners wage a constant war. Paul said he punished his body.

Do you want to win? Then begin today.
1. Win by beginning your day with Bible reading and prayer.
2. Win by showering, bathing, shaving, doing your hair, and splashing on a dash of cologne.
3. Win by wearing something fresh. Even old clothes can look sharp with a little washing and ironing.
4. Win by having something good for breakfast. Whether you eat a lot or a little, start the day with food that makes your body feel alive.
5. Win by smiling and greeting the people you meet on your way to work, school, or the store. (I've developed a thumbs-up sign that seems to give people more of a boost than just a wave. Try it!)
6. Win by speaking aloud, "This is going to be a great Day for God! Christ is in my heart and life and He has all power in heaven and earth to make me a winner!"
7. Win by sharing Christ with someone.

●

Remember: HE THAT WINNETH SOULS IS WISE. WINNING THE LOST IS AN ALL TIME THING.

323/WORSHIP THE LORD—LOUDLY!

"And they blew the trumpet...and piped with pipes, and rejoiced with great joy, so that the earth rent (split in two) *with the sound of them"* (1 Kings 1:39 & 40).

Also read: 2 Chron. 5:13-14; Psa. 47:1; 109:30; 149:1-6

When it comes to worship, God likes things to be loud. I know this is contrary to worldly minds, but it is true. The Bible makes this fact very clear.

The Holy Spirit inspired David to write, *"Praise him upon loud cymbals...Let every thing that hath breath praise the Lord"* (Psa. 150:5-6).

Through the 29 years of my ministry I have noticed that too many Christians "freeze up" when the worship of God gets noisy. This should not be. God enjoys worship when you put everything into it.

When King David brought the ark of God into Jerusalem the Bible says, *"Thus all Israel brought up the ark of the covenant of the Lord with shouting, and with the sound of the cornet, and with trumpets, and with cymbals, MAKING A NOISE with psalteries and harps"* (1 Chron. 15:28, emphasis mine).

Whenever a church service gets this loud and noisy there's surely someone who will criticize. This time it was David's own wife, *"And it came to pass, as the ark of the... Lord came to the city of David, that Michal* (David's wife), *the daughter of Saul looking out at a window saw king David dancing and playing: and she despised him in her heart"* (1 Chron. 15:29).

When David returned Michal met him and sarcastically said, *"How glorious was the King of Israel to day, who uncovered himself to day in the eyes of the handmaids of his servants."* (David was obviously dancing and kicking his feet so high that his skirt-like kilt flapped high enough to see his bare legs.)

Then David said, *"It was before the Lord, which chose me before thy father, and before all his house, to appoint me ruler over the people of the Lord, over Israel: therefore will I play before the Lord."*

●

Remember: GOD WANTS YOUR WORSHIP TO BE ENTHUSIASTIC. IT REVEALS THAT, LIKE DAVID, YOU HAVE A HEART AFTER GOD.

GLORY IN THE GRAY!

"White hair is a crown of glory and is seen most often among the godly" (Proverbs 16:31, TLB).

Also read: Ps. 71:9; Matt. 10:30

Hair is a multi-billion dollar business in North America. A wife asked her husband this question one day after coming home from the beauty shop, "Honey, do you think you'll love me when I'm gray?"

He replied, "I don't know why not—I've loved you through seven shades already."

Once at a convention, a young preacher was poking fun of an older minister who was bald. When the older pastor got his turn at the lectern he said, "Years ago they buried a man who was bald and 3 years later when they dug him up he had a little hair. From this they've come to the conclusion that hair grows best on a dead head."

Today's text tells us that gray hair is a crown of glory. This doesn't mean that every Christian should have gray hair—but when the time comes and you don't feel like fighting the battle with tints and dyes anymore, just let it go gray and rejoice you've got some there that CAN turn gray. I'm going to do this when that time comes.

How do you view older people? Once I read that the elderly are just teenagers trapped in old bodies. Suddenly I realized this was true. Just because a person is old doesn't mean he's lost the passions and desires of youth.

If the years are mounting up on you, don't be discouraged. The Bible says, *"The glory of young men is their strength; and the beauty of old men is the gray head"* (Prov. 20:29).

•

Remember: WEAR YOUR AGE WITH PRIDE, GLORY IN THE GRAY.

325/EVERYONE NEEDS A DREAM

"and when Jesus beheld him, he said, Thou art Simon the son of Jona: thou shalt be called Cephas, which is by interpretation, A stone" (John 1:42).

Also read: Prov. 16:9; Ps. 37:5

Maybe you've heard the story of two men in prison looking out from behind the bars. One man looked down and saw mud. The other looked up and saw the stars.

Every one of us can look at the limitations in our life and say, "I can't. I have too many problems." You have to look up and see the stars beyond your bars. You need a dream that will help you soar above life's struggles.

I once heard about a man who died at 42 and was buried at 71. At 42, he lost his wife and his job. He went on living physically, but he could just as well have been buried then, because he didn't do anything significant from that time on. He just existed. He had no dream, or hope.

We all need a dream of becoming more than we are. I've always said, "The hand that doesn't reach, shrivels." And that's not God's will. God wants you to become more than you are.

Walking by the Sea of Galilee, Jesus saw Peter and his brother Andrew fishing, and He said to them, *"Follow me, and I will make you fishers of men"* (Matt. 4:19).

"I will make you!" Jesus said.

It is following Jesus that makes a person what he ought to be. The "making" power of God never goes into action until Jesus Christ is followed. Only God knows who you really are deep down inside. Only God can give you a dream and bring out your full potential. When God gives you a dream, it's not some figment of your imagination. It's real! And it's life-changing!

•

Remember: JESUS GAVE PETER A DREAM OF BECOMING MORE THAN HE WAS. THE DREAM CAME TRUE FOR PETER, AND IT CAN COME TRUE FOR YOU!

326/PAIN IS A PROCESS

"Beloved, think it not strange concerning the fiery trial which is to try you, as though some strange thing happened to you; But rejoice, inasmuch as you are partakers of Christ's sufferings; that, when his glory shall be revealed, you may be glad also with exceeding joy" (1 Peter 4:12 & 13).

Also read: Ps. 25:18; 77:10-14; 2 Cor. 4:15-18; Heb. 12:11

Spiritual and emotional pain is a part of the process by which God produces saints, just like heat is part of the process by which men produce gold.

This is why Peter says, *"Ye greatly rejoice, though now for a season, if need be, ye are in heaviness through (many) temptations: That the trial of your faith, being much more precious than of gold that perisheth, though it be tried with fire, might be found unto praise and honour and glory at the appearing of Jesus Christ"* (1 Pet. 1:6, 7).

Can you imagine how the gold would feel, if it were human, when the refiner begins to boil it? "Ouch! Hey, you're hurting me! Help! Aaaaaaaaaaah! I'm dying! Oh no! What's happened to me?"

Why does a refiner melt the gold and bring it to a boil? So the impurities will float to the top and be skimmed off. This is the reason for the fire.

The same is true for the fiery trial you are going through. God may be working to melt you down even further so the impurities of your heart will surface. Then He will skim them off and make you more like Jesus.

A tourist in the Mideast was watching a man refining silver and noticed the pot of silver simmering on the flames. It prompted him to ask, "How long will you boil it?" The refiner looked up and said, "Until I can see my reflection."

You can see that pain is a process by which God refines us until Jesus Christ can see His reflection in our lives.

Not all pain comes from God—some is caused by misguided self-will and other times by Satan. But after you have prayed and determined the source, if your pain has not been caused by the evil one, it could be God is processing you into a perfect saint.

●

Remember: PAIN IS A PROCESS.

327/DARE MIGHTY THINGS!

"...time would fail me to tell of Gideon...and of Samson...and of David...and of the prophets: Who through faith subdued kingdoms, wrought righteousness, obtained promises, stopped the mouths of lions, quenched the violence of fire, escaped the edge of the sword, out of weakness were made strong, waxed valiant in fight—turned to flight the armies of the aliens" (Hebrews 11:32-34).

Also read: Acts 4:31; Eph. 6:18-20

Would you like to be a hero of the Christian faith—not for your ego but for the glory of God? Would you like to write a few dynamic chapters in the 20th Century Book of Acts?

Then DARE mighty things! I have found that most Christians, just like seals basking in the sun on the Alaskan shores, have a "comfort zone." They seldom venture out where it's risky.

It doesn't take much strength for a fish to swim along with the current, but if it wants to swim *against* the current, it needs great strength and power.

You don't need faith and courage to huddle with the cowardly crowd. You can appear "normal" to others while actually being "abnormal" to God.

Why do we thrill to the stories of David, Samson, Daniel, Elijah and others? Because they dared mighty things.

What mighty things do you have planned? I'm not talking about doing foolish and presumptuous things, but I do think you'd better not play it so safe that your life is just a blah.

Are you willing to become a champion for God? Then dare something great today—even if it is to witness to the hardest roughest person you know.

> *"Far better is it to dare mighty things,*
> *To win glorious triumphs,*
> *Een though checkered with failure*
> *Than to live in the gray twilight that knows not*
> *Victory or defeat."*
>
> —Teddy Roosevelt

Remember: TODAY, DARE MIGHTY THINGS!

328/TROUBLES WILL MAKE YOU BITTER OR BETTER

"We glory in tribulations also: knowing that tribulation worketh patience" (Romans 5:3).

Also read: Is. 30:21; 58:11

The Bible says there is *"a time to weep"* (Ecc. 3:4). If you're not weeping now, should the Lord tarry, the time will come when tears will stain your cheeks.

Solomon told young men and women, *"Remember now thy Creator in the days of thy youth, while the evil days come not, nor the years draw nigh, when thou shalt say, I have no pleasure in them"* (Ecc. 12:1).

Solomon was saying, "Rejoice at the sunrise of your youth, for sorrows will come at sundown." As you mature, trouble will come to try you. It's God's plan for building your spiritual man. And during these dark times you may cry out, "Why, God, if You love me, must I suffer so?"

Suffering is a necessary part of the human experience. It is so vital to your Christian life that God outlines it as one of the most important stages of you spiritual growth.

The early Christians had a positive view regarding tribulation and suffering. They knew that they work for the good of the believers. Paul says in our Scripture text, "Tribulation worketh!" Trials accomplish much more than you realize at first. However, if you are not careful, they will spoil your soul. Troubles will make you bitter or better!

Sorrows are too precious for us to waste. The devil wants us to overlook this marvelous truth. You may think the disappointment, loss, pain, and loneliness you are experiencing will mar your life. But God is using it to mold and shape you into a vessel of glory and honor to Him.

If you are experiencing sorrow in your life, don't become bitter. Become better. Allow the heartache to strengthen you and draw you nearer to God.

•

Remember: TROUBLES WILL MAKE YOU BITTER OR BETTER. YOU CAN CHOOSE WHICH IT WILL BE.

329/IT'S FUN TO BEAR FRUIT

"I have chosen you, and ordained you, that ye should go and bring forth fruit, and that your fruit should remain" (John 15:16).

Also read: Matt. 13:23; John 15:2, 8; Rom. 7:4; Col. 1:5-6

Are you having a struggle in your walk with God? Is it difficult for you to live the Christian life?

If so, then your problem may be one of positioning—you need to get your roots deeper into the Word of God and deeper into prayer. A fruitful tree needs abundant resources.

It's not hard for an apple tree to have apples or an orange tree to have oranges. But these trees would really struggle if they tried to have pears. The reason why is obvious—they lack the nature and nutrients of a pear tree.

If you are struggling to live the Christian life, ask yourself, "Am I really a Christian? Does Jesus really live in my heart, or is it just a fact in my head?"

If you are sure that Jesus lives in your heart, then ask yourself, "Am I really studying the Scriptures, praying and walking in the Spirit?"

If not—then start today. An apple tree doesn't move its branches back and forth, moaning and groaning, trying to have apples—never! Apples simply spring forth from the nutrients carried in its branches.

If you're struggling to live the Christian life—don't! Simply sink your roots deeper into God's Word, prayer and the Holy Spirit. You'll bear fruit without much effort.

●

Remember: IT'S FUN TO BEAR FRUIT FOR THE LORD.

330/DO YOU HAVE A FIRE IN YOUR BELLY?

"He shall baptize you with the Holy Ghost, and with fire" (Matthew 3:11).

Also read: Matt. 5:14-16; 28:18-20; Acts 1:8

When someone asked Hubert Humphrey about Walter Mondale's chances for running for the presidency of the United States, the elder politician said he didn't think Mondale would make it because he lacked "the fire in his belly."

History shows that Walter Mondale did have the determination to run for the presidency. And even if you don't appreciate his politics you must admire his dedication because he ran the gamut of presidential primaries—an exhausting experience.

Do you have a fire in your belly? Do you have the courage to fight the world, flesh and the devil to win lost souls to Jesus Christ? Jesus said, *"The kingdom of heaven suffereth* (allows) *violence, and the violent take it by force"* (Matt. 11:12).

I have found during my 29 years in evangelism that very few people have fire in their bellies. There are few who are willing to actually go out and win sinners.

Many are afraid of having a door slammed in their face, or having someone laugh or curse them. But the fact is, if you are going to be a commando for Christ you're going to get some ridicule and persecution. Jesus said, *"Blessed are they which are persecuted for righteousness' sake: for theirs is the kingdom of heaven.*

"Blessed are ye, when men shall revile you, and persecute you, and shall say all manner of evil against you falsely, for my sake.

"Rejoice, and be exceeding glad: for great is your reward in heaven: for so persecuted they the prophets which were before you" (Matt. 5:10-12).

If you lack the boldness to witness as you should, seek Jesus Christ for the great baptism in the Holy Spirit. Acts 1:5 says Jesus baptizes with the Holy Ghost and fire.

•

Remember: YOU NEED A FIRE IN YOUR BELLY!

331/WHERE YOUR TREASURE IS, YOUR HEART IS!

"Lay not up for yourselves treasures upon earth, where moth and rust doth corrupt, and where thieves break through and steal: but lay up for yourselves treasures in heaven, where neither moth nor rust doth corrupt, and where thieves do not break through nor steal: for where your treasure is there will your heart be also" (Matthew 6:19-21).

Also read: Is. 40:8; Matt. 24:35; Prov. 3:6

The Lord says that wherever you have your treasure, your heart is going to follow.

I'll never forget a minister in a city where I once conducted a crusade. He had about $15,000 invested in the stock market. Every day when I rode with this pastor to make his calls, he would say, "Lowell, I think we need to drive downtown."

I learned that downtown, outside a brokerage firm, the Dow Jones stock averages were displayed on a marquee, and he wanted to see how his investment was doing. He made sure we drove by that marquee each day so he could get one last up-to-the-minute check on his investment. That's where his heart was.

Jesus, in the Scripture, is not telling you to give away your treasures, only to transfer them from earth to heaven.

A man once said, "All my life I've heard that we should lay up treasures in heaven, but no one has ever told me how."

You get treasures into heaven by investing your time, your money, and your energy with eternity in mind. Think about it for a moment. The material things that people knock themselves out to acquire—houses, cars, boats, clothes—are not going to heaven. They are used here on earth. They have no eternal value.

The only thing that is going to heaven is people. People are going to last forever, Their souls are going to live throughout eternity...somewhere.

•

Remember: PEOPLE ARE HEAVEN'S TREASURES!

332/OUR COMPASSIONATE SAVIOR

"A bruised reed shall he not break, and smoking flax shall he not quench" (Matthew 12:20).

Also read: Psa. 18:2; Isa. 40:29, 31; 41:10; Dan. 10:19

Jesus is our compassionate Savior. He is always doing everything He can to help restore us to fullness of life. Today's text is one of the greatest in the Bible: *"A bruised reed shall he not break, and smoking flax shall he not quench."*

I have gone fishing and hunting a lot and have seen broken reeds about to sink beneath the water. Jesus is saying to us, "When you're broken and about to go under—I will not break you. I'll lift you up and restore you."

The same is true of smoking flax: When the fire has almost gone out, it's so easy to smother it. But Jesus doesn't quench us when the fire of hope is almost gone in our souls—He gently blows upon us by the breath of the Holy Spirit and rekindles the flame again.

If you're going through a tough time, if you feel like you're going under, if the fire in your soul has almost died, let Jesus lift you up by His Word—spend extra time reading the Bible. God's promises will help strengthen you. Also, spend extra time in prayer so the Holy Spirit can breathe upon you. As the gentle Spirit begins to breathe upon your smouldering soul, you will feel the flames of hope ignite and come to life again.

Jesus knows how events in life can break your will and quench your fire. So He is standing by, this very moment, to help you to be restored again.

•

Remember: JESUS IS LIFTING YOU UP THIS VERY MOMENT. HE IS BLOWING UPON YOU BY THE HOLY SPIRIT. ABSORB ALL OF HIM THAT YOU CAN—FOR HE IS YOUR COMPASSIONATE SAVIOR!

333/FEAR IS WHERE FAITH IS BORN!

"So then faith cometh by hearing, and hearing by the word of God" (Romans 10:17).

Also read: Psa. 27:1, 3; Prov. 3:25-26; Rom. 8:15; 2 Tim. 1:7

The greatest faith is often born out of fear. You can see this illustrated in the life of Peter in Matthew, chapter 14.

One night the disciples were trying to cross Galilee in their fishing boat when a storm overtook them. They battled the winds and the waves all night. *"And in the fourth watch of the night Jesus went unto them, walking on the sea"* (verse 25). Watch the progression of faith.

First, PETER WAS AFRAID. *"And when the disciples saw (Jesus) walking on the sea, they were troubled, saying, It is a spirit; and they cried out for fear"* (verse 26). Peter was the spokesman for the twelve and I'm sure that he yelled the loudest. They had been battling the storm all night, fighting for their very lives, and now Jesus appears in the night—and it filled them with fright.

Notice how Jesus built their faith: *"But straightway Jesus spake unto them, saying, Be of good cheer* (or courage); *it is I; be not afraid"* (verse 27). These words from Jesus built Peter's faith, and he moved from fear to honest doubt.

Second, PETER WAS IN DOUBT. *"And Peter answered him and said, "Lord. if it be thou, bid me come unto thee on the water"* (verse 28). If you have fears, fill your mind with the Word of God—you'll move out of fear into honest doubt. Notice how Jesus spoke one more word and moved Peter from doubt to faith. *"And (Jesus) said, Come"* (verse 29).

Third, PETER HAD FAITH. *"And when Peter was come down out of the ship, he walked on the water, to go to Jesus"* (verse 29).

Wow! Peter walked on the water! He is doing the impossible. How? Because he launched out on the words of Jesus to "come."

If you're afraid, mix your fears with God's word. Soon you'll be filled with faith and your fears will disappear.

•

Remember: FEAR IS WHERE FAITH IS BORN.

"Christ hath redeemed us from the curse of the law, being made a curse for us..that the blessing of Abraham might come on the Gentiles through Jesus Christ" (Galatians 3:13 & 14).

Also read: Heb. 10:23; 1 Jn. 1:7; Is. 53:5

Are you hurting? Do you need God's healing touch in your body? If your answer is yes, I have some wonderful news for you. Jesus wants to heal you. It's His will to heal you.

I know Jesus wants to heal you, because He died to take away your sins and your sicknesses. Healing is part of God's salvation package. Isaiah 53:4 & 5 says, *"Surely he hath borne our griefs, and carried our sorrows: yet we did esteem him stricken, smitten of God, and afflicted. But he was wounded for our transgressions, he was bruised for our iniquities: the chastisement of our peace was upon him; and with his stripes we are healed."*

If Jesus bore our sicknesses, we need not bear them any longer. Sickness is part of the curse and Jesus came to destroy the curse. He suffered in our stead, because He did not want us to suffer sin, sickness, and disease. Jesus redeemed us not only from our sins, but also from our sicknesses.

Provision for your healing is in the present tense. *"With his stripes we are healed!"* Christ has already paid the price so that every illness in your body—the pain of arthritis, deafness, poor eyesight, cancer, high blood pressure, heart trouble, you name it—can be healed. Whatever pain or affliction you're suffering was laid upon Jesus. Now it's up to you to reach out and receive your healing by faith.

●

Remember: HEALING IS PART OF GOD'S SALVATION PACKAGE!

335/THE BENEFITS OF BELIEVING

"But of him are ye in Christ Jesus, who of God is made unto us wisdom, and righteousness, and sanctification, and redemption" (1 Corinthians 1:30).

Also read: 1 John 2:13; 5:4-5; Rev. 2:7-9

You will run into difficulties and temptations as a believer, but there are also many wonderful benefits.

First, JESUS GIVES YOU WISDOM. Through the eyes of Christ you can see eternity: heaven, hell, angels, demons, Judgment Day, etc. When you are wise about eternal realities you are truly wise.

I was trying to win a man to Christ one day who said, "How do you know all these things are true? No one has gone to hell and come back. No one has died and risen again to prove these things are true."

I was glad to tell him that Jesus has already been to hell and back and has told us what horrible judgment awaits the wicked. Thank God, Jesus makes you eternally wise.

Second, JESUS MAKES YOU RIGHTEOUS! *"For (God) hath made him to be sin for us, who knew no sin: THAT WE MIGHT BE MADE THE RIGHTEOUSNESS OF GOD IN HIM"* (2 Cor. 5:21, emphasis mine). Jesus makes you perfect in the eyes of God. Because His blood was shed for your sin, God looks as favorably upon you as He looks upon His own Son.

Third, JESUS BRINGS SANCTIFICATION. If you want to drive the darkness out of your life, allow the light of Jesus to shine in your heart. Immediately you will think, feel and live differently. Paul wrote, *"To them that are sanctified in Christ Jesus"* (1 Cor. 1:2). John wrote, *"Whosoever abideth in him sinneth not"* (1 John 3:6). If you want to be holy, pure and clean, abide in Jesus Christ; He has all power over sin and Satan.

Fourth, IN CHRIST WE HAVE REDEMPTION! We are His purchased possession. You and I have been bought with a price, the blood of Jesus. Do you realize how much you mean to God and Christ? *You* are God's greatest treasure upon earth, and He will end up giving *you* everything when this world is finished (see Rev. 21:7).

•

Remember: PRAISE GOD TODAY FOR HIS BENEFITS TO YOU AS A BELIEVER!

HOW TO HANDLE YOUR TEMPER

"Be ye angry, and sin not" (Ephesians 4:26).

Also read: Eccl. 7:9; Psa. 37:8; Prov. 14:29; Eph. 4:31-32

My temper has to be one of my greatest problems. I believe all strong-willed people probably have difficulty in this area. And it is a fact that when you lose your temper—you lose.

Here's how I have tried to win over my temper. (Notice I say TRIED—because I haven't always won.)

1. *I must saturate my mind with God's Word and my soul with His spirit.* There's no ifs, ands or buts about it: If I don't have devotions each day and saturate my soul with God's Spirit, the fuse of my temper will be too short to handle. I'll explode before I realize it.

2. *I consider the results of my actions.* Stopping long enough to think—rather than react to the situation—helps me to get a grip on my emotions.

I told a man recently, "When you're tempted to blow up, pray the Lord's Prayer before you speak." It helps make an angry person calm.

3. *Consider the fact that Satan may be manifesting himself through your spirit.*

James and John were strong-minded men (and God needs these kind). One day Jesus came to a Samaritan village to heal the sick and preach the Gospel. But the villagers were so ungrateful they would not receive Him. The Bible says, *"And when his disciples James and John saw this, they said, Lord, will you that we command fire to come down from heaven, and (destroy) them, even as Elijah did?*

"But he turned and rebuked them, and said, You know not what manner of spirit (or nature) you are of.

"For the Son of man is not come to destroy men's lives, but to save them. And they went to another village" (see Luke 9:54-56).

•

Remember: IF YOU WANT TO CONTROL YOUR TEMPER, THINK OF SAVING PEOPLE INSTEAD OF REBUKING THEM.

337 / ARE YOU ANGRY WITH GOD?

"Do you think it is right for you to claim, 'I haven't sinned, but I'm no better off before God than if I had?" (Job 35:2, TLB).

Also read: Is. 26:3; Jn. 12:46; Ps. 37:24

If you've been going through a tough time, take a moment to study the life of Job. The Bible says he was, *"...perfect and upright, and one that feared God and* (shunned) *evil"* (Job 1:1). He was very rich and had a loving family of seven sons and three daughters.

However, Satan accused God of bribing Job with blessings. He said, *"Why shouldn't he* (serve you), *when you pay him so well?...You have always protected him and his home and his property from all harm...But just take away his wealth and you'll see him curse you to your face!'*

"The Lord replied, 'You may do anything you like with his wealth, but don't harm him physically" (verses 9-12, TLB).

So Satan stirred up robbers who stole all of Job's livestock in one day. He sent a tornado that struck the building where Job's children were feasting, and they were all killed.

Did Job cause these problems? Not at all. For God declared Job totally innocent (see Job 2:3). Yet, as Job's problems increase, he became bitter in his soul. *"I haven't sinned, but I'm no better off before God than if I had"* (Job 32:1, TLB).

Maybe this is where you're at today. You've lived a holy life, tried your best, and yet everything has gone wrong. Let me share with you the same words of encouragement that Job's friend shared with him:

1. *"God will not do wrong by those who trust in him"* (Job 34:10).
2. *"When you say, 'I've done my best but God hasn't done His best for me' you are saying you are more righteous than God"* (Job 35:2).
3. Look at the Heavens and all of creation—everything God does is good, so trust He will do good by you!

•

Remember: YOU MAY NOT UNDERSTAND THE EVENTS TAKING PLACE, BUT GOD WILL DO RIGHT BY YOU!

338/HOW TO MAKE YOUR MONEY LAST FOREVER!

"Make to yourselves friends of the mammon of unrighteousness; that, when ye fail, they may receive you into everlasting habitations" (Luke 16:10).

Also read: Psa. 96:8; Matt. 13:44-46; Luke 16:10-11

How long will your money last? Jesus tells us there is a way you can make your money last forever.

Today's text, broken down into literal language says, "Win converts with your money, so that when you die, the converts you have won with your money will receive you unto everlasting habitations."

When you give money to win lost souls to Jesus Christ, you are making certain that your money will last forever. In fact, you're making sure that your money will walk around heaven—in the persons of those you helped win to Jesus Christ.

Why do you give to God?
1. *Out of obligation?* Do you feel you must pay your 10% "God-tax" or things will go wrong?
2. *To protect your reputation?* Do you give so others won't think you're cheap?
3. *To relieve your conscience?* Do you give because you should give and do so simply to make yourself feel better?
4. *As an investment?* A small number of Christians, like very wise investors, look for soulwinning opportunities where they can invest their money to bring eternal dividends. This way they are sure their money will last forever.

Don't dump your money into any place without carefully considering what kind of results you are going to get from your investment.

•

Remember: WISE GIVERS CAN MAKE THEIR MONEY LAST FOREVER.

339/FOR SUCH AN HOUR AS THIS

"And who knows whether you are come to the kingdom for such a time as this?" (see Esther 4:14).

Also read: Mark 3:34-37; Luke 9:61-62; 14:27-33

I believe this is your hour to do something great for God. Queen Esther had to be reminded of this when her people, the Jews, were about to be destroyed.

Haman, who hated the Jews, was a personal advisor to the King of Persia. Satan used him to persuade King Ahasuerus to wipe out all of the Jewish people.

Queen Esther was a Jew. Her Jewish uncle, Mordecai, urged her to plead with the king on behalf of her people. He said, *"Think not...that you shall escape in the king's house, more than all the Jews. For if you...hold your peace at this time, then shall there arise deliverance from another place; but you and your father's house shall be destroyed: and who knows whether you are come to the kingdom for such a time as this?"* (see Est. 4:13 & 14).

Christian, you are part of the Kingdom of God. You need to recognize that you have come to the Kingdom FOR THIS VERY HOUR. Jesus said, *"You have not chosen me, but I have chosen you, and ordained you, that you should go and bring forth fruit, and that your fruit should remain: that whatsoever you shall ask of the Father in my name, he may give it you"* (see John 15:16).

These facts are clear:
1. You are chosen.
2. You are ordained.
3. You are to bring forth fruit (works of righteousness as well as winning lost souls to Christ).
4. Your fruit will remain throughout eternity.
5. Everything you need is made possible through prayer.

Today you will meet many people who are lost in sin and need your testimony. Remember today that the work of God needs your prayers and financial support.

●

Remember: YOU HAVE BEEN BROUGHT INTO THE KINGDOM OF GOD—FOR SUCH A TIME AS THIS.

340/WHAT IS GRACE?

"For by grace are ye saved through faith; and that not of yourselves: it is the gift of God: not of works, lest any man should boast" (Ephesians 2:8 & 9).

Also read: Matt. 5:44; 6:12; 7:1 & 2

You and I are saved by the grace of God, but what exactly is grace? The best definition I have ever found is: God's Riches At Christ's Expense—G.R.A.C.E!

Jesus gave the best illustration of grace when he said, *"The Kingdom of Heaven can be compared to a king who decided to bring his account up to date. In the process, one of his debtors was brought in who owed him $10,000,000! He couldn't pay, so the king ordered him sold for the debt, also his wife and children and everything he had.*

"But the man fell down before the king, his face in the dust, and said, 'Oh, sir, be patient with me and I will pay it all.' Then the king was filled with pity for him and released him and forgave his debt."

"But when the man left the king, he went to a man who owed him $2,000...and demanded instant payment. The man fell down before him and begged him to give him a little time...but his creditor wouldn't wait. He had the man arrested and jailed until the debt would be paid in full.

"Then the man's friends went to the king and told him what had happened. And the king called before him the man he had forgiven and said, 'You evil-hearted wretch! I forgave you all that tremendous debt...shouldn't you have mercy on others, just as I had mercy on you?'

"Then the angry king sent the man to the torture chamber until he had paid every last penny due. So shall my heavenly Father do to you if you refuse to truly forgive your brothers" (Matt. 18:23-35).

Because God has forgiven us fully and freely, we should do the same for others. Is there someone you should forgive? Act like the King of Glory and extend you pardon today.

•

Remember: GRACE IS GOD'S RICHES AT CHRIST'S EXPENSE!

341/SEEK WISDOM!

"A wise man will hear, and will increase learning; and a man of understanding shall attain unto wise counsels" (Proverbs 1:5).

Also read: Ex. 31:3; Job 28:12-28; Psa. 37:30; 90:12

There are two ways you can learn. First, you can learn from your own experience of suffering. Second, you can learn from the experience of others. The first way will bloody your head—the second is to learn from others so you can move ahead.

This is why it is important to read good books and make friends with wise people. They all help you move ahead of the pack who are still beating their heads against obstacles.

I have found that 10 minutes with a wise man or woman equals 4 hours of study in books or 5 years of trying to learn it on your own. People who have graduated from the "University of Adversity" can give you tips that save you years of struggling.

Learn how to ask intelligent questions. Rather than wasting time on pitter-patter, ask, "What would you do differently if you had your life to live over again?" or "What mistakes are young people my age making today?" or "What is the most meaningful experience you've ever had—and what did you learn from it?"

Another way I love to learn is by reading books that others have read and marked. They usually mark the meat and it saves me a lot of time!

It is also interesting to meet people who have worked for many years at unusual jobs. Try to zero in on one key question. For instance, I met a man recently who worked in a cancer research laboratory in Maryland for most of his life. I asked him, "Please explain cancer in one sentence." He said he couldn't answer it so simply.

Then I asked, "Doesn't cancer begin when one cell goes berzerk and begins eating and infecting another cell?" He laughed and said "That's right!" and we were off and running with an interesting, informative conversation.

•

Remember: TO BECOME WISE, SEEK ADVICE FROM WISE PEOPLE.

342/BEWARE OF COMPROMISERS!

"Some godless teachers have wormed their way in among you, saying that after we become Christians we can do just as we like without fear of God's punishment" (Jude 4, TLB).

Also read: Prov. 14:12; Rom. 8:2-13, 37; 12:1-2

Be cautious of the friends you keep. I have Christian friends I like very much, but I will not go near them. Why? Because they are compromisers.

Their standards are slippery; they have a way of appealing to my weaker nature in such a way that when I'm with them, I am less holy than when I'm not. They tell slightly off-color stories and are critical of other Christians. They also make subtle "tongue-in-cheek" comments that dirty my spirit.

Jude wrote the early Christians to beware of godless teachers who had wormed their way into their midst, teaching the liberal theology that Christians could sin without being punished. The same thing is happening today. Your carnal friends may not be teachers, but they are saying by their actions that God will not punish sin. Stay away from them!

Paul wrote the Thessalonians, *"If any man obey not our word by this epistle, note that man, AND HAVE NO COMPANY WITH HIM, that he may be ashamed.*

"Yet count him not as an enemy, but admonish him as a brother" (2 Thess. 3:14 & 15, emphasis mine).

If you know someone who is not living holy before God, speak to him kindly. Don't count him as an enemy, but urge him to leave his compromising ways.

More than that, you know that some people appeal to the "God-side" of you and others will appeal to the "dark-side" of you. Stay away from compromisers as far as you can—for they will corrupt your soul.

•

Remember: BEWARE OF COMPROMISERS!

343/PRESSED!

"For we would not, brethren, have you ignorant of our trouble which came to us in Asia, that we were pressed out of measure, above strength insomuch that we despaired even of life" (2 Corinthians 1:8).

Also read: Prov. 20:30; Ja. 1:2-4, 12

Do you feel under pressure? Paul the apostle had an experience so horrible in Asia that he thought he was going to die. But, he went on to say, *"We felt we were doomed to die and saw how powerless we were to help ourselves; but that was good, for then we put everything unto the hands of God, who alone could save us, for he can even raise the dead. And he did help us, and saved us from a terrible death; yes, and we expect him to do it again and again"* (2 Cor. 1:9 & 10, TLB).

God will do it for you, too. I believe you will make it through every trial that comes your way. And the pressure you may be experiencing now will help to make you the person God intends you to be. Don't look at your trial as a reprimand but as God's redemptive refinement.

I'll never forget some of the terrible pressures I have undergone in this ministry. There have been times when, because of pressure, I've had asthma attacks, my skin has felt like it was burning, I've felt like crying uncontrollably, and I thought I was losing my mind. But God brought me through them all.

Pressure is part of God's plan. This poem explains why.

Pressed

Pressed out of measure and pressed to all length;
Pressed so intensely, it seems beyond strength;
Pressed in the body and pressed in the soul;
Pressed in the mind til the dark surges roll;
Pressure by foes and pressure from friends
Pressure on pressure til life nearly ends.
Pressed into knowing no helper but God;
Pressed into loving the staff and the rod;
Pressed into living a life in the Lord;
Pressed into giving a Christ-life outpoured!

(copied)

●

Remember: PAUL EXPERIENCED GREAT PRESSURE AND CAME OUT VICTORIOUS; YOU WILL TOO!

344/THERE'S A PLAN BEHIND YOUR PROBLEMS

"For whom he did foreknow, he also did predestinate to be conformed to the image of his Son" (Romans 8:29).

Also read: Psa. 34:17-19; 56:11-13; Jas. 1:12; 24:1

If you are having problems in your life more is happening than you realize. God is working out His plan in you and will use every problem to make you more like Jesus Christ. This doesn't mean that God plans your problems, no more than a sailor plans the direction of the wind. But Christ, the great captain of your soul, will use every wind to help you move forward.

You've often read, *"We know that all things work together for good to them that love God, to them who are the called according to his purpose"* (Rom. 8:28). The purpose of all things (both good and bad) is to help you be conformed to the *image* of Jesus Christ.

Pressure is one of the methods God uses to change people. This is why you must be careful when trouble comes your way. If you allow your problems to get you down, you'll become bitter instead of better.

It's encouraging to know that God himself is watching over every event that takes place in your life. He hears each prayer, sees each tear, and feels each pain. Because God withheld Himself and allowed Jesus to suffer (think of the many times Jesus had to leave certain villages because of rejection) don't be surprised if you must suffer too.

But you are not suffering as a *victim* of circumstances—you are a *victor* in all circumstances. Problems and pains are the pressures God allows to make you just like Jesus Christ. This is why Paul the apostle said, *"I am exceeding joyful in all our tribulation"* (2 Cor. 7:4).

If you will rejoice in your problems, and then with prayer, persistence, and patience solve them—you'll become like Jesus Christ.

•

Remember: THERE'S A PLAN BEHIND YOUR PROBLEMS.

345/HOW TO GET THE MONKEY OFF YOUR BACK

"Greater is he that is in you, than he that is in the world" (1 John 4:4).

Also read: Psa. 18:2; 27:1; Isa. 40:29; Eph. 6:13

Are you trying to break a bad habit? If you're trying to get the monkey off your back why don't you let the Lion take more control of your life?

John the apostle saw a vision of heaven. When he could see that no one was worthy to open the sealed book he said, *"I wept much"* (Rev. 5:4).

If you have been weeping over a habit that seems to have you defeated (overeating, lust, temper, greed, etc.) notice the next thing that happened:

"And one of the elders saith unto me, Weep not: behold, the Lion of the tribe of Juda...hath prevailed" (verse 5).

The Lion of Judah, Jesus Christ, prevailed to open up the sealed book.

Jesus Christ will do the same for you. You may have asked Jesus Christ to come into your heart but now you must give Him more complete control of your life.

The next time you are tempted, say aloud, "Jesus Christ, You are the Lion of Judah. Now I'm asking You to drive this habit out of my life. You have all power in heaven and earth; and I surrender my lusts and urges to Your great power this very moment!"

Try it! You'll find that "monkey-habits" flee when the Lion is on the loose. There is no habit more powerful than Jesus Christ.

This suggestion may also help you: Don't try to hold out against your urges for one hour, but try it for only ten seconds. If you can hold off for a few seconds to get your faith in focus, you will give the Lord enough time to drive the monkeys away.

•

Remember: MONKEYS RUN WHEN THE LION IS LOOSE.

346/THE ROYAL LAW!

"Fulfill the royal law according to the scripture, Thou shalt love thy neighbor as thyself" (James 2:8).

Also read: Prov. 20:3; 21:23; 25:14

Today's devotional is a short course on human relations. It's called the Royal Law; *"You must love and help your neighbors just as much as you love and take care of yourself"* (TLB).

Here are the ten commandments of getting along with people.

1. Always say less than you think. Cultivate a low persuasive voice. How you say it often counts more than what you say.
2. Make promises sparingly and keep them faithfully.
3. Never let an opportunity pass to say a kind and encouraging word to or about someone. Praise good work, regardless of who did it.
4. Be interested in others. Make merry with those who rejoice; with those who weep, mourn. Let everyone you meet, however humble, feel that you regard them as persons of importance.
5. Be cheerful. Don't burden those around you by dwelling on your aches and pains and disappointments. Remember, everyone is carrying some kind of burden.
6. Keep an open mind. Discuss, but don't argue.
7. Let your virtues speak for themselves. Refuse to talk about the vices of others. Discourage gossip.
8. Take into consideration the feelings of others. Wit and humor at the expense of another is never worth the pain that may be inflicted.
9. Pay no attention to ill-natured remarks about you. Remember the person who carried the message may not be the most accurate reporter in the world. Simply live so that nobody will believe him.
10. Don't be anxious about the credit owed you. Do your best and be patient. Forget about yourself and let others praise you.

●

Remember: TO GET ALONG WITH OTHERS, JUST PRACTICE THE "ROYAL LAW."

347/GOD IS NEVER LATE!

"And shall not God avenge his own elect, which cry day and night unto him, though he bear long with them? I tell you that he will avenge them speedily" (Luke 18:7 & 8).

Also read: Psa. 145:18-19; Prov. 15:29; Isa. 65:24

When Glenn Cunningham was a small boy his legs were terribly burned and deformed. He and his brother unknowingly tossed gasoline onto a live fire. When it exploded Glenn's legs were crippled with scar tissue.

But Glenn didn't give up. By sheer determination and prayer he gradually learned to walk and run until he became a star runner in high school. Then in the 1939 Berlin Olympics Glenn won the silver medal and the admiration of millions.

Recently Glenn appeared on our TV program and shared a truth that has blessed me over and over again. Looking back on his life, Glenn said, "God may wait—but He's never late!"

WOW! Have you been praying earnestly about a situation and there hasn't been a change? Don't give up or be discouraged; just remember this phrase, "God may wait—but He's never late!"

Today's text brings out that God may delay (He may "bear long" with us), but when He starts moving, things happen quickly. He will avenge us "speedily!"

Prayer could be likened to filling a barrel with water. You keep filling it and filling it, without making much progress, then suddenly it runs over. (NOTE: The first gallon was just as important as the last, even though it appeared you hadn't accomplished much.)

So keep praying! Barnstorm heaven. Cry out and keep crying until you get your answer. There are some things that take time. God knows what He's doing—His timing is perfect!

•

Remember: GOD MAY WAIT—BUT HE'S NEVER LATE!

348/ARE YOU IN GOD'S BUSINESS OR THE "GOD-BUSINESS?"

"Not every one that saith unto me, Lord, Lord, shall enter into the kingdom of heaven; but he that doeth the will of my Father which is in heaven" (Matthew 7:21).

Also read: Matt. 7:15-20; Rom. 12:1, 2; 1 John 2:15-17

Sometime ago I attended Gospel Music Week in Nashville, Tennessee. Many concerts were held in a beautiful theatre in downtown Nashville. One night I struck up a conversation with 3 of the ushers and ticket takers.

One of them asked, "Who are all these people? Are they all Christians, or what?" I could see the girl was genuinely confused because there are all types of people involved in Gospel music—promoters, salesmen, writers, photographers, musicians, etc. And the fact is that not all of them are living for God.

I answered the girl's question this way: "You have to be careful when you attend a Gospel event, because not all of the people are committed Christians. Some are in 'God's Business' while others are in the 'God-business.' "

Jesus said that people who are in the God-business will face a horrible judgment. *"Many will say to me in that day, Lord, Lord, have we not prophesied* (or preached) *in your name? and in thy name have cast out devils? and in thy name done many wonderful works?*

"And then will I profess unto them, I never knew you: depart from me, ye that work iniquity" (Matt. 7:22 & 23).

The question you and I should always ask ourselves is "Are we in God's business—or the God-business?" If you and I serve God for any other reason than to further His cause or to help others—we're in trouble.

•

Remember: ONLY THOSE IN GOD'S BUSINESS WILL BE REWARDED; ALL OTHERS WILL BE CAST AWAY!

349/LORD, MAKE A BETTER MAN OUT OF ME!

"When we arrived in Macedonia there was no rest for us; outside, trouble was on every hand and all around us; within us, our hearts were full of dread and fear" (2 Corinthians 7:5, TLB).

Also read: Phil. 3:13 & 14

The apostle Paul was an ordinary man who struggled with his fears just like you and me. The verse above shows that. Here's an anonymous poem I rewrote about a regular man.

Lord, Make a Better Man Out of Me!

I really would like to be braver and bolder,
A little bit wiser, because I am older;
I wish to be kinder to these whom I meet
And just a bit manlier taking defeat.

This is my New Year's wish and my plea:
Lord, make a better man out of me.

You know I would like to be just a bit finer,
More of a smiler and less of a whiner;
Just a bit quicker to stretch out my hand
Helping another who's struggling to stand.

This is my prayer the New Year to be:
Lord, make a better man out of me.

This I have prayed to be: just a bit fairer,
Just a bit better and just a bit squarer;
Not quite so ready to censure and blame,
Quicker to help every man in the game.

Not quite so eager men's failings to see.
Lord, make a better man out of me.

This I would like to be: just a bit truer,
Less of a wisher and more of a doer;
Broader and bigger, more willing to give
And always helping my neighbors to live.

This is my New Year's prayer and my plea:
Lord, make a better man out of me!

●

Remember: AS YOU READ GOD'S WORD, PRAY, AND OBEY GOD, HE'LL MAKE A BETTER PERSON OUT OF YOU!

350/THE WOMAN WHO HAD THE COURAGE TO SAY "NO!"

"But the queen Vashti refused to come at the king's commandment" (Esther 1:12).

Also read: Psa. 31:24; Prov. 3:26; Isa. 41:10; Rom. 8:37

"No" is one of the hardest words to say in the English language. In this day when so many are yielding to compromise and peer pressure it's refreshing to read of someone who had the grit to stand up and say "No," even though it cost her the throne of Persia.

Queen Vashti was a lady. When her husband, the king, gave a great feast for the princes of his kingdom it was a wild drunken affair. In the midst of their drinking, the king, full of pride and liquor, decided to show off his queen—a beautiful lady of impeccable taste and judgment.

But when he sent his servants to bring the queen she refused. She said in effect, "No, I won't go to your party to be lusted after by your drunken princes."

This angered the king and all his advisors so much that they decided to take away her throne. They deposed Queen Vashti and found another woman for the king.

But the character of this queen far outshines the power of the king. Her willingness to risk her position to maintain her honor is awe-inspiring—especially when you consider she was not a Jew and did not understand the principles of the Scriptures.

Have you been tempted to give in to pressure? Have you been tempted to compromise?

If so then remember Queen Vashti, who had the courage to maintain her convictions and say "No," even when her position as queen was at stake.

●

Remember: DON'T SELL OUT OR YOU'LL BELONG TO THE HIGHEST BIDDER.

351/SECRET IMAGINATIONS

"Then he said unto me, Son of man, have you seen what the elders of Israel do in the dark, every man in the secret chambers of his imagination? for they say, 'the Lord seeth not" (Ezekiel 8:12, Literal).

Also read: Psa. 10:4; 94:11; Isa. 55:7-9

As Christians, we believe that God is omniscient (all-knowing); that He is aware of everything we think as well as what we do.

So often we forget God's "power-to-know" and consider ourselves righteous while we entertain evil thoughts. It's what we do in the dark chambers of our imaginations that reveals whether or not we are holy or impure.

The Bible says God gave Ezekiel a vision; He gave him the power to look through a hole in a wall and said, *"Go in, and behold the wicked abominations that they* (the people of Israel) *do here"* (verse 7).

Ezekiel says, *"So I went in and saw; and behold every form of creeping things, and abominable beasts, and all the idols of the house of Israel, portrayed upon the wall round about"* (verses 9, 10).

Then God noticed the people were saying, *"The Lord doesn't see us; he has gone away!"* (verse 12, TLB).

What are you doing in the dark chambers of your mind? Are you partaking of lustful thoughts, plans of revenge, jealous urges, dirty jokes, or curse words?

The way to rid your mind of all these evil creeping cockroaches is to open up your mind to the light of Jesus Christ. Confess every unclean thought that comes into your mind the moment it appears. Then Jesus Christ will destroy these snakes and lizards of the flesh.

God brought the flood upon Noah's world because of evil thoughts. *"And God saw that the wickedness of man was great in the earth, and that every imagination of the thoughts of his heart was only evil continually"* (Gen. 6:5).

•

Remember: GOD SEES YOUR SECRET IMAGINATIONS. GUARD WHAT YOU THINK ABOUT IN THE DARK!

352/YOU HAVE HIS NAME!

"That at the name of Jesus every knee should bow" (Philippians 2:10).

Also read: 1 Chron. 16:8; Psa. 69:36; 105:1; 148:13

There is great power in the name of Jesus. The Bible says, *"Wherefore God also hath highly exalted him, and given him a name which is above every name:*

"That at the name of Jesus every knee should bow, of things in heaven, and things in earth, and things under the earth;

"And that every tongue should confess that Jesus Christ is Lord, to the glory of God the Father" (Phil. 2:9-11).

I used to think that every knee would bow when Jesus returned in glory. I could see Satan and his demons, all worldly dictators, presidents and emperors, and all of the heavenly host bowing their knees before Jesus Christ.

But a friend of mine pointed out something wonderful to me. He said, "Lowell, have you noticed that the Scripture doesn't say that people will bow only at the physical presence of Jesus—but 'at the name of Jesus'? We have His name—and the God-given authority to use His name today."

Hallelujah! This truth exploded on my heart with great glory as I hope it has on yours. You have the power of Jesus' name at your disposal. Because Jesus has all power in heaven and in earth, you can use it to bind and loose according to Matthew 16:19.

You are not the victim of the powers on this earth. You have the Name that causes kings and queens to bow. Even the devil and his demons must obey when you use the name "JESUS" with power and authority.

Praise God, you're not the vanquished—you are the VICTOR! This is why Jesus said, *"And whatsoever you shall ask in my name, that will I do, that the Father may be glorified in the Son.*

"If you shall ask anything in my name I will do it" (John 14:13-14).

•

Remember: YOU HAVE HIS NAME!

353/YOU HAVE WHAT IT TAKES!

"I am with you; that is all you need. My power shows up best in weak people.' Now I am glad to boast about how weak I am; I am glad to be a living demonstration of Christ's power, instead of showing off my own power and abilities" (2 Corinthians 12:9, TLB).

Also read: Prov. 16:9; Phil. 4:13; Ps. 34:17

George Washington Carver was a black man who struggled and came up the hard way. He fought for every inch of ground he ever gained in life. He wrote this unusual poem:

You Have What It Takes!
Figure it out for yourself, my lad,
You've all that the greatest of men have had;
Two arms, two hands, two lips, two eyes,
And a brain to use if you would be wise.
Don't be discouraged and without a plan—
Just start from the top and say, "I CAN!"

Look them over, the wise and the great,
They all take their food from a common plate,
And similar knives and forks they use,
With similar laces they tie their shoes;
The world considers them brave and smart,
But you've all they had when they made their start.

Courage must come from the soul within,
The man must furnish the will to win.
So figure it out for yourself, my lad,
You were born with all they the great have had;
With your equipment they all began.
Get a hold of yourself and say, "I CAN!"

The Lord told Paul, *"I am with you; that is all you need."* The apostle went on to say, *"I am quite happy about 'the thorn'* (of his personal problems), *and about insults and hardships, persecutions and difficulties; for when I am weak, then I am strong—the less I have, the more I depend on him"* (2 Cor. 12:10, TLB).

You can win if you will set your mind to it. You must act—not react! You must plan and say, "I CAN!"

•

Remember: THE LORD IS WITH YOU AND YOU'VE GOT WHAT IT TAKES!

354/MISS AMERICA MISSES

"Be not deceived; God is not mocked; for whatsoever a man soweth, that shall he also reap" (Galatians 6:7).

Also read: Prov. 11:18; 22:8; 2 Cor. 9:6; Gal. 6:8

Vanessa Williams was voted the first black Miss America in the history of the pageant. Suddenly every dream of Vanessa's seemed to be coming true: travel, television appearances, celebrity status, money. You name it—the world was knocking at Vanessa's door. She was the "pride" of Americans who looked up to her shining example.

But then the bombshell went off. Months before Vanessa entered the Miss America pageant, she had posed in the nude for photos with another nude woman. The obvious lesbian tones of these scandalous photos prompted officers of the Miss America pageant to take away Vanessa's crown.

The poor taste she had sowed, she had to reap. Vanessa was forced to resign as Miss America; a true American tragedy of a Miss America who missed.

It's easy for you and me to throw stones at Vanessa, but this is not the object of this devotional. But, because of her national status as a beauty queen, maybe others will take note and watch the seeds they sow.

The Bible says, *"While the earth remaineth, seedtime and harvest, and cold and heat, and summer and winter, and day and night shall not cease"* (Gen. 8:22).

God's Word says that as long as the earth remains the laws of sowing and reaping will not change.

What are you sowing? If Vanessa's mistake took away her crown, will your act of sowing indiscretion take away your crown at Judgment Day? Jesus says, *"Behold, I come quickly: hold fast what you have that no man take (your) crown"* (Rev. 3:11).

Remember that the law of sowing and reaping not only applies to seeds of evil being reaped, but also applies to the good seed you sow.

Today is your chance to sow love, forgiveness, peace, joy and kindness. Sow as much good as you can and you'll have an abundant harvest.

•

Remember: WHAT YOU SOW, GROWS.

355/LET GO!

"Commit thy way unto the Lord; trust also in him; and he shall bring it to pass" (Psalm 37:5).

Also read: Prov. 3:6; Ps. 139: 9 & 10; Is. 58:11

Do you need divine deliverance? Are you facing a problem that is beyond your ability to solve? Then you must let go.

The day God illuminated this verse to my soul I marked it in my Bible: September 28, 1984. The verse says, *"Commit thy way unto the Lord; trust also in him; and HE shall bring it to pass."* Notice, you must commit and trust your situation to God before He will act.

The Bible also says, *"Rest in the Lord, and wait patiently for him:* (and) *fret not..."* (vs. 7). Have you really committed your problem to the Lord? Have you let go?

One day I took my car to a mechanic because it would not run right. After he opened the hood and began searching for the problem, I poked my head under it, too, and began tapping on the carburetor and pulling wires. He became so frustrated he stepped back and gave me a stare that said, "Sir, if you want me to get this thing running again, you've got to get out of my way."

I meekly retreated to the lobby until he had it running again.

You and I are tempted to do the same thing with God. We've done all we can and have failed, and so we bring the situation to Him, but instead of letting go, we harass Him with our meddling. The Bible tells us to:
- Commit
- Trust
- Rest
- Wait Patiently
- And Fret Not

•

Remember: LET GO AND GOD WILL BEGIN TO WORK!

WHAT THEY SAID OF JESUS

"Whom do men say that I the Son of man am? And (the disciples) *said, Some say that thou art John the Baptist, some, Elias: and others, Jeremias, or one of the prophets"* (Matthew 16:13 & 14).

Also read: John 13:14-15; Heb. 12:2-3; Phil. 2:5-8

Recently the Holy Spirit gave me an exciting illumination on this passage of Scripture. I saw through the eyes of the people a description of Jesus that I had never seen before.

First, *They thought Jesus was John the Baptist.* John the Baptist was a fearless prophet of God. He preached to the soldiers that they should be kind to people and not to demand more pay. He preached to King Herod that it was a sin for him to have his brother Phillip's wife (See Matt. 14:3-4). John rebuked the Pharisees for their hypocrisy and entreated them to repent (see Luke 3:7-8). The people thought that Jesus preached like John the Baptist—with the same fearless commitment to please only God.

Second, *They thought Jesus was like Elijah.* Elijah was another fearless prophet of God who was also a great miracle-worker. He was able to pray and call fire down from heaven and to heal the sick. Jesus worked miracles—opening blind eyes, casting out demons, cleansing lepers and raising the dead. The people thought Jesus was Elias (Elijah) come back from the dead.

Third, *They thought Jesus was like Jeremiah.* Jeremiah was a weeping prophet—deeply touched by the tragic condition of his people. He said, *"For these things I weep; mine eye runneth down with water, because the comforter that should relieve my soul is far from me: my children are desolate, because the enemy prevailed"* (Lam. 1:16). Jesus also wept for the needs of the people. He beheld the city of Jerusalem and wept over it (see Luke 19:41). There was a sadness in the eyes of Jesus that reminded the people of what they had read of Jeremiah, the broken-hearted prophet.

Does this give you a better idea of what Jesus was like? He was like John the Baptist, Elijah and Jeremiah—what a wonderful manifestation of God wrapped up in one man.

•

Remember: WHAT WAS SAID OF JESUS SHOULD BE SAID (IN PART) OF YOU AND ME.

357 /THE SIN POLL

"For sin is the transgression of the law" (1 John 3:4).

Also read: 1 Jn. 1:9; Ex. 20:1-17

People magazine ran a survey to see what it's readers considered to be the top ten sins of today.

One thousand responses were selected at random for analysis. Four out of five were women. Eighty percent said they believed in God, although only forty-three percent said they attended church at least once each month. Half of the respondents were married and seventy-nine percent were employed. Fifty-four percent said they were Protestant, thirty percent Catholic and five percent Jewish.

Readers were also asked to rank the Ten Commandments by degree of difficulty. The results were, from hardest to easiest:

1. Thou shalt not take the name of the Lord thy God in vain.
2. Remember the Sabbath Day (to keep it holy).
3. Thou shalt not covet thy neighbor's house, (nor) thy neighbor's wife; nor anything that is thy neighbors.
4. Thou shalt not bear false witness against thy neighbor.
5. Thou shalt not commit adultery.
6. Thou shalt not steal.
7. Honor thy father and thy mother.
8. Thou shalt not make unto thee any graven image.
9. Thou shalt have no other gods before me.
10. Thou shalt not kill.

The Bible says that sin is the transgression of the law. If you break one of the commandments, you are guilty of breaking them all. This is why God says, *"All have sinned and come short of the glory of God"* (Rom. 3:23). We all need to repent and receive Jesus Christ as the sacrifice for our sins and as Lord of our lives.

•

Remember: THE SIN POLL REVEALS THAT WE NEED THE SAVIOR!

358/DO WHAT THE LORD DESIRES!

"And David longed, and said, Oh that one would give me drink of the water of the well at Bethlehem, that is at the gate!" (1 Chronicles 11:17).

Also read: Psa. 147:11; Ez. 36:26 & 27; Col. 1:10; Heb. 11:6

David and his soldiers were fighting the Philistines and things were not going well. The Philistines were in possession of Bethlehem and David and his men were held up in the cave of Adullam.

If you have ever been in a cave you know what a dark, depressing place it can be. The dampness and the continual dripping of the water can wear down your spirit. Also the drinking water of the cave of Adullom must have been terrible (it was probably loaded with minerals).

One day David became so depressed he sighed and said to himself, *"Oh that someone would give me a drink of water from the well at Bethlehem"* (2 Chron. 11:17).

He did not command anyone to do it, for he knew the Philistines were in possession of the city. But three of his men overheard his remark. They loved David so much they crept out quietly that night, made their way through enemy lines and returned with water from Bethlehem's well.

When they brought the water to David it touched his heart so deeply he would not drink it—but poured it out as an offering to the Lord.

Do you and I love our King, the Lord Jesus Christ, enough that we will sacrifice ourselves and take risks to please Him—even when He does not command us to do certain things? Are we close enough to Jesus to know the secret longings of His heart? Are we devoted enough to Him to fulfill those longings without being commanded to do so? This is true love.

Has the Holy Spirit challenged your heart to move past the point where the Lord has to command you to do His will? I hope so, for then you'll have a whole new relationship with God.

•

Remember: DO WHAT THE LORD DESIRES WITHOUT WAITING FOR A COMMAND.

359/BEWARE, LEST GOD BREAK IN UPON YOU!

"And let the priests also, which come near to the Lord, sanctify themselves, lest the Lord break forth upon them" (Exodus 19:22).

Also read: Is. 1:18; 1 Jn. 1:7; 2 Sam. 22:21

Today, many have lost sight of the holiness and power of God. We have imagined Him to be a tenderhearted diety that smiles down sympathetically and always says, "I forgive!"

Nothing could be further from the truth. As Abraham said of the pagans around him, *"Surely the fear of God is not in this place"* (Gen. 20:11). The prophet Isaiah said, *"Sanctify the Lord of hosts himself; and let him be your fear, and let him be your dread"* (Isa. 8:13).

When God was about to appear to the children of Israel at Mount Sinai, He told them to sanctify themselves. They were to prepare their hearts and wash their clothes (read all of Exodus 19). Then He set boundaries around the mountain, telling the people not to touch it lest they die. God even commanded the men not to be intimate with their wives, so they would be holy and prepared for His appearing.

On the third morning when God descended upon the mountain, *"There were thunders and lightnings, and a thick cloud upon the mount, and the voice of a trumpet exceeding loud; so that all of the people in the camp trembled"* (Ex. 19:16).

Verse 22 says even the priests were to sanctify themselves lest the Lord break forth upon them. Why would He do that? For the same reason a mother washes the face of a dirty child—she cannot stand to see dirt on the face of her loved one!

God is holy and He loves us so much that if we come near with filthy hearts, He cannot resist the urge to cleanse us. Is God holding you away from himself because of unclean things in your life? If so, repent of everything that is not right and you'll be able to ascend the mount as Moses did.

●

Remember: GOD MAY BE HOLDING YOU OFF SO HE WILL NOT BREAK IN ON YOU!

360/GOD IS ONLY AS BIG AS YOU MAKE HIM

"How often they provoked Him in the wilderness, And grieved Him in the desert! Yes again and again they tempted God, And limited the Holy One of Israel" (Psalm 78:40 & 41, NKJ).

Also read: Na. 1:7; Ps. 138:7; Rom. 8:28; 2 Cor. 1:3 & 4

How big is God? You could say He is immeasurably mighty—but God is only as big as you make Him when you're confronted with a problem.

The Israelis believed in God but when they faced problems (the need for food, water, or deliverance) they wavered and wanted to turn back. They restricted the great power of God on their behalf; they limited the Holy One of Israel.

It's true that God is all-powerful, but as far as your experience is concerned, He is only as big as He appears to be when you're facing a problem.

What problems are you facing now? Sickness, debt, loved ones who are not living for the Lord, a rebellious son or daughter, a mate who is stubborn or unfaithful, or a difficult situation at work?

Whatever crisis you're facing, the God you will experience is as great as you confess Him to be at this moment of crisis.

This is why the Psalmist David continually declared, *"Thou art my rock and my fortress"* (Psa. 71:3).
"Thou art my strong refuge" (verse 7).
"I will go in the strength of the Lord God" (verse 16).

What are you confessing God to be?

* If you're sick, say, "The Lord is my healer. He is working even now to restore me to health."
* If you're in debt, say, "The Lord is my counsellor, showing me how to develop my skills to pay bills. He is also working even now to provide for my needs."
* If your loved ones are lost, say, "The Lord is my Shepherd and He is searching for my lost sheep today."

Whatever your need is this moment, confess out loud that God is the Lord of your situation.

●

Remember: GOD IS ONLY AS BIG AS YOU MAKE HIM!

361/LOVE IS THE GREATEST

"There are three things that remain—faith, hope and love—and the greatest of these is love" (1 Corinthians 13:13 TLB).

Also read: 1 Jn. 4:7-11

Albert Schweitzer was a great humanitarian. He turned his back on a successful career as a classical concert pianist and went to the jungles of Africa where he built a hospital for the needy.

When Yousuf Karsh, the great portrait photographer, asked Schweitzer which was the greatest of the Ten Commandments, he said, "Christ gave only one commandment—and that was love."

Are you having some difficult situations with people? If so—try love.

Emmet Fox has written these golden lines:

Love

There is no difficulty that enough love will not conquer; No disease that enough love will not heal; No door that enough love will not open; No gulf that enough love will not bridge; No wall that enough love will not throw down; No sin that enough love will not redeem ...

It makes no difference how deeply seated may be the trouble, How hopeless the outlook, How muddled the tangle, How great the mistake, A sufficient realization of love will dissolve it all ... If only you could love enough you would be the happiest and most powerful being in the world ...

— *Emmet Fox*

●

Remember: TRY UNLOCKING SOME OF THE CLOSED DOORS IN YOUR LIFE THE GREATEST WAY—WITH LOVE.

362/WHEN GOD CAME CLOSE TO KILLING MOSES!

"And it came to pass by the way in the inn, that the Lord met him, and sought to kill him" (Exodus 4:24).

Also read: Phil. 4:9; Ps. 24:4 & 5; 2 Cor. 9:7

Can you imagine God trying to kill Moses? Why would the Lord seek to destroy his servant?

Here's what had happened. Moses had failed to circumcise his son. God's covenant with Abraham was that all the male children be circumcised. *"And the uncircumcised man child whose flesh of his foreskin is not circumcised, that soul shall be cut off from his people; he hath broken my covenant"* (Gen 17:14).

Remember, Moses was going down to Egypt as a keeper of God's covenant and his own son wasn't even circumcised. And because the boy was too young, and uninformed, it was Moses' responsiblity. So God was chasing him down, angered at his neglect, and was about to kill him.

Not only this, but there was obviously a division between Moses and his wife, Zipporah, about circumcision, because she complained about this rite that night. When she heard her husband crying out because he was about to be destroyed by the hand of God, Zipporah *"took a flint knife and cut off the foreskin of her young son's penis, and threw it against Moses' feet, remarking disgustedly, 'What a blood smeared husband you've turned out to be!" Then God let him alone"* (Ex. 4:25-26, TLB).

Has God become your enemy because you have failed to keep your covenant with Him? If it appears that God is working against you, if everything is going wrong, or if God appears to be ignoring your prayers, take an inventory.

1. Are you obeying God—keeping His commandments?
2. Is your life clean—or have you been compromising your principles of purity?
3. Have you honored God by water baptism, communion, church attendance, and giving generously?

•

Remember: GOD IS A COVENANT-KEEPING GOD AND IF YOU FAIL TO KEEP YOUR PROMISE, HE WILL WORK AGAINST YOU!

363 /HAVE FAITH IN GOD!

"He staggered not at the promise of God through unbelief: but was strong in faith, giving glory to God; and being fully persuaded that, what he had promised, he was able also to perform" (Romans 4:20 & 21).

Also read: Phil. 4:13; Is. 46:11; Ps.84:11

Above all else, God is trying to develop your faith. Because *"without faith it is impossible to please him: for he that cometh to God must believe that he is, and that he is a rewarder of them that diligently seek him"* (Heb. 11:6).

If you'll study the great men and women of God in the Bible, you'll see that everyone of them had to struggle with their doubts until they conquered them.

- Abraham was childless until he was one-hundred years old, even though God had promised him a son many years earlier.
- Moses struggled because he felt he couldn't speak well enough to stand before Pharoah. Then he struggled with Pharoah, who almost destroyed him at the Red Sea. Later, he struggled with the children of Israel on their way to the Promised Land.
- David had been told he would one day be king, but he spent years hiding from King Saul who wanted to kill him. Then he wrestled with his own sin after committing adultery with Bathsheba. Finally, he had family problems and his own son turned against him.

The list of those who fought for their faith could go on and on. Every hero has had his hell; every champion, his pit. Every winner has had his wasteland; every victor, his valley.

Are you having a hassle keeping your faith in God today? Welcome to the club! God is trying to develop your faith and strengthen you by the trials He allows to come your way.

How can you stand the pressure?

•

Remember: HAVE FAITH IN GOD'S FAITHFULNESS. WHEN THE GOING GETS ROUGH, TRUST IN GOD'S CHARACTER MORE THAN IN THE CIRCUMSTANCES. GOD HAS NEVER LET ONE OF HIS CHILDREN DOWN!

364/DO RIGHT IN THE SIGHT OF THE LORD!

"Hezekiah began to reign when he was twenty-five years old..and he did that which was right in the sight of the Lord" (2 Chronicles 29:1 & 2).

Also read: Rom. 8:6; 12:2; Prov. 21:21

One day as I was studying in the Old Testament, I read this passage about Hezekiah, one of the kings of Israel. It says that he did right in the sight of the Lord. What did he do that was right? Here's what I found:

1. *"He opened the doors of the house of the Lord and repaired them"* (vs. 3). The new king fixed up the house of God that had fallen into ruin. You and I will do right if we make certain that the church we attend is painted, the lawn mowed, the carpet cleaned, etc. In fact your church may need a new carpet, piano, or organ. You might even need a new church.
2. *"He sanctified the house of the Lord and commanded that the filthiness be carried out of the holy place"* (vs. 5). Holiness pleases God. If you have allowed any impure thoughts or habits to creep up into your mind or life, carry out the filthiness. Repent of all that is unpleasing to God.
3. *"He made a covenant with God so that the Lord would turn his anger away"* (vs. 10). God is a covenant-making God. He made covenants with Noah, Abraham, Jacob, David, Solomon, etc. If you really want God to get serious with you, make a covenant. But be careful that you think it through so you don't make a rash vow.
4. *"He called people to prayer, to stand before the Lord and burn incense"* (vs. 11). Prayer pleases God because it enables Him to show mercy upon transgressors. When you become an intercessor you are entering the holy chambers of the Almighty. Jesus is our full time intercessor in heaven (see Heb. 7:25), and prayer enables you to become an intercessor on earth.

Hezekiah pleased God because he put God and God's house and worship first in his life. He did everything he knew to be right, and the Lord honored him.

•

Remember: GOD IS PLEASED WHEN WE PUT HIM FIRST.

365/PLEASE GO BY ACTING NOW!

"Hezekiah began to reign when he was five and twenty years old...And he did that which was right in the sight of the Lord" (2 Chronicles 29:1 & 2).

Also read: Ps. 47:1, 66:1-4, 104:33,34

As I explained in the previous devotional, Hezekiah did what was right in the sight of the Lord. Here are some other things he did:

5. *"Hezekiah gathered the rulers of the city together and went up to the house of the Lord"* (2 Chronicles 29:20). He became politically active. He knew it would be impossible to have reform without changing city hall.
6. *"He brought in musicians to the House of the Lord"* (verses 25-27). I know a lot of gospel musicians and singers who are allowing their musical gifts to lie idle. If God has given you abilities in this area, start using your talents. There are churches that want and need good guitar players, drummers, horn players, pianists, and singers.

   If your church doesn't have a band, find one that does. Or start using your music for jail services, rest homes, and evangelistic rallies.
7. *"Hezekiah's actions prompted the congregation to worship"* (vs. 28). When you lift up your hands and pray aloud it pleases God. (see Psalm 134, 1 Tim. 2:8, and Acts 4:24.) Worship works wonders with the Lord. Sometimes people think this style of worship is charismatic, but the Scriptures show that it is originally Jewish.
8. *"Hezekiah commanded the Levites to sing"* (vs. 30). It is important that you make an extra effort to lift up your voice in church when the congregation is singing. Don't drag along—give it all you've got.
9. *"The king commanded that offerings be received"* (vs. 31). God's work is worthy of your support. Don't slack off on your giving. Make certain the Lord is receiving His ten percent, plus offerings.

The Bible says, *"So the service of the house of the Lord was set in order. And Hezekiah and all the people rejoiced, that God had prepared the people: for the thing was done suddenly"* (vs. 36).

•

Remember: IF YOU WANT TO PLEASE GOD, DO WHAT YOU KNOW IS RIGHT.

Books to help you grow!

by Lowell Lundstrom

SUPERNATURAL PROSPERITY
Are you facing a financial crisis? Would you like to increase your income? In this life-changing book, Lowell Lundstrom tells how you can fight inflation by applying the principles of supernatural prosperity. Here is a step-by-step approach for gaining control of your spiritual and financial life. You can enjoy supernatural prosperity!!

B-41 $3.50

HOW YOU CAN PRAY WITH POWER AND GET RESULTS
God wants to answer your prayers. God wants to meet your needs. If your prayer life has not been as rewarding as you'd like it to be, you'll find much help in this 263-page large print Christian growth book.

MB-44 $4.00

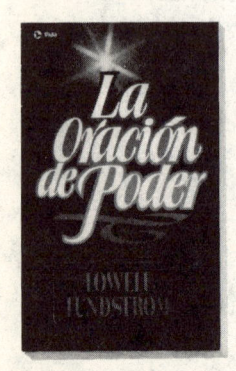

LA ORACIÓN DE PODER
(How You Can Pray With Power and Get Results)
This life-changing book on prayer is now available in Spanish! In just six months after being printed, the publishers have placed it on their Best-Seller list. A great gift to reach out to Spanish-speaking people.

MB-68 $4.00

HEAVEN'S ANSWER FOR THE HOME
Enrich your marriage! Make your home a happier place. Learn to prepare your children for the days ahead. Find personal fulfillment through life's most intimate relationship. These topics and more are discussed in this helpful volume.

TB-39 $3.50

LOWELL
What compels a man to spend over 300 nights a year for 25 years traveling across the country singing and preaching the Gospel? Here, in the words of his family and friends, is unique insight into a special man and his ministry.

MB-34 $3.50

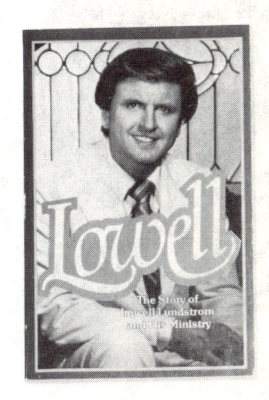

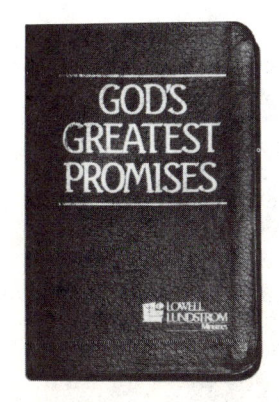

GOD'S GREATEST PROMISES
Over 330 pages of God's promises printed topically—a must for everyone. Here is a quick and easy guide to the promises of God (KJV). This special edition is bound by a beautiful genuine bonded leather cover. A great devotional aid—an excellent gift.

MB-50 $19.95

OUR FAVORITE RECIPES
Here are over 400 delicious recipes collected from friends all over the United States and Canada who have shared their favorite dishes with the Lundstroms during their past 25 years on the road. Arranged in easy-to-follow categories, this cookbook—with photos, inspirational thoughts and scripture verses—will be an exciting addition to every kitchen. Unique spiritual helps section included.

MB-17 $9.95

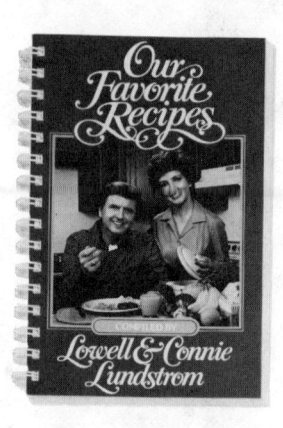

WHAT'S COMING NEXT?
An encouraging look into the exciting future God has planned for you! If you have avoided Bible prophecy because you thought it was too difficult, too speculative, or simply because it didn't inspire you, then you will enjoy reading this captivating book. Lowell Lundstrom shares easy-to-understand biblical prophecies along with exciting spiritual truths. 360-page large "speed-read" type.

MB-49 $4.95

IF YOU'RE OVER THE HILL YOU OUGHTA' BE GOIN' FASTER
by Carl Malz
Carl Malz, associate evangelist of Lowell Lundstrom, explains how to get the best out of the rest of your life! This delightful book will help you laugh at the past and give you courage to face your future. Chapter titles include: Gray Is Great!; Feeling Better God's Way; The Antidote for Loneliness and Counterattack. This book is a great resource for friends or loved ones who are retiring or looking forward to it.

MB-70 $3.50

FREE AT LAST
by Gloria Lundstrom
Gloria Lundstrom, wife of Larry Lundstrom, shares how to be set free through forgiveness. God has given her a special ability to help people be released from harmful and hurtful emotions collected over the years. You can experience the peace and excitement of personal freedom by reading and responding to this great book of ministry.
MB-72 $5.00

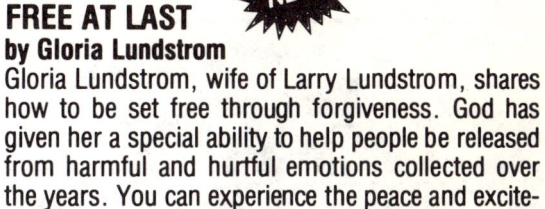

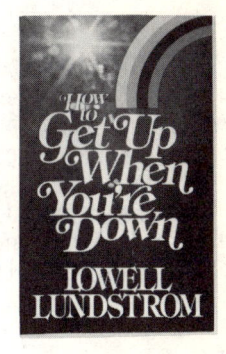

HOW TO GET UP WHEN YOU'RE DOWN
Nine great chapters including: How to Defeat Depression, When Trouble Works for Good, What to Do When You Don't Know What to Do, The Blessings of Troubles, Blessed Are the Tempted, and Faith in the Face of Defeat.
MB-26 $2.00

Tapes to help you grow!

WITH YOU THROUGH THE WORD
NEW
Lowell reads completely through Psalms Proverbs and Ephesians. On these 12-60 minute cassette tapes he explains many difficult passages. You will receive encouragement, guidance and strength from the Scriptures and Lowell's personal life teaching. This powerful commentary will be a great help for your personal devotions and Bible study.   **TC-76 $35.00**

PASTORS' SEMINAR
One of the greatest gifts a person could give his pastor! These six tapes include: The Power of Positive Pastoring, Ministerial Conflicts and Organizing for Success by Carl Malz; and The Importance of Unconditional Commitment, How to Be an Effective Communicator and How to Increase Your Church Finances by Lowell Lundstrom.
MC-22 $20.00

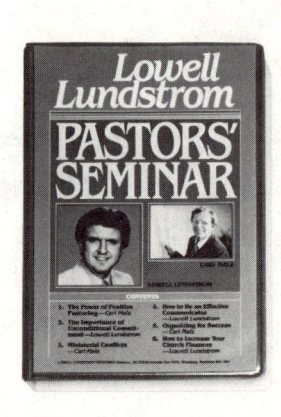

CRUSADE CASSETTE LIBRARY
You can relive the spirit and excitement of the best of Lowell Lundstrom's preaching. These light crusade sermons have changed thousands of lives. For personal enjoyment and growth and outreach to friends, listen to these messages by Lowell Lundstrom: Why We Know That Jesus Christ Is the One True Way to God, The Secrets of Success and Happiness, Signs That Show the Return of Christ Is at Hand, How You Can Have a Happier Home, How God Wants to Heal Your Hurts, Is Your Soul for Sale?, The Benefits of Being a Christian, and Lowell's Testimony: From Rock 'n' Roll to Christ.   **CC-01 $26.00**

LIVING TO WIN SEMINAR
Listen to these life-changing sessions: Feeling Better God's Way, How Tough Love Wins and Developing Your Faith by Carl Malz; How to Discover God's Purpose in Your Life, Secrets That Will Help You to Win Others to Christ, Surviving and Thriving in the Last Days and How to Develop Your Faith for Finances by Lowell Lundstrom; Winning in Life as a Wife by Connie Lundstrom; The Keys to Winning Your Family to Christ by Larry Lundstrom; and Free to Be Me Through Inner Healing by Gloria Lundstrom.

MC-26 $30.00

FAMILY LIFE SEMINAR
Hundreds of lives have been transformed at the Lundstrom Family Life Seminar—now you too can enjoy the most popular sessions. These scriptural insights and personal experiences are very helpful in solving problems facing families today. Topics include: Differences and How to Handle Them, How to Handle the Problems of Raising Teen-agers and How to Handle the Hassle in Your Castle by Carl Malz; Building Bridges of Communication, How to Experience the Ultimate of the Intimate Side of Marriage, Discovering God's Purpose in Your Life and Principles of Prosperity by Lowell Lundstrom; How to Handle Impossible Situations by Connie Lundstrom; Self Acceptance—The Key to Inner Healing by Gloria Lundstrom; and How to Establish Family Devotions for Your Home by Larry Lundstrom.

MC-01 $30.00

Music to lift your spirit

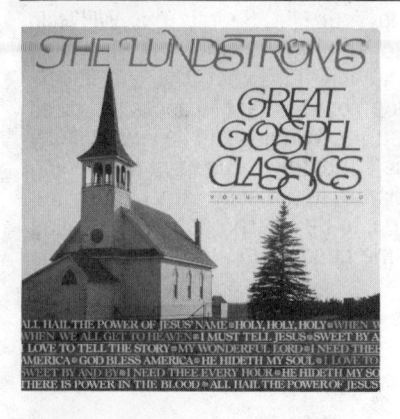

GREAT GOSPEL CLASSICS — NEW
Volume Two
All Hail the Power of Jesus' Name • Holy, Holy, Holy • My Wonderful Lord • I Must Tell Jesus • I Love to Tell the Story • When We All Get to Heaven • America—God Bless America • He Hideth My Soul • Sweet By and By • I Need Thee Every Hour • There Is Power in the Blood
MR-65 $8.00

GREAT GOSPEL CLASSICS
Volume One
How Great Thou Art • More About Jesus • My Jesus I Love Thee-Fairest Lord Jesus • In The Garden • Love Lifted Me • The Old Rugged Cross • Amazing Grace-Precious Lord Take My Hand • What A Friend • A Mighty Fortress • Sweet Hour of Prayer • Where Could I Go-I Feel Like Travelin' On
MR-34 $8.00

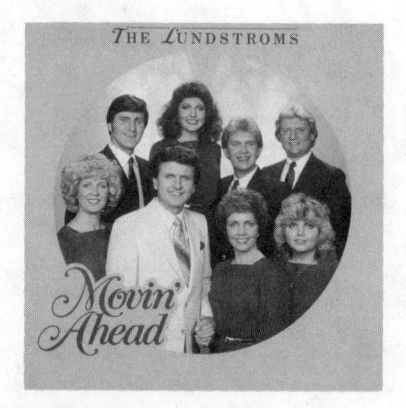

MOVIN' AHEAD
Walking Gold • Out of the Ordinary Man • You Can Be A Winner • Everything to Me • Win the Lost • Be Ready for the Day When Jesus Comes • Stand Tall • Rain Into a Rainbow • He Didn't Lift Us Up to Let Us Down • A New Song • I Sing Jesus • We're Happy Christians
MR-38 $8.00

A FRESH TOUCH
It's A Great Thing to be Saved • Jesus Stood By Me • The Preacher • Just Imagine A World Without Jesus • You Will Never Know • Lord, I Really Need a Song Today • I Am Loved • Beautiful Music • I Am Protected • Praise the Lord
                    SR-33 $8.00

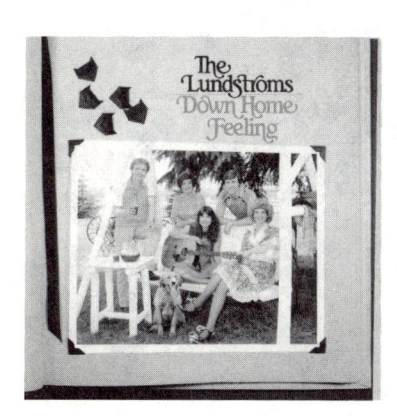

DOWN HOME FEELING
Be Nice To The Little Guy • Born Again • Rise Again • I Have Returned • It's Great To Be A Christian • O Give Thanks • How Do You Spell Love • I Am Persuaded • He Was There All the Time • It's A Good Life
                    MR-24 $8.00

MUSIC/MUSIC/MUSIC
Music, Music, Music • I'll Shine Again • Butterfly • More of You • Jesus, He is the Son of God • Lord I Want to Spend Eternity With You • He Will Not Fail Me Now • I Know That Jesus Can • I'm On My Way to Heaven • Cherished Moments
                    MR-23 $8.00

THE VERY BEST OF THE LUNDSTROMS

Walking in the Sunshine of His Love • The Storm • Suzy's Prayer • I've Tasted and I Know the Lord is Good • Make Calvary Real • The Messiah Has Come • Play, Guitar, Play • A Rich Man Am I • Tommy's Prayer • A Fugitive From God • Now You Know • He Will Not Fail Me Now • Our Traveling Song

MR-29 $8.00

OLD-TIME CHRISTMAS FAVORITES

Hark the Herald Angels Sing • Joy to the World • The First Noel • O Little Town of Bethlehem • Away in a Manger • O Come All Ye Faithful • Jingle Bells • Angels We Have Heard on High • We Three Kings • Silent Night • It Came Upon the Midnight Clear

MR-31 $8.00

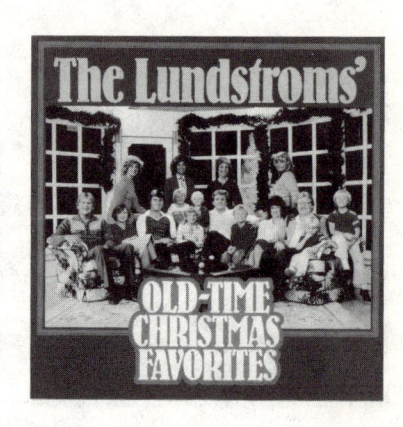

BEST OF CHRISTMAS

A Double Record Album of Christmas Memories • 24 Of The Most Requested Songs • Plus A Nostalgic Collection of Lundstrom Photos

MR-36 $12.00

YOU GAVE ME A SONG
You Gave Me A Song • Lord, I Want to Spend Eternity With You • I'll Never Go Away Again • How Do You Spell Love? • Butterfly • Hosanna • Jesus Is Coming Back • Make Me An Instrument • Born Again • Heaven's Heroes

MR-28 $8.00

YOU GAVE ME A SONG SONGBOOK
Now you can enjoy all the music and words for each song on Londa's first solo album. A special personal photo section is included.

MB-48 $2.00

HEAVENLY LOVE
NEW

Heavenly Love • Flow Like A River • Alleluia to the King • Lord I Need You • I Will Sing Unto The Lord • Nobody Loves Me Like You • You've Never Given Up On Me • You Don't Have To Make Believe • We Three Are One • Look To Him

MR-39 $8.00

NEW

HEAVENLY LOVE SONGBOOK
Londa's latest release!
All the sheet music including words for this great album are written here for your enjoyment and use.

MB-78 $4.00

JUST FOR KIDS SONGBOOK
A beautifully illustrated songbook containing words and music to all the songs from the "Just For Kids" record album. A great gift to help little singers and musicians get excited about music and improve their singing and listening skills.

MB-67 $3.95

JUST FOR KIDS
Praising the Lord • The Fastest Song • Little David • Jesus Loves Me • It's A Happy Day • The B-I-B-L-E • Pound, Pound, Pound • Grandma and Grandpa • Butterfly • Suzy's Prayer • I'm Not Afraid of the Dark • That's Why I Love the Lord • He's Watching Over Me • I'm His Friend Each Day • God Sent an Angel

MR-35 $12.00

THE LARRY LUNDSTROM FAMILY COLLECTION
NEW

I'm on My Way to Heaven • When I Prayed Through • Praise the Lord • I Sing Jesus • The B-I-B-L-E • Come Spring • It's Great to Be a Christian • Bigger Than Any Mountain • Tears Are a Language • I'll See You in the Rapture • That's Why I Love the Lord • A Happy Way to Live • Now You Know • This Old House

MR-64 $8.00

THE LUNDSTROM'S CHRISTMAS SONGBOOK

This special Christmas songbook contains many of the songs from the television production, "The Lundstrom's Country Christmas." Thirteen great songs including: Daddy Will Be Home For Christmas, Didn't He Shine, I Know Now and It's Christmas. The songbook features a family photo section.

MB-24 $1.00

I'M HAPPY

I'm Happy • My Best Friend • I'm Jesus' Soldier Boy • Little by Little • You Can't Keep a Good Man Down • Oh How I Love Jesus/Jesus Loves the Little Children • Inside Out • Wake up, Little Sleepyhead • I Know Jesus Lives in My Heart • I Was Raised a Gospel Singer • God's Not Finished With Me Yet • Jesus Told Me That He Loved Me • You'll be Happy When You're Serving Jesus Christ • Praise God for the Good Things

MR-76 $12.00

ORDER FORM

QTY.	ITEM NO.	DESCRIPTION	PRICE EACH	TOTAL PRICE

Method of Payment

☐ Money Order ☐ Master Card ☐ Visa ☐ Check

Credit card No. ☐☐☐☐☐☐☐☐☐☐☐☐☐

Expiration date ☐☐☐☐

Telephone No. ( ) _____

Signature _____

TOTAL AMT. ENCLOSED
(in U.S. dollars)

NAME _____

ADDRESS _____

CITY _____ STATE _____ ZIP _____

Send order to:

LOWELL LUNDSTROM MINISTRIES
Sisseton, South Dakota 57262
Canada: Box 4000, Winnipeg, Manitoba R3C 3W1